PROPERTY LAW AND ECONOMICS

ENCYCLOPEDIA OF LAW AND ECONOMICS, SECOND EDITION

General Editor: Gerrit De Geest
School of Law, Washington University, St Louis, MO, USA

1. Tort Law and Economics
   Edited by Michael Faure
2. Labor and Employment Law and Economics
   Edited by Kenneth G. Dau-Schmidt, Seth D. Harris and Orly Lobel
3. Criminal Law and Economics
   Edited by Nuno Garoupa
4. Antitrust Law and Economics
   Edited by Keith N. Hylton
5. Property Law and Economics
   Edited by Boudewijn Bouckaert

Future titles will include:

Procedural Law and Economics
Edited by Chris William Sanchirico

Regulation and Economics
Edited by Roger Van den Bergh

Contract Law and Economics
Edited by Gerrit De Geest

Methodology of Law and Economics
Edited by Thomas S. Ulen

Corporate Law and Economics
Edited by Joseph A. McCahery and Erik P.M. Vermeulen

Production of Legal Rules
Edited by Francesco Parisi

Intellectual Property Law and Economics
Edited by Ben Depoorter

For a list of all Edward Elgar published titles visit our site on the World Wide Web at http://www.e-elgar.co.uk

Property Law and Economics

Edited by

Boudewijn Bouckaert

Professor of Law, University of Ghent, Belgium

ENCYCLOPEDIA OF LAW AND ECONOMICS,
SECOND EDITION

Edward Elgar

Cheltenham, UK • Northampton, MA, USA

Published by
Edward Elgar Publishing Limited
The Lypiatts
15 Lansdown Road
Cheltenham
Glos GL50 2JA
UK

Edward Elgar Publishing, Inc.
William Pratt House
9 Dewey Court
Northampton
Massachusetts 01060
USA

A catalogue record for this book is available from the British Library

Library of Congress Control Number: 2009941414

Mixed Sources
Product group from well-managed forests and other controlled sources
www.fsc.org Cert no. SA-COC-1565
© 1996 Forest Stewardship Council
FSC

ISBN 978 1 84720 565 0

Printed and bound by MPG Books Group, UK

Contents

Contributors

Bram Akkermans, Assistant Professor European Private Law and post-doctoral fellow, Faculty of Law, Maastricht University, the Netherlands

Boudewijn Bouckaert, Professor of Law, Centre for Advanced Studies in Law and Economics, University of Ghent, Belgium

James W. Bowers, Oliver P. Stockwell Professor of Law, Louisiana State University Law Center, USA

Daniel H. Cole, Indiana University School of Law, Indianapolis, USA

Ben Depoorter, Ghent University Law School, the Netherlands and University of Miami Law School, USA

Jeffrey Evans Stake, Robert A. Lucas Chair of Law, Indiana University Maurer School of Law, USA

Charlotte Hess, Associate Dean for Research, Collections, and Scholarly Communication, Syracuse University Library, Syracuse, NY, USA

Kim Hoofs, Junior Researcher, Faculty of Law, Maastricht University, the Netherlands

Andreas Kontoleon, Department of Land Economy, University of Cambridge, UK

Elinor Ostrom, Workshop in Political Theory and Policy Analysis, Indiana University, USA

Timothy Swanson, Department of Economics, University College of London, UK

Sjef van Erp, Professor of Civil Law and European Private Law, Maastricht University, the Netherlands

Jenny Wahl, Professor of Economics, Carleton College, USA

1 Introduction

Boudewijn Bouckaert

Property Law and Economics is the fifth volume of the second edition of the Encyclopedia of Law and Economics series. The second edition continues the ambitions of the first edition which is to provide a reference work surveying most of the law and economics literature. The Encyclopedia allows the researcher to get efficiently acquainted with the literature on his research topic and look for publications of possible interest. Consulting the Encyclopedia puts the saying 'standing on the shoulders of the former generation' in practice and avoids duplicate efforts within the research community.

As with the first edition, the chapters of this volume contain two parts. First a review of the literature on the subject. The review is written by an authority in the field. On average the length of these reviews is 30 pages. Second, a quasi complete bibliography.

In the reviews the authors discuss the basic questions concerning the institutions involved, compare the legal solutions across different legal families (mainly common and civil law) and jurisdictions and provide an outline of the genesis of economic theories concerning the institutions within their focus. In Chapter 12 ('Security Interests, Creditors' Priorities, and Bankruptcy'), for instance, Bowers provides us with an outline of the evolution of the economics of bankruptcy law starting from the seminal insights of Jackson and the further directions the literature developed from Jackson's insights. The bibliography starts from the beginning of the law and economics literature and is updated until the end of 2007. Most listed publications are in English but as English is the 'lingua franca' of law and economics many publications, although in English, are of a non-Anglo-Saxon origin. For non-English publications a translation of the title is provided.

Concerning the quotation style the system prevailing in most economic literature was chosen. Within the text of the review the name of the author(s), the year of publication and eventually the page are mentioned while within the bibliographical list the full title of the book or article, the name of the journal, the volume number of the issue, the year of publication and the number of the first and last page are mentioned. Also the court cases, discussed within the reviews, are listed at the end of the bibliography.

Selection of entries and structure

Unlike the first edition in 2000 the volumes of the Encyclopedia are conceived as independent publications covering all the legal topics in one more or less delineated field of the law. Beside the chapters dealing with the law and economics literature on the different legal subjects, entries on the legal history of property rights and comparative property law were also added. The addition of the legal historian chapter allows the reader of this to put some legal subjects, mentioned in the law-and-economics-entries, in a historical perspective which may enrich the multi-disciplinary approach of his study. The addition of the comparative law chapter allows the reader, especially the reader without legal training, to place legal-technical problems, dealt with in the law-and-economics chapters, within the larger framework of the legal tradition. The legal historian and the comparative law chapters may also generate suggestions for further law-and-economics research. In the comparative law chapter (Chapter 3) for instance Van Erp and Akkermans mention several tendencies in modern property law, common to most national jurisdictions. They mention the indirect impacts of European law on property law, the dematerialization of property, the rise of party autonomy and the erosion of the *numerus clausus*-principle. These tendencies could be interesting subjects for further law-and-economic analysis.

As far as the selection of the topics of the chapters is concerned, some difficult choices had to be made. The borderline of property law with other branches of the law is often porous and unclear. This problem, existing in the legal tradition, reflects also on the subdivision of the legal-economic literature.

There are, however, legal chapters whose belonging to the domain of property law is beyond any discussion. On all these chapters a law-and-economics entry was written. These non-discussed property law-subjects are: private and common property rights (Elinor Ostrom and Charlotte Hess); original assignment of private property (Boudewijn Bouckaert); decomposition of property rights (Jeffrey Evans Stake); nuisance (Timothy Swanson and Andreas Kontoleon); adverse possession (Ben Depoorter); title systems and recordation of interests (Boudewijn Bouckaert).

Besides these 'classics' we included chapters on three other topics, the belonging to the domain of property law is not so evident at all, especially for classical lawyers.

Consider in the first place Chapter 10 on the economics of slavery, written by Jenny Wahl. Classical lawyers will classify this subject rather within the field of human rights than under property rights. This classification is of course largely influenced by the normative position law, and especially international law, took on slavery by taking human personality as such out of the field of patrimonial rights and the sphere of commodification by the market. Property rights on human beings and the marketization of human beings were, however, historical realities in the Roman Empire, in Europe from the sixteenth to the eighteenth century and in the American South until 1865. As markets in human beings can be analyzed in the same way as markets in goods and services, the economics of slavery may generate insights into the phenomenon, a mere moral-philosophical approach cannot.

Chapter 11 on 'New forms of private property: property rights in environmental goods', written by Daniel Cole, deals mainly with environmental regulations, a subject classical lawyers would classify under the administrative law. As is shown in this chapter, the regulatory framework in this field evolved often towards a property approach, in which the administrative permits were considered as a kind of rights, in many respects similar to classical property rights. These permits can be traded and are considered as an asset, being part of the collateral of the holder. Consequently the inclusion of this chapter in a property volume is largely justified from an evolutionary point of view.

Chapter 12 on 'Security interests, creditors' priorities, and bankruptcy', written by James Bowers, covers at the contrary a set of rights classified, especially by civil lawyers, within the field of property law. Mortgages, pledges, liens and other contractual priority rights are considered to be 'dependant real rights' as they are dependant on a debt obligation of which they are a security. This is in contrast to the 'independent real rights', aiming at the organisation of an orderly use and transfer of corporeal goods. From a mere conceptual viewpoint these rights are indeed property rights as they have a holder, as there is a certain power of the holder on the concerned asset, as they are tradable and belong to the patrimony of the holder. From a mere functional analysis the classification within the field of property rights can be challenged however. The rationale of these rights is so closely connected with the functioning of credit markets and the functioning of corporations that inclusion into a volume on corporate law could be justified.

Finally there are also some subjects for which there are good reasons to include them into a volume on property rights but which were, also for some good reasons, not included. The subject of takings for instance has many links with property law as it deals with a way of acquisition of real property by the government. Most often classical lawyers will classify this subject under constitutional law (the general principles) and the administrative law (the technical details on the reasons for taking and its procedure). Both classifications are justified. As more elements in the law on takings rather lean towards public law, an entry on taking will appear in the volume on public law. Also for zoning law there are arguments to include it in a property volume. Zoning law involves limitations on land use through a system of planning and permits. Most often these permits are tied to the land and as a consequence tradable. In this sense they follow the logic of the tradable permits, discussed within Chapter 11 by Daniel Cole. Also here, however, the administrative element seems to be the most important so that a chapter on zoning was not included. In so far as zoning law is related with more classical property rights, the subject is discussed in this volume, as for instance in Chapter 6 by Jeffrey Evans Stake, where zoning law is compared with other legal instruments to order land use like easements and restrictive covenants.

2 Property rights in legal history

Kim Hoofs

Introduction

Since time immemorial, the reach and the content of property rights change with society. These continual adjustments to the practical needs of society are concomitant to the purpose of these rights: serving society. The right of ownership is the most extensive and variable property right in the course of history. It has had many different meanings. These can only be understood by examining the particular society it served. The historical content of the right of ownership can be understood by studying codifications and statutes. These are important for the specific periods of history. The historical codifications often had major influences on later codifications and sometimes even on later civilizations.

In general, textbooks concerning the history of property law begin with Roman law, because of its major influence on modern private law of Western civilization. However, the ancient Egyptian and the ancient Greek cultures also had their influence on the Western legal systems. Greek civilization was greatly influenced by older civilizations, especially by Mesopotamian societies. The oldest code of law originates from this period of Mesopotamian dynasties and is known as the Code of Urukagina.

The two most famous and influential codifications of Roman law are the Lex Duodecim Tabularum (Law of the Twelve Tables) and the Corpus Iuris Civilis. Though the time difference between these codifications is over nine centuries, they resemble each other in several ways; contentwise as well as structurewise. The Lex Duodecim Tabularum became part of the cultural, historical consciousness of the Romans. This explains Gaius' excessive interest in the Lex Duodecim Tabularum during the first century A.D., which resulted in an extensive comment (Spruit, 2003, p. 8).

The Roman right of ownership, *dominium*, has been cultivated over the course of time, from indefinite to extensive. Because of the gradual development of the right of ownership one single definition will not satisfy. However, absoluteness can be mentioned as *the* fundamental characteristic of the right of ownership (Zwalve, 2000, p. 100). Although Roman law exerted a strong influence on Germanic law, the Germanic right of ownership kept its own substance and can, in contrast to the Roman right of ownership, be characterized as social, meaning that the reach of the Germanic right of ownership was bordered by the rights of others (Dooyeweerd, 1957).

During the Middle Ages, the Corpus Iuris Civilis was of great importance to the explanation of the different ownership relations between vassals and lords, which existed under the feudal system. These relations were explained by referring to the *actio directum* and the *actio utile* to be found in the Corpus Iuris Civilis. The clarification of these different ownership relations was founded on the concept of divided ownership (Feenstra, 1989, pp. 111–122). The use of the concept of divided ownership ended abruptly, at least on the mainland of Europe, by the entry of the French Revolution. The main reason to bring an end to the concept of divided ownership was the uncertainty and inequality brought along by this concept of ownership. Seen in the light of the feudal system, divided ownership often led to infringement of personal and individual freedom. From that moment the principle of a uniform concept of ownership became a fact (Zwalve, 2003, p. 156; Van den Bergh, 1979, p. 29).

The English right of ownership went through a wholly different development. After the Conquest of England by William the Conqueror in 1066 the feudal system was established. As a result of the feudal system the concept of divided ownership was introduced (G. Smith, 1990, p. 46). In contrast to the history of ownership on the mainland of Europe, the concept of divided ownership in England survives to this day.

1. The Mesopotamian codes

The oldest codes by far originated from the Middle East, to be more specific from Mesopotamia, an area geographically located between the rivers Tigris and the Euphrates. These codes give an insight into the societies which they served and derived from.

The oldest code known is the Code of Urukagina of Lagash which dates from around 2350 B.C. This code has never been retrieved but its existence is known from later codifications by other Mesopotamian kings. This code dealt with the reformation of abuses by previous rulers. The oldest code that came down to us is the Code of Ur-Nammu and dates from 2100 B.C., containing sanctions in case of serious personal injuries. Both codes are not familiar with the idea of ownership.

The idea of ownership was first codified in the Code of Eshnunna, around 1930 B.C. The idea of ownership was already rooted in this society. A free person was able to own a variety of objects and was capable to protect, if necessary with the help of society, his right of ownership. The Code of Eshnunna was a compilation of legal rules, such as rules on the administration of the kingdom, classes and persons, marriage and divorce, misdemeanours, contract and property (Yaron, 1988).

Following after the appearance of the Code of Eshnunna, the Code of Hammurabi was created around 1760 B.C. and strongly influenced by the Eshnunna's Code. The Code of Hammurabi is the best-kept Mesopotamian code. The Eshnunnian idea of ownership was also incorporated in the Code of Hammurabi. This code was created with the idea to please the Gods and written to foster social justice, basically 'an eye for an eye'. The script is written on a basalt stone containing 282 legal provisions of various areas of law, as matrimonial law, law of slaves, law of women and law of children. The code also includes provisions with regard to theft, damages and property (Diamond, 2004, pp. 82–103; Yoffee, 2005, pp. 102–109)

2. A brief insight into property law during the ancient Egyptian and Greek periods

2.1 Ancient Egyptian law

In ancient Egyptian societies religious beliefs encroached in every aspect of society. This resulted in an inextricable amalgamation between religion and politics. In the area of law this amalgamation brought about a remarkable interaction between the different 'main characters of society'; the king and the goddess of law, Ma'at. The king was inferior to Ma'at and although the king was charged with creating legal rules, he could not be held responsible for them, only Ma'at. The major part of law concerned social customs and behaviour, and the rules of law were usually designed to protect families (David, 2000, p. 39).

Ancient Egyptian society was traditionally agricultural. Because of the limited fertile land, real property was extremely important. In the earliest history the king was an absolute monarch, with full powers over life, death, labour and property of all his subjects. He owned all real property.

Nevertheless, private law existed in practice, and property could be the object of private legal transactions. The land was treated as if it was privately owned by individuals themselves. They could own land, use the land as they chose, such as burning the land for fertility purposes, and were able to transfer the land. Thus, ancient Egyptian law did recognize the concept of private property.

Besides this concept of private ownership, the law also recognized a number of derivative concepts relating to property, such as bailment and servitudes (VerSteeg, 2002, p. 123; Theodorides, 1971, p. 299). The presence of these concepts is proof of a strong property law system.

2.2 Ancient Greek law

The ancient Greek property law can, just as the ancient Egyptian law, be characterised as a strong property law system. Ancient Greek law was also influenced by religion, although in a different manner as in ancient Egypt (Parker, 2005, pp. 61–81).

Agriculture played a leading role in Greek society, which led to a very well-developed right of ownership regarding land (Isager and Skydsgaard, 1992, p. 3). The law drew a clear distinction between movable and immovable property. There were no restrictions to the ownership of movables in contrast with the ownership of immovable objects like land and houses. The latter was conserved for citizens. Citizens of foreign origin and foreigners were only able to own real estate when the right to acquire ownership was allocated to them. For real estate the obligation to record the transfer of ownership in a property register existed. Besides the privately owned estate, ancient Greek law knew also publicly owned estate and sacred real estate.

The owner of an object, movable or immovable, was able to use the object and sell it. Transferring partial enjoyment of the object was possible, as in the case of *misthosis* (lease). The owner was also entitled to offer the object as security. Ancient Greek law knew two types of security: personal and real security. Through personal security the person was pledging himself. By real security the object was offered as security. The oldest form of real security was *enechyron* (pawning). In the case of pawning the ownership passed to the creditor by selling the right to recovery to the creditor. The debtor retained possession of the object. When the debtor paid his debt to the creditor the property returned to him. If the debtor was unable to pay, the creditor retained ownership and had the right to possession (Maffi, 2005, pp. 259–263).

3. Developments of Roman society and law

3.1 The Roman political trilogy

Roman history traditionally discerns three main periods, each characterized by its own polity: the Monarchy, the Republic and the Principate. The beginning of the Monarchy is dated around 750 B.C. During this period the king was chosen for life by the people of Rome, the *comitia*. According to tradition, the rules of law were promulgated by the king in the quality of supreme priest. These rules are often indicated as *leges regiae*. However, these *leges regiae* cannot be considered as a result of considered legal politics.

With the fall of the Monarchy, in 510 B.C., the Republic was brought into being. The political power was taken by the Roman aristocracy, the Patricians, and divided between several officials, named *magistratus*. The assumption of the political power by the Patricians led to a conflict with the Plebeians, a prosperous part of the Roman population, who were not assuming political powers. Not until 287 B.C. was this dispute settled by the Lex Hortensia, which put an end to the inequality of justice and legal insecurities (Spruit, 1994, p. 56; Spruit, 2003, p. 7).

In the atmosphere of the Republic the area of property law experienced an enormous growth. This growth is, to a certain extent, expressed in the Lex Duodecim Tabularum in 450 B.C. The Lex Duodecim Tabularum was the first codification in Roman law containing rules of private, public and procedural law. In spite of the incompleteness concerning the different rules and the lack of content, this codification has been of great importance. Even six centuries later an extensive comment on the Lex Duodecim Tabularum was written by Gaius (Hanenburg, 1972; Spruit, 2003, p. 15).

During the second part of the Republic polity, the Roman realm developed in a tearing rush. The territory of the Roman Republic was made of Western and Southern Europe, a part of Central Europe and Asia, Northern Africa and Egypt. This extension led to a social-economical and cultural development, which resulted in further civilization of private law.

At the start of the Principate in 27 B.C. the political powers were reunited in the hands of one man, Augustus, born as Octavianus, to restore the powers of state and the Republic establishments. The rules of Roman private law were spread out in an even bigger realm than during the Republic. Britannia and large pieces of the Middle East became part of the Roman realm. In this period the rules of private law became enlarged and refined. Many legal relations were controlled by the *bona fides* (good faith) whereby a concrete and just solution was placed in the hands of a judge, whom often was counselled by lawyers. Through this counselling the science of law flourished (Ankum, 1976, p. 3).

After a peaceful start the Principate became a very turbulent period. It brought on the division of the Roman empire into a West Roman and an East Roman empire, and in 476 A.D. the existence of the West Roman empire came to an end caused by an invasion of barbarian tribes.

The recapture of a part of the territory of the former West Roman empire by the East Roman emperor Justinian in 553 A.D. resulted in a renewed expansion of Roman law. Justinian was determined to systemize Roman law by creating a comprehensive Code. The Justinian Code, afterwards named the Corpus Iuris Civilis, became also valid in the recaptured areas. The West Roman territory was lost again in 568 A.D. and between the geographic borders of the formal West Roman empire the Corpus Iuris Civilis was lost sight of. The Corpus Iuris Civilis can be considered as the rounding off of the development of Roman law (Spruit, 2002, pp. 4–10).

3.2 Corpus Iuris Civilis

The Corpus Iuris Civilis was the first codification since the Lex Duodecim Tabularum which attempted to control all the different fields of law. The Corpus Iuris Civilis consisted of four parts; the *Codex Constitutionum*, the *Digesta*, the *Institutiones* and the *Novellae Constitutiones.*

The *Codex Constitutionum* contained a collection of imperial legislation of the Roman emperors. The *Digesta*, also named *Pandectae*, embraced a collection of legal writings containing private opinions from legal scholars such as Gaius, Ulpian and Papinian and was intended for practitioners and judges. The *Institutiones* were developed for a practical purpose, namely as a manual for students containing a general survey of the whole field of Roman law. The last part of the Corpus Iuris Civilis, the *Novellae Constitutiones*, was a compilation of later imperial legislation and added later (W. Smith, 1859, p. 302). The Corpus Iuris Civilis serves as one of the most revealing sources to gain an insight into Roman law.

3.3 Roman law

3.3.1 The actio *as the foundation of the Roman legal system* In modern legal systems, the foundation for legal actions is found in subjective rights. Roman law on the other hand was unfamiliar with a legal system of rights: the legal system was based on *actiones* (actions or writs). It is mainly a difference in legal technique. The Roman way to start a civil proceeding was by appealing on an *actio*. An *actio* in Roman law can be defined as a person's rights to make his right object of a legal dispute. The *actio* includes the right to an *actio* and the *actio* itself. By working with *actiones*, Roman law made postulated procedural law. The term *actio* was also used to indicate a lawsuit.

Roman law made a distinction between *actiones in rem*, real legal claims, and *actiones in personam*, personal legal claims. The difference between the *actiones* is laid down in the answer to the question whether there is a contract between the parties. If there is a contract, it is a matter of an *actio in personam*, otherwise it is a matter of an *actio in rem*.

This distinction between *actiones in rem* and *actiones in personam* is quite similar to, and has been the basis for, the distinction between absolute and relative rights in modern, European mainland law. An absolute right gives a legal status to the owner of the absolute right, meaning that the absolute right can be defended against everybody. These absolute rights can be created only in certain circumstances, in contrast to relative rights. The latter being only bipartite, they can be created in any circumstances. A relative right cannot be invoked against any person, but only against a specific person. In contrast to relative rights, the choice of absolute rights is limited in two ways: there is a limitation of the number of absolute rights and the content of the absolute rights is largely dictated by law. This limitation is named *numerus clausus* (closed number). The distinction between absolute and relative rights is the foundation for the distinction between property law and contract law (Derine, 1982, pp. 117–118; Kaser and Knütel, 2003, pp. 46–7; Mousourakis, 2003, p. 130).

The Corpus Iuris Civilis made a distinction between physical and non-physical objects. A physical object, indicated as *res corporalis*, is an object that can be touched, such as land, slaves, garments, gold, silver and innumerable other goods. Non-physical objects, *res incorporales*, on the other hand, cannot be touched, such as real and personal rights and usufructs. Only a legal, separate, independent and physical object can be the subject of an *actio in rem* (Kaser and Wubbe, 1971, p. 93).

Certain specific objects did not come under a *res*, namely *res divini iuris*, *res communes omnium* and *res publicae*. *Res divini iuris* were objects belonging to the Gods, as sanctuaries. *Res communes omnium* (common things) sufficiently satisfied the needs of people, but should not be a subject of power, like the air. *Res publicae* (public things) were objects owned by 'the people'. These objects could be used by all people of a state, like public roads and harbours (Kaser and Knütel, 2003, pp. 119–120; Van der Steur, 2003, p. 111).

Another object-distinction made by the Corpus Iuris Civilis could be found in *res mancipi* and *res nec mancipi*. *Res mancipi* were those objects which the Romans most highly praised, as Italian soil, rural servitudes and slaves. A slave was not considered to be a person, but a thing. All other objects were *res nec mancipi*. This distinction was very important when it concerned a proper transfer of an object. A *res mancipi* was transferred through *mancipatio*, containing formal acts. The *mancipatio* had a restricted appropriateness; just Roman citizens could transfer and receive objects by *mancipatio*. Transferring a *res nec mancipi* occurred by merely transferring the possession of the object (Kaser and Knütel, 2003, pp. 119–120; Potjewijd, 1998, p. 12; Spruit, 2003, p. 179).

3.3.2 The complicated content of dominium The most important *actio in rem* according to Roman law is the *rei vindicatio*. The purpose of this legal claim was to protect ownership. During the Monarchy and the Republic, ownership was called *meum esse* (it is mine). The reach of the *meum esse* was not clear, which led to a vague boundary line between ownership and possession. As a result of the juridical development during the Republic, the extensive meaning of ownership was restructured in a more defined concept. Around the start of the first century A.D., ownership was named *dominium* and a distinction made between *dominium* and *possessio* on the one hand, and *dominium* and limited real rights on the other hand (Kaser and Knütel, 2003, pp. 138–139; Mäkinen, 2001, pp. 11–15).

Although no definition of *dominium* was found in the Roman law, certain characteristics were given, such as the absoluteness of the *dominium*. Absoluteness contained the independence of ownership relating to other 'rights' and the absolute power of the owner to dispose of the object (Zwalve, 2000, p. 100). The absoluteness of *dominium* can be found in two *actiones*, offered to the owner when experiencing interference of his property. The first *actio* is the already mentioned *rei vindicatio*, which made it possible to claim movable goods or land from any possessor. The second *actio* is the *actio negatoria* that made it possible to sue any person who was interfering in the control of the property. Both *actiones* could be initiated against any possible possessor (Bouckaert, 1990, p. 782).

Until the fall of the West Roman empire several forms of ownership existed. First of all, Quiritarian ownership acquired under the *ius civile Quiritium* (civil law), the original Roman legal system. Besides quiritarian ownership there was praetorian ownership, which was extended by the *ius naturale* (natural law). Natural law consists of rules, which are common to all peoples, and are based upon objective and eternal norms. Praetorian ownership would only come into being when strict appliance of general rules would lead to an unreasonable outcome. In these cases praetorian ownership took precedence over civilian ownership. Even though the term ownership is used, the core praetorian ownership is not equal to quiritarian ownership. Actually, praetorian ownership should not be seen as ownership, but only as an absolute, exclusive right.

The praetor could allow praetorian ownership in two situations. First, when the possession of the object was provided by a person who was not appropriate to dispose of the object and second, when the acquisition of the possession of the object, a *res mancipi*, was not recognized by the *ius civile*. In the second situation the person did not become owner of the object, but merely possessor because the formal acts for transferring the object were not fulfilled. In that case the term 'praetorian ownership' was often replaced by the term 'bonitarian ownership'.

Roman law knew, besides the praetorian ownership and the bonitarian ownership, two other kinds of ownership, namely ownership attributed to foreigners and ownership concerning immovables in the province. The above mentioned different forms of ownership were merged by the Corpus Iuris Civilis into one form of ownership, which excluded ownership where the possession of the property of the object was provided by a person who was not permitted to dispose of the object (Ankum, 1976, p. 39; Kaser and Knütel, 2003, pp. 139–140).

4. Canon law, a powerful source besides Roman law

In the course of the fourth century A.D. another source of law, based on Roman law, unfolded: Canon law. Despite the fact that Canon law did not have a substantial influence on the right of ownership, this new source should be discussed shortly in the interest of the development of private law.

The beginning of the development of Canon law was the promulgation of the tolerance of religion by emperor Constantine the Great in 313 A.D., which brought about the restoration of Christian property that had been confiscated during a long period of persecution (Coleman, 1914, pp. 29–35; Van de Wiel, 1991, p. 29).

During the second part of the Middle Ages the scope of Canon law was large. Canon law emerged as a working international law and applied everywhere in Latin Christianity in contrast to the ordinary legal systems which were limited to a particular region. The rules of Canon law, *canones*, were applied equally to everyone, regardless of gender, class or social status. These *canones* were not published in official collections but only in various private collections such as the Decretum, written by Gratianus around 1140 A.D. By writing this comprehensive work Gratianus tried to eliminate the differences between the various private collections. The influence of the Decretum has been enormous. The Decretum was incorporated in the Corpus Iuris Canonici in 1582 and did not lose its validity until the twentieth century.

Since its reception, Canon law was fully separated from Roman law and became a separate source of law in its own right. The importance of Canon law grew, not only because of the expansion of the *canones* but also through the moral author compared with Roman law (Brundage, 1995, pp. 44–69; Lokin and Zwalve, 2001, pp. 124–137).

Until the development of Canon law, the main sources of law according to the Catholic Church were the *ius divinum* (divine law), positive law and *ius naturale* (natural law). Natural law prevailed through its dignity as divine source above all other sources. Even after the creation of Canon law, natural law remained of major importance. Natural law brought about the possibility to rectify positive law by appealing on the principle of equity. In the area of property law, Canon lawyers assigned great authority to the *bona fides* (good faith) (Lokin and Zwalve, 2001, pp. 23–29).

5. Germanic law

Around 400 A.D. the Germanic tribes invaded the West Roman empire. Finally this resulted in the abdication of the last West Roman emperor, Romulus Augustus, in 476 A.D. It resulted in the fall of the West Roman empire. Notwithstanding the conquests by the Germanic tribes, Roman law and Canon law remained in force. As Roman and Canon law were much more developed than the Germanic laws and each Germanic tribe had its own laws, it was undesirable to impose the rather primitive Germanic laws upon the original inhabitants of the West Roman empire. As a consequence, the people remained under the Roman legal system and the Germanic people under Germanic laws. The co-existence of different systems of law for different people residing within the same territory is often referred to as the principle of personality of law (Gilissen and Gorlé, 1991, pp. 155–172).

Primitive Germanic law consisted of unwritten immemorial customs. With the emergence of new Germanic kingdoms on the seized land of the West Roman empire these customs were, more and more, written down and referred to as *leges nationum Germanicarum.* The Codex Euricianus is the oldest Germanic codification and dates around 480 A.D. Germanic law developed under the influence of Roman and Canon law and, vice versa, Germanic law influenced Roman law. As a result, Roman law degenerated and the original Roman law gradually disappeared.

Consequently, the principle of personality of law was replaced by the principle of territoriality, under which the law of an area was applicable to all who lived in this certain area (Van Caenegem, 1992, pp. 18–20).

Although Germanic law and Roman law grew together, a fundamental difference between their concepts of ownership remained. The Roman concept of ownership was characterized by absoluteness, containing the independence of ownership as against other 'rights' and the absolute power of the owner to dispose of the object, as discussed in paragraph 3.3.2 (Zwalve, 2000, p. 100). The Germanic right of ownership, on the other hand, contained a strong social element, meaning that by exercising the right of ownership the owner had to consider the interests of third parties within the community.

This social element comes from the collective right of ownership that underlies the Germanic society. An example of this social element is to be found when studying the power to destroy an object. When destroying an object there was always another person that was hindered in his rights. Destruction was against the Germanic notion of ownership (Wesel, 1997, p. 182). This does not mean that individual ownership did not exist at all under Germanic law. Individual ownership has been developed in the course of time, next to the already existing collective ownership, but it was limited to clothing, weapons and other objects necessary for daily life (Kunst, 1968, pp. 190–198; Wesel, 1997, p. 182).

6. England's remarkable (law) transformation

While the European continent was stocked in the 'Dark Ages', William the Conqueror invaded England in 1066 A.D. The existing English constitutional and legal history and major diversity of law ended abruptly. The Norman conquest was the starting point for the development of current English law. The introduction of the full-grown feudal system led to a whole new classification of English society. William had an uncompromising view about the land of his conquered kingdom; all the land belonged to him and in this view he placed himself on top of the feudal pyramid. William seized the land and distributed it among his followers but he also allowed the Englishmen to redeem their estates by paying for them (G. Smith, 1990, pp. 39–57).

6.1 England's remarkable law transformation

During the twelfth and thirteenth centuries common law originally developed as the collective judicial decisions that were based in tradition, custom and precedent. Under the reign of King Henry II (1154–1189) common law was further developed. This king introduced the first national courts, known as the Royal Courts. At the beginning the competence of the Royal Courts was very restricted, but in a short time the competence extended enormously which finally resulted in one common English law.

A civilian was only competent to go to court when he had a writ. A writ was a letter containing a command of the king, set up by his chancellory. The writ was only granted when the court was competent. But this system had a flaw: it seemed that the Royal Court had no competence if there was no writ available. The solution was found in expanding the competence of the Lord Chancellor, head of the Chancery and by this decision the Court of Chancery was born. At the start of this 'new way of jurisdiction' the person of the Chancellor was a high-placed cleric, who based his decisions on 'equity', in meaning of reasonableness and fairness. By equity the shortcomings of common law could be overcome.

Since the sixteenth century, equity became, besides common law and the statutes, the third legal source in England. During the seventeenth century, the judgments of the Chancellor were collected. In the eighteenth century it became clear that equity was not equal to reasonableness and fairness; equity exists of several solid and accurately formulated legal rules and was conceived as a corrective system of justice.

By the Judicature Acts of 1876 the two courts, the common law courts and the equity courts, lost their independence, and they were joined together in the Supreme Court of Judicature (Zwalve, 2000, pp. 29–33; Lokin and Zwalve, 2001, pp. 358–380; Gray and Gray, 2007, pp. 20–22). This reformation, however, did not lead to any alteration in material law.

The most remarkable equitable development is the trust. The core of the trust is splitting of the ownership of an object and assigning it to different persons, so that the legal ownership of an object goes to the trustee, and the equitable ownership of the same object to another person, the beneficiary. The beneficiary can enjoy all the benefits of the object (R. Smith, 2006, pp. 18–20). The trust was, even before the Conquest of 1066, developed in practice, but was not recognized by the courts. An example: person (A) was leaving his land for a specific period and he transferred the land to a friend (B), with the intention that B would take care of the land during this period. After returning to the land, A expected B to transfer the land back to him. Mostly B was willing to do so, but sometimes B refused. At common law A did not have any rights against B since he had transferred the estate to B, so B became the owner of the estate.

In the fourteenth and fifteenth century the trust went through a remarkable development. The Chancellor decided that parties could be forced, when demanded by one of the primary parties, to act according to the agreement. Recourse to this agreement was also possible when a third party was entitled as new legal owner of the property. In favour of the original owner A the Chancellor accepted another type of ownership: ownership in equity. So, in equity A was recognised as the owner. This development resulted in two possible types of ownership; one at common law and one in equity (Edwards and Stockwell, 2005, pp. 6–8).

6.2 The characteristics of English law

English law deviates strongly from the judicial systems on the European mainland. The main distinguishing characteristics of English property law will be discussed below.

The first distinguishing characteristic of English property law can be found in the distinction between *actiones in rem* and *actiones in personam*, discussed earlier in 3.3.1. On the European mainland this division leads to a division in absolute and relative rights in the judicial systems. In English law this division leads to a different structure, which can be explained on the basis of the writs.

During the thirteenth century it was Bracton who made a distinction between writs *in rem* and writs *in personam*, which resulted in the distinction between immovable and movable objects. In case of a writ *in rem*, the object to which a person was entitled could only concern an immovable object. A writ *in rem* is seen as a real action and this part of property law is indicated as the law of real property. When it concerned a writ *in personam*, there was a movable object involved, and a demand for compensation was the only option. The writ *in personam* is indicated as personal property. In contrast to the European mainland the distinction of the actions *in rem* and *in personam* did not lead to the division of property law on the one hand and the law of obligations on the other hand but led to a distinction in property law itself (Zwalve, 2000, pp. 97–100).

The above mentioned distinction between movables and immovables leads to the second characteristic of English property law. This characteristic is the structural difference between property law relating to land and property law relating to other property.

Personal property at common law knows an absolute ownership, whereby the ownership cannot be divided. In equity, ownership can be divided under a trust of personal rights. All objects of personal property can be defined as chattels, in contrast to the objects of land property which are indicted with the term estate. These chattels can, with the exception of leasehold, be divided into tangible and intangible movables (Goode, 2004, pp. 27–55). Tangible property has a physical substance and can be touched. Real estate and money though cannot be indicated as a tangible. Intangible property exists in a claim to land, to goods or to money.

Personal property is not entrusted with the inheritance of the feudal system, in contrast to the rules of English real property law. These latter rights grew in an era where the king was lord of all the land and land stood for wealth (Gleeson, 1997, pp. 3–14). Property land law will discussed hereafter.

The third characteristic of English property law, that is also a deviation from all the modern concepts of ownership in continental Europe, is the approach of the concept of ownership concerning the property of land. Ownership was in Roman law, just as in modern law systems as discussed above, absolute. English law on the other hand is not familiar with an absolute right of ownership, which is characterized by its independence from other rights and is not related to time. This appears not only from the already discussed split ownership, where ownership is always divided in ownership and possession, but also from the still maintained feudal land structure from which various estates are generated.

Concerning real property land law, the formal structure is nowadays still feudal, so the king is formally still the only lord of all the land. The holder of the estate can have an estate in fee simple absolute in possession, an estate in fee tail or an estate for life. The estate in fee simple absolute in possession is often indicated with *fee simple* and is, as discussed below, correspondingly close to the continental ownership (Burn, Cartwright and Cheshire, 2006, pp. 27–28; Zwalve, 2000, p. 100).

The estate in fee simple is the most extensive right one can have in land. Fee simple indicates that this estate does not know any limitation in time, so that it will not end with the death of the holder of the estate as, for example, the estate for life, as will be discussed later on. The Law of Property Act 1925 points out that this estate is one of the two primary estates in modern land law, but that it can be a legal estate only when it satisfies the demand of 'absolute and in possession'. 'Absolute' implies that the rights concerning the estate are exclusive, meaning that there are no restrictions whatsoever. 'In possession' signifies that the holder of the estate has the enjoyment of the property right. No one can have a stronger title to the land than the holder of the estate who has the estate in fee simple.

The estate in fee tail and the estate for life are equitable rights and are not comparable to the absolute ownership of the European mainland. The estate in fee tail can be defined as an estate in land that is limited in inheritance, whereby only direct heirs could be eligible for this estate. Besides the limitation of the class of heirs, there was also a limitation concerning the tenant's competence to act; the class of heirs had a certain expectation and with regard to this expectation the acts of the tenant were limited. The estate in fee tail is as legal estate not allowed anymore since the Law of Property Act 1925, but only possible as equitable estate.

The estate for life can be compared with usufruct. This estate is linked to the life of the holder of the estate and the estate comes to an end at the moment of his death. From the moment of death of the original holder of the estate the estate returns to the person, the grantor, who established the estate. Even when the original holder of the estate has conveyed the estate, the estate still lasts only for the time of the life of the original holder of the estate. This regression of the estate is often indicated with the term 'reversion'. The estate for life has the logical result that it cannot be inherited (Zwalve, 2000, pp. 113–155; Burn, Cartwright and Cheshire, 2006, pp. 167–182; Gray and Gray, 2007, pp. 16–18)

Besides the above-mentioned division of estates there is another commonly used distinction; the freehold and the non-freehold estates. The above-mentioned estates are all freehold estates, implying that the king has granted an interest over the land. This freehold estate represents real property. At common law the primary estate in land is the freehold, meaning the above-mentioned estate in fee simple absolute in possession. The non-freehold estates give their holder the 'using rights' of the estate for a certain period of time, also indicated with the term lease. These estates are personal property (Zwalve, 2000, pp. 125–129). The above-mentioned characteristics of English property law do not cover all its characteristics but cover the most important interests for this chapter.

7. The resurrection of Roman law

As seen above, England received a uniform law much earlier than the mainland of Europe. The development of this uniform law did not experience any (immediate) influence of the Corpus Iuris Civilis. On the mainland of Europe, the development of law went completely different.

From the twelfth century onwards mainland lawyers became interested in the Corpus Iuris Civilis, which led to developments in all the areas of law, especially in the area of private law. This period is characterized as 'the reception of Roman law' and can be considered as a point of departure of the European legal science since the Middle Ages. The reason for this growing interest in the Corpus Iuris Civilis can be found in the weakness of local laws and the lack of unity of the Germanic laws (Huebner, 2000, pp. 1–16). The Corpus Iuris Civilis was not treated as a codex but as an object of intellectual reflection. In this way the Corpus Iuris Civilis made a big contribution to the development of private law. The validity of the Corpus Iuris Civilis existed until the start of the nineteenth century, when the different European mainland countries introduced their own codes. Nevertheless, the Corpus Iuris Civilis remained a source of inspiration (Spruit, 2003, pp. 90–97).

The first lawyers who studied and taught the Corpus Iuris Civilis, also known as Glossators, were living in Bologna, Italy between 1100 and 1250 A.D. They treated each individual text separately, and put their comments down in glosses and summaries. The Glossators used the Corpus Iuris Civilis as a practical application, but they often forgot to take into consideration the differences between Roman society and the society of the Middle Ages. This often led to adaptation of Roman law to the needs of the medieval society.

As an example of adaptation the expression *ius in re* can be mentioned. The Glossators related a *ius in re* (a property right in modern terms) to all cases where the Corpus Iuris Civilis speaks of an *actio in rem*. But in the Corpus Iuris Civilis itself the expression *ius in re* was unknown, because Roman law did not even know rights; it only knew actions.

A very confusing and important adaptation can be found in splitting the *dominium*. The Glossators were searching for a solution to explain the situation and the rights in a feudal relation between vassals and their lords. Feudal law was developed from the eighth century on as an original system of law. It was created independently of Roman or Germanic law and was mainly developed on customs (Van Caenegem, 1992, p. 20).

The Glossators found two *actiones* in the Corpus Iuris Civilis that could function as an interpretation of this feudal relationship, namely the *actio directum* and the *actio utile*. The *actio directum* was treated as the right of main *dominium*, and the *actio utile* as the right to use the *dominium*, *usus fructus* (Coing, 1953, p. 351; Feenstra, 1979, pp. 6–20; Visser, 1985, pp. 39–40). As seen above, Roman law knew different kinds of ownership, but did not split the core of the ownership as has been done by the Glossators. Splitting ownership in the core is only possible by approaching ownership as a bundle of rights.

Bartolus de Saxoferrato (1313–1357) struggled with fitting the feudal system into the terms of *dominium*. Bartolus defined ownership as a right to have access to an object in *perfecte disponendi*, which can be translated as full disposal. By defining ownership as *perfecte disponendi* Bartolus had the intention to make a distinction between the rights of *dominium* on the one hand and the right of possession on the other hand. In contrast to the Glossators, Bartolus distinguished three forms of ownership; *dominium directum*, *dominium utile* and *quasi dominium* (Coing, 1953, pp. 364–371).

The meaning of the *dominium directum* and the *dominium utile* can be compared with the *dominium directum* and the *dominium utile* as defined by the period of the Glossators. The third kind of dominium, the *quasi dominium*, was less accepted than the *dominium directum* and the *dominium utile*. This *quasi dominium* was used to protect a person who did not have the *usucapio* (ownership acquired by possession during a certain period of time) yet and was protected by the *actio Publiciana*. The *actio Publiciana* was brought into being for the protection of the praetorian owner (Feenstra, 1989, pp. 111–113).

One of the followers and student of Bartolus was Baldus de Ubaldis (1327–1400). His considerations have been very important with regard to the further development of the law of property. Baldus used the term *iura realia* instead of *iura in re*, which he defined as rights without the existence of any commitment. Baldus was the first lawyer who came up with an enumeration of the *iura realia*. This enumeration existed of *dominium*, the right of succession, personal servitudes, (real) servitudes and hypothec, including the pignus. A further distinction between these rights was not made by Baldus.

It was Hugo Donellus in the sixteenth century who made a distinction between *dominium* on the one hand and limited real rights on the other hand. This distinction became the basis for Grotius's theory of *dominium*, which became a leading principle in the legal systems on the European mainland. Grotius's theory will be discussed hereunder (Feenstra, 1979, p. 20; Smits, 1996, pp. 52–53).

8. The influence of natural law on property law and the run-up to the Age of Reason

During the sixteenth and seventeenth century the insights changed. The Corpus Iuris Civilis was not the main source of law anymore. Its leading position was taken over by natural law, which content was set by nature and therefore it was valid everywhere. The change was brought about by the growing opinion that the rules of the Corpus Iuris Civilis were not timeless. Many solutions from the Corpus Iuris Civilis were sensed as irrational and therefore replaced by rational solutions found in natural law (Lokin and Zwalve, 2001, pp. 30–33).

The spiritual father of natural law in modern times was Hugo Grotius, who lived from 1583 to 1645. Two of his most important works were 'Inleydinge tot de Hollantsche regts-geleertheyt' (Introduction to Dutch jurisprudence) and 'De jure belli ac pacis' (On the Law of War and Peace). In these works he lays down his concept of natural law. According to Grotius the meaning of natural law is to be found in the reason (Scruton and Daalder, 2000, p. 37; Heirbaut, 2000, p. 85).

Grotius proposed some remarkable changes to private law. These proposals deviated from the rules of the Corpus Iuris Civilis. The theory of Grotius concerning ownership and limited property rights is an excellent example of his ideas on private law. Grotius's ideas on ownership did not deviate much from the concept of ownership known in the Middle Ages. Grotius made a distinction between *dominium* or full ownership on the one hand and incomplete ownership on the other hand. With full ownership he meant the position of the juridical owner, during the Middle Ages indicated with the term *dominium directum*. Incomplete ownership corresponded with the medieval term *dominium utile* and was according to Grotius a descent from the full ownership and therefore also enforceable against everyone. Grotius sees incomplete ownership as the same concept as Donellus, namely as *ius in re aliena*. Grotius's theoretical development was responsible for the disappearance of divided ownership (Van der Walt, 1995, pp. 20–22; Feenstra, 1989, pp. 118–122).

Another example of Grotius's different point of view was his theory on the moment of transferring property. In Roman law the ownership of an object transferred at the moment that the possession of the object was given to the buyer. The opinion of Grotius was that according to natural law the ownership was already transferred at the moment that the parties agreed on the transfer of ownership; at the moment of closing the contract (Lokin and Zwalve, 2001, p. 33).

In the extent of the ideas of Grotius, natural law flourished during the eighteenth century in all the European academies. Grotius's ideas on natural law continued to be revered and expanded by philosophers like John Locke (1632–1704) and Jean-Jacques Rousseau (1712–1778). Discussion of these philosophers would, however, go beyond the scope of this chapter.

The flourishing period is called 'the Age of Reason' and was a period of rationalism. In the thought of rationalism the law needed, for the sake of legal security, to be reformed because of its very divided and chaotic law structure; the law consisted of custom law, royal legislation, Canon law and Roman law.

9. How the history of property law became French toast. . . .

The starting point for the French Revolution was the threat of bankruptcy of the French state in 1788, and the way in which King Louis XVI tried to turn this disaster aside by calling the Etats Généraux together. The Etats Généraux met on 5 May 1789, for the first time since 1614, holding several meetings with the intention of presenting reforms to prevent bankruptcy. In the past the Etats Généraux, represented by the three classes; the nobility, the clerical order and the bourgeoisie, were only called together for special occasions, especially when an additional flow of money was needed.

During one of the meetings, the bourgeoisie was not satisfied with the procedures concerning the counting of the votes. They separated themselves from the nobility and the clerical order and adopted the name: 'Assemblée Nationale Constituante' or National Assembly. The Assembly strived for a constitution, an idea that was a remaining product of natural law. This constitution should make an end to the different rules of law existing for the different classes and should bring the number of legal systems existing back to one; the constitution should bring equality before the law (Lesaffer, 2004, pp. 367–368).

Equality was not found in feudal relations during the eighteenth century. The society of the eighteenth century was, just as during the Middle Ages, controlled by the feudal system. But the feudal obligations accompanied by the feudal relations could not be compared with the obligations during the Middle Ages. The lord, holder of the *dominium directum*, lost his right more and more to the tenant, holder of the *dominium utile*. The obligations from the tenant to the lord, which were set in return for the *dominium utile*, did not increase, but they actually decreased. Financial obligations became worthless because of inflation; personal obligations on the other hand became near to useless because of a changing society. Besides the decreased value of the obligations, the content of the tenants' obligations was often unclear, which resulted in confusion. As a result of the shift of the amount of rights between the lord and the tenant and the unclearness of the content of the obligations, the value of the right of the lord became worthless. By the abolition of the feudal system, the *duplex dominium* (double ownership) was rejected and from that moment on the only kind of ownership accepted was the *dominium utile* (Heirbaut, 2003, pp. 301–320).

The first major step to equality was made by the National Assembly decree of 4 August 1789. With the decree feudalism and the attached privileges of the nobility were abolished. The abolition of feudalism was recommended by the nobility. The consequence was that all Frenchmen became citizens, and recognized as 'libres et égaux' (Lokin and Zwalve, 2001, pp. 182–210). Equality came to expression in the 'Déclaration des Droits de l'Homme et du Citoyen', that was accepted by the National Assembly on 26 August 1789. The Declaration consisted of a preamble and 17 articles, containing a set of individual and collective rights intended to give an enumeration of the most important rights.

Article 2 gave an enumeration of human rights and also mentioned freedom of ownership. The juridical explanation of freedom of ownership was discussed in article 17: 'La propriété étant un droit inviolable et sacré, nul ne peut en être privé, si ce n'est lorsque la nécessité publique, légalement constatée, l'exige évidemment, et sous la condition d'une juste et préalable indemnité'.

Boersema discusses in his book 'Mens mensura iuris' the content and the relation between these two articles. Although the relationship and the content of these articles are beyond the reach of this chapter, it needs to be pointed out that article 17 deals with the terms 'inviolable' and 'sacral'. These terms mean that the ownership concerning an object is given by God, and that the ownership is inviolable. Ownership can only be meant to be inviolable when it is taken out of a social environment, otherwise the inviolability cannot be guaranteed. So article 17 does not refer to a positive right of ownership, but only to ownership placed outside the social environment (Boersema, 1998, pp. 45–81).

The Déclaration des Droits de l'Homme et du Citoyen has been of major importance since it came into effect. With the introduction of the first written Constitution, in the autumn of 1791, the Declaration was incorporated in the Constitution as a preamble. From that moment on France became a parliamentary and constitutional monarchy (Lesaffer, 2004, pp. 370–373). But the days of the monarchy were numbered and it was finally abolished on 21 September 1792. The abolition of the monarchy marked at the same time a new polity, the republic. As a result of this new polity, society demanded a new constitution. The ratification of the Constitution took place in June 1793. It was suspended because of the ongoing war, which finally resulted in the fact that it never came into force (Lokin and Zwalve, 2001, pp. 186–188).

After the Constitution of 1793 several drafts followed, but none of them has had such a major influence on the codification history of the European mainland as the 'Code civil des Français', in short: the Code civil. The Code civil, during the Napoleonic era also named the Code Napoleon, entered into force on 21 March 1804. This codification contained a definition of a property right in article 544 C.C.: 'La propriété est le droit de jouir et disposer des choses de la manière la plus absolue, pourvu qu'on n'en fasse pas un usage prohibé par les lois ou par les règlements'. This article gives a very far-reaching review of individual freedom concerning the use of the right of ownership. Only through a conflicting situation by law or regulation will the freedom to use the right be put aside. With the clause 'la manière la plus absolue' is meant that an object can only be owned by one owner. The property right of the owner can only be divided when the Code civil approves (Danet, 2002, pp. 215–225). By this phrase the feudal system was definitively abolished.

In the countries which Napoleon conquered the legal power of the Code civil was introduced. After the defeat of Napoleon many of these countries decided to apply the Code civil until they had completed their own codex. Each country came up with its own code, containing its own rules of law and based on its own principles; the solutions for the many different legal questions were very diverse. However, the different codes all hold on to the uniform concept of ownership, fearing the return of the unfair consequences of the feudal system.

10. . . . Or not?

The previous pages show that the main characteristics of the concept of ownership, as it exists on the European mainland, are uniformity and absoluteness. The following pages display the limitations to these characteristics.

10.1 Infringements on the absoluteness of ownership

In principle third parties are not allowed to infringe on the right of ownership, because it would alienate the characteristic of absoluteness. Nevertheless, there are certain infringements an owner has to tolerate. These are the infringements that find their justification in the balancing of the interests of the owner on the one side and interests of a third party on the other side. The balancing may result in a lawful infringement of the right of ownership under rules of private or public law (Van Dam, Mijnssen and van Velten, 2002, pp. 35–54).

Public law infringements on the right of ownership follow from laws, decrees and rules of unwritten public law. These rules of public law may limit the owner's right to use the property as well as the right to dispose of it. Furthermore, authorities may have specific rights concerning the objects of ownership. The most far-reaching infringement by public law is expropriation. In the case of expropriation the right of ownership is taken away from the owner for the sake of the public interest (Van Dam, Mijnssen and van Velten, 2002, pp. 26–34).

Private law infringements derive from the rights of third parties and rules of unwritten private law. Under certain circumstances the exercise of property rights may amount to abuse of competence and be unlawful for that reason. In a case of abuse of competence the owner exceeds the competence linked to his property right. Moreover, causing nuisance give the neighbours a tort action against the person causing this nuisance. Nuisance is an act which interferes with the enjoyment of the neighbouring property. Not every act of nuisance can be considered to be unlawful: this depends on the nature, extent and duration of the impediment and also on the damage caused by it. If the nuisance is regarded as unlawful the law will normally give the neighbours a tort action against the troublemaker (Van Dam, 2006, pp. 389–396; Pitlo, Gerver and Hidma, 1995, pp. 199–205).

Article 1, First Protocol of the European Convention on Human Rights (ECHR), expresses the protection of the right of ownership against infringements of third parties. Article 1, subsection 1 provides that 'every natural or legal person is entitled to the peaceful enjoyment of his possessions. No one shall be deprived of his possessions except in the public interest and subject to the conditions provided for by law and by the general principles of international law'. By recognizing the right of peaceful enjoyment, article 1 guarantees the right of property, according to the European Court of Human Rights (*Marckx v. Belgium*, application no. 6833/74). The right of property has to be understood in a broad sense. The Court stresses that: 'possession has an autonomous meaning which is certainly not limited to ownership of physical goods: certain other rights and interests constituting assets can also be regarded as "property rights", and thus as "possessions"', (*Gasus Dosier- und Fördertechnik GmbH v. The Netherlands*, application no. 15375/89). Rights and interests that do not have a financial or economic value are not covered by article 1 (Barkhuysen, van Emmerik and Ploeger, 2005, pp. 109–112).

The second sentence of article 1, subsection 1, provides that no one can be deprived of his or her property, except when the deprivation is in the public interest and can be justified by an action permitted by law. This sentence gives the states a certain margin of appreciation when judging if the law governs the aim of any interference, as well as its proportionality and the preservation of a fair balance (*J.A. Pye (Oxford) Ltd v. The United Kingdom*, application no. 44302/02). The legal measure taken has to be reasonable and proportional having regard to the goal aimed for: there has to be a 'fair balance' between the public interest on the one side and the protection of individual property rights on the other side (Van der Pot, Elzinga and de Lange, 2006, pp. 440–443). The protection offered by article 1 against expropriation by a state is a minimum standard. The states are free to offer additional protection.

10.2 Infringements on the uniformity of ownership

Many codes that had been developed in the countries on the European mainland following the French Revolution contained the principle of uniform ownership. However, the legal development in several countries during the last two centuries casts doubt on the validity of uniformity as a characteristic feature of ownership. More and more uniform ownership was regarded as rigid and inflexible. This development results from the demand of society that struggles with the uniform concept. As a consequence of this development the distinction between relative or personal rights on the one hand and absolute rights on the other hand has become vague, which in several cases led to divided ownership. There are many examples to name. Almost every country has its own exception to the principle of uniform ownership, but a complete enumeration goes beyond the reach of this chapter.

The German foundation of a uniform concept of ownership is laid down in §903 Bürgerliches Gesetzbuch (German civil code): 'The owner of a thing may, to the extent that a statute or third-party rights do not conflict with this, deal with the thing at his discretion and exclude others from every influence'. But also the German legislator created deviations on the uniform concept of ownership. A remarkable example of divided ownership in German law is the *Treuhand* (trust).

With *Treuhand* the *Treugeber* (settlor) transfers the Treuhand-ownership to the *Treuhänder* (trustee). The Treuhand-ownership can be seen as the juridical ownership with regard to an object. Although the *Treugeber* has transferred his juridical ownership to the *Treuhänder*, he retains the economic ownership (Schulte-Bunert, 2005, pp. 14–27; Wieling, 2006, pp. 799–818). The concept of *Treuhand* shows major similarities to the common law express trust.

A recent development in the field of divided ownership is the French *fiducie*. The *fiducie* was introduced into the French civil code by statute of 19 February 2007. The *fiducie* is defined in article 2011 of the civil code: 'La fiducie est l'opération par laquelle un ou plusieurs constituants transfèrent des biens, des droits ou des sûretés, ou un ensemble de biens, de droits ou de sûretés, présents ou futurs, à un ou plusieurs fiduciaires qui, les tenant séparés de leur patrimoine propre, agissent dans un but déterminé au profit d'un ou plusieurs bénéficiaires'.

In the case of *fiducie* the property is transferred by the settlor to the fiduciary, under an obligation to hold it for the benefit of another, the beneficiary. This type of *fiducie* is often defined with the term *fiducie-gestion*. Besides the *fiducie-gestion*, French law distinguishes another two types of *fiducie*, the *fiducie-sûreté* (security trust) and the *fiducie-transmission* (transmission trust).

The *fiducie-gestion* gives the opportunity to create arrangements equivalent to the common law trust already discussed above. The *fiducie-gestion* is often indicated as the French trust (Bell, Boyron and Whittaker, 2007, pp. 340–341).

As we have seen above, both developments, the German *Treuhand* as well as the French *fiducie*, lead to divided ownership.

Conclusion

Ownership is the most comprehensive right a person can have regarding an object. There has always been a strong interaction between law on the one side and the needs of society on the other side. Therefore, ownership cannot be precisely defined because its meaning and reach adapt to the social needs. This interaction is reflected clearly in Roman and Germanic ownership.

Although Roman ownership has been refined during the three main historical periods, each characterized by its own polity: the Monarchy, the Republic and the Principate, the characteristic of absoluteness should be mentioned as *the* fundamental characteristic of the right of ownership. Absoluteness can be defined as the independence of ownership relating to other rights and the absolute power of the owner to exercise authority over the object.

On the contrary, Germanic ownership cannot be characterized as absolute, but is, more than Roman law ownership, restricted by interests of the community; the Germanic owner has to take account of the interests of third parties within the community. This social content derives from the notion of collective ownership that was the basis for the Germanic individual ownership.

The interaction between the social needs on the one hand and ownership on the other hand underlies the different forms of ownership in a particular society. The reasons for acknowledgement of the plurality of ownership differed per society. Roman society was familiar with different types of ownership, such as ownership attributed to foreigners and ownership concerning immovables in the province. But the two most important types of ownership were the quiritarian ownership and the praetorian ownership. Quiritarian ownership can be defined as civil ownership. Praetorian ownership comes into being only when strict appliance of general rules would lead to an unreasonable outcome. In the praetorian ownership the social need is laid down to amend the hardship caused occasionally by the quiritarian ownership.

The medieval feudal system also knew different types of ownership which were called *dominium directum* and *dominium utile*. In contrast to the Roman *dominium* these were not different types of ownership which existed next to each other, but types of ownership that emerged after the division of the original ownership. The *dominium directum* was treated as the actual, but bare right of ownership, of which the *dominium utile*, the right of exclusive use of the object, was separated.

These different types of ownership, often referred to as *duplex dominium*, were not created out of the need to correct hardship, as was the case in Roman law, but out of the need to give expression to the relations between vassals and lords in the feudal system.

English ownership concerning land is, like medieval ownership, based on the feudal system and can be defined as divided. As in the Middle Ages on the European continent divided ownership can be explained as splitting of the right of ownership in a right of use and in a right of bare ownership.

With the French Revolution the natural interaction between society and ownership ended abruptly. One of the core notions of the French Revolution was equality, but equality was not found in the feudal system. The commitments derived from the feudal system were in general formulated in the interest and advantage of the aristocracy. The legal basis for these commitments was given by the possibility to split the ownership. By bringing down the feudal system, divided ownership was abolished; the only kind of ownership accepted was the *dominium utile*. From that moment on ownership was defined as absolute and unitary.

The unitary and absolute concept of ownership has, even after the Napoleonic era, been continued by the different countries on the mainland of Europe, mainly out of fear of inequality. The English divided ownership, on the other hand, was not replaced by the unitary concept of ownership, because England was not involved in the French Revolution.

The consequence of strict adherence to the unitary and absolute ownership is that ownership can no longer adapt freely to the needs of society. However, in the centuries following the introduction of the absolute and uniform ownership the possibilities to restrict the absoluteness of ownership have grown. Infringements on the absolute ownership characteristic are possible when they result out of written or unwritten law, or when resulting from the rights of others. In this way the social needs are reflected in the reach of ownership.

Concerning the unitary ownership characteristic, society has created different kinds of ownership, which can be seen as forms of divided ownership, as the *Treuhand (German trust)* and the *fiducie-gestion (French trust)*. Both forms of divided ownership are codified.

With the possibility to limit absolute ownership and with the increase of the number of different kinds of ownership, the unitary and absolute concept of ownership has in fact come to an end.

Bibliography

Ankum, J. (1976), *Elementen van Romeins recht*, Zwolle: W.E.J. Tjeenk Willink.

Barkhuysen, T., M. van Emmerik and H. Ploeger (2005), *De eigendomsbescherming van artikel 1 van het Eerste Protocol bij het EVRM en het Nederlandse burgerlijk recht*, Deventer: Kluwer.

Bell, John, Sophie Boyron and Simon Whittaker (2007), *Principles of French Law*, Oxford: Oxford University Press.

Van den Bergh, G. (1979), *Eigendom, grepen uit de geschiedenis van een omstreden begrip*, Deventer: Kluwer.

Boersema, D. (1998), *Mens mensura iuris*, Deventer: Kluwer.

Bouckaert, Boudewijn (1990), 'What's property?', *Harvard Journal of Law & Public Policy*, **13**, 775–816.

Brundage, James (1995), *Medieval Canon Law*, Harlow: Pearson Education Limited.

Burn, E., J. Cartwright and G. Cheshire (2006), *Cheshire and Burn's Modern Law of Real Property*, Oxford: Oxford University Press.

Van Caenegem, R. (1992), *An Historical Introduction to Private Law*, Cambridge: Cambridge University Press.

Coing, Helmut (1953), 'Zur Eigentumslehre des Bartolus', *Zeitschrift der Savigny-Stiftung für Rechtsgeschichte*, **70**, 348–371.

Coleman, Christopher (1914), *Constantine the Great and Christianity, three phases: the historical, the legendary and the spurious*, New York: The Columbia University Press.

Van Dam, C. (2006), *European Tort Law*, Oxford: Oxford University Press.

Van Dam, C., F. Mijnssen and A. van Velten (2002), *Mr. C. Asser's Handleiding tot de beoefening van het Nederlandse Burgerlijk Recht, Goederenrecht, Tweede Deel: zakelijke rechten*, Deventer: Kluwer.

Danet, Didier (2002), 'Does the Code Civil matter?', *European Journal of Law and Economics*, **14**, 215–225.

David, Ann (2000), *The Experience of Ancient Egypt*, London: Routledge.

Derine, Raymond (1982), *Schets van het Romeins Privaatrecht: uitwendige geschiedenis*, Antwerpen: Kluwer rechtswetenschappen.

Diamond, A. (2004), *Primitive Law, Past and Present*, London: Routledge.

Dooyeweerd, H. (1957), *De verhouding tussen individu en gemeenschap in de Romeinse en Germaanse eigendomsopvatting*, Amsterdam: H.J. Paris.

Edwards, Richard and Nigel Stockwell (2005), *Trusts and Equity*, Harlow: Pearson Education.

Feenstra, Robert (1979), *Ius in re, het begrip zakelijk recht in historisch perspectief*, Zwolle: W.E.J. Tjeenk Willink.

Feenstra, Robert (1989), 'Dominium and ius in re aliena: the origins of a civil law distinction', in Birks, Peter, *New Perspectives in the Roman Law of Property: Essays for Barry Nicholas*, Oxford: Clarendon Press, pp. 111–122.

Gilissen, John and Frits Gorlé (1991), *Historische inleiding tot het recht, deel I: Ontstaan en evolutie van de belangrijkste rechtsstelsels*, Antwerpen: Kluwer.

Gleeson, Simon (1997), *Personal Property Law*, London: FT Law and Tax.

Goode, Roy (2004), *Commercial Law*, London: Penguin Books.

Gray, Kevin and Susan Gray (2007), *Land Law*, Oxford: Oxford University Press.

Hanenburg, Jacoba (1972), *De wet der twaalf tafelen*, Gent: Story-Scientia.

Heirbaut, Dirk (2000), *Europese juristen en oud recht*, Gent: Academia Press.

Heirbaut, Dirk (2003), 'Feudal law: the real ius commune of property in Europe, or: Should we reintroduce duplex dominium?', *European Review of Private Law*, 301–320.

Huebner, Rudolf (2000), *A History of Germanic Private Law*, New Jersey: The Lawbook Exchange Ltd.

Isager, Signe and Jens Skydsgaard (1992), *Ancient Greek Agriculture: An Introduction*, London: Routledge.

Kaser, Max and F. Wubbe (1971), *Romeins Privaatrecht*, Zwolle: N.V. W.E.J. Tjeenk Willink.

Kaser, Max and Rolf Knütel (2003), *Römisches Privatrecht*, München: Verlag C.H. Beck.

Kunst, A. (1968), *Historische ontwikkeling van het recht, deel II*, Zwolle: N.V. uitgeversmaatschappij W.E.J. Tjeenk Willink.

Lesaffer, Randall, (2004), *Inleiding tot de Europese rechtsgeschiedenis*, Leuven: Universitaire Pers Leuven.

Lokin, J. and W. Zwalve (2001), *Hoofdstukken uit de Europese Codificatiegeschiedenis*, Deventer: Kluwer.

Maffi, Alberto (2005), 'Family and property law', in Gagarin, Michael and David Cohen, *The Cambridge Companion to Ancient Greek Law*, Cambridge: Cambridge University Press, pp. 254–266.

Mäkinen, Virpi (2001), *Property Rights in the Late Medieval Discussion on Franciscan Poverty*, Leuven: Peeters.
Mousourakis, George (2003), *The Historical and Institutional Context of Roman Law*, Aldershot and Dartmouth: Ashgate Publishing.
Parker, Robert (2005), 'Law and Religion', in Gagarin, Michael and David Cohen, *The Cambridge Companion to Ancient Greek Law*, Cambridge: Cambridge University Press, pp. 61–81.
Pitlo, A., P. Gerver and T. Hidma (1995), *Het systeem van het Nederlandse Privaatrecht*, Deventer: Kluwer.
Van der Pot, C., D. Elzinga and R. de Lange (2006), *Handboek van het Nederlandse staatsrecht*, Deventer: Kluwer.
Potjewijd, Geert (1998), *Beschikkingsbevoegdheid, bekrachtiging en convalescentie: een romanistische studie*, Deventer: Kluwer.
Schulte-Bunert, Kai (2005), *Das Vertragsstatut der Treuhand im internationalen Privatrecht*, Frankfurt am Main: Peter Lang.
Scruton, Roger and Hessel Daalder (2000), *Spinoza*, Rotterdam: Lemniscaat Publisher.
Smith, Goldwin (1990), *A Constitutional and Legal History of England*, New York: Dorset Press.
Smith, Roger (2006), *Property Law*, Harlow: Longman.
Smith, William (1859), *A Dictionary of Greek and Roman Antiquities*, Boston: Little, Brown and Company.
Smits, Jan (1996), 'Van partijen en derden; over interpretatie van de numerus clausus van zakelijke rechten', *Groninger Opmerkingen en Mededelingen XIII*, 41–64.
Spruit, J. (1994), *Enchiridium, overzicht van de geschiedenis van het Romeins privaatrecht*, Deventer: Kluwer.
Spruit, J. (2002), *Metopen: verzamelde essays over het Romeinse recht en zijn geschiedenis*, Deventer: Kluwer.
Spruit, J. (2003), *Cunabula iuris, Elementen van het Romeinse privaatrecht*, Deventer: Kluwer.
Van der Steur, J. (2003), *Grenzen van rechtsobjecten, een onderzoek naar de grenzen van objecten van eigendomsrechten en intellectuele eigendomsrechten*, Deventer: Kluwer.
Theodorides, Aristide (1971), 'The concept of law in Egypt', in Harris, J., *The Legacy of Egypt*, Oxford: Clarendon Press, pp. 291–322.
VerSteeg, Russ (2002), *Law in Ancient Egypt*, Durham: Carolina Academic Press.
Visser, D. (1985), 'The "Absoluteness" of ownership: the South African common law in perspective', *Acta Juridica*, 39–52.
Van der Walt, A. (1995), 'Unity and pluralism in property theory – a review of property theories and debates in recent literature, part 1', *Tydskrif vir die Suid-Afrikaanse reg*, 15–42.
Wesel, Uwe (1997), *Geschichte des Rechts, Von den Frühformen bis zum Vertrag von Maastricht*, München: Verlag C.H. Beck.
Van de Wiel, Constant (1991), *History of Canon Law*, Louvain: Peeters Press.
Wieling, Hans (2006), *Sachenrecht, Band 1 Sachen, besitz und Rechte an beweglichen Sachen*, Berlin: Springer.
Yaron, Reuven (1988), *The Laws of Eshnunna*, Israel: The Magnes Press.
Yoffee, Norman (2005), *Myths of the Archaic State: Evolution of the Earliest Cities, States and Civilizations*, Cambridge: Cambridge University Press.
Zwalve, W. (2000), C.Æ. *Uniken Venema's Common Law & Civil Law*, Deventer: W.E.J. Tjeenk Willink.
Zwalve, W. (2003), *Hoofdstukken uit de geschiedenis van het Europese privaatrecht*, Deventer: Kluwer.

Cases

Marckx v. Belgium, 13 June 1979, application no. 6833/74.
Gasus Dosier- und Fördertechnik GmbH v. The Netherlands, 23 February 1995, application no. 15375/89.
J.A. Pye (Oxford) Ltd v. The United Kingdom, 8 June 2004, application no. 44302/02.

3 Property rights: a comparative view

Sjef van Erp and Bram Akkermans

1. Introduction

Property rights take a central place in any legal system. These rights offer the holder exclusive power over an object with effect against the whole world. Property rights are therefore different from personal rights, which generally only have effect between the parties who create them. Parties are, therefore, far more free to create contractual relations (rights and duties) than they are in the creation of property relations. Because of their far-reaching effect property rights are limited in number and content and their creation, transfer and extinguishment requires that a special, mandatory, procedure is followed. Property law is therefore different from contract law, characterised more by limitations than by freedom.

Property law still is very nationally (in the sense of: locally) oriented. Each legal system has its own property law, which, although it may be rooted in a particular legal tradition, still follows its own path based upon its own policy choices. This element of localism in property law systems, aggravated by a tendency to argue along doctrinal lines and develop the law in a highly technical and black letter rule-oriented way, makes the comparison of these systems complicated. At the same time, however, all (Western) property law systems seem to share a basic framework. The constituent elements of this framework can be classified in terms of general principles, policy choices, ground rules and technical rules (Van Erp 2006a, 13). This distinction in constituent elements enables a multi-level comparison and brings divergences in national property law traditions down to the level of technical differences, which can, if the political will is present to create, for instance, a European property law, be overcome. Generally, comparison is highly possible at the level of general principles, ground rules and the various policy choices which, as such, have to be made.

There are four basic general principles of property law. First of all – we only repeat what was said earlier – every property law system imposes limitations on the number and content of property rights. Parties are not free to create just any property right with any content. Instead, property rights function in a closed system that is known as the *numerus clausus* of property rights. Depending on the legal system the principle of *numerus clausus* takes the form of an absolutely closed list (in such a case the legal system applies a *rule* of *numerus clausus*) or of a set of general limitations (the respective legal system applies only a *principle* of *numerus clausus*) (Akkermans 2008, 403). Secondly, once it has been established that the right which was created is a property right, a fundamental starting point of property law is that a property right cannot exist without a specific object. This general starting point is known as the principle of specificity (Johansson 2009, 88). Thirdly, connected to the principle of specificity, another fundamental starting point is that, because of the 'against the whole world' effect of property rights, third parties must be able to know about the existence of such a right. This is the principle of publicity and can take the form of possession, e.g. in case of movable objects, or registration, e.g. in case of immovable objects (Cámara-Lapuente 2005, 798; Cantero 1998, 363). Together, these two principles are also known as the principle of transparency (Van Erp 2006a, 14). Finally, there is the principle of accessority. This concept is more controversial as a principle and has been classified as a technical rule before (Van Erp 2006a, 14–17). Accessority explains dependence between two elements in the law of property. Traditionally this concerns the intricate relation between a property security right and the claim the performance of which is being secured by such right. However, accessority is also used, especially in the Romanic legal tradition, to describe the relationship between the object of a property right and the property right itself.

Ground rules are also of a general nature and apply in all legal systems. These ground rules are the following. First, a holder of a right cannot transfer more than he has, known as the *nemo dat* rule. Second, the rule that older rights come before newer rights, the *prior tempore* rule. Third, the rule that limited property rights have priority over fuller rights, and, final and fourth, the rules that protect property rights.

These principles and ground rules create the basic framework that is characteristic of Western systems of property law. Taking this framework as a starting point offers a structured approach to find and analyse similarities and differences. Throughout this contribution these principles and ground rules will therefore be as a basis for comparison. What is highly intriguing to see is that systems of property law seem to share a common catalogue of property rights. Although differences exist, the core body of property rights in the various property law traditions is very similar. The explanation used for this similarity that the civil law systems share is that they are all rooted in Roman law and that certain aspects of the Roman law catalogue of rights seem to have influenced the development of the common law (Akkermans 2008, 411). Still, the differences at a technical level between the civil law and the common law traditions should not be forgotten or underestimated (Van Erp 2006b, 1043). This chapter therefore will first consider this common body of property rights. After that some important developments in the law of property, which is not a static area of law at all, but, on the contrary a highly dynamic legal field, will be discussed before the principles and ground rules will return once more in the conclusion.

2. Property rights

Property rights are rights that have effect against the whole world. It is this characteristic that distinguishes them from personal rights, which generally only take effect between the parties that create them (Reid 1997, 225). Consequently, property law and the law of obligations are separate areas of private law, each providing their own rules on creation, enforcement and destruction (Füller 2006, 10). Furthermore, in property law party autonomy is limited, whereas it is cherished in the law of contract.

The limitations on party autonomy in the law of property are best visible when looking at the *numerus clausus* of property rights. Parties are not free to create any property right they desire. Instead, they must comply with the requirements set forth by property law and choose one of the property rights made available in the legal system (*Typenzwang*) and abide by the restrictions the law imposes on the content of these rights (*Typenfixierung*) (Wiegand 1987, 633). These limitations make it possible to provide an overview of the property rights that are usually available. In this overview, the law of France, Germany, the Netherlands and England will be taken into account. French, German, and English law represent three of the major legal traditions in Europe (Glenn 2006, 125). The law of the Netherlands, which originally followed the French tradition, but which since 1992 is more in line with the German tradition, offers interesting insights into a system that attempts to combine these traditions.

2.1 Primary rights: ownership

In any legal system there is one property right that forms the source from which the other property rights may be derived. This can be done on the basis of a subtraction of powers from the most extensive right or on the basis of limiting the powers contained in the most extensive right (Struycken 2007, 361). This most extensive property right has also been named primary right to emphasise its importance in respect to the other property rights, which have been named lesser rights (Akkermans 2008, 298). These lesser rights are also called limited property rights as they limit the owner in exercising his powers and the right itself is more limited than the right of ownership.

The most extensive or primary right in civil law systems is the right of ownership. This right is the paramount entitlement a person can have with regard to an object. Whether such an object may be tangible, movable and immovable, or intangible, depends on the legal system. In French law all of these objects can be subject matter of the right of ownership, in German and Dutch law the right of ownership is restricted to tangible objects. Intangible objects, especially claims, are subjects of property law, but incapable of being owned. Instead, the term entitlement is used. In practical terms the differences between 'owning' a movable or immovable tangible object and being 'entitled' to a claim may be limited, as both rights can be transferred and used as security by creating a limited security right (Gretton 2007, 802).

The right of ownership as the paramount entitlement provides its holder the right to use, enjoy and dispose of his right. Moreover, in French doctrine the right of ownership is awarded three characteristics. First, the right is absolute, it cannot be fragmented into two types of ownership (Terré and Simler 1998, 107). This characteristic should be seen as a rejection of the *duplex dominium*, i.e. fragmented ownership, that was known under the *ancien régime*, i.e. the law that applied in France before the French Revolution. Secondly, the right of ownership is an exclusive right (Chabas 1994, 84). This indicates that only the owner is entitled to use, enjoy and dispose of the object of ownership and only he may exclude anyone from interfering with these powers. Thirdly, the right of ownership is perpetual (Chabas 1994, p. 103). The perpetuity of the right of ownership is perhaps its most important characteristic; it exists as long as the object of ownership exists. When a limited property right is created that is derived from the right of ownership the right of ownership will always exist longer than the limited property right. Would the right of ownership cease to exist, the limited property right will automatically be extinguished also. This has been named the residuary characteristic of the right of ownership (Honoré 1961, 126–128).

Finally, the right of ownership is protected with a special action known as revindication, originating from the Roman *rei vindicatio* (Watson 1968, 96). This action enables the owner to take back the control of the object of his ownership. The revindication, contrary to the actions granted in contract law, entails specific enforceability only. Furthermore, the right of ownership is protected with a special action to stop interference with the enjoyment of the right. This action, known as the *actio negatoria*, stems from Roman law and also entails specific enforceability only (Kaser and Knütel 2003, 171). The right of ownership can therefore be protected in a positive way, against unlawful possessors such as thieves, as well as in a negative way, against interferers such as trespassers.

Because of its perpetual nature and the specific enforceability of the right of ownership, English law does not recognise such a right (Swadling 2007, 280–282). English property law follows a more fragmented approach and a distinction should be made between land law and personal property law. This distinction originates from the historical development of the common law. Real actions, i.e. those actions that were specifically enforceable, were only available in respect to land (Pollock and Maitland 1898, 570). A real action awarded *seisin*, i.e. actual power over the land. Therefore land law is also known as real property law. Tangible objects other than land, however, were not protected by real actions. Instead these objects are protected by the law of obligations, in particular through specific torts (Bridge 2002, 47).

In order to gain a better understanding of the differences between civil law and common law a brief excursion into legal history may be useful. When, in 1066, the common law began its development, William the Conqueror claimed ownership of all the land. Consequently, land in England can no longer be owned but is held from the King in what remains of a feudal structure (Holdsworth 1927, p. 3). Originally, a person would hold land from the King in tenure (from the French *tenir*) in the form of a feudal grant. This grant was strictly personal, but later developed into a transferable right called estate. The different feudal grants became standardised over time until, with the Law of Property Act 1925, the legislature confirmed this limitation of the available estates at common law (Swadling 2007, 234). The estate most comparable to civil law ownership is known as the fee simple absolute in possession (the 'freehold'). 'Fee' denotes the origin of the right as a feudal grant, 'simple' means that the right will pass to the heirs of the holder without any conditions, 'absolute' indicates that the right is not subject to any condition and 'in possession' signals that the holder of the right is actually in control over the land (Burn and Cartwright 2006, 167–170). The fee simple is the most extensive entitlement to land in English law and can therefore be qualified as a primary right.

In English personal property law, the feudal terminology does not apply. Instead, the most extensive right is known as title, which is short for entitlement (Bridge 2002, 28). Title in English property law is similar to ownership in civil law systems, but is not considered the same by English lawyers, because of the relativity of title. Relativity of title means that several persons can be entitled to an object at the same time and that English lawyers approach a possible conflict between two entitlements by looking at who has the stronger right. However, the outcome only answers the order of importance between the two rights in question and not in general (Bridge 2002, 29). Title is protected through the law of tort, which does not lead to specific enforceability, but rather to liability to pay damages. Because of these two reasons, English lawyers maintain that title and ownership are not the same. With regard to personal property law 'title' can nevertheless still be qualified as a primary right.

From a functional point of view the right of ownership as the primary right in a civil law system of property law finds its equivalents in the common law concepts of fee simple in land law and title in personal property law (Akkermans 2008, 404–407). These rights form the paramount entitlement a person can have in respect to an object.

The right of ownership or its English equivalents are normally exercised to use and enjoy an object. However, the right of ownership also represents a value that can be used to secure the performance of an obligation. This use of the right of ownership for security purposes can be achieved in two ways. First, a transfer of the right of ownership may be reserved until the performance of an obligation, usually payment of the purchase price. This type of security-ownership is known as retention of title or reservation of ownership. Retention of title or reservation of ownership is known in most legal systems, especially as Member States of the European Union are obliged under EU law to have such a security right. Secondly, the right of ownership can also be transferred under the obligation to re-transfer the right of ownership when an obligation has been performed. This type of security-ownership is known as a transfer of ownership for security purposes or *fiducia cum creditore*. This use of the right of ownership or fee simple is not allowed in all legal systems. Dutch law prohibits the transfer of ownership for security purposes; English law by operation of law transforms such a transfer of land into a property security right known as a charge. However, a transfer of title to a movable object for security purposes is allowed in the form of a mortgage.

2.2 Property rights to use

Most property law systems recognise rights to use. These rights grant the holder of the right, who is someone other than the owner, the right to use and/or enjoy the object of ownership. Generally speaking, these rights to use exist for a limited (short) duration of time with an extensive content or for a longer period of time with a more limited content (Akkermans 2008, 407–408).

Property rights to use for a limited amount of time include the right of usufruct in civil law systems. The right of usufruct is the right to use and enjoy an object for the duration of the life of the person holding the right or, when the person holding the right is a legal person, for a determined period of time, usually 30 years. The right of usufruct grants the holder the same powers to use and enjoy the object as the owner, but with the obligation to maintain the object and its value. When the objects of the right of usufruct are shares or other objects that may be invested, maintaining their value implies an investment duty for the holder of the right, the usufructuary. In exchange the usufructuary is entitled to the fruits the object produces for the duration of the existence of the right. These fruits can be apples from a tree in case of natural fruits, but also income from rent or dividend on a share in case of civil fruits. The right of ownership, when a right of usufruct is created, is deprived of or limited in its power to use and enjoy and is therefore known as bare-ownership for the duration of existence of the right (Terré and Simler 1998, 591). English law does not recognise a right of usufruct, but the same result can be achieved through the use of trust law (Swadling 2007, 234). A trust is a legal device which enables that someone is appointed as the manager of a fund of trust assets (the 'trustee') for the benefit of someone else (the 'beneficiary'). Within English law (the common law in a broad sense) two legal systems apply at the same time, which both can give rise to the creation of property rights: common law in a strict sense and equity. The trustee is frequently described as a person who holds a property right at common law, whereas the beneficiary is described as the holder of a property right in equity.

In English law the right of lease (the 'term of years absolute' or 'leasehold'), which, besides the fee simple (or freehold), the other estate known at common law under Section 1 of the Law of Property Act 1925, is a right to use and enjoy land for a limited period of time, which must be determined but which may be almost forever. The right of lease grants exclusive possession to its holder to the detriment of the holder of the fee simple. His right is, similar to bare-ownership in civil law systems, known as a remainder. The remainder can, as bare-ownership, be transferred to another person. In such a situation the remainder is known as reversion (Burn and Cartwright 2006, 510). With regard to the right of lease it can be seen how in a particular legal system a contractual right (lease) can develop into a right that is given such a strong protection that it becomes proprietary in nature. The civil law still considers lease to be a purely personal right, although generally – in particular with regard to immovables – the lessee is protected in his rights in case the owner/lessor transfers his right of ownership. The new owner then becomes lessor by force of law.

The leasehold in its turn resembles civil law property rights of *emphyteusis* and *superficies*. The right of *emphyteusis* is the right to use and enjoy a piece of land in the same way as the owner. The right of *superficies* is a property right that separates the right of ownership from a building or other construction from the ownership of the land. The holder of the property right of *superficies* becomes owner of the building or construction on the land on which the property right is created. The rights of *emphyteusis* and *superficies* generally exist for a limited period of time only. Usually a maximum of 99 years applies (Dupichot 2007, 5).

Besides these property rights for a limited period of time, there are also property rights to use for a very long duration of time. In civil law systems this is the right of servitude, in English law the right of easement. Although only civil law systems share a basis in Roman law the House of Lords in its landmark decision *Re Ellenborough Park* has applied very similar criteria as in the civil law for the existence of servitudes (Swadling 2007, 252). A right of servitude or easement grants a specific right to its holder that must be tolerated by the owner of another piece of land. These rights can be a right of view or a right of way over the land of someone else. In order to create such a right it must be held by two parties, one who benefits, one who is burdened. These two parties must either hold a primary right or a property right to use on the land. A right of servitude can only be created in respect to land. Instead of the holders themselves, it should be one of the pieces of land that benefits and one of the pieces of land that is burdened by the existence of the right of servitude. The pieces of land must therefore, generally, be in vicinity to each other (Borkowski 1997, 170).

Alternatively, servitudes exist that are not real servitudes, i.e. dependent on two pieces of land, but which are personal. A personal servitude is a right that burdens a piece of land, but, different from a right of real servitude, benefits any specified person. The requirement of two pieces of land therefore does not apply to this category of servitudes. These personal servitudes are not recognised by all legal systems. In German law they are known as *beschränkte persönlische Dienstbarkeit* and in English law as restrictive covenants (Schwab and Prütting 2003, 431; Burn and Cartwright 2006, 668).

In English law there is also a property right that entitles a person to take something from the land of someone else. These rights are known as profits à prendre, and include a right to access the land of someone else in order to exercise the profit. The profit generally exists for a longer duration of time (Swadling 2007, 255). Similarly to profits, German law recognises real burdens in the form of a *Reallast*: a right that entitles its holder to a periodic payment in the form of a duty for the holder of the burden to pay. Performance of a *Reallast* will, because of this positive duty that the right imposes, not lead to specific enforceability. Instead it leads to liability (Amann 1993, 222).

Finally, legal systems also award a right to use and enjoy an apartment. Apartments create specific problems to property lawyers because of the technical rules concerning accession. In civil law systems, when a building is placed on a piece of land the ownership of the land comprises the ownership of the building, unless a right of *superficies* is created. However, an apartment is only a small part of the building for which a right of *superficies* cannot be used. Moreover, apartment buildings require a special management regime, different from a single building used by only one owner. Apartment rights are therefore needed to solve this problem.

These rights exist in the exclusive use of a certain space in the building, the co-entitlement to the common parts, and a membership of a compulsory association of apartment-owners. This is either created through a special type of co-ownership as is done in French law, a separate property right as is done in Dutch law and modification of the law dealing with ownership or fee simple in case of apartments, as is done in German and English law (Van der Merwe, De Waal and Carey Miller 2002).

2.3 Property rights as security

Besides property rights that entitle to the use and enjoyment of an object, property rights are also used to strengthen the performance of an obligation in the form of a security right. A property security right entitles its holder to, if not already, take possession, sell the object and compensate the claim on the debtor of the obligation with the proceeds of the sale. As a general prohibition most legal systems prohibit the holder of the property security right to keep the object for himself after non-performance by the debtor. An agreement to such extent is known as a *pactum commissoria* and already stems from Roman law. It is only allowed in France and under the application of European Union legislation in case of financial collateral arrangements between banks and other financial institutions (Van Vliet 2005, 190; Johansson 2009, 21–22).

Because property rights are used to secure the performance of an obligation, their existence is usually dependent on the existence of that obligation. This dependence is known as accessority and results in destruction of the property right if the obligation underlying the right extinguishes, for instance through payment of a claim. However, not all legal systems impose accessority in all cases. Property security rights can be divided in rights with respect to immovable objects (land or buildings) and in rights with respect to movable objects and claims.

In civil law systems the property security right that is used to secure the performance of a, usually monetary, obligation is a right of pledge or a right of mortgage (hypothec). A right of pledge can exist with and without the transfer of possession. In the first case, the right of pledge is known as a possessory pledge and implies that the holder of the right will be, for the duration of the underlying obligation, in possession of the object. The disadvantage of a possessory pledge is that the owner can no longer use his object. This can in particular be problematic if the object is needed to trade in order to earn income to perform the monetary obligation underlying the property security right. A non-possessory pledge is therefore a solution for this (Legeais 2006, 359). It is the same right as a possessory right of pledge, but without the requirement of a transfer of possession. Therefore, the owner of the object remains in possession, but with the risk that in realisation of the right of pledge in case of non-performance of the underlying obligation, the holder of the right of pledge takes possession and the object is sold in order to compensate the claim of the holder of the right of pledge.

The possessory pledge originates in Roman law, it is therefore recognised in all civil law systems, but is also known in English law, where it is a specific type of bailment, a way of holding rights on behalf of another (Kaser 1971, 458; Swadling 2007, 269). The non-possessory pledge is recognised in particular as an alternative to the transfer of ownership for security purposes. It is therefore recognised in Dutch law, but also, since 2006, in French law. In English law, non-possessory security rights also exist in the form of charges. Any object may be charged to secure the performance of an obligation. This can be a fixed charge, in which case it is immediately clear what objects fall under the charge. However, a charge may also be floating in which case it hovers over objects that can be substituted until realisation of the charge, in which case the floating charge becomes fixed (Goode 2004, 587).

In respect to immovables, civil law systems recognise a right of hypothec. A right of hypothec is a non-possessory security right that entitles its holder to the value of the immovable or land. The right of hypothec, like the right of pledge, dates back to Roman law, and is traditionally accessory to the claim the performance of which it seeks to secure (Kaser 1971, 462). However, exceptions exist in relaxation of accessority to enable the use of the right of hypothec to secure a future claim and to enable the re-use of the right of hypothec. Securing a future claim is necessary to allow credit facilities. Re-using the right of hypothec achieves what is known in France as a rechargeable hypothec modelled to the rechargeable mortgage in German law and the so-called 'euro-mortgage' proposed by a European Union working group. The rechargeable hypothec was introduced in France in 2006 together with the reversed hypothec. A reversed hypothec is a right of hypothec for a claim that increases instead of decreases in value and is used, primarily, as supplementary income to pension benefits (Grimaldi 2005, 33).

German law also recognises a strictly non-accessory property security right on immovable objects in the form of a right of *Grundschuld*. The *Grundschuld* is a right that entitles its holder to take possession and sell the object. The right is not dependent on any claim and is usually created by the owner himself, before the right is transferred for security purposes to a creditor in the same way as ownership can be transferred for security purposes. The result is a security-*Grundschuld* right (Baur, Baur and Stürner 1999, 505).

In English law the right of mortgage was originally a transfer of the fee simple for security purposes. However, because such a security transfer was considered to give the creditor too much power, the Law of Property Act 1925 changed this type of transfer into a legal charge by operation of law. As a result a mortgage on land is a charge, i.e. a non-possessory property security right and no longer a transfer of the fee simple for security purposes. Mortgages of movable objects remain allowed (Burn and Cartwright 2006, 724).

2.4 *Other property rights*

The above catalogue of property rights allows a classification along the traditional lines of property law. However, due to societal changes property law systems are moving away from a classical system of property law (Van Erp 2009). This movement away from the classical system of property law also brings the rise of new property rights and the acceptance of new objects of property law, such as emission rights and 'virtual' property (domain names, but also a protected position in Internet computer games or in virtual worlds such as 'Second Life').

The most important example of these new property rights are those that entitle its holder to the acquisition of a property right. Different from classical property rights that are derived from an existing more extensive property right, these acquisition rights look towards a right that must still be acquired. Acquisition rights do not limit, e.g., the right of ownership in its content, but force the transfer of such right. German law is most famous for these rights in the recognition of *Anwartschaftsrechte* (Strauch 1984, 288). These acquisition rights emerge when a personal right arises to which the German Civil Code provides additional protection. The best example of this is the position of the acquirer in a situation of reservation of ownership. The right of ownership in such a situation remains with the owner and the other party will only have a personal right to expect the acquisition of the right of ownership. The expectation right is protected in the German Civil Code in such a way that the only requisite for the transfer of ownership is the fulfilment of the condition under which it was created. The expectation right is therefore awarded proprietary status through the case law of the German Federal Supreme Court (BGH). Other examples of acquisition rights are estate contracts in English law, that give rise to a property right, because English law allows specific enforceability of contracts relating to land (Swadling 2007, 259). The same applies to options to purchase that are recognised in English law, because of the same reason, but also in German law under the heading of the *dingliche Vorkaufsrecht* (Staudinger and Wolfsteiner al 2002, 769).

A second type of property right that does not fit very well in the classical distinctions is the suretyship in France. A suretyship is a contract by which one party declares himself liable for the debt of another party (Aynès and Crocq 2003, 15). In a regular suretyship agreement, which is classified as a personal security right, as there are no property rights involved, the surety is liable with his full set of assets (whole estate or patrimony). However, when the surety creates a limited property right, a right of pledge or hypothec, on his own asset that serves as security for the payment of a debt of someone else this is known as a *cautionnement réelle* or real suretyship (Aynès & Crocq 2003, 43). The legal nature of a real suretyship has been much debated in France, and several decisions of the French *Cour de Cassation* have made the classification of the right even more difficult (Grimaldi 2005, 454). Eventually the French *Cour de Cassation* classified the real suretyship as a distinct property security right.

The classification by the French Supreme Court is remarkable, because in other legal systems existing property security rights may also be used to secure payment of the debt of another. However, until 2006, this was not possible under French law and therefore the need to classify this distinct property right arose. Since 2006 the right of pledge and hypothec may also be used for this purpose, but the classification of the French *Cour de Cassation* remains (Legeais 2006, 57–61).

3. Developments

Comparing property law systems becomes more and more important. The traditional assumption that property law systems diverge and cannot be harmonised is proven false by comparative legal analysis (Van Erp 2006b, 1043). Moreover, through comparative analysis common developments that bring property law systems closer to each other can be discovered (Van Erp 2009). Some of these developments will be dealt with here.

3.1 The increasing importance of European and global economic and legal integration

Property law has traditionally escaped the influence of harmonising measures from a European level. There has, in other words, been almost no European legislation dealing with the core of property law. Exceptions to this include directives on the protection of cultural goods and on financial collateral arrangements. However, there is more European legislation that, although it does not affect the core of property law, touches upon aspects of property law. Examples are the Directive combating late payments that forced Member States to recognise a reservation of ownership or retention of title, the Insolvency Regulation that does the same, but also European legislation dealing with soil protection and the trade in emission rights. It can, therefore, be said that a growing body of European Union property law exists (Sagaert 2007, 301; Akkermans 2008, 486).

Property law is also covered by the current revision of the European Union consumer *acquis*, the existing European Union law in the area of consumer transactions and, more specifically, consumer protection. Under an 2001 Action Plan from the European Commission a large group of academics has been researching the core of European private law in order to draft a Common Frame of Reference (Von Bar et al 2009). Certain areas of property law have also been included in the review, although in these areas not much European property law in a strict sense can be found (Von Bar and Drobnig 2002, 442). These are areas of property law that have a direct impact on contract law. They include transfer of ownership of movable objects, property security rights on movable objects and trusts (Von Bar et al 2009, 24). The Draft Common Frame of Reference (DCFR) is therefore a possible source for future European Union property law.

Finally, property law is now increasingly dealt with on a global level. Examples are the 2001 Cape Town Convention on international interests in mobile equipment (aircraft, railway rolling stock, space objects), the 2008 draft Convention on substantive rules regarding intermediated securities (both the work of Unidroit, an international organisation for unification of the law <www.unidroit.org>) and the 2007 Legislative guide on secured transactions (under the responsibility of Uncitral, a United Nations organisation for unification of the law <www.uncitral.org>).

3.2 Changes in objects of property law

A general problem that all property law systems are facing is the rise of new objects in property law (Reich 1964, 733; Libchaber 2004, 239). Property law systems are generally old systems of law that have hardly changed over time. The catalogue of property rights that deals with objects is mostly quite old. However, since the French Revolution and, especially, since the Industrial Revolution the importance of land as an object of property law has decreased and the importance of movable objects and, most recently, immaterial objects has increased (Libchaber 2004, 239). These immaterial, or intangible, objects are, for example, ideas and other intellectual property rights and, especially, claims. Claims are rights to the performance of an obligation usually derived from a contract. Although these claims are personal in nature – they only apply between the parties – they represent a value that can be an object of property law. Claims are used in modern finance to serve as subject matter for property security rights. This development from material to immaterial objects has been named dematerialisation (Libchaber 2004, 329; Johansson 2009, 2).

The problem with dematerialisation is that the old rules of property law do not always apply adequately to these new objects of property law. For example, money is now, in the last few decades, held in bank accounts rather than in a collection of coins and paper notes. A bank account is, in terms of property law, classified as a claim on a bank for the payment of money in coins and bank notes. When money is transferred from one bank account to another, the rules of property law apply. However, the transfer rules of property law generally require a transfer of possession, i.e. factual control, over the object from the transferor to the transferee. However, modern banking practice makes a transfer of money on a bank account into an administrative act where one account is credited and the other is indebted, without any transfer of possession of any object. In terms of property law, in any case, the claim of the transferor is certainly not transferred to the transferee (Heermann 2003, 167; Delebecque and Germain 2004, nr. 2303–2312). The rules of property law therefore barely apply here anymore. Comparable remarks can be made about intermediated securities. Shares, stocks and bonds, are no longer kept physically by, e.g., a bank, but have been reduced to book entries (Johansson 2009, 14). Transfer of shares is therefore a process of crediting one account and debiting another.

3.3 Party autonomy in property law (numerus clausus)

One of the distinguishing features between contract law and the law of property is the limited role of party autonomy in the law of property. In classical contract law, the freedom of contract, as the supreme expression of party autonomy, is seen as the most valuable starting point (Atiyah 1979; Gordley 1991). In property law, the starting point is completely the opposite: limitation on party autonomy in order to safeguard legal certainty (Van Erp 2006a, 5–6). According to the *numerus clausus* principle of property rights only those property rights can be created that are set forth by, at least in principle, legislation and only the content as laid down in legislation can be given to property rights created by the parties. However, that is not to say that parties may not make clever use of party autonomy to achieve certain effects in the law of property.

First of all, parties may use the law of property in combination with the law of contract to enforce the performance of a contractual obligation. Although originally the law of property only allows the use of property security rights for this, also other property rights are being used for this purpose. It is especially in German law that this use has been invented (Baur, Baur and Stürner 1999, 370–371). The best example is the use of a right of real servitude. A right of servitude may only contain a negative duty. It is therefore almost impossible to enforce a positive duty with property effects. Nonetheless, when a servitude is negatively formulated, such as a prohibition to have a petrol station on a piece of land, and that right of servitude is combined with a contract that limits the holder of that right to enforce it, the practical effect can be the imposition of a positive duty. This can be done by formulating the contract in such a way that the right of servitude will only be exercised when the holder of the servient land, on which an actual petrol station exists, stops buying a specific brand of petrol from the holder of the dominant land, i.e. in this case the petrol company. In the latter situation, the petrol company can demand removal of the petrol station. The final outcome in practice is a positive duty for the owner of the petrol station to buy his petrol from that specific petrol company, secured by a right of servitude. These servitudes are therefore known as security servitudes (Füller 2006, 505–506).

A second example of how parties by making autonomous choices can use property law to attain results which may not have been envisaged by the drafters of, e.g., civil codes can be found when looking at the 'stacking' of property rights. The use of stacking is controversial (Struycken 2007, 368–378). An example of this is a municipality that does not want to transfer ownership of the land it is selling to, e.g., a developer, because it wants to control land use also in its capacity as private law owner. Instead of transferring the right of ownership, the municipality will use a long lease or right of *emphyteusis*, that will grant the holder of the right control over the land, but not the primary property law entitlement. However, in order to obtain finance it might be necessary for the holder of the right of *emphyteusis* to have ownership of the buildings that are to be constructed on the land. To attain this purpose a right of *superficies* can be created on the right of *emphyteusis*. Further, when the building that is constructed is an apartment building the right of ownership that is created by the right of *superficies* on the right of *emphyteusis* will be separated into rights of apartment, which can each, in their turn, be subject to a right of hypothec to finance the acquisition of the apartment right on the right of *superficies* on the right of *emphyteusis* on the right of ownership of the municipality.

3.4 Flexibilisation of the specificity principle

The principle of specificity prescribes that each object of property law must be identifiable. In the classical model of property law an unidentified object leads to the impossibility to hold a property right on such an object. This fundamental starting point of a legal system originates from a time where land was the most valuable and important object of property law. However, with the changes in objects of property law and the movement towards the recognition of immaterial objects, in particular claims, as subject matter of property law, the principle of specificity has come under pressure (Van Erp 2006a, 14–16).

First of all, claims are a-typical objects of property law. They are fundamentally different from tangible objects, as they exist for a short duration of time only and cannot as easily as physical objects, i.e. by handing over factual control, be transferred to another person. Nevertheless, claims are the primary source of business finance today. The principle of specificity determines that for each object of property law a separate property right must exist. When a trader has several thousands of claims he wishes to provide as security for the payment of a loan, according to the specificity principle each claim would need to be identified as well as to be described individually *ex ante* in order to create a valid right of pledge. A steady pressure from legal practice has led to a relaxation of the principle of specificity in respect to security rights on claims. It is generally considered sufficient that the claims can be described *ex post*, in other words at the moment of enforcement of the security right. It is now in several legal systems possible to transfer claims, especially for security purposes, by making use of a list, in which these claims are described in generic terms. In French law this is known as a *cession Dailly* after the name of the law that introduced this possibility (Crocq 1995, 27; Legeais 2006, 377). In the Netherlands a further flexibilisation occurred through the recognition of valid rights of pledge on claims that have been 'specified' by a general reference to the administration of the debtor/security provider.

Another development that affects the specificity principle is related to how the transfer of large quantities of bulk objects, such as grain, takes place. In these situations it can be difficult to identify the object and it is unclear what exactly belongs to a certain bulk. To solve this problem it is made possible to transfer a quantity of goods by identifying the bulk, rather than the individual parts the bulk comprises (Van Vliet 2000, 93).

As a consequence – next to what can be seen with regard to the principle of *numerus clausus* – also the principle of specificity is no longer applied rigorously. A strict identification in case of security rights on multiple and shifting claims is not necessary and in case of a transfer of quantities of the same material that cannot be easily separated from each other (transfer of goods ex bulk) a meticulous identification of the goods is also not required. Instead, one single transaction suffices to create or transfer rights in respect to these objects.

3.5 Flexibilisation of the publicity principle

The principle of publicity, which demands that a property right is visible to third parties, fulfils a very important function in the law of property: it offers justification for the third party effect. Therefore in the classical model of property law all property rights are subject to publicity. When movable objects are involved, publicity is achieved by factual control. The owner of an object is also the person in factual control. When, for some reason, the factual control has been handed over to someone else, this is a sign of changed property relations; either a transfer of ownership or the creation of, for instance, a right of pledge. In respect to immovables there is land registration. In the classical model the creation, existence and termination of property rights in respect to land are to be registered so that third parties may inform themselves before acquiring a property right in a piece of land.

However, especially in the area of property security rights developments have taken place that have resulted in a less strict application of the publicity principle and the development of alternative techniques, other than transfer of factual control and registration, to inform third parties. This development was caused, among others, by the rise of a transfer of ownership of movables and claims for security purposes, whereby factual control remains with the debtor, rather than with the creditor/security-owner. To the outside world the debtor, although no longer owner, still seems owner. This is known as reputed ownership and requires protection by third parties in good faith, wishing to acquire property rights in these movables or claims. It may also require new techniques to inform third parties, such as a duty to provide information by the transferor of a property right to the transferee. The same applies to the creation of non-possessory property security rights such as the non-possessory pledge and charges. Also there, the impression remains that the owner of the object is in full, i.e. unburdened or unlimited, control and the other party will need to be informed otherwise.

In respect to property security rights in respect to land, registration already offers a solution for non-possessory security rights, such as the rights of hypothec and mortgage. However, the flexibilisation of the law on hypothecs, for instance the recognition of a rechargeable hypothec, also leads to a different approach whereby a right of hypothec may still be in the register although it is completely repaid, waiting for another creditor on whose behalf the right may be recharged (Grimaldi 2005, 33–36).

3.6 Less importance of the accessority principle in the law on security rights

Another important development concerns the principle of accessority. Accessority means that a link exists between a property security right and the underlying (secured) claim. A repayment of the claim will lead to a loss of the security right. This principle protects the debtor from undesired use of the security right by the creditor. Recent developments in Germany with non-accessory property security rights have shown how dangerous the lack of accessority can be (Clemens 2007, 737). There, non-accessory property security rights on land, rights of *Grundschuld*, had fallen into the hands of companies that were not bound by the corresponding underlying contractual relationship due to a lack of accessority. As a result the rights of *Grundschuld* were sometimes realised in a situation where the debtor had paid off his debt. Legislation to remedy this is now being considered, now that it became clear that contractualisation of property law also has its negative side effects.

Interestingly enough, this non-accessory property security right has, for many years, been envisaged by the European Commission as a model for a Euro-mortgage, a pan-European property security right in respect to land (Stöcker 1992). Whether, after these developments the emphasis on the need for a non-accessory security right remains, is to be seen. In the meantime, the principle of accessority remains strong in most legal systems.

Many legal systems nevertheless relax the principle of accessority to make it possible that a property security right can be created in order to secure the performance of a future claim. This is particularly useful when credit is given, which can fluctuate. In such a situation a credit facility may be opened which, at the moment of its creation, is not used instantly. In other words, at the moment of creation, the claim which the security right seeks to secure does not yet exist, but will come into existence once money is actually borrowed. The principle of accessority does, as a matter of principle, forbid the immediate creation of a property security right under these circumstances, but the principle is more and more relaxed in the interest of commerce to allow the creation of a valid security right at the moment of the opening of the credit facility. Examples are the legal systems of the Netherlands and, since 2006, of France.

3.7 Growing acceptance of general and fluid security rights

A final development in the law of property concerns the acceptance of general security rights. In the classical model of property law there is only room for a single set of property rights per object. However, there is a growing need in legal practice to be able to use one and the same property right on a set of objects (a changing 'fund' of assets), rather than having to use one property right per object. The principle of specificity does not allow this. Moreover, creditors are treated equally, the *paritas creditorum*, unless the law explicitly gives a creditor priority. This priority is limited to a specific asset or group of assets of the debtor's patrimony. An example of priority is a creditor secured by a security property right. The limitation of the priority is, again, an expression of the specificity principle, which in this case protects ordinary, i.e. unsecured, creditors against creditors who may be over-secured. Recognising a general security right would violate the specificity principle, as this would hardly leave any other objects for the other creditors in, e.g., an insolvency procedure.

Nonetheless, general security rights do exist. The best example is the English floating charge, a property security right on land, movable objects and claims (also known as 'chattels' and 'choses in action' in English property law terminology), that only becomes a fixed charge when it 'crystallises' upon default by the debtor. Once the charge becomes a fixed charge, the chargee is entitled to take possession and sell objects to compensate his claim with the proceeds of sale (Goode 2004, 676). In French law a similar situation is achieved, but with a different technique. The principle of specificity does not allow the creation of a single property right in respect to multiple objects. However, it is possible to combine certain objects into one group which, as a group, can be subject of a single property security right. The group is known as a *fonds de commerce* or fund of commercial assets and can be the object of a special right of pledge (Malaurie and Aynès 2005, 33–35). German law recognises an *Unternehmen*, or undertaking, that can, under conditions be the object of a single right of pledge (Hattenhauer 1989, 101).

4. Conclusion

The various property law traditions, particularly civil law and common law, share leading principles and ground rules. These principles and ground rules create a basic framework, within which further policy choices have to be made, such as how far third parties in good faith should be protected in the interest of commerce. The major differences between the property law traditions are not so much the result of divergence regarding the basic framework, but regarding the technical rules which have been formulated over centuries. In other words: the existing divergence is primarily the result of historical development. On the continent of Europe a major historical moment was the French Revolution, whereas all property law traditions underwent the changes caused by the Industrial Revolution. Developments continue as a result of regional and global economic and legal integration. This even affects the application of the leading principles, which nevertheless, in spite of these changes, show a remarkable resilience.

Property law is therefore slowly developing into a system fit for the twenty-first century, although much work needs to be done to ensure coherence both at national level as well as in the European and international legal order. The analysis of property rights in terms of principles, policy choices, ground rules and technical rules have proven to be a model that can be worked with.

Bibliography

Akkermans, B., *The Principle of Numerus Clausus in European Property Law* (Ius Commune Europaeum; Antwerpen/Oxford/Portland: Intersentia, 2008).

Amann, H., 'Durchsetzung der Reallast ohne Verlust der Reallast', *Deutsche Notar-Zeitschrift (DNotZ)* (1993), 222–32.
Atias, Christian, *Droit Civil – Les Biens* (8th edn.; Paris: Lexis Nexis S.A., 2005).
Atiyah, P.S., *The Rise and Fall of Freedom of Contract* (Oxford: Clarendon Press, 1979).
Aynès, Laurent and Crocq, Pierre, *Droit Civil: Les Sûretés, la Publicité Foncière* (Paris: Defrénois, 2003).
Bar, Christian von and Drobnig, U., *Study on Property Law and Non-contractual Liability Law as they relate to Contract Law* (http://europa.eu.int/comm/consumers/cons_int/safe_shop/fair_bus_pract/cont_law/study.pdf, 2002).
Bar, Christian von, et al. (eds.), *Principles, Definitions and Model Rules of European Private Law. Draft Common Frame of Reference (DCFR).* (Outline edn.) (Munich: Sellier European Law Publishers, 2009).
Bartels, S.E. and Milo, J.M., 'Contents of Real Rights: Personal or Proprietary. A Principled History', in S.E. Bartels and J.M. Milo (eds.), *Contents of Real Rights* (Nijmegen: Wolf Legal Publishers, 2004), 5–23.
Baur, F., Baur, J.F., and Stürner, R., *Sachenrecht* (17. neubearbeite Auflage edn.; München: C.H. Beck'sche Verlagsbuchhandlung, 1999).
Borkowski, Andrew, *Textbook on Roman Law* (2nd edn.; London: Blackstone Press Ltd., 1997), 152 ff.
Bridge, Michael, *Personal Property Law* (3rd edn.; Oxford: Oxford University Press, 2002).
Burn, E.H. and Cartwright, J., *Cheshire and Burns's Modern Law of Real Property* (17th edn.; Oxford: Oxford University Press, 2006).
Cabrillac, Michel and Mouly, Christian, *Droit des sûretés* (Paris: Litec, 2004).
Cámara-Lapuente, Sergio, 'Registration of Interests as a Formality of Contracts: Comparative Remarks on Land Registers within the Frame of European Private Law', *European Review of Private Law,* 13/6 (2005), 797–839.
Cantero, Gabriel Garcia, 'Les Différentes Fonctions de la Possession en Droit Privé', *European Review of Private Law,* 6/4 (1998), 363–83.
Chabas, François, 'Biens: Droit de Propriété et ses Démembrements', in Jean Mazeaud, et al. (eds.), *Leçons de Droit Civil, Tome 2* (8th edn.; Paris: Montchrestien, 1994).
Clemens, Clemente, 'Verwertung der nicht akzessorischen Grundschuld im Rahmen eines Forderungsverkaufs', *Zeitschrift für Immobilienrecht,* 21 (2007), 737–46.
Crocq, Pierre, *Propriété et garantie*, eds Henry Solus and Jacques Ghestin (*Bibliothèque de Droit Privé* – Tome 248; Paris: Librarie Générale de Droit et de Jurisprudence (L.G.D.J.), 1995).
Delebecque, Philippe, Germain, Michel et al., *Traité de Droit Commercial: Tome 2, Effets de Commerce, Banque, Contrats Commerciaux, Procedures Collectives* (Paris: LGDJ, 2004).
Dupichot, Philippe, 'Opération Fiducie sur le Sol Français', *La Semaine Juridique Edition Générale,* 81/11 (2007), 5–8.
Erp, J.H.M. van, 'De osmose van Nederlands en Europees goederenrecht', *NTBR,* 10 (Special Issue)/N. 94 (2004), 533–46.
Erp, J.H.M. van, *European and National Property Law: Osmosis or Growing Antagonism?* (Walter van Gerven Lectures, 6; Groningen: Europa Law Publishing, 2006a).
Erp, J.H.M. van, 'Comparative Property Law', in Mathias Reimann and Reinhard Zimmermann (eds.), *The Oxford Handbook of Comparative Law* (Oxford: Oxford University Press, 2006b), 1043–70.
Erp, J.H.M. van, 'From "classical" to modern European property law?', *FS Kerameus* (2009).
Füller, Jens Thomas, *Eigenständiges Sachenrecht?* (Jus Privatum. Beitrage zum Privatrecht, Band 104; Tubingen: Mohr Siebeck, 2006).
Glenn, H. Patrick, 'Legal Families and Legal Traditions', in Mathias Reimann and Reinhard Zimmermann (eds.), *The Oxford Handbook of Comparative Law* (Oxford: Oxford University Press, 2006), 421–40.
Goode, Roy, *Commercial Law* (3rd edn.; London: Penguin Books, 2004).
Gordley, James, *The Philosophical Origins of Modern Contract Doctrine* (Oxford: Clarendon Press, 1991).

Gordley, James, 'Myths of the French Civil Code', *The American Journal of Comparative Law,* 42 (1994), 459–505.
Gordley, James, *Foundations of Private Law. Property, Tort, Contract, Unjust Enrichment* (Oxford: Oxford University Press, 2006).
Gray, Kevin and Gray, Susan Francis, *Elements of Land Law* (4th edn.; Oxford: Oxford University Press, 2005).
Gretton, George, 'Ownership and its Objects', *Rabels Zeitschrift für Auslandisches und Internationales Privatrecht,* 71/4 (2007), 802–51.
Grimaldi, M., et al., *Rapport relatif à la réforme du droit des sûretés remis au garde des Sceaux par le groupe de travail présidé par M. Michel Grimaldi* (2005).
Hattenhauer, H., 'Über vereintes und entzweites Eigentum', in J.F. Baur (ed.), *Das Eigentum. Vorträge gehalten auf der Tagung des Joachim Jungius-Gesellschaft der Wissenschaften Hamburg am 10, 11 und 12 December 1987* (Göttingen: Vandenhoeck & Ruprecht, 1989), 83–101.
Heerman, Peter H., *Geld und Geldgeschäfte [Money and Money Transactions]* (Tübingen: Mohr Siebeck, 2003).
Holdsworth, William, *An Historical Introduction to the Land Law* (Oxford: Oxford University Press, 1927).
Honoré, A.M., 'Ownership', in A.G. Guest (ed.), *Oxford Essays in Jurisprudence* (Oxford: Oxford University Press, 1961), 107–47.
Johansson, Erica, *Property Rights in Investment Securities and the Doctrine of Specificity (Diss.)* (Heidelberg: Springer Verlag, 2009).
Kaser, Max, *Das römische Privatrecht; 1. Abschnitt* (2. neubearb. Auflage; München: C.H. Beck'sche Verlagsbuchhandlung, 1971).
Kaser, M. and Wubbe, F.B.J., *Romeins Privaatrecht*, trans. F.B.J. Wubbe (2nd revised and updated edn.; Zwolle: Tjeenk Willink, 1971), 93–155.
Kaser, Max and Knütel, Rolf, *Römisches Privatrecht* (17th renewed and extended edn.; München: C.H. Beck, 2003).
Lawson, Frederic H. and Rudden, Bernard, *The Law of Property* (3rd edn.; New York: Oxford University Press, 2002).
Legeais, Dominique, *Sûretés et garanties du crédit* (5th edn.; Paris: Librarie Générale de Droit et de Jurisprudence (L.G.D.J.), 2006).
Libchaber, Rémy, 'La Recodification du Droit des Biens', *Le Code Civil 1804–2004; Livre du Bicentenaire* (Paris: Dalloz/Lexis Nexis Litec, 2004), 297–372.
Malaurie, Philippe and Aynès, Laurent, *Les biens*, eds Philippe Malaurie and Laurent Aynès (2nd edn., Droit civil; Paris: Defrénois, 2005).
Merwe, C.G. van der, De Waal, M.J. and Carey Miller, D.L., 'Property and Trust Law – South Africa – Suppl. 2 (July 2002)', in R. Blanpain (ed.), *International Encyclopaedia of Laws* (Deventer: Kluwer Law International, 2002).
Piedelièvre, Stéphane, *Les sûretés* (4th edn.; Paris: Dalloz, 2004).
Pollock, F. and Maitland, F.W., *The History of English Law – Before the Time of Edward* (2nd edn., Volume II; Cambridge: Cambridge University Press, 1898).
Reich, Charles A., 'The New Property', *Yale Law Journal,* 73/5 (1964), 733–87.
Reid, Kenneth G.C., 'Obligations and Property: Exploring the Border', *Acta Juridica,* 227 (1997), 225–45.
Rudden, Bernard, 'Economic Theory v. Property Law: The *Numerus Clausus* Problem', in J. Eekelaar and J. Bell (eds.), *Oxford Essays on Jurisprudence* (3rd edn.; Oxford: Clarendon Press, 1987), 239–63.
Sagaert, V., 'Real rights and real obligations in Belgian and French law', in S.E. Bartels and J.M. Milo (eds.), *Contents of Real Rights* (Nijmegen: Wolf Legal Publishers, 2004), 47–70.
Sagaert, Vincent, 'De Verworvenheden van het Europese Goederenrecht', in A.S. Hartkamp, C.H. Sieburgh and L.A.D. Keus (eds.), *De Invloed van het Europese Recht op het Nederlandse Privaatrecht* (Deventer: Kluwer, 2007), 301–33.
Schwab, Karl Heinz and Prütting, Hanns, *Sachenrecht. Ein Studienbuch* (31st edn.; München: Verlag C.H. Beck, 2003).

Snijders, W., 'Ongeregeldheden in het vermogensrecht (I)', *WPNR,* 6607 (2005), 79–85.
Staudinger, J, von and Wolfsteiner, H., 'Buch 3 Sachenrecht – §§ 1113–1203', in W. Wiegand (ed.), *J. von Staudinger's Kommentar zum Bürgerlichen Gesetzbuch mit Einfürungsgesetz und Nebengesetzen* (Berlin: Sellier: de Gruyter, 2002).
Stöcker, O.M., *Die Eurohypothek* (Berlin: Duncker & Humblot, 1992).
Strauch, Dieter, 'Das geteilte Eigentum in Geschichte und Gegenwart', in G. Baumgärtel, et al. (eds.), *Festschrift für Heinz Hübner zum 70. Gerburtstag am 7. November 1984* (Berlin – New York: Walter de Gruyter, 1984), 273–93.
Struycken, T.H.D., *De numerus clausus in het goederenrecht (Diss.)*, eds S.C.J.J. Kortmann and N.E.D. Faber (Serie Onderneming en Recht; Deventer: Kluwer, 2007).
Swadling, W.J., 'Property: General Principles', in Andrew Burrows (ed.), *English Private Law* (Oxford: Oxford University Press, 2007), 219–401.
Terré, François and Simler, Philippe, *Droit Civil – Les Biens* (5th edn.; Paris: Dalloz, 1998).
Velten, A.A., van, *Privaatrechtelijke aspecten van onroerend goed* (Ars Notariatus 120; Deventer: Kluwer, 2003).
Vliet, L.P.W., *Transfer of Movables in German, French, English and Dutch Law* (Nijmegen: Ars Aequi Libri, 2000).
Vliet, L.P.W., van, 'De Financiëlezekerheidsovereenkomst, een Tussenbalans', *NTBR,* May (2005), 190–204.
Waal, M.J. de, 'Identifying Real Rights in South African Law: the "Subtraction from the *Dominium*" Test and its Application', in S.E. Bartels and J.M. Milo (eds.), *Contents of Real Rights* (Nijmegen: Wolf Legal Publishers, 2004), 83–98.
Walt, A.J. van der and Kleyn, D.G., 'Duplex Dominium: The History and Significance of the Concept of Divided Ownership', in D.P. Visser (ed.), *Essays on the History of Law* (Cape Town: Juta & Co, 1989), 213–60.
Watson, Alan, *The Law of Property in the Later Roman Republic* (Oxford: Oxford University Press, 1968).
Wiegand, W., '*Numerus clausus* der dinglichen Rechte. Zur Entstehung und Bedeutung eines zentralen zivilrechtlichen Dogmas', in G. Köbler (ed.), *Wege europäischer Rechtsgeschichte – Festschrift Kroeschell* (Frankfurt a.M., 1987), 623–43.
Wiegand, W., 'Funktion und systematische Stellung des Sachenrechts im BGB', in M. Martinek and P.L. Sellier (eds.), *100 Jahre BGB – 100 Jahre Staudinger. Beiträge zum Symposion vom 18–20. Juni 1998 in München* (J. von Staudingers Kommentar zum Bürgerlichen Gesetzbuch mit Einführungsgesetz und Nebengesetzen; Berlin: De Sellier Gruyter, 1999), 107–27.
Wolff, Martin and Raiser, Ludwig, *Sachenrecht. Ein Lehrbuch* (10. Auflage edn.; Tübingen: J.C.B. Mohr (Paul Sibeck), 1957).
Zenati, Frédéric and Revet, Thierry, *Les biens* (2e edn.; Paris: Presse Universitaires de France, 1997).

4 Private and common property rights

Elinor Ostrom and Charlotte Hess

1. Introduction

The relationship between private property and common property has engaged both legal and economic scholars in a long series of controversies over the meaning, the sequence of development, and the superiority of private vs. common property. The issues debated relate to the efficiency, equity and sustainability of private property as contrasted to common property. The scholarship in both professions has been characterized by formulations that are adopted by each generation of scholars without much effort to examine their foundations or to test them by empirical research. Both have their doctrinal aspects. And, the dominant view in both disciplines has been that private property is clearly superior to common property. Many scholars think of contemporary examples of common property as remnants of the past, likely to disappear during the twenty-first century (see Atran 1993). Recent research, however, has challenged the presumption that private property is necessarily superior to common property.

2. The legal debate over private vs. common property

Prior to the publication in 1861 of *Ancient Law* by the distinguished English jurist, Henry Sumner Maine, the accepted view among Western jurists was that the origin of the concept of property in ancient times was the occupation of land by a single proprietor and his family (Grossi 1981). Further, the superiority of individual property holdings was so well accepted in the legal literature of the early nineteenth century that the possibility of other forms of property existing on the European continent threatened juridical views about the origins of social order. Maine drew not only on his own extensive research in India but also on the work of Georg Ludwig von Maurer (1854, 1856) on the primitive Germanic village communities, the Mark, and of the pioneering work of William Blackstone (1766). Maine concluded that: 'it is more than likely that joint ownership, and not separate ownership, is the really archaic institution, and that the forms of property that will afford us instruction will be those that are associated with the rights of families and of groups of kindred' ([1861] 1963, p. 252). This set off a flurry of publications challenging and supporting his conclusion (see extensive bibliographic citations in Grossi

1981). The great debate had much more than academic importance, as major political struggles continued throughout the nineteenth century over the status of the many remaining forms of common property on the European continent. A legal and political belief system that saw the origin of property itself in the efforts of individual proprietors to occupy land gave the landed proprietor a special role in society. These beliefs helped to justify the passage of legislation to eliminate collective landholding rights and to authorize enclosures and the takeover of communal properties by individual proprietors.

The meaning of private property in comparison to common property remains a contested issue in modern legal scholarship. Ellickson, Rose, and Ackerman (1995), for example, start their textbook on property law with a first chapter devoted to 'The Debate over Private Property'. The second chapter addresses 'The Problem of the Commons'. In the latter chapter, they include parts of the famous article by Hardin (1968) on 'The Tragedy of the Commons', but then ask students the following questions: 'Private property is often said to avert the tragedy of the commons. But does it? Who enforces property limitations? Does another kind of "commons" problem lurk in the organization and maintenance of a property regime?' (Ellickson, Rose, and Ackerman 1995, p. 141). In an earlier volume, Rose (1994, p. 37) points to the 'kicker' in a sharp distinction between private and common property when she stresses that a private-property *regime* as a system 'has the same structure as a common property' (see also Epstein 1979, 1994, 2002).

3. The economic debate over private vs. common property

Economists tend to view common-property institutions as having a longer history than private-property institutions and to explain the growth of modern, Western societies in part as the result of changing from common property to private property (North and Thomas 1976; North, Anderson, and Hill 1983). Private property is considered by most economists to be an essential ingredient in economic development due to the incentives associated with diverse kinds of property relationships (see, for example, Welch 1983). A farmer who owns his own labor, land and other factor inputs, for example, is likely to see a direct relationship between investments and the level of benefit achieved over the long term. A farmer who belongs to an agricultural production cooperative, on the other hand, may see only a loose connection between personal contributions and benefits. The more individuals in a society whose work is only loosely connected to their benefits, the more pervasive an attitude of free riding can become. If everyone tends to free ride on the work of others, overall economic productivity will be low.

Private-property rights, however, cannot simply emerge spontaneously from a common-property system. Private-property rights depend upon the existence and enforcement of a set of rules that define who has a right to undertake which activities on their own initiative and how the returns from that activity will be allocated (V. Ostrom 2008). In other words, rules and rulers are required to establish, monitor and enforce a property system. While some rules generate incentives that greatly increase the welfare of most participants in an economy, there are always individuals who resist changes because of benefits they receive from a prior system or propose changes that particularly benefit themselves. Rulers may also receive substantial returns from making rules that benefit some to the detriment of others. Thus, rent-seeking behavior is expected on the part of both entrepreneurs and rulers.

Common-property regimes are, therefore, presumed by many economists to be inefficient due to three problems. One is rent dissipation, because no one owns the products of a resource until they are captured, and everyone engages in an unproductive race to capture these products before others do (Knight 1924; Gordon 1954; Scott 1955; Schaefer 1957; Cheung 1970; C. Clark 1976, 1980; Dasgupta and Heal 1979). The second is the high transaction and enforcement costs expected if communal owners were to try to devise rules to reduce the externalities of their mutual overuse (Demsetz 1967; Coase 1960). The third is low productivity, because no one has an incentive to work hard in order to increase their private returns (North 1990). Common-property regimes are presumably retained by rulers who do not understand the enhancement in overall economic welfare that will result from a change to private property or who are supported by those who benefit from these 'archaic' regimes. A common policy prescription is articulated by R. Smith (1981, p. 467) when he stated that 'the only way to avoid the tragedy of the commons in natural resources and wildlife is to end the common-property system by creating a system of private property rights'.

4. Confusions that generate misunderstanding

The debate about the relative merits of private and common property has been clouded by a troika of confusions that hinder scholarly communication. Different meanings are assigned to terms without clarifying how multiple aspects relate to one another. The source of confusion relates to the differences between (1) common-property and open-access regimes, (2) common-pool resources and common-property regimes, and (3) a resource system and the flow of resource units. All three sources of confusion reduce clarity in assigning meaning to terms and retard theoretical and empirical progress.

The confusion between common-property and open-access regimes

In a now classic article, Ciriacy-Wantrup and Bishop (1975) clearly demarked the difference between property regimes that are *open access*, where no one has the legal right to exclude anyone from using a resource, from *common property*, where the members of a clearly demarked group have a legal right to exclude nonmembers of that group from using a resource (see also Bromley 1991). Open-access regimes (*res nullius*) – including the classic cases of the open seas and the atmosphere – have long been considered in legal doctrine as involving no limits on who is authorized to use a resource. If anyone can use a resource, no one has an incentive to conserve their use or to invest in improvements. If such a resource generates highly valued products, then one can expect that the lack of rules regarding authorized use will lead to misuse and overconsumption. Some local grazing areas, inshore fisheries and forests are effectively open-access resources, but many fewer than presumed in the literature.

Some open-access regimes lack effective rules defining property rights by default (Dales 1968). Either the resources affected by these open-access regimes are not contained within a nation-state or no entity has successfully laid claim to legitimate ownership. Other open-access regimes are the consequence of conscious public policies to guarantee the access of all citizens to the use of a resource within a political jurisdiction. The concept of *jus publicum* applies to their formal status, but effectively these resources are open access. The state governments of Oregon and Washington intervened in the early twentieth century to prevent local salmon fishermen from devising rules that would have limited entry and established harvesting limits (Higgs 1996). Fishing unions along the US coastal areas tried to organize inshore fisheries so as to limit entry and establish harvesting limits during the 1950s. Even though their efforts could not have had a serious impact on prices due to the presence of an active international market for fish, the fishing unions were prosecuted by the US Department of Justice and found in violation of the Sherman Antitrust Act (Johnson and Libecap 1982). Thus, US inshore fisheries have effectively been open-access resources during much of the twentieth century as a result of governmental action to prevent local fishing groups from establishing forms of common-property regimes within those political jurisdictions. In more recent times, however, both the national and state governments have reversed their prior stands and have actively sought ways of creating forms of co-management in inshore fisheries (see Pinkerton 1989, 1994; Acheson 2003; Wilson, Yan, and Wilson 2007).

A third type of open-access regime results from the ineffective exclusion of nonowners by the entity assigned formal rights of ownership. In many developing countries, the earlier confusion between open-access and common-property regimes paradoxically led to an increase in the number and extent of local resources that are effectively open access. Common-property regimes controlling access and harvesting from local streams, forests, grazing areas, and inshore fisheries had evolved over long periods of time in all parts of the world, but were rarely given formal status in the legal codes of newly independent countries (Wiersma 2005).

As concern for the protection of natural resources mounted during the 1960s, many developing countries nationalized all land and water resources that had not yet been recorded as private property. The institutional arrangements that local users had devised to limit entry and use lost their legal standing, but the national governments lacked monetary resources and personnel to monitor the use of these resources effectively. Thus, resources that had been under a de facto common-property regime enforced by local users were converted to a de jure government-property regime, but reverted to a de facto open-access regime. When resources that were previously controlled by local participants have been nationalized, state control has usually proved to be less effective and efficient than control by those directly affected, if not disastrous in its consequences (Curtis 1991; Hilton 1992; Panayotou and Ashton 1992; Ascher 1995). The harmful effects of nationalizing forests that had earlier been governed by local user groups have been well documented for Thailand (Feeny 1988), Niger (Thomson 1977; Thomson, Feeny, and Oakerson 1992), Nepal (Arnold and Campbell 1986; Messerschmidt 1986), and India (Gadgil and Iyer 1989; Jodha 1990). Similar results have occurred in regard to inshore fisheries taken over by state or national agencies from local control by the inshore fishermen themselves (Cordell and McKean 1992; Cruz 1986; Dasgupta 1982; Higgs 1996; Pinkerton 1989).

The confusion between a resource system and a property regime

The problems resulting from confusing open-access regimes with common-property regimes are particularly difficult to overcome due to a second terminological problem. The term 'common-property resource' is frequently used to describe a type of economic good that is better referred to as a 'common-pool resource'. All common-pool resources share two attributes of importance for economic activities: (1) it is costly to exclude individuals from using the good either through physical barriers or legal instruments and (2) the benefits consumed by one individual subtract from the benefits available to others (V. Ostrom and E. Ostrom 1977b; E. Ostrom, Gardner, and Walker 1994). Recognizing a class of goods that shares these two attributes enables scholars to identify the core theoretical problems facing individuals whenever more than one individual or group utilizes such resources for an extended period of time. Using 'property' in the term used to refer to a type of good reinforces the impression that goods sharing these attributes tend everywhere to share the same property regime.

Common-pool resources share with public goods the difficulty of developing physical or institutional means of excluding beneficiaries. Unless means are devised to keep nonauthorized users from benefiting, the strong temptation to free ride on the efforts of others will lead to a suboptimal investment in improving the resource, monitoring use, and sanctioning rule-breaking behavior. Second, the products or resource units from common-pool resources share with private goods the attribute that one person's consumption subtracts from the quantity available to others. Thus, common-pool resources are subject to problems of congestion, overuse and potential destruction unless harvesting or use limits are devised and enforced. In addition to sharing these two attributes, particular common-pool resources differ on many other attributes that affect their economic usefulness including their size, shape and productivity and the value, timing and regularity of the resource units produced.

Common-pool resources may be owned by national, regional, or local governments; by communal groups; by private individuals or corporations; or used as open access resources by whomever can gain access. Each of the broad types of property regimes has different sets of advantages and disadvantages, but at times may rely upon similar operational rules regarding access and use of a resource (Feeny et al. 1990). Examples exist of both successful and unsuccessful efforts to govern and manage common-pool resources by governments, communal groups, cooperatives, voluntary associations, and private individuals or firms (Bromley et al. 1992; K. Singh 1994; K. Singh and Ballabh 1996). Thus, as discussed below, there is no automatic association of common-pool resources with common-property regimes – *or, with any other particular type of property regime*. Further, common-property arrangements are essentially share contracts (Lueck 1994; Eggertsson 1990, 1992, 1993) and, as such, face similar problems of potential opportunistic behavior and moral hazard problems.

The confusion between the resource and the flow of resource units

Common-pool resources are composed of resource systems and a flow of resource units or benefits from these systems (Blomquist and Ostrom 1985). The resource system (or alternatively, the stock or the facility) is what generates a flow of resource units or benefits over time (Lueck 1995). Examples of typical common-pool resource systems include lakes, rivers, irrigation systems, groundwater basins, forests, fishery stocks and grazing areas. Common-pool resources may also be facilities that are constructed for joint use, such as mainframe computers and the Internet. The resource units or benefits from a common-pool resource include water, timber, medicinal plants, fish, fodder, central processing units, and connection time. Devising property regimes that effectively allow sustainable use of a common-pool resource requires rules that limit access to the resource system and other rules that limit the amount, timing, and technology used to withdraw diverse resource units from the resource system.

5. Property as bundles of rights

A property right is an enforceable authority to undertake particular actions in a specific domain (Commons 1968). Property rights define actions that individuals can take in relation to other individuals regarding some 'thing'. If one individual has a right, someone else has a commensurate duty to observe that right. Schlager and Ostrom (1992) identify five property rights that are most relevant for the use of common-pool resources, including access, withdrawal, management, exclusion, and alienation. These are defined as:

Access:	The right to enter a defined physical area and enjoy nonsubtractive benefits (for example, hike, canoe, sit in the sun).
Withdrawal:	The right to obtain resource units or products of a resource system (for example, catch fish, divert water).
Management:	The right to regulate internal use patterns and transform the resource by making improvements.
Exclusion:	The right to determine who will have access rights and withdrawal rights, and how those rights may be transferred.
Alienation:	The right to sell or lease management and exclusion rights (Schlager and Ostrom 1992).

In much of the economics literature, private property is defined as equivalent to alienation. Property-rights systems that do not contain the right of alienation are considered to be ill-defined. Further, they are presumed to lead to inefficiency since property-rights holders cannot trade their interest in an improved resource system for other resources, nor can someone who has a more efficient use of a resource system purchase that system in whole or in part (Demsetz 1967). Consequently, it is assumed that property-rights systems that include the right to alienation will be transferred to their highest valued use. Larson and Bromley (1990) challenge this commonly held view and show that much more information must be known about the specific values of a large number of parameters before judgments can be made concerning the efficiency of a particular type of property right.

Table 4.1 Bundles of rights associated with positions

	Owner	Proprietor	Claimant	Authorized User	Authorized Entrant
Access	X	X	X	X	X
Withdrawal	X	X	X	X	
Management	X	X	X	X	
Exclusion	X	X			
Alienation	X				

Source: E. Ostrom and Schlager (1996, p. 133).

Instead of focusing on one right from the bundle, it is more useful to classify five types of property-rights holders as shown in Table 4.1. In this view, individuals or collectivities may hold well-defined property rights that include or do not include all five of the rights defined above. This approach separates the question of whether a particular right is well-defined from the question of the effect of having a particular set of rights. 'Authorized entrants' include most recreational users of national parks who purchase an operational right to enter and enjoy the natural beauty of the park, but do not have a right to harvest forest products. Those who have both entry and withdrawal use-right units are 'authorized users'. The presence or absence of constraints upon the timing, technology used, purpose of use and quantity of resource units harvested are determined by operational rules devised by those holding the collective-choice rights (or authority) of management and exclusion.

The operational rights of entry and use may be finely divided into quite specific 'tenure niches' (Bruce 1995) that vary by season, by use, by technology, and by space. Tenure niches may overlap when one set of users owns the right to harvest fruits from trees, another set of users owns the right to the timber in these trees, and the trees may be located on land owned by still others (Bruce, Fortmann, and Nhira 1993). Operational rules may allow authorized users to transfer access and withdrawal rights either temporarily through a rental agreement, or permanently when these rights are assigned or sold to others.

'Claimants' possess the operational rights of access and withdrawal plus a collective-choice right of managing a resource that includes decisions concerning the construction and maintenance of facilities and the authority to devise limits on withdrawal rights. The net fishers of Jambudwip, India, for example, annually regulate the positioning of nets so as to avoid interference, but do not have the right to determine who may fish along the coast (Raychaudhuri 1980). Fishing territories are a frequent form of property for indigenous, inshore fishers (Durrenberger and Palsson 1987). Farmers on large-scale government irrigation systems frequently devise rotation schemes for allocating water on a branch canal (Benjamin et al. 1994; Shivakoti and Ostrom 2002).

'Proprietors' hold the same rights as claimants with the addition of the right to determine who may access and harvest from a resource. Most of the property systems that are called 'common-property' regimes involve participants who are proprietors and have four of the above rights, but do not possess the right to sell their management and exclusion rights even though they most frequently have the right to bequeath it to members of their family and to earn income from the resource (see Berkes 1989; Bromley et al. 1992; McCay and Acheson 1987; McCarthy 2006).

Empirical studies have found that some proprietors have sufficient rights to make decisions that promote long-term investment and harvesting from a resource. Place and Hazell (1993) conducted surveys in Ghana, Kenya, and Rwanda to ascertain if indigenous land-rights systems were a constraint on agricultural productivity. They found that having the rights of a proprietor as contrasted to an owner in these settings did not affect investment decisions and productivity. Other studies conducted in Africa (Migot-Adholla et al. 1991; Bruce and Migot-Adholla 1994) also found little difference in productivity, investment levels, or access to credit. In densely settled regions, however, proprietorship over agricultural land may not be sufficient (Feder et al. 1988; Feder and Feeny 1991; Anderson and Lueck 1992). As land is densely settled, the absence of a title reduces the options for farmers to sell their land and reap a return on this asset. Further, without a title, farmers lack collateral to obtain credit to invest more intensively in the productive potential of their land (see Alston, Libecap, and Schneider 1996).

Thus, a key finding from an overview of many studies is that no type of property-rights regime works equivalently in all types of settings (Quinn et al. 2007). For private-property systems in land to make a difference in productivity gains, one probably needs (1) a somewhat dense population so competition for use is present and (2) the existence of effective markets related to credit, inputs, and the sale of commodities (see further discussion in Section 7). In a series of studies of inshore fisheries, self-organized irrigation systems, forest user groups and groundwater institutions, proprietors tended to develop clear boundary rules to exclude noncontributors; established authority rules to allocate withdrawal rights; devised methods for monitoring conformance; and used graduated sanctions against those who do not conform to these rules (Blomquist 1992; Tang 1994; Lam 1998; T. Yandle 2003; Weinstein 2000).

'Owners' possess the right of alienation – the right to transfer a good in any way the owner wishes that does not harm the physical attributes or uses of other owners – in addition to the bundle of rights held by a proprietor. An individual, a private corporation, a government, or a communal group may possess full ownership rights to any kind of good including a common-pool resource (Montias 1976). The rights of owners, however, are never absolute. Even private owners have responsibilities not to generate particular kinds of harms for others (Demsetz 1967).

What should be obvious by now is that the world of property rights is far more complex than simply government, private and common property. These terms better reflect the status and organization of the holder of a particular right than the bundle of property rights held. All of the above rights can be held by single individuals or by collectivities. Some communal fishing systems grant their members all five of the above rights, including the right of alienation (Miller 1989). Members in these communal fishing systems have full ownership rights. Similarly, farmer-managed irrigation systems in Nepal, the Philippines and Spain have established transferable shares to the systems. Access, withdrawal, voting and maintenance responsibilities are allocated by the amount of shares owned (Maass and Anderson 1986; Martin 1986; Siy 1982). On the other hand, some proposals to 'privatize' inshore fisheries through the devise of an Individual Transferable Quota (ITQ), allocate transferable use rights to authorized fishers but do not allocate rights related to the management of the fisheries, the determination of who is a participant, nor the transfer of management and exclusion rights. Thus, proposals to establish ITQ systems, which are frequently referred to as forms of 'privatization', do not involve full ownership.

With new commons, such as the Internet, the bundle may include other types of rights. Hess and Ostrom (2007, pp. 52–53) found that electronic information resources often have more than five types of rights. Drawing on Schlager and Ostrom (1992), seven major types of property rights were identified. The following rights are defined for an online institutional repository.

Access	The right to enter a defined physical area and enjoy nonsubtractive benefits.
Contribution	The right to contribute to the content.
Extraction	The right to obtain resource units or products of a resource system.
Removal	The right to remove one's artifacts from the resource.
Management/ Participation	The right to regulate internal use patterns and transform the resource by making improvements.

Exclusion	The right to determine who will have access, contribution, extraction, and removal rights and how those rights may be transferred.
Alienation	The right to sell or lease management and exclusion rights.

Other examples are the Creative Commons (CC) licenses that were established to allow authors to different rights for their works rather than the 'one size fits all' standard copyright agreement. CC defines the spectrum of possibilities between full copyright – *all rights reserved* – and the public domain – *no rights reserved.* Rights given to users by the authors are Attribution, Noncommercial, No derivative works and Share alike (see http://creativecommons.org/about/license/).

The next two sections are devoted to a discussion of the attributes of common-pool resources that are conducive to communal proprietorship or communal ownership as contrasted to individual ownership. Groups of individuals are considered to share communal property rights when they have formed an organization that exercises at least the collective-choice rights of management and exclusion in relationship to some defined resource system and the resource units produced by that system. Where communal groups are full owners, members of the group have the further right to sell their access, use, exclusion and management rights to others, subject in many systems to the approval of the other members of the group. Some communal proprietorships are formally organized and recognized by legal authorities as having a corporate existence that entails the right to sue and be sued, the right to hold financial assets in a common bank account, and to make decisions that are binding on members. Other communal proprietorships are less formally organized and may exercise de facto property rights that may or may not be supported by legal authorities if challenged by nonmembers. Obviously, such groups hold less well-defined bundles of property rights than those who are secure in their de jure rights even though the latter may not hold the complete set of property rights defined as full ownership. In other words, well-defined and secure property rights may not involve the right to alienation.

6. Attributes of common-pool resources conducive to the use of communal proprietorship or ownership

Even though all common-pool resources share the difficulty of devising methods to achieve exclusion and a sustainable level of harvesting of resource units, the variability of common-pool resources is immense in regard to other attributes that affect the incentives of resource users and the likelihood of achieving outcomes that approach optimality. Further, whether it is difficult or costly to develop physical or institutional means to exclude nonbeneficiaries depends on the availability and cost of technical and institutional solutions to the problem of exclusion and the relationship of the cost of these solutions to the expected benefits of achieving exclusion from a particular resource.

Let us start initially with a discussion of land as a resource system. Where population density is extremely low, land is abundant, and land generates a rich diversity of plant and animal products without much husbandry, the expected costs of establishing and defending boundaries to a parcel of land of any size may be greater than the expected benefits of enclosure (Demsetz 1967; Feeny 1993). Settlers moving into a new terrain characterized by high risk due to danger from others, from a harsh environment, or from lack of appropriate knowledge, may decide to develop one large, common parcel prior to any divisions into smaller parcels (Ellickson 1993). Once land becomes scarce, conflict over who has the rights to invest in improvements and reap the results of their efforts can lead individuals to want to enclose land through fencing or institutional means to protect their investments. There are tradeoffs in costs to be considered, however. The more land included within one enclosure, the lower the costs of defending all the boundaries, but the higher the costs of regulating the use of the enclosed parcel.

The decision to enclose may be taken by the joint owners to divide the commons into a series of private plots owned exclusively by single families (Field 1984, 1985, 1989; Ellickson 1993). The benefits of enclosing land depend on the scale of productive activity involved. For some agricultural activities, as discussed below, there may be considerable benefits associated with smaller parcels fully owned by a family enterprise. For other activities, the benefits may not be substantial. Moving all the way to private plots is an efficient move when the expected marginal returns from enclosing numerous plots exceed the expected marginal costs of defending a much more extended system of boundaries and the reduced transaction costs of making decisions about use patterns (Nugent and Sanchez 1989).

In a classic study of the diversity of property-rights systems used for many centuries by Swiss peasants, Netting (1976, 1981) observed that the same individuals fully divided their agricultural land into separate family-owned parcels, but that grazing lands located on the Alpine hillsides were organized into communal property systems. In these mountain valleys, the *same* individuals used different property-rights systems side-by-side for multiple centuries. Each local community had considerable autonomy to change local rules, so there was no problem of someone else imposing an inefficient set of rules on them. Netting argued that attributes of the resource affected which property-rights systems were most likely for diverse purposes. Netting identified five attributes that he considered to be most conducive to the development of communal property rights:

1. low value of production per unit of area;
2. high variance in the availability of resource units on any one parcel;
3. low returns from intensification of investment;
4. substantial economies of scale by utilizing a large area; and
5. substantial economies of scale in building infrastructures.

Steep land where rainfall is scattered may not be suitable for most agricultural purposes, but can be excellent land for pasture and forests if aggregated into sufficiently large parcels. By developing communal property rights to large parcels of such land, those who are members of the community are able to share environmental risks due to the unpredictability of rain-induced growth of grasses within any smaller region. Further, herding and processing of milk products is subject to substantial economies of scale. If individual families develop means to share these reduced costs, all can save substantially (Agrawal 1999). Building the appropriate roads, retaining walls and processing facilities may also be done more economically if these efforts are shared.

While the Swiss peasants were able to devote these harsh lands to productive activities, they had to invest time and effort in the development of rules that would reduce the incentives to overgraze and would ensure that investments in shared infrastructure were maintained over time. In many Swiss villages, rights to common pasturage were distributed according to the number of cows that could be carried over the winter using hay supplies produced on the owners' private parcels. In all cases, the village determined who had use rights, what the specific access and withdrawal rights were, how investment and maintenance costs were to be shared, and how the annual returns from common processing activities were to be shared. All of these systems included at least village proprietorship rights, but some Swiss villages developed full ownership rights by incorporating and authorizing the buying and selling of shares (usually with the approval of the village). Netting's findings are strongly supported by studies of mountain villages in Japan, where thousands of rural villages have held communal property rights to extensive forests and grazing areas located in the steep mountainous regions located above their private agricultural plots (McKean 1982, 1992a, 1992b). Similar systems have existed in Norway for centuries (Ørebech et al. 2005; Sandberg 1998).

The importance of sharing risk is stressed in other theoretical and empirical studies of communal proprietorships (Gupta 1986; Nugent and Sanchez 1993). Unpredictability and risk are increased in systems where resource units are mobile and where storage facilities, such as dams, do not exist (Schlager, Blomquist, and Tang 1994). Institutional facilities for sharing risk, such as formal insurance systems or institutionalized mechanisms for reciprocal obligations in times of plenty, also affect the kinds of property-rights systems that individuals can devise. When no physical or institutional mechanisms exist for sharing risk, communal property arrangements may enable individuals to adopt productive activities not feasible under individual property rights. In the Sudan, for instance, the variance in the productivity of land over space – due largely to the fluctuation in rainfall from year to year – is strongly associated with the size of communally held parcels allocated to grazing (Nugent and Sanchez 1993). Ellickson (1993) compares the types of environmental and personal security risks faced by new settlers in New England, in Bermuda, and in Utah to explain the variance in the speed of converting jointly held land to individually held land in each of these settlements.

A consistent finding across many studies of communal property-rights systems is that these systems do not exist in isolation and are usually used in conjunction with individual ownership. In most irrigation systems that are built and managed by the farmers themselves, for example, each farmer owns his or her own plot(s) while participating as a joint proprietor or owner in a communally organized irrigation system (Coward 1980; Sengupta 1991, 1993; Tang 1992; Vincent 1995; Wade 1992). Water is allocated to individual participants using a variety of individually tailored rules, but those irrigation systems that have survived for long periods of time tend to allocate water and responsibilities for joint costs using a similar metric – frequently the amount of land owned by a farmer (E. Ostrom 1990, 1992). In other words, benefits are roughly proportional to the costs of investing and maintaining the system itself.

Further, formally recognized communal systems are usually nested into a series of governance units that complement the organizational skills and knowledge of those involved in making collective-choice decisions in smaller units (O. Johnson 1972). Since the Middle Ages, most of the Alpine systems in both Switzerland and Italy have been nested in a series of self-governing communities that respectively governed villages, valleys, and federations of valleys (Merlo et al. 1989). In modern times, cantonal authorities in Switzerland have assumed an added responsibility to make periodic, careful monitoring visits to each alp on a rotating basis and to provide professional assessments and recommendations to local villages, thereby greatly enhancing the quality of knowledge and information about the sustainability of these resources.

Contrary to the expectation that communal property systems lacking the right to alienate ownership shares are markedly less efficient than property-rights systems involving full ownership, substantial evidence exists that many communal proprietorships effectively solve a wide diversity of local problems with relatively low transaction costs (Gaffney 1992; Hanna and Munasinghe 1995a, 1995b; Kaul 1996; Sandberg 1998). Obtaining valid and reliable measures of outputs and costs for a large number of property-rights systems covering similar activities in matched environmental settings is extremely difficult. In regard to irrigation, a series of careful studies of the performance of communal proprietorship systems as contrasted to government-owned and managed systems, clearly demonstrates the higher productivity of the communal systems controlling for relevant variables (Tang 1992; Benjamin et al. 1994; Lam 1998). Schlager's (1994) studies of inshore fisheries demonstrate that fishers who have clearly defined proprietorship are able to solve difficult assignment problems and assign the use of space and technology so as to increase both the efficiency and equity of their systems. James Wilson and colleagues' studies also demonstrate that communal proprietorship systems are more efficient than frequently thought (Wilson et al. 1994; Wilson, Yan, and Wilson 2007).

Performance of communal property-rights systems varies substantially, however, as do the performance of all property-rights systems. Some communal systems fail or limp along at the margin of effectiveness just as private firms fail or barely hang on to profitability over long periods of time. In addition to the environmental variables discussed above that are conducive in the first place to the use of communal proprietorship or ownership, the following variables related to the attributes of participants are conducive to their selection of norms, rules, and property rights that enhance the performance of communal property-rights systems (E. Ostrom 1993):

1. Accurate information about the condition of the resource and expected flow of benefits and costs is available at low cost to the participants (Blomquist 1992; Gilles and Jamtgaard 1981).
2. Participants share a common understanding about the potential benefits and risks associated with the continuance of the status quo as contrasted with changes in norms and rules that they could feasibly adopt (E. Ostrom 1990; Sethi and Somanathan 1996).
3. Participants share generalized norms of reciprocity and trust that can be used as initial social capital (Cordell and McKean 1992).
4. The group using the resource is relatively stable (Seabright 1993).
5. Participants plan to live and work in the same area for a long time (and in some cases, expect their offspring to live there as well) and, thus, do not heavily discount the future (Grima and Berkes 1989).
6. Participants use collective-choice rules that fall between the extremes

of unanimity or control by a few (or even bare majority) and, thus, avoid high transaction or high deprivation costs (E. Ostrom 1990).
7. Participants can develop relatively accurate and low-cost monitoring and sanctioning arrangements (Berkes 1992).

Many of these variables are, in turn, affected by the type of larger regime in which users are embedded. If the larger regime recognizes the legitimacy of communal systems, and is facilitative of local self-organization by providing accurate information about natural resource systems, providing arenas in which participants can engage in discovery and conflict-resolution processes, and providing mechanisms to back up local monitoring and sanctioning efforts, the probability of participants adapting more effective rules over time is higher than in regimes that ignore resource problems or presume that all decisions about governance and management need to be made by central authorities.

Two additional variables – the size of a group and its homogeneity – have been noted as conducive to the initial organization of communal resources and to their successful performance over time (Agrawal 2000; Libecap 1989a, 1989b). As more research has been conducted, however, it is obvious that much more theoretical and empirical work is needed since both variables appear to have complex effects (Poteete and Ostrom 2004, 2008). Changing the size of a group, for example, always involves changing some of the other variables likely to affect the performance of a system. Increasing the size of a group is likely to be associated with at least the following changes: (1) an increase in the transaction costs of reaching agreements; (2) a reduction of the burden borne by each participant for meeting joint costs such as guarding a system, and maintenance; and (3) an increase in the amount of assets held by the group that could be used in times of emergency. Libecap (1995) found that it was particularly hard to get agreements to oil unitization with groups greater than four. Blomquist (1992), on the other hand, documents processes conducted in the shadow of an equity court that involved up to 750 participants in agreeing to common rules to allocate rights to withdraw water from groundwater basins in Southern California. The processes took a relatively long period of time, but they have now also survived with little administrative costs for half a century (Blomquist, Schlager, and Heikkila 2004). Agrawal and Goyal (2001) have shown that communal forestry institutions in India that are moderate in size are more likely to reduce overharvesting than are smaller groups because they tend to utilize a higher level of guarding than smaller groups.

Group heterogeneity is also multifaceted in its basic causal processes and effects. Groups can differ along many dimensions including their assets, their information, their valuation of final products, their production technologies, their time horizons, their exposure to risk (for example, headenders versus tailenders on irrigation systems), as well as their cultural belief systems (Varughese and Ostrom 2001). Libecap's (1989b) research on inshore fisheries has shown that when fishers have distinctively different production technologies and skills, all potential rules for sharing withdrawal rights have substantial distributional consequences and are the source of conflict that may not easily be overcome. Libecap and Wiggins's (1984) studies of the prorationing of crude oil production reveal an interesting relationship between the levels and type of information available to participants and the likelihood of agreement at various stages in a bargaining process. In the early stages of negotiation, all oil producers share a relatively equal level of ignorance about the relative claims that each might be able to make under private-property arrangements. This is the most likely time for oil unitization agreements to be reached successfully. If agreement is not reached early, each participant gains asymmetric information about their own claims as more and more investment is made in private information. Agreements are unlikely at this stage. If producers then aggressively pump from a common oil pool, all tend to be harmed by the overproduction and are willing late in the process to recognize their joint interests. Libecap's (1995) study of marketing agreements among orange growers also shows a strong negative impact of heterogeneity. The theoretical work of Mancur Olson (1965) on privileged groups, on the other hand, predicts that when some participants have substantial assets and whose interests are aligned with achieving an agreement, such groups are more likely to be organized. The empirical support for this proposition comes more from studies of global commons (Mitchell 1995; Oye and Maxwell 1995).

Heterogeneity in the knowledge and acceptance of local common-property regimes is likely to lead to their undoing. In frontier regions, new migrants increase the number of people sharing the return from a common-pool resource. Further, migrants are unlikely to recognize the legitimacy of extant, de facto, property-rights systems (see Alston, Libecap, and Schneider 1996). Thus, the common agreement necessary for the sustenance of any property-rights system may rapidly disappear if settlement patterns undergo a rapid change. Similarly, common-property systems related to inshore fisheries have also proved to be unstable when trawlers from other locations start to visit on a regular basis without recognizing the de facto property rights of local fishers.

7. Attributes of common-pool resources conducive to the use of individual rights to withdrawal, management, exclusion, and alienation

The advantage of individual ownership of strictly private goods – where the cost of exclusion is relatively low and one person's consumption is subtractive from what is available to others – is so well established that it does not merit attention here. Industrial and agricultural commodities clearly fit the definition of private goods. Individual rights to exclusion and to transferring control over these goods generate incentives that lead to higher levels of productivity than other forms of property arrangements.

It has frequently been assumed that land also is clearly always a private good and therefore best allocated using market mechanisms based on individual ownership rights. Agricultural land in densely settled regions is usually best allocated by a system of individual property rights. Gaining formal title to land, however, may or may not increase efficiency. Feder et al. (1988) conducted an important econometric study that showed that agricultural land in Thailand without a formal title was worth only one-half to two-thirds of land with a formal title. Further, increasing the security of private-property rights also led to an increased value of the crops produced (between one-tenth and one-fourth higher than those without secure title). More secure titling also provided better access to credit and led to greater investments in improved land productivity (see also Feder and Feeny 1991). Insecure property rights may lead potential users to arm and engage in violent conflict so as to gain control over land through force or by negotiation to avoid force. Several types of economic losses result from conflict over ownership (Umbeck 1981a, 1981b).

Title insurance is another mechanism used to reduce the risk of successful challenges to ownership of land. Registering brands is still another technique used to increase the security of ownership over resource units in the form of cattle that may range freely over a large area until there is a communal effort to undertake a round-up. Gaining formal titles is, however, costly. In societies that do not yet have high population densities and where customary rights are still commonly understood and accepted, formal titling may be an expensive method of increasing the security of a title that is not associated with a sufficiently higher return to be worth the economic investment (see Migot-Adholla et al. 1991). In addition, it should now be clear that the cost of fencing land by physical and/or institutional means is nontrivial and that there are types of land and land uses that may be more efficiently governed by groups of individuals rather than single individuals.

A commonly recommended solution to problems associated with the governance and management of mobile resource units, such as water and fish, is their 'privatization' (Christy 1973; C. Clark 1980). Implementing operational and efficient individual withdrawal rights to mobile resources is far more difficult in practice than demonstrating the economic efficiency of hypothetical systems. Simply gaining valid and accurate measurements of 'sustainable yield' is a scientifically difficult task. In systems where resource units are stored naturally or by constructing facilities such as a dam, the availability of a defined quantity of the resource units can be ascertained with considerable accuracy, and buying, selling, and leasing rights to known quantities is relatively easy to effectuate in practice. Many mobile resource systems do not have natural or constructed storage facilities, and gaining accurate information about the stock and reproduction rates is very costly and involves considerable uncertainty (Allen and McGlade 1987; J. Wilson et al. 1991). Further, as Copes (1986) has clearly articulated, appropriators from such resources can engage in a wide diversity of evasive strategies that can destabilize the efforts of government agencies trying to manage these systems. Further, once such systems have allocated individual withdrawal rights, efforts to further regulate patterns of withdrawal may be very difficult and involve expensive buy-back schemes. Experience with these individual withdrawal-rights systems has varied greatly in practice (see McCay 1992; Wilson and Dickie 1995).

Exactly which attributes of both physical and social systems are most important to the success of individual withdrawal rights from common-pool resources is not as well established as the attributes of common-pool resource systems conducive to group proprietorship or ownership. On the physical side, gaining accurate measurements of the key variables (quantity, space, technology) that are to be involved in management efforts is essential. Resource systems that are naturally well-bounded facilitate measurement as well as ease of observing appropriation behavior. Storage also facilitates measurement. Where resource units move over vast terrain, the cost of measurement is higher than when they are contained (for example, it is easier to develop effective withdrawal-rights systems for lobsters than for whales).

Considerable recent research has also stressed the importance of involving participants in the design and implementation of such property-rights systems. When participants do not look upon such rules as legitimate, effective, and fair, the capacity to invent evasive strategies is substantial (Seabright 1993). The size of the group involved and the heterogeneity of participants also affect the costs of maintaining withdrawal-rights systems (Edwards 1994). And, the very process of allocating quantitative and transferable rights to resource units may undo some of the common understandings and norms that allowed communal ownership systems to operate at lower day-to-day administrative costs.

8. Communal property regimes in the twenty-first century

The focus of this chapter has been primarily on natural resources. Many of the lessons learned from the operation of communal property regimes in these sectors, however, are quite relevant for a wide diversity of similar property regimes that are currently in wide use and likely to have a substantial presence in the next century. A very large number of housing developments – both apartment houses and individual family dwellings – involve individual property to the housing unit itself combined with communal property to the grounds, recreational facilities, and other joint facilities. While individuals can buy and sell their individual housing units, at the time of purchase they assume a set of duties in respect to the closely related communal properties. Monthly assessments for the repair and maintenance of these common facilities are not unlike the assessments made by a community of irrigators on themselves for the maintenance of their own system. Further, purchase and sales frequently require the permission of other members of the group. Similarly, many sports clubs allocate use quotas to members and assess members' regular fees for the maintenance of the commonly owned facilities.

The modern corporation is frequently thought of as the epitome of private property. While buying and selling shares of corporate stock is a clear example of the rights of alienation at work, relationships within a firm are far from being 'individual' ownership rights. Since the income that will be shared among stockholders, management, and employees is itself a common pool to be shared, all of the incentives leading to free riding (shirking) and overuse (padding the budget) are found within the structure of a modern corporation (Ghoshal and Moran 1996; Putterman 1995; Seabright 1993). Thus, where many individuals will work, live, and play in the next century will be governed and managed by mixed systems of communal and individual property rights.

Acknowledgments

Support from the National Science Foundation (Grant Nos. SBR-9319835 and SBR-95 21918), the Ford Foundation, and the Andrew W. Mellon Foundation is gratefully acknowledged. Comments on an initial draft of this entry by Arun Agrawal, David Feeny, Vincent Ostrom, Peter Ørebech, and Jimmy Walker are gratefully acknowledged. The comments of two anonymous reviewers were of considerable value. The editing skills of Patty Lezotte have been, as usual, of immense assistance – particularly in a paper involving such an extensive bibliography as Charlotte Hess and I have prepared for this chapter. Thanks also to Emily Castle for her assistance in updating the information in footnote 1.

Notes on the bibliography

The updated and revised bibliography[1] adds well over 200 additional citations to the earlier version. We have selected articles and books that continue the tradition of common property scholarship as well as those that reflect new trends in this area of study. Noteworthy stronger foci are sustainability, the global commons, property regimes in transition, and the intersection of intellectual property rights and environmental goods.

The crucial questions surrounding common-property management have continued to be ones of equity, efficiency and sustainability. Since the turn of this past century, however, the issue of sustainability has increased in its importance and visibility in the commons literature (see, for instance, Agrawal 2001; Anderies et al. 2007; Bressers and Kuks 2004; Costanza et al. 2001; Kamara, Kirk, and Swallow 2004; Marshall, Fritsch, and Dulhunty 2005; McMahon 2006; Meinzen-Dick and Di Gregorio 2004; Ørebech et al. 2005; Oses-Erasoa and Viladrich-Grau 2007; Pasqual and Souto 2003; Smajgl and Larson 2007; Veeman and Politylo 2003). Ecological economist Robert Costanza (2000) writes:

> The most critical task facing humanity today is the creation of a shared vision of a sustainable and desirable society, one that can provide permanent prosperity within the biophysical constraints of the real world in a way that is fair and equitable to all of humanity, to other species, and to future generations.

Some authors argue that developing new common-property regimes may be helpful in achieving sustainability (Brunckhorst 2003; Buck 2002; Buxton 2004; Marshall, Fritsch, and Dulhunty 2005; Williamson, Brunckhorst, and Kelly 2003).

New research demonstrates the urgent need for effective approaches to commons problems that are global in scale (E. Ostrom et al. 1999). Particular areas of focus on the global commons in this bibliography are biodiversity (Choudry 2005; Coban 2004; Goeschl and Igliori 2006; Tisdell 2004; Trommetter 2005) and water resources (Becker and Easter 1999; Dilworth 2007; Dinar 2000; Fisher 2004; Smets 2004).

Common-property regimes in transition is another noteworthy recurrent theme (see Banner 2002; Dekker 2003; Majumdar 2007; J. Marshall 2001; John McCarthy 2000; Moyo 2005; Muñoz Piña, de Janvry, and Sadoulet 2003; Mwangi 2006, 2007a, 2007b; Okello 2005; Rao et al. 2005; D. Thompson 2006). Mwangi (2007b), for instance, illustrates the complexity of regime change in her research on the transition from collective to individualized rights in Kenya's Maasailand and the complications of politics and procedural problems. The ambiguity of certain property regimes leads a number of researchers to examine 'who owns' various resources (Barnes 2001 [sky]; M.F. Brown 2003 [native culture]; Gepts 2004 [biodiversity]; Ho 2001 [land]; Macinko and Bromley 2002 [fisheries]). Privatization is another kind of regime transition of great concern regardless of which kind of resource is involved (for representative works see Hannesson 2006; Hedlund 2001; Lesorogol 2003; Mansfield 2004; National Research Council 2001).

Another growing area of study is the intersection of traditional property rights and intellectual property rights. Drahos and Mayne (2003) write that patents, as types of intellectual property rights, can reduce access to knowledge in such life-sustaining areas as genetics, health, and agriculture – a problem even worse in developing countries. Aoki calls one of these intersections 'seed wars' – battles 'over the ownership of intellectual property rights of germplasm – arguments over weeds, seeds and deeds' (Aoki 2003; see also Borowiak 2004; Dutfield 2000; C. Thompson 2004). A number of works focus on rights to plant genetic resources and threats to indigenous knowledge and systems of agriculture (Barnett 2000; Dickenson 2004; Eyzaguirre et al. 2004; Kennedy 2006; Rifkin 2002; Spier 2001).

Note

1. The commons database in the library of the Workshop in Political Theory and Policy Analysis contains 59,192 records of literature on the commons, common-pool resources, and common property. Of those, 848 have 'common property' in the title.

Bibliography

Acheson, James M. (1988), *The Lobster Gangs of Maine*, Hanover, NH: University Press of New England.

Acheson, James M. (2000), 'Clearcutting Maine: Implications for the theory of common property resources', *Human Ecology*, **28**, 145–169.

Acheson, James M. (2003), *Capturing the Commons: Devising Institutions to Manage the Maine Lobster Industry*, Lebanon, NH: University Press of New England.

Adger, W. Neil and Cecilia Luttrell (2000), 'Property rights and the utilisation of wetlands', *Ecological Economics*, **35**, 75–89.

Adhikari, Bhim (2005), 'Poverty, property rights and collective action: Understanding the distributive aspects of common property resource management', *Environment and Development Economics*, **10**, 7–31.

Agrawal, Arun (1999), *Greener Pastures: Politics, Markets, and Community among a Migrant Pastoral People*, Durham, NC: Duke University Press.

Agrawal, Arun (2000), 'Small is beautiful, but is larger better? Forest-management institutions in the Kumaon Himalaya, India', in Clark Gibson, Margaret McKean, and Elinor Ostrom (eds), *People and Forests: Communities, Institutions, and Governance*, Cambridge, MA: MIT Press, pp. 57–86.

Agrawal, Arun (2001), 'Common property institutions and sustainable governance of resources', *World Development*, **29**, 1649–1672.

Agrawal, Arun (2005), *Environmentality: Technologies of Government and the Making of Subjects*, Durham, NC: Duke University Press.

Agrawal, Arun and Elinor Ostrom (2001), 'Collective action, property rights, and decentralization in resource use in India and Nepal', *Politics and Society*, **29**, 485–514.

Agrawal, Arun and Sanjeev Goyal (2001), 'Group size and collective action: Third-party monitoring in common-pool resources', *Comparative Political Studies*, **34** (1), 63–93.

Aguilera-Klink, Federico (1994), 'Some notes on the misuse of classic writings in economics on the subject of common property', *Ecological Economics*, **9** (3), 221–228.

Alchian, Armen A. (1965), 'Some economics of property rights', *Il Politico*, **30**, 816–829.

Alchian, Armen A. and Harold Demsetz (1973), 'The property rights paradigm', *Journal of Economic History*, **33**, 16–27.

Alcock, F. (2002), 'Bargaining, uncertainty, and property rights in fisheries', *World Politics*, **54**, 437–461.

Alcorn, J.B. and A.G. Royo (eds) (2000), *Indigenous Social Movements and Ecological Resilience: Lessons from the Dayak of Indonesia*, Washington, DC: World Wildlife Fund.

Allen, P.M. and J.M. McGlade (1987), 'Modelling complex human systems: A fisheries example', *European Journal of Operational Research*, **30**, 147–167.

Alston, Lee J., Thráinn Eggertsson, and Douglass C. North (eds) (1996), *Empirical Studies in Institutional Change*, New York: Cambridge University Press.

Alston, Lee J., Gary Libecap, and Robert Schneider (1996), 'The determinants and impact of property rights: Land titles on the Brazilian frontier', *Journal of Law, Economics and Organization*, **12**, 25–61.

Altman, Jon C. (2004), 'Economic development and indigenous Australia: Contestations over property, institutions and ideology', *Australian Journal of Agricultural and Resource Economics*, **48**, 513–534.

Andelson, Robert V. (ed.) (1991), *Commons without Tragedy: The Social Ecology of Land Tenure and Democracy*, London: Centre for Incentive Taxation.

Anderies, John M., Armando A. Rodriguez, Marco A. Janssen, and Oguzhan Cifdaloz (2007), 'Panaceas, uncertainty, and the robust control framework in sustainability science', *Proceedings of the National Academy of Sciences*, **104** (39), 15194–15199.

Anderson, C.L. and E. Swimmer (1997), 'Some empirical evidence on property rights of first peoples', *Journal of Economic Behavior and Organization*, **33** (1), 1–22.

Anderson, Terry L. (2004), 'Donning Coase-colored glasses: A property rights view of natural resource economics', *Australian Journal of Agricultural and Resource Economics*, **48**, 445–462.

Anderson, Terry L. and Peter J. Hill (eds) (2001), *The Technology of Property Rights*, Lanham, MD: Rowman & Littlefield.

Anderson, Terry L. and Peter J. Hill (2004), *The Not So Wild, Wild West: Property Rights on the Frontier*, Stanford, CA: Stanford University Press.

Anderson, Terry L. and Dean Lueck (1992), 'Land tenure and agricultural productivity on Indian reservations', *Journal of Law and Economics*, **35**, 427–454.

Anderson, Terry L. and Fred S. McChesney (eds) (2003), *Property Rights: Cooperation, Conflict, and Law*, Princeton, NJ: Princeton University Press.

Aoki, Keith (1998), 'Neocolonialism, anticommons property, and biopiracy in the (not-so-brave) new world order of international intellectual property protection', *Indiana Journal of Global Legal Studies*, **6** (1), 11–38.

Aoki, Keith (2003), 'Weeds, seeds & deeds: Recent skirmishes in the seed wars', *Cardozo Journal of International and Comparative Law*, **11**, 247–331.

Apostle, Richard, Bonnie McCay, and Knut H. Mikalsen (2002), *Enclosing the Commons: Individual Transferable Quotas in the Nova Scotia Fishery*, St. John's, Newfoundland: ISER Books.

Arnason, Ragnar (2005), 'Property rights in fisheries: Iceland's experience with ITQs', *Reviews in Fish Biology and Fisheries*, **15**, 243–264.

Arnold, Craig Anthony (2002), 'The reconstitution of property: Property as a web of interests', *Harvard Environmental Law Review*, **26**, 281–364.

Arnold, Gwen (2003), 'Collective action for common pool resource management in Michigan inland lake communities', *Michigan Journal of Political Science*, **2**, 1–97.

Arnold, J.E.M. (1993), 'Management of forest resources as common property', *Commonwealth Forestry Review*, **72**, 157–161.

Arnold, J.E.M. and J. Gabriel Campbell (1986), 'Collective management of hill forests in Nepal: The community forestry development project', in National Research Council, *Proceedings of the Conference on Common Property Resource Management*, Washington, DC: National Academies Press, pp. 425–454.

Arnold, J.E.M. and W.C. Stewart (1989), *Common Property Resource Management in India*, Oxford: Oxford Forestry Institute, University of Oxford, Department of Plant Sciences, Tropical Forestry Papers no. 24.

Ascher, William (1995), *Communities and Sustainable Forestry in Developing Countries*, San Francisco, CA: ICS Press.

Ashenafi, Zelealem, and N. Leader-Williams (2005), 'Indigenous common property resource management in the central highlands of Ethiopia', *Human Ecology*, **33**, 539–563.
Atran, Scott (1993), 'Itza Maya tropical agro-forestry', *Current Anthropology*, **34**, 633–700.
Axelby, Richard (2007), '"It takes two hands to clap": How Gaddi shepherds in the Indian Himalayas negotiate access to grazing', *Journal of Agrarian Change*, **7**, 35–75.
Baack, Bennett (1982), 'Testing the impact of exclusive property rights: The case of enclosing commons fields', in Roger Ransom, Richard Sutch, and Gary Walton (eds), *Explorations in the New Economic History: Essays in Honor of Douglass C. North*, New York: Academic Press.
Baden, John (1977), 'A primer for the management of common pool resources', in Garrett Hardin and John Baden (eds), *Managing the Commons*, San Francisco, CA: W.H. Freeman.
Baird, John S. (1982), 'Conservation of the commons: Effects of group cohesiveness and prior sharing', *Journal of Community Psychology*, **10**, 210–215.
Baker, Kenneth and Michael McKee (2000), 'Increasingly contested property rights and trading in environmental amenities', *Land Economics*, **76**, 333–344.
Baker, Matthew, Thomas Miceli, C.F. Sirmans, and Geoffrey K. Turnbull (2001), 'Property rights by squatting: Land ownership risk and adverse possession statutes', *Land Economics*, **77**, 360–370.
Baland, Jean-Marie and Patrick Francois (2005), 'Commons as insurance and the welfare impact of privatization', *Journal of Public Economics*, **89**, 211–231.
Baland, Jean-Marie and Jean-Philippe Platteau (1996), *Halting Degradation of Natural Resources: Is There A Role for Rural Communities?*, New York: Oxford University Press and FAO.
Baland, Jean-Marie and Jean-Philippe Platteau (1998), 'Division of the commons: A partial assessment of the new institutional economics of land rights', *American Journal of Agricultural Economics*, **80** (3), 644–657.
Baland, Jean-Marie and Jean-Philippe Platteau (2003), 'Economics of common property management regimes', *Handbook in Economics*, **20**, 127–184.
Banks, Tony (2001), 'Property rights and the environment in pastoral China: Evidence from the field', *Development and Change*, **32**, 717–740.
Banks, Tony (2003), 'Property rights reform in rangeland China: Dilemmas on the road to the household ranch', *World Development*, **31**, 2129–2142.
Banner, Stuart (2002), 'Transitions between property regimes', *Journal of Legal Studies*, **31**, S359–S371.
Barbanell, Edward M. (2001), *Common-Property Arrangements and Scarce Resources: Water in the American West*, Westport, CT: Praeger.
Bardhan, Pranab K. (ed.) (1989), *The Economic Theory of Agrarian Institutions*, Oxford: Clarendon Press.
Bardhan, Pranab K. (2005a), 'Institutions matter, but which ones?', *Economics of Transition*, **13**, 499–532.
Bardhan, Pranab K. (ed.) (2005b), *Scarcity, Conflicts, and Cooperation: Essays in the Political and Institutional Economics of Development*, Cambridge, MA: MIT Press.
Barnes, Peter (2001), *Who Owns the Sky? Our Common Assets and the Future of Capitalism*, Washington, DC: Island Press.
Barnes, Peter (2006), *Capitalism 3.0: A Guide to Reclaiming the Commons*, San Francisco, CA: Berrett-Koehler.
Barnett, Jonathan M. (2000), 'Cultivating the genetic commons: Imperfect patent protection and the network model of innovation', *San Diego Law Review*, **37** (4), 987–1067.
Barzel, Yoram (1991), *Economic Analysis of Property Rights*, New York: Cambridge University Press.
Barzel, Yoram (2002), *A Theory of the State: Economic Rights, Legal Rights, and the Scope of the State*, New York: Cambridge University Press.
Beck, Tony and Cathy Nesmith (2001), 'Building on poor people's capacities: The case of common property resources in India and West Africa', *World Development*, **29**, 119–133.

Becker, Marc (2007), 'Indigenous struggles for land rights in twentieth-century Ecuador', *Agricultural History*, **81**, 159–181.

Becker, Nir and K. William Easter (1999), 'Conflict and cooperation in managing international water resources such as the Great Lakes', *Land Economics*, **75** (2), 233–245.

Behnke, Roy H., Jr. (1985), 'Open-range management and property rights in pastoral Africa: A case of spontaneous range enclosure in South Darfur, Sudan', London: Overseas Development Institute.

Béné, Christophe, A. Neiland, T. Jolley, B. Ladu, S. Ovie, O. Sule, M. Baba, et al. (2003), 'Natural resource institutions and property rights in inland African fisheries: The case of the Lake Chad basin region', *International Journal of Social Economics*, **30**, 275–301.

Bengwayan, Michael A. (2003), *Intellectual and Cultural Property Rights of Indigenous and Tribal Peoples in Asia*, London: Minority Rights Group.

Benjamin, Paul, Wai Fung Lam, Elinor Ostrom, and Ganesh Shivakoti (1994), *Institutions, Incentives, and Irrigation in Nepal*, Decentralization: Finance & Management Project Report, Burlington, VT: Associates in Rural Development.

Benjaminsen, Tor Arve, Ben Cousins, and Lisa Thompson (eds) (2002), *Contested Resources: Challenges to the Governance of Natural Resources in Southern Africa*, Cape Town: Programme for Land and Agrarian Studies (PLAAS).

Benjaminsen, Tor A. and Christian Lund (eds) (2001), *Politics, Property and Production in the West African Sahel: Understanding Natural Resources Management*, Uppsala and London: Nordic Africa Institute and Global.

Benjaminsen, Tor A. and Christian Lund (2002), 'Formalisation and informalisation of land and water rights in Africa: An introduction', *European Journal of Development Research*, **14**, 1–10.

Berck, P. (1979), 'Open access and extinction', *Econometrica*, **47**, 877–882.

Berge, Erling (ed.) (1993), *Common Property Regimes: Law and Management of Non-Private Resources: Proceedings of the Conference; Vols. I-II*, Ås, Norway: Agricultural University of Norway.

Berge, Erling and Nils Stenseth (eds) (1995), *Law and the Management of Renewable Resources*, Trondheim, Norway: University of Trondheim, Department of Sociology and Political Science.

Berkes, Fikret (ed.) (1989), *Common Property Resources; Ecology and Community-Based Sustainable Development*, London: Belhaven.

Berkes, Fikret (1992), 'Success and failure in marine coastal fisheries of Turkey', in Daniel W. Bromley, et al. (eds), *Making the Commons Work: Theory, Practice, and Policy*, San Francisco, CA: ICS Press, pp. 161–182.

Berkes, Fikret (2004), 'Rethinking community-based conservation', *Conservation Biology*, **18**, 621–630.

Berkes, Fikret (2007), 'Community-based conservation in a globalized world', *Proceedings of the National Academy of Sciences*, **104** (39), 15188–15193.

Berry, Sara S. (2000), *Chiefs Know Their Boundaries: Essays on Property, Power, and the Past in Asante, 1896–1996*, Westport, CT: Heinemann.

Blackstone, William (1766), *Commentaries on the Laws of England, Book II*, Chicago: University of Chicago Press.

Blaikie, Piers M. and Harold C. Brookfield (eds) (1987), *Land Degradation and Society*, New York: Methuen.

Blomley, N. (2007), 'Making private property: Enclosure, common right and the work of hedges', *Rural History*, **18**, 1–22.

Blomquist, William (1992), *Dividing the Waters: Governing Groundwater in Southern California*, San Francisco, CA: ICS Press.

Blomquist, William and Elinor Ostrom (1985), 'Institutional capacity and the resolution of a commons dilemma', *Policy Studies Review*, **5**, 383–393.

Blomquist, William, Edella Schlager, and Tanya Heikkila (2004), *Common Waters, Diverging Streams: Linking Institutions and Water Management in Arizona, California, and Colorado*, Washington, DC: Resources for the Future.

Bolle, F. (1986), 'On the oligopolistic extraction of non-renewable common-pool resources', *Economics*, **53**, 519–527.

Borowiak, Craig (2004), 'Farmers' rights: Intellectual property regimes and the struggle over seeds', *Politics and Society*, **32**, 511–543.

Brandt, Sylvia (2007), 'Evaluating tradable property rights for natural resources: The role of strategic entry and exit', *Journal of Economic Behavior and Organization*, **63**, 158–176.

Brandt, Sylvia and D. McEvoy (2006), 'Distributional effects of property rights: Transitions in the Atlantic herring fishery', *Marine Policy*, **30**, 659–670.

Brara, Rita (2006), *Shifting Landscapes: The Making and Remaking of Village Commons in India*, New York: Oxford University Press.

Breemer, J.D. (2004), 'What property rights: The California coastal commission's history of abusing land rights and some thoughts on the underlying causes', *UCLA Journal of Environmental Law and Policy*, **22**, 247–300.

Bressers, Hans and Stefan Kuks (eds) (2004), *Integrated Governance and Water Basin Management: Conditions for Regime Change and Sustainability*, Boston, MA: Kluwer Academic.

Brock, William A. and Stephen R. Carpenter (2007), 'Panaceas and diversification of environmental policy', *Proceedings of the National Academy of Sciences*, **104** (39), 15206–15211.

Bromley, Daniel W. (1991), *Environment and Economy: Property Rights and Public Policy*, Cambridge, MA: Basil Blackwell.

Bromley, Daniel W. (1992), 'The commons, common property, and environmental policy', *Environmental and Resource Economics*, **2**, 1–17.

Bromley, Daniel W. (2000), 'Property regimes and pricing regimes in water resource management', in A. Dinar (ed.), *The Political Economy of Water Pricing Reforms*, New York: Oxford University Press, pp. 29–48.

Bromley, Daniel W., David Feeny, Margaret McKean, Pauline Peters, Jere Gilles, Ronald Oakerson, C. Ford Runge, and James Thomson (eds) (1992), *Making the Commons Work: Theory, Practice, and Policy*, San Francisco, CA: ICS Press.

Brooks, R., S. Davidson, and R. Faff (2003), 'Sudden changes in property rights: The case of Australian native title', *Journal of Economic Behavior and Organization*, **52**, 427–442.

Brown, G., B. Berger, and M. Ikiara (2005), 'Different property rights regimes in the Lake Victoria multiple species fishery', *Environment and Development Economics*, **10**, 53–65.

Brown, K.M. (2006a), 'New challenges for old commons: The role of historical common land in contemporary rural spaces', *Scottish Geographical Journal*, **122**, 109–129.

Brown, K.M. (2006b), 'The role of moral values in contemporary common property enactment', *Norsk Geografisk Tidsskrift*, **60**, 89–99.

Brown, Michael F. (2003), *Who Owns Native Culture?*, Cambridge, MA: Harvard University Press.

Brox, Ottar (1990), 'The common property theory: Epistemological status and analytical utility', *Human Organization*, **49**, 227–235.

Bruce, John W. (1995), *Legal Bases for the Management of Land-Based Natural Resources as Common Property*, Forests, Trees and People Programme, Rome, Italy: Food and Agriculture Organization of the United Nations.

Bruce, John W., Louise Fortmann, and Calvin Nhira (1993), 'Tenures in transition, tenures in conflict: Examples from the Zimbabwe social forest', *Rural Sociology*, **58**, 626–642.

Bruce, John W. and Shem E. Migot-Adholla (eds) (1994), *Searching for Land Tenure Security in Africa*, Dubuque, IA: Kendall/Hunt.

Brunckhorst, David J. (2003), 'Factors in the success of common property resource institutions', *Ecological Management and Restoration*, **4**, 72–73.

Bruns, Bryan Randolph and Ruth Meinzen-Dick (eds) (2000), *Negotiating Water Rights*, New Delhi, India: Vistaar for the International Food Policy Research Institute.

Bruns, Bryan Randolph, Claudia Ringler, and Ruth Meinzen-Dick (eds) (2005), *Water Rights Reform: Lessons for Institutional Design*, Washington, DC: International Food Policy Research Institute.

Buchanan, James M. and Gordon Tullock (1965), *The Calculus of Consent: Logical Foundations of Constitutional Democracy*, Ann Arbor: University of Michigan Press.
Buck, Stuart (2002), 'Replacing spectrum auctions with a spectrum commons', *Stanford Technology Law Journal* 2, http://stlr.stanford.edu/STLR/Articles/02_STLR_2
Burger, Joanna, Elinor Ostrom, Richard Norgaard, David Policansky, and Bernard Goldstein (eds) (2000), *Protecting the Commons: A Framework for Resource Management in the Americas*, Covelo, CA: Island Press.
Burling, J.S. (2002), 'Private property rights and the environment after Palazzolo', *Boston College Environmental Affairs Law Review*, **30**, 1–64.
Burling, J.S. (2006), 'First we need real property rights', *Environmental Forum*, **23**, 23–27.
Burton, P.S. (2004), 'Hugging trees: Claiming de facto property rights by blockading resource use', *Environmental and Resource Economics*, **27**, 135–163.
Butler, L.L. (2000), 'The pathology of property norms: Living within nature's boundaries', *Southern California Law Review*, 73, 927–1015.
Buxton, Carol R. (2004), 'Property in outer space: The common heritage of mankind principle vs. the "first in time, first in right" rule of property law', *Journal of Air Law and Commerce*, **69**, 689–707.
Cahir, John (2004), 'The withering away of property rights', *Oxford Journal of Legal Studies*, **24**, 619–641.
Calabresi, Guido and A. Douglas Melamed (1972), 'Property rules, liability rules, and inalienability: One view of the cathedral', *Harvard Law Review*, **85**, 1089–1128.
Caleys, Eric R. (2006), 'Natural property rights and privatization: A comment on Professor Rose', *Saint Louis Law Journal*, **50**, 721–734.
Campbell, Bruce, Alois Mandondo, Nontokozo Nemarundwe, Bevlyne Sithole, Wil De Jong, Marty Luckert, and Frank Matose (2001), 'Challenges to proponents of common property resource systems: Despairing voices from the social forests of Zimbabwe', *World Development*, **29**, 589–600.
Caputo, M.R. and D. Lueck (2003), 'Natural resource exploitation under common property rights', *Natural Resource Modeling*, **16**, 39–68.
Carpenter, Kristin A. (2005), 'A property rights approach to sacred sites cases: Asserting a place for Indians as nonowners', *UCLA Law Review*, **52**, 1061–1148.
Casari, Mario (2007), 'Emergence of endogenous legal institutions: Property rights and community governance in the Italian Alps', *Journal of Economic History*, **67**, 191–226.
Casimir, Michael J. (1990), 'The determinants of rights to pasture: Territorial organization and ecological constraints', in M.J. Casimir and A. Rao (eds), *Mobility and Territoriality*, New York: Berg.
Cernea, Michael M. (ed.) (1991), *Putting People First: Sociological Variables in Rural Development*, 2nd ed., New York: Oxford University Press.
Chakraborty, Rabindra Nath (2001), 'Stability and outcomes of common property institutions in forestry: Evidence from the Terai region of Nepal', *Ecological Economics*, **36**, 341–353.
Chan, Nelson (2001), 'How new land use rights are changing communal property and China's cities', *Australian Property Journal*, **36**, 629–635.
Chaudhry, Shivani and Owen J. Lynch (eds) (2002), *Amplifying Local Voices, Striving for Environmental Justice: Proceedings of the African Public Interest Law and Community-Based Property Rights Workshop, Usa River, Arusha, Tanzania, August 1–4, 2000*, Washington, DC: Center for International Environmental Law.
Chavez, Carlos and Hugo Salgado (2005), 'Individual transferable quota markets under illegal fishing', *Environmental and Resource Economics*, **31**, 303–324.
Cheever, F. (2002), 'Property rights and the maintenance of wildlife habitat: The case for conservation land transactions', *Idaho Law Review*, **38**, 431–452.
Cheikbossian, G. (2003), 'Property rights, rent-seeking and aggregate outcomes in transition economies', *Economic Systems*, **27**, 271–288.
Chen, C.H. (2002), 'Property rights and rural development in China's transitional economy', *Economics of Planning*, **35**, 349–363.

Chen, F. (2002), 'An analysis of water transaction by the way of economics of property rights', *Chinese Rural Economy*, **10**, 25–29.
Chen, J. (2004), 'Webs of life: Biodiversity conservation as a species of information policy', *Iowa Law Review*, **89**, 495–608.
Cheung, S.N.S. (1970), 'The structure of a contract and the theory of a nonexclusive resource', *Journal of Law and Economics*, **13**, 49–70.
Chimhowu, Admos and Phil Woodhouse (2006), 'Customary vs. private property rights? Dynamics and trajectories of vernacular land markets in sub-Saharan Africa', *Journal of Agrarian Change*, **6**, 346–371.
Chopra, Kanchan and S.C. Gulati (2001), *Migration, Common Property Resources and Environmental Degradation: Interlinkages in India's Arid and Semi-Arid Regions*, Thousand Oaks, CA: Sage.
Choudry, Aziz (2005), 'Privatizing nature: Plundering biodiversity', in Ernst Ulrich von Weizsäcker, Oran R. Young, and Matthias Finger (eds), *Limits to Privatization: How to Avoid too Much of a Good Thing*, Sterling, VA: Earthscan, pp. 58–61.
Christy, Francis T. (1973), *Fisherman Quotas: A Tentative Suggestion for Domestic Management*, Kingston: University of Rhode Island, Law of the Sea Institute.
Ciriacy-Wantrup, Siegfried V. (1963), *Resource Conservation: Economics and Policies*, rev. ed., Berkeley: University of California, Division of Agricultural Sciences.
Ciriacy-Wantrup, Siegfried V. and Richard C. Bishop (1975), '"Common property" as a concept in natural resource policy', *Natural Resources Journal*, **15**, 713–727.
Clark, Colin W. (1976), *Mathematical Bioeconomics: The Optimal Management of Renewable Resources*, New York: Wiley.
Clark, Colin W. (1980), 'Restricted access to common-property fishery resources: A game theoretic analysis', in Pan-Tai Liu (ed.), *Dynamic Optimization and Mathematical Economics*, New York: Plenum, pp. 117–132.
Clark, J. Stephen and Gerald A. Carlson (1991), 'Testing for common versus private property: The case of pesticide resistance', *Discussion*, **21**, 92–96.
Cleaver, Frances (2000), 'Moral ecological rationality, institutions and the management of common property resources', *Development and Change*, **31**, 361–383.
Co, Catherine Y., John A. List, and Larry D. Qui (2004), 'Intellectual property rights, environmental regulations, and investment', *Land Economics*, **80**, 153–173.
Coase, Ronald H. (1960), 'The problem of social cost', *Journal of Law and Economics*, **3**, 1–44.
Coban, Aykut (2004), 'Caught between state-sovereign rights and property rights: Regulating biodiversity', *Review of International Political Economy*, **11**, 736–762.
Colchester, M. (2003), 'Indigenous peoples and protected areas: Rights, principles and practice', *Nomadic Peoples*, **7**, 33–51.
Cole, Daniel H. (2002), *Pollution and Property: Comparing Ownership Institutions for Environmental Protection*, New York: Cambridge University Press.
Cole, Daniel H. and Peter Z. Grossman (2002), 'The meaning of property rights: Law versus economics?', *Land Economics*, **78**, 317–330.
Commons, John R. (1968), *Legal Foundations of Capitalism*, Madison: University of Wisconsin Press.
Congost, Rosa (2003), 'Property Rights and Historical Analysis: What Rights? What History?', *Past and Present*, **181**, 73–106.
Copes, Parzival (1984), 'The market as an open access commons: A neglected aspect of excess capacity', *Economist*, **132**, 49–60.
Copes, Parzival (1986), 'A critical review of the individual quota as a device in fisheries management', *Land Economics*, **62**, 278–291.
Cordell, John C. and Margaret A. McKean (1992), 'Sea tenure in Bahia, Brazil', in Daniel W. Bromley, et al. (eds), *Making the Commons Work: Theory, Practice, and Policy*, San Francisco, CA: ICS Press, pp. 183–205.
Cornes, Richard, Charles F. Mason, and Todd Sandler (1986), 'The commons and the optimal number of firms', *Quarterly Journal of Economics*, **101**, 641–646.

Cornes, Richard and Todd Sandler (1986), 'On commons and tragedies', *American Economic Review*, **83**, 787–792.
Costanza, Robert (2000), 'Visions of alternative (unpredictable) futures and their use in policy analysis', *Ecology and Society*, **4** (1), http://www.ecologyandsociety.org/vol4/iss1/art5/
Costanza, Robert, Bobbi S. Low, Elinor Ostrom, and James Wilson (eds) (2001), *Institutions, Ecosystems, and Sustainability*, New York: Lewis Publishers.
Coulibaly, Cheibane (ed.) (2006), *Questions de Gouvernance*, Bamako, Mali: Editions Le Cauri d'Or (Les Cahiers de Mande Bukari, Numéro 04).
Coward, E. Walter, Jr. (ed.) (1980), *Irrigation and Agricultural Development in Asia: Perspectives from the Social Sciences*, Ithaca, NY: Cornell University Press.
Cox, Susan (1985), 'No tragedy on the commons', *Environmental Ethics*, **7**, 49–61.
Coyle, Sean and Karen Morrow (2004), *The Philosophical Foundations of Environmental Law: Property, Rights and Nature*, Portland, OR: Hart Publishing.
Crawford, Sue E.S. and Elinor Ostrom (2005), 'A grammar of institutions', in Elinor Ostrom, *Understanding Institutional Diversity*, Princeton, NJ: Princeton University Press, pp. 137–174. Originally published in *American Political Science Review* **89**(3) (September 1995), 582–600.
Cremers, Leontien, Marjolein Ooijevaar, and Rutgerd Boelens (2005), 'Institutional reform in the Andean irrigation sector: Enabling policies for strengthening local rights and water management', *Natural Resources Forum*, **29**, 37–50.
Croson, Rachel and Jason Scott Johnston (2000), 'Experimental results on bargaining under alternative property rights regimes', *Journal of Law, Economics, and Organization*, **16**, 50–73.
Cruz, S.D. and A.V. Raikar (2006), 'Democratic management of common property in Goa: From "Gaonkarias" and "Communidades" to Gram Sabhas', *Economic and Political Weekly*, **41**, 439–445.
Cruz, Wilfrido D. (1986), 'Overfishing and conflict in a traditional fishery: San Miguel Bay, Philippines', in National Research Council, *Proceedings of the Conference on Common Property Resource Management*, Washington, DC: National Academies Press, pp. 115–135.
Cullet, P. (2001), 'Property-rights regimes over biological resources', *Environment and Planning C*, **19**, 651–664.
Cummings, Sarah, Minke Valk, and Henk van Dam (eds) (2001), *Gender Perspectives on Inheritance and Property: Rights and Reality: A Global Source Book*, Oxford, UK: Oxfam.
Curran, Sara R. and Tundi Agardy (2002), 'Common property systems, migration, and coastal ecosystems', *Ambio*, **31**, 303–305.
Curry, Janel M. and Steven McGuire (2002), *Community on Land: Community, Ecology, and the Public Interest*, Lanham, MD: Rowman & Littlefield.
Curtis, Donald (1991), *Beyond Government: Organizations for Common Benefit*, London: Macmillan.
Cutting, R.H. (2001), '"One man's ceilin' is another man's floor": Property rights as the double-edged sword', *Environmental Law*, **31**, 819–900.
Dabla-Norris, Era and Scott Freeman (2004), 'Enforcement of property rights and underdevelopment', *Review of Development Economics*, **8**, 391–405.
Dadibhavi, R.V. (2000), 'Management of common property resources: A review and some policy issues', *Journal of Rural Development*, **19**, 199–217.
Dales, John H. (1968), *Pollution, Property, and Prices: An Essay in Policy-Making and Economics*, Toronto: University of Toronto Press.
Dalton, T.R., R.M. Coats, and B.R. Asrabadi (2005), 'Renewable resources, property rights regimes and endogenous growth', *Ecological Economics*, **52**, 31–41.
Damodaran, A. (2001), 'WTO agriculture agreement, common property resources and income diversification strategy', *Economic and Political Weekly*, **36**, 3633–3642.
Daniels, Brigham A. (2007), 'Emerging commons and tragic institutions', *Environmental Law*, **37**, 515–571.

Dasgupta, Partha (1982), *The Control of Resources*, Cambridge, MA: Harvard University Press.
Dasgupta, Partha (2005), 'Common property resources: Economic analytics', *Economic and Political Weekly*, **40**, 1610–1622.
Dasgupta, Partha and Geoffrey M. Heal (1979), *Economic Theory and Exhaustible Resources*, Garden City, NJ: J. Nisbet.
De Alessi, Louis (1980), 'The economics of property rights: A review of the evidence', *Research in Law and Economics*, **2**, 1–47.
De Alessi, Louis (1982), 'On the nature and consequences of private and public enterprises', *Minnesota Law Review*, **67**, 191–209.
Deere, Carmen Diana and Magdalena León (2001), *Empowering Women: Land and Property Rights in Latin America*, Pittsburgh, PA: University of Pittsburgh Press.
Dekker, Henri A.L. (2003), *Property Regimes in Transition: Land Reform, Food Security and Economic Development: A Case Study in the Kyrgyz Republic*, Burlington, VT: Ashgate.
de Moor, Martina and P. Warde (eds) (2002), *The Management of Common Land in North West Europe, c. 1500–1850*, Turnhout, Belgium: Brepols.
Demsetz, Harold (1964), 'The exchange and enforcement of property rights', *Journal of Law and Economics*, **7**, 11–26.
Demsetz, Harold (1967), 'Toward a theory of property rights', *American Economic Review*, **62**, 347–359.
de Soto, Hernando (2000), *The Mystery of Capital: Why Capitalism Triumphs in the West and Fails Everywhere Else*, New York: Perseus.
Devany, A.S., R. Eckert, C. Meyers, D. O'Hara, and R. Scott (1969), 'A property system for market allocation of electro-magnetic spectrum: A legal-economic-engineering study', *Stanford Law Review*, **30**, 1499–1561.
deWaal, Clarissa (2004), 'Post-socialist property rights and wrongs in Albania: An ethnography of agrarian change', *Conservation and Society*, **2**, 19–50.
Dickenson, Donna (2004), 'Consent, commodification and benefit-sharing in genetic research', *Developing World Bioethics*, **4**, 109–124.
Dietz, Thomas, Elinor Ostrom, and Paul C. Stern (2003), 'The struggle to govern the commons', *Science*, **302** (5652), 1907–1912.
Dilworth, Richardson (2007), 'Privatization, the world water crisis, and the social contract', *PS: Political Science and Politics*, **40**, 49–54.
Dinar, Ariel (ed.) (2000), *The Political Economy of Water Pricing Reforms*, New York: Oxford University Press.
Dincer, Oguzhan C. (2007), 'The effects of property rights on economic performance', *Applied Economics*, **39**, 825–837.
Dixon, Kathrine (2007), 'Working with mixed commons/anticommons property: Mobilizing customary land in Papua New Guinea the Melanesian way', *Harvard Environmental Law Review*, **31**, 219–277.
Dolšak, Nives and Elinor Ostrom (eds) (2003), *The Commons in the New Millennium: Challenges and Adaptations*, Cambridge, MA: MIT Press.
Doolittle, Amity A. (2001), 'From village land to "native reserve": Changes in property rights in Sabah, Malaysia', *Human Ecology*, **29**, 69–98.
Doolittle, Amity A. (2005), *Property and Politics in Sabah, Malaysia: Native Struggles over Land Rights*, Seattle: University of Washington Press.
Drahos, Peter (2004), 'The regulation of public goods', *Journal of International Economic Law*, **7**, 321–339.
Drahos, Peter and Ruth Mayne (eds) (2003), *Global Intellectual Property Rights: Knowledge, Access and Development*, New York: Palgrave Macmillan.
Drobak, John N. (ed.) (2006), *Norms and the Law*, New York: Cambridge University Press.
Duany, Julia and Wal Duany (2001), 'War and women in the Sudan: Role change and adjustment to new responsibilities', *Northeast African Studies*, **8**, 63–82.
Duchrow, Ulrich and Franz J. Hinkelammert (2004), *Property for People, Not for Profit: Alternatives to the Global Tyranny of Capital*, Geneva: WCC Publications.

Duke, Joshua M. and Ryan P. Jost (2003), 'Promoting mediation in property rights conflicts', *Land Economics*, **79**, 29–37.

Duke, Joshua M. and Lori Lynch (2006), 'Farmland retention techniques: Property rights implications and comparative evaluation', *Land Economics*, **82**, 189–213.

Durant, Robert F., Daniel J. Fiorino, and Rosemary O'Leary (eds) (2004), *Environmental Governance Reconsidered: Challenges, Choices, and Opportunities*, Cambridge, MA: MIT Press.

Durrenberger, E.P. and G. Palsson (1987), 'Ownership at sea: Fishing territories and access to sea resources', *American Ethnologist*, **14**, 508–522.

Dutfield, Graham (2000), *Intellectual Property Rights, Trade and Biodiversity: Seeds and Plant Varieties*, London: Earthscan.

Edney, Julian J. and P.A. Bell (1983), 'The commons dilemma: Comparing altruism, the golden rule, perfect equality of outcomes, and territoriality', *Social Science Journal*, **20**, 23–33.

Edwards, S.F. (1994), 'Ownership of renewable ocean resources', *Land Economics*, 9, 253–273.

Edwards, S.F. (2001), 'Rent-seeking and property rights formation in the U.S. Atlantic Sea scallop fishery', *Marine Resource Economics*, **16**, 263–276.

Edwards, S.F. (2003), 'Property rights to multi-attribute fishery resources', *Ecological Economics*, **44**, 309–323.

Eggertsson, Thráinn (1990), *Economic Behavior and Institutions*, Cambridge: Cambridge University Press.

Eggertsson, Thráinn (1992), 'Analyzing institutional successes and failures: A millennium of common mountain pastures in Iceland', *International Review of Law and Economics*, **12**, 423–437.

Eggertsson, Thráinn (1993), 'The economics of institutions: Avoiding the open-field syndrome and the perils of path dependence', *Acta Sociologica*, **36**, 223–237.

Eggertsson, Thráinn (2005), *Imperfect Institutions: Possibilities and Limits of Reform*, Ann Arbor: University of Michigan Press.

Ellerbusch, Fred (2006), 'Brownfields: Risk, property, and community value', *Local Environment*, **11**, 559–576.

Ellickson, Robert C. (1991), *Order without Law: How Neighbors Settle Disputes*, Cambridge, MA: Harvard University Press.

Ellickson, Robert C. (1993), 'Property in land', *Yale Law Journal*, **102**, 1315–1344.

Ellickson, Robert C., Carol M. Rose, and Bruce A. Ackerman (1995), *Perspectives on Property Law*, Boston, MA: Little, Brown.

Ellis, Elisabeth (2006), 'Citizenship and property rights: A new look at social contract theory', *Journal of Politics*, **68**, 544–555.

Ely, J.W. (2004), 'Property rights and environmental regulation: The case for compensation', *Harvard Journal of Law and Public Policy*, **28**, 51–60.

Emel, Jacques L. and Elizabeth Brooks (1988), 'Changes in form and function of property rights institutions under threatened resource scarcity', *Annals of the Association of American Geographers*, **78**, 241–252.

Ensminger, Jean (1992), *Making a Market: The Institutional Transformation of an African Society*, New York: Cambridge University Press.

Epstein, Richard A. (1979), 'Possession as the root of title', *Georgia Law Review*, **13**, 1221–1243.

Epstein, Richard A. (1994), 'On the optimal mix of private and common property', in E.F. Paul, F.D. Miller, and Jeffrey Paul (eds), *Property Rights*, New York: Cambridge University Press.

Epstein, Richard A. (2002), 'The allocation of the commons: Parking on public roads', *Journal of Legal Studies*, **31**, S515–S544.

Eyzaguirre, Pablo, Nancy McCarthy, Monica Di Gregorio, and Evan Dennis (2004), 'Property rights, collective action and plant genetic resources', in Ruth Meinzen-Dick and Monica Di Gregorio (eds), *Collective Action and Property Rights for Sustainable Development*, Washington, DC: International Food Policy Research Institute.

Falcon, W.P. and C. Fowler (2002), 'Carving up the commons – Emergence of a new international regime for germplasm development and transfer', *Food Policy*, **27**, 197–222.
Falque, Max, Michael De Alessi, and Henri Lamotte (eds) (2002), *Marine Resources: Property Rights, Economics, and Environment*, New York: Elsevier.
Feder, Gershon and David Feeny (1991), 'Land tenure and property rights: Theory and implications for development policy', *World Bank Economic Review*, **5**, 135–153.
Feder, Gershon, T. Onchan, Y. Chalamwong, and C. Hangladoran (1988), *Land Policies and Form Productivity in Thailand*, Baltimore, MD: Johns Hopkins University Press.
Feeny, David (1988), 'Agricultural expansion and forest depletion in Thailand, 1900–1975', in John F. Richards and Richard P. Tucker (eds), *World Deforestation in the Twentieth Century*, Durham, NC: Duke University Press, pp. 112–143.
Feeny, David (1993), 'The demand for and the supply of institutional arrangements', in Vincent Ostrom, David Feeny, and Hartmut Picht (eds), *Rethinking Institutional Analysis and Development*, San Francisco, CA: ICS Press, pp. 159–209.
Feeny, David, Fikret Berkes, Bonnie J. McCay, and James M. Acheson (1990), 'The tragedy of the commons: Twenty-two years later', *Human Ecology*, **18**, 1–19.
Feldman, T.D. and A.E.G. Jonas (2000), 'Sage scrub revolution? Property rights, political fragmentation, and conservation planning in Southern California under the federal endangered species act', *Annals of the Association of American Geographers*, **90**, 256–292.
Fernandez, Linda (2006), 'Natural resources, agriculture and property rights', *Ecological Economics*, **57**, 359–373.
Ferreira, Susana (2004), 'Deforestation, property rights, and international trade', *Land Economics*, **80**, 174–193.
Field, Barry C. (1984), 'The evolution of individual property rights in Massachusetts agriculture, 17th–19th centuries', *Northeastern Journal of Agricultural and Resource Economics*, **14**, 97–109.
Field, Barry C. (1985), 'The optimal commons', *American Journal of Agricultural Economics*, **67**, 364–367.
Field, Barry C. (1989), 'The evolution of property rights', *Kyklos*, **42**, 319–345.
Fisher, D.E. (2004), 'Rights of property in water: Confusion or clarity?', *Environmental and Planning Law Journal*, **21**, 200–226.
Fitzpatrick, Daniel (2005), '"Best practice" options for the legal recognition of customary tenure', *Development and Change*, **32**, 361–371.
Fitzpatrick, Daniel (2006), 'Evolution and chaos in property rights systems: The Third World tragedy of contested access', *Yale Law Journal*, **115**, 996–1049.
Folke, Carl and Fikret Berkes (1995), 'Mechanisms that link property rights to ecological systems', in Susan Hanna and Mohan Munasinghe (eds), *Property Rights and the Environment*, Stockholm and Washington, DC: The Beijer International Institute of Ecological Economics and The World Bank.
Fortmann, Louise and John W. Bruce (1988), *Whose Trees? Proprietary Dimensions of Forestry*, Boulder, CO: Westview Press.
Fox, Jefferson (2002), 'Siam mapped and mapping in Cambodia: Boundaries, sovereignty, and indigenous conceptions of space', *Society and Natural Resources*, **15**, 65–78.
Fox, K.J., R.Q. Grafton, J. Kirkley, and D. Squires (2003), 'Property rights in a fishery: Regulatory change and firm performance', *Journal of Environmental Economics and Management*, **46**, 156–177.
Francis, Michael (2005), 'Trade and the enforcement of environmental property rights', *Journal of International Trade and Economic Development*, **14**, 281–298.
Frey, Bruno S. (1990), 'Institutions matter: The comparative analysis of institutions', *European Economic Review*, **34**, 443–449.
Freyfogle, Eric T. (2002), 'Property rights, the market, and environmental change in 20th century America', *Environmental Law Reporter News and Analysis*, **32**, 10254–10266.
Freyfogle, Eric T. (2003a), *The Land We Share: Private Property and the Common Good*, Washington, DC: Island Press.
Freyfogle, Eric T. (2003b), 'Private property rights in land: An agrarian view', in N. Wirzba

(ed.), *The Essential Agrarian Reader: The Future of Culture, Community, and the Land*, Lexington: University Press of Kentucky.
Friedman, Alan E. (1971), 'The economics of the common-pool: Property rights in exhaustible resources', *UCLA Law Review*, **18**, 855–873.
Frischmann, Brett M. (2005a), 'An economic theory of infrastructure and commons management', *Minnesota Law Review*, **89** (4), 917–1030.
Frischmann, Brett M. (2005b), 'Infrastructure commons', *Michigan State Law Review*, **89**, 121–136.
Frohlich, Norman, Joe Oppenheimer, and Oran Young (1971), *Political Leadership and Collective Goods*, Princeton, NJ: Princeton University Press.
Furubotn, Eirik G. (1987), 'Privatizing the commons: Comment, with reply by Terry L. Anderson and Peter J. Hill', *Southern Economic Journal*, **54**, 219–224.
Furubotn, Eirik G. and Svetozar Pejovich (1972), 'Property rights and economic theory: A survey of recent literature', *Journal of Economic Literature*, **10**, 1137–1162.
Futemma, Celia, Fabio DeCastro, Maria Clara Silva-Forsberg, and Elinor Ostrom (2002), 'The emergence and outcomes of collective action: An institutional and ecosystem approach', *Society and Natural Resources*, **15**, 503–522.
Gadgil, Madhav and Prema Iyer (1989), 'On the diversification of common-property resource use by Indian society', in Fikret Berkes (ed.), *Common Property Resources: Ecology and Community-Based Sustainable Development*, London: Belhaven Press, pp. 240–272.
Gaffney, Mason (1992), 'The taxable surplus in water resources', *Contemporary Policy Issues*, **10**, 74–82.
Gallardo Fernández, Gloria L. (2002), *Communal Land Ownership in Chile: The Agricultural Communities in the Commune of Canela, Norte Chico (1600–1998)*, Aldershot: Ashgate.
Gambaro, Antonio (2002), 'Public vs. private land property or complex regimes of rights on land', in M.E. Sánchez Jordan and A. Gambaro (eds), *Land Law in Comparative Perspective*, New York: Kluwer Law International.
Gardner, Roy and Elinor Ostrom (1991), 'Rules and games', *Public Choice*, **70**, 121–149.
Gardner, Roy, Elinor Ostrom, and James M. Walker (1990), 'The nature of common-pool resource problems', *Rationality and Society*, **2**, 335–358.
Gaudet, G., M. Moreaux, and S.W. Salant (2002), 'Private storage of common property', *Journal of Environmental Economics and Management*, **43**, 280–302.
Geisler, Charles and Gail Daneker (eds) (2000), *Property and Values: Alternatives to Public and Private Ownership*, Washington, DC: Island Press.
Gelcich, Stefan, Gareth Edwards-Jones, Michel J. Kaiser, and Elizabeth Watson (2004), 'Using discourses for policy evaluation: The case of marine common property rights in Chile', *Society and Natural Resources*, **18**, 377–391.
Gepts, Paul (2004), 'Who owns biodiversity, and how should the owners be compensated?', *Plant Physiology*, **134**, 1295–1307.
Ghate, Rucha (2004), *Uncommons in the Commons: Community Initiated Forest Resource Management*, New Delhi: Concept.
Ghate, Rucha and Harini Nagendra (2005), 'Role of monitoring in institutional performance: Forest management in Maharashtra, India', *Conservation & Society*, **3**, 509–532.
Ghoshal, Sumantra and Peter Moran (1996), 'Bad for practice: A critique of the transaction cost theory', *Academy of Management Review*, **21**, 13–47.
Gibson, Clark C., Krister Andersson, Elinor Ostrom, and Sujai Shivakumar (2005), *The Samaritan's Dilemma: The Political Economy of Development Aid*, New York: Oxford University Press.
Gibson, Clark C., Fabrice Lehoucq, and John Williams (2002), 'Does privatization protect natural resources? Property rights and forests in Guatemala', *Social Science Quarterly*, **83**, 206–225.
Gibson, Clark C., Margaret A. McKean, and Elinor Ostrom (eds) (2000), *People and Forests: Communities, Institutions, and Governance*, Cambridge, MA: MIT Press.
Gibson, Clark C., John Williams, and Elinor Ostrom (2005), 'Local enforcement and better forests', *World Development*, **33** (2), 273–284.

Gibson, Johanna (2005), *Community Resources: Intellectual Property, International Trade and Protection of Traditional Knowledge*, Burlington, VT: Ashgate.
Gilles, Jere L. and Keith Jamtgaard (1981), 'Overgrazing in pastoral areas: The commons reconsidered', *Sociologia Ruralis*, **2**, 335–358.
Gimelli, F. (2000), 'Intellectual property rights in agriculture in the light of the debate on biotechnology: Historical evolution and current situation', *Italian Journal of Biochemistry*, **49**, 41–51.
Gimenez-Maceda, Teresita, Rosario M. Espino, and Shivani Chaudhry (eds) (2001), *Marine and Coastal Resources and Community-Based Property Rights: A Philippine Workshop*, Quezon City, Philippines: Tanggol Kalikasan, Inc.
Gissurarson, Hannes H. (2000), *Overfishing: The Icelandic Solution*, London: Institute of Economic Affairs.
Gitter, Donna M. (2004), 'Ownership of human tissue: A proposal for federal recognition of human research participant's property rights in their biological material', *Washington and Lee Law Review*, **61**, 257–346.
Gluck, P. (2002), 'Property rights and multipurpose mountain forest management', *Forest Policy and Economics*, **4**, 125–134.
Godshall, L.E. (2003), 'Making space for indigenous intellectual property rights under current international environmental law', *Georgetown International Environmental Law Review*, **15**, 497–530.
Godwin, R. Kenneth and W. Bruce Shepard (1977), 'Population issues and commons dilemmas', *Policy Studies Journal*, **6**, 231–238.
Godwin, R. Kenneth and W. Bruce Shepard (1979), 'Forcing squares, triangles, and ellipses into a circular paradigm: The use of the commons dilemma in examining the allocation of common resources', *Western Political Quarterly*, **32**, 265–277.
Goeschl, Timo and Danilo Camargo Igliori (2006), 'Property rights for biodiversity conservation and development: Extractive reserves in the Brazilian Amazon', *Development and Change*, **37**, 427–451.
Goetze, David B. (1987), 'Identifying appropriate institutions for efficient use of common pools', *Natural Resources Journal*, **27**, 187–191.
Goldsmith, E., N. Hildyard, P. Bunyard, and P. McCully (eds) (1992), *Whose Common Future? A Special Issue of The Ecologist, Vol. 22, No.4, July/August 1992*, Dorset: Agriculture House.
Gordon, H. Scott (1954), 'The economic theory of a common-property resource: The fishery', *Journal of Political Economy*, **62**, 124–142.
Graff, G.D., S.E. Cullen, K.J. Bradford, D. Zilberman, and A.B. Bennett (2003), 'The public-private structure of intellectual property ownership in agricultural biotechnology', *Nature Biotechnology*, **21**, 989–995.
Grafton, R. Quentin (2000), 'Governance of the commons: A role for the state?', *Land Economics*, **76**, 504–517.
Grafton, R. Quentin, Dale Squires, and Kevin J. Fox (2000), 'Private property and economic efficiency: A study of a common-pool resource', *Journal of Law and Economics*, **43**, 679–713.
Grima, A.P. Limo and Fikret Berkes (1989), 'Natural resources: Access, rights to use and management', in Fikret Berkes (ed.), *Common Property Resources; Ecology and Community-Based Sustainable Development*, London: Belhaven, pp. 33–54.
Grossi, Paolo (1981), *An Alternative to Private Property; Collective Property in the Juridical Consciousness of the Nineteenth Century*, Chicago: University of Chicago Press.
Grossman, M.R. (2002), 'Biotechnology, property rights and the environment', *American Journal of Comparative Law*, **50**, 215–248.
Guadagni, Marco (2002), 'Trends in customary land property', in M.E. Sánchez Jordan and A. Gambaro (eds), *Land Law in Comparative Perspective*, New York: Kluwer Law International.
Guillet, David W. (1992), *Covering Ground: Communal Water Management and the State in the Peruvian Highlands*, Ann Arbor: University of Michigan Press.

Guillet, David (2000a), 'Reconsidering institutional change: Property rights in northern Spain', *American Anthropologist*, **102**, 713–725.

Guillet, David (2000b), 'Water property rights and resistance to demand management in northwestern Spain', in B.R. Bruns and Ruth Meinzen-Dick (eds), *Negotiating Water Rights*, New Delhi: Vistaar, pp. 222–244.

Guloksuz, E. (2002), 'Negotiation of property rights in urban land in Istanbul', *International Journal of Urban and Regional Research*, **26**, 462–476.

Gupta, Anil K. (1986), 'Socioecology of stress: Why do common property resource management projects fail?', in National Research Council, *Proceedings of the Conference on Common Property Resource Management*, Washington, DC: National Academies Press, pp. 305–322.

Gwartney, James D. and Richard Stroup (1988), 'Communal vs. private property rights', *The Freeman*, **38**, 58–59.

Haas, Peter M., Robert O. Keohane, and Marc A. Levy (eds) (1993), *Institutions for the Earth; Sources of Effective International Environmental Protection*, Cambridge, MA: MIT Press.

Haber, Stephen, Armando Razo, and Noel Maurer (2003), *The Politics of Property Rights: Political Instability, Credible Commitments, and Economic Growth in Mexico, 1876–1929*, New York: Cambridge University Press.

Habron, G. (2003), 'Role of adaptive management for watershed councils', *Environmental Management*, **31**, 29–41.

Haddad, Brent M. (2003), 'Property rights, ecosystem management, and John Locke's labor theory of ownership', *Ecological Economics*, **46**, 19–31.

Hafer, Catherine (2006), 'On the origins of property rights: Conflict and production in the state of nature', *The Review of Economic Studies*, **73**, 119–143.

Hagedorn, Konrad (2004), 'Property rights reform on agricultural land in Central and Eastern Europe', *Quarterly Journal of International Agriculture*, **43**, 409–438.

Halkos, G.E. and N.C. Kyriazis (2003), 'Property rights and game-theory implications of satellite communications: The bilateral case of Greece and Russia', *European Journal of Law and Economics*, **15**, 233–250.

Haller, Tobias (2002), 'Common property resource management, institutional change and conflicts in African floodplain wetlands: Presentation of a research project and reflections on institutional change and conflicts', *African Anthropologist*, **9**, 25–35.

Hanisch, Markus (2003), *Property Reform and Social Conflict*, Aachen, Germany: Shaker Verlag.

Hanna, Susan (2006), 'Will structural reform fix fishery management? Commission policy recommendations and the U.S. regional fishery management council system', *Bulletin of Marine Science*, **78**, 547–562.

Hanna, Susan, Carl Folke, and Karl-Göran Mäler (eds) (1996), *Rights to Nature: Ecological, Economic, Cultural, and Political Principles of Institutions for the Environment*, Washington, DC: Island Press.

Hanna, Susan and Mohan Munasinghe (eds) (1995a), *Property Rights and the Environment*, Stockholm and Washington, DC: The Beijer International Institute of Ecological Economics and The World Bank.

Hanna, Susan and Mohan Munasinghe (eds) (1995b), *Property Rights in a Social and Ecological Context; Case Studies and Design Applications*, Stockholm and Washington, DC: The Beijer International Institute of Ecological Economics and The World Bank.

Hannesson, Rögnvaldur (2005), 'Rights based fishing: Use rights versus property rights to fish', *Reviews in Fish Biology and Fisheries*, Mäler, 231–241.

Hannesson, Rögnvaldur (2006), *The Privatization of the Oceans*, Cambridge, MA: MIT Press.

Hardin, Garrett (1968), 'The tragedy of the commons', *Science*, **162**, 1243–1248.

Hardin, Garrett (1991), 'The tragedy of the unmanaged commons: Population and the disguises of providence', in R.V. Andelson (ed.), *Commons without Tragedy*, Savage, MD: Barnes and Noble.

Hardin, Garrett and John Baden (eds) (1977), *Managing the Commons*, San Francisco, CA: W.H. Freeman.
Harford, J.D. (2000), 'Methods of pricing common property use and some implications for optimal child-bearing and the social discount rate', *Resource and Energy Economics*, **22**, 103–124.
Hastings, E.M., S.K. Wong, and Megan Walters (2006), 'Governance in a co-ownership environment: The management of multiple-ownership property in Hong Kong', *Property Management*, **24**, 293–308.
Hayami, Yujiro and Keijiro Otsuka (1993), *The Economics of Contract Choice*, Oxford: Clarendon Press.
Hazari, B.R. and A. Kumar (2003), 'Basic needs, property rights and degradation of commons', *Pacific Economic Review*, **8**, 47–56.
Heaney, A. and S. Beare (2002), 'Property rights and externalities in water trade', *ACIAR Proceedings*, **106**, 254–268.
Hedlund, Stefan (2001), 'Property without rights: Dimensions of Russian privatisation', *Europe-Asia Studies*, **53**, 213–238.
Heller, Michael A. (1998), 'The tragedy of the anticommons: Property in the transition from Marx to markets', *Harvard Law Review*, **111** (3), 622–688.
Heller, Michael A. (2000), 'Critical approaches to property institutions: Three faces of private property', *Oregon Law Review*, **79**, 417–434.
Heltberg, Rasmus (2002), 'Property rights and natural resource management in developing countries', *Journal of Economic Surveys*, **16**, 189–214.
Herrera, P.A., G. van Huylenbroek, and R.L. Espinel (2004), 'An application of the contingent valuation method to assess the efficiency of the institutional structure of irrigation property rights: The case of the peninsula of Santa Elena, Ecuador', *International Journal of Water Resources Development*, **20**, 537–552.
Herring, Ronald J. (1990), 'Resurrecting the commons: Collective action and ecology', *Items*, **44**, 64–68.
Hess, Charlotte (2007), *The Comprehensive Bibliography of the Commons*, The Digital Library of the Commons, http://dlc.dlib.indiana.edu/cpr/index.php
Hess, Charlotte and Elinor Ostrom (2003), 'Ideas, artifacts, and facilities: Information as a common-pool resource', *Law and Contemporary Problems*, **66**, 111–146.
Hess, Charlotte and Elinor Ostrom (eds) (2007), *Understanding Knowledge as a Commons: From Theory to Practice*, Cambridge, MA: MIT Press.
Higgs, Robert (1996), 'Legally induced technical regress in the Washington salmon fishery', in L.J. Alston, Thráinn Eggertsson, and Douglass North (eds), *Empirical Studies in Institutional Change*, New York: Cambridge University Press.
Hilton, Rita (1992), 'Institutional incentives for resource mobilization: An analysis of irrigation schemes in Nepal', *Journal of Theoretical Politics*, **4**, 283–308.
Hinteregger, Monika and Barbara Pozzo (2002), 'Property and environment', in M.E. Sánchez Jordan and A. Gambaro (eds), *Land Law in Comparative Perspective*, New York: Kluwer Law International.
Ho, Peter (2001), 'Who owns China's land? Property rights and deliberate institutional ambiguity', *China Quarterly*, **166**, 394–411.
Ho, Peter (2005), *Institutions in Transition: Land Ownership, Property Rights, and Social Conflict in China*, New York: Oxford University Press.
Hodgson, Geoffrey M. (2003), 'The enforcement of contracts and property rights: Constitutive versus epiphenomenal conceptions of law', *International Review of Sociology*, **13**, 375–391.
Hoffman, Irene (2004), 'Access to land and water in the Zamfara Reserve: A case study for the management of common property resources in pastoral areas of West Africa', *Human Ecology*, **32**, 77–105.
Holder, C.D. (2004), 'Changes in structure and cover of a common property pine forest in Guatemala, 1954–1996', *Environmental Conservation*, **31**, 22–29.
Holland, S.P. and M.R. Moore (2003), 'Cadillac Desert revisited: Property rights,

public policy, and water-resource depletion', *Journal of Environmental Economics and Management*, **46**, 131–155.
Hotelling, Harold (1931), 'The economics of exhaustible resources', *Journal of Political Economy*, **39**, 137–175.
Hotte, Louis (2001), 'Conflicts over property rights and natural-resource exploitation at the frontier', *Journal of Development Economics*, **66**, 1–21.
Hotte, Louis (2005), 'Natural-resource exploitation with costly enforcement of property rights', *Oxford Academic Papers*, **57**, 497–521.
Hsu, S.L. (2003), 'A two-dimensional framework for analyzing property rights regimes', *University of California Davis Law Review*, **36**, 813–894.
Hsueh, Vicki (2006), 'Cultivating and challenging the common: Lockean property, indigenous traditionalisms, and the problem of exclusion', *Contemporary Political Theory*, **5**, 193–214.
Hughes, David M. (2001), 'Cadastral politics: The making of community-based resource management in Zimbabwe and Mozambique', *Development and Change*, **32**, 741–768.
Hulme, D. and M. Murphree (eds) (2001), *African Wildlife and Livelihoods: The Promise and Performance of Community Conservation*, Oxford, UK: James Currey.
Husain, Zakir and Rabindra N. Bhattacharya (2004), 'Common pool resources and contextual factors: Evolution of a fishermen's cooperative in Calcutta', *Ecological Economics*, **50**, 201–217.
Hutchinson, Steven and Daniel O'Connor (2005), 'Policing the new commons: Corporate security governance on a mass private property in Canada', *Policing and Society*, **15**, 125–144.
Igoe, Jim (2004), *Conservation and Globalization: A Study of National Parks and Indigenous Communities from East Africa to South Dakota*, Belmont, CA: Wadsworth.
Inman, K. and D.M. McLeod (2002), 'Property rights and public interests: A Wyoming agricultural lands study', *Growth and Change*, **33**, 91–114.
Innes, Robert (2000), 'The economics of takings and the compensation when land and its public use value are in private hands', *Land Economics*, **76**, 195–212.
Irrera, F.G., M.J. Oneto, and J. Rabinovich (2001), 'Property rights of public natural resources: A new legal alternative for developing countries', *Monographs in Systematic Botany*, **84**, 304–311.
Jodha, Narpat S. (1990), 'Depletion of common property resources in India: Micro-level evidence', in G. McNicoll and M. Cain (eds), *Rural Development and Population: Institutions and Policy*, Oxford: Oxford University Press, pp. 261–283.
Jodha, Narpat S. (2007), 'Common property resources and the rural poor', in M. Rangarajan (ed.), *Environmental Issues in India: A Reader*, New Delhi: Pearson Longman, pp. 206–246.
Johannesen, A.B. and A. Skonhoft (2004), 'Property rights and natural resource conservation: A bio-economic model with numerical illustrations from the Serengeti-Mara ecosystem', *Environmental and Resource Economics*, **28**, 469–488.
Johnson, Craig (2004), 'Uncommon ground: The "poverty of history" in common property discourse', *Development and Change*, **35**, 407–434.
Johnson, K.A. and K.C. Nelson (2004), 'Common property and conservation: The potential for effective communal forest management within a national park in Mexico', *Human Ecology*, **32**, 703–733.
Johnson, Omotunde E.G. (1972), 'Economic analysis: The legal framework and land tenure systems', *Journal of Law and Economics*, **15**, 259–276.
Johnson, Ronald N. (1985), 'Restraint under open access: Are voluntary incentives sufficient or is coercion required?', *American Journal of Agricultural Economics*, **67**, 373–376.
Johnson, Ronald N. and Gary D. Libecap (1982), 'Contracting problems and regulation: The case of the fishery', *American Economic Review*, **72**, 1005–1022.
Johnston, Jason Scott (2000), 'On the commons of common law', in R.E. Meiners and A.P. Morriss (eds), *The Common Law and the Environment: Rethinking the Statutory Basis for Modern Environmental Law*, New York: Rowman and Littlefield, pp. 211–241.

Jones, Eric C. (2003), 'Building on Ostrom's "the rudiments of a theory of the origins, survival, and performance of common-property institutions"', *Journal of Ecological Anthropology*, **7**, 65–72.

Jones, Gareth A. and Peter M. Ward (1998), 'Privatizing the commons: Reforming the ejido and urban development in Mexico', *International Journal of Urban and Regional Issues*, **22** (1), 76–93.

Judge, Rebecca P. (2002), 'Restoring the commons: Toward a new interpretation of Locke's theory of property', *Land Economics*, **78**, 331–338.

Juul, Kristine and Christian Lund (eds) (2002), *Negotiating Property in Africa*, Portsmouth, NH: Heinemann.

Kadekodi, Gopal K. (2004), *Common Property Resource Management: Reflections on Theory and the Indian Experience*, New York: Oxford University Press.

Kafumbe, A.L. (2006), 'Women's property rights and the laws of succession in Uganda: Reform propositions', *East African Journal of Peace and Human Rights*, **12**, 65–90.

Kalinoe, Lawrence Kuna and James Leach (eds) (2004), *Rationales of Ownership: Transactions and Claims to Ownership in Contemporary Papua New Guinea*, Wantage, UK: Sean Kingston.

Kamara, A., M. Kirk, and B. Swallow (2004), 'Property rights and land use change: Implications for sustainable resource management in Borana, Southern Ethiopia', *Journal of Sustainable Agriculture*, **25**, 45–62.

Kaplowitz, Michael D. (ed.) (2000), *Property Rights, Economics, and the Environment*, Stamford, CT: JAI Press.

Karp, Larry S. (1992), 'Efficiency inducing tax for a common property oligopoly', *The Economic Journal*, **102**, 321–332.

Katz, Elizabeth G. (2000), 'Social capital and natural capital: A comparative analysis of land tenure and natural resource management in Guatemala', *Land Economics*, **76**, 114–132.

Kaul, Minoti Chakravarty (1996), *Common Lands and Customary Law: Institutional Change in North India over the Past Two Centuries*, Oxford: Oxford University Press.

Kazianga, Harounan and William A. Masters (2006), 'Property rights, production technology, and deforestation: Cocoa in Cameroon', *Agricultural Economics*, **35**, 19–26.

Kebede, Bereket (2002), 'Land tenure and common pool resources in rural Ethiopia: A study based on fifteen sites', *African Development Review*, **14**, 113–149.

Kendrick, A. (2003), 'The flux of trust: Caribou co-management in northern Canada', *Environments*, **31**, 43–60.

Kennedy, Ronan (2006), 'International conflicts over plant genetic resources: Future developments?', *Tulane Environmental Law Journal*, **20**, 1–42.

Keohane, Robert O. and Elinor Ostrom (eds) (1995), *Local Commons and Global Interdependence: Heterogeneity and Cooperation in Two Domains*, London: Sage.

Khan, M.H. (2004), 'Power, property rights and the issue of land reform: A general case illustrated with reference to Bangladesh', *Journal of Agrarian Change*, **4**, 73–106.

Kim, Jongwook and Joseph T. Mahoney (2006), 'How property rights economics furthers the resource-based view: Resources, transaction costs and entrepreneurial discovery', *International Journal of Strategic Change Management*, **1**, 40–52.

Kiser, Larry L. and Elinor Ostrom (1982), 'The three worlds of action: A metatheoretical synthesis of institutional approaches', in Elinor Ostrom (ed.), *Strategies of Political Inquiry*, Beverly Hills, CA: Sage, pp. 179–222.

Kissling-Näf, Ingrid and Stefan Kuks (eds) (2004), *The Evolution of National Water Regimes in Europe: Transitions in Water Rights and Water Policies*, Boston, MA: Kluwer.

Kleinen, John (2003), 'Access to natural resources for whom? Aquaculture in Nam Dinh, Vietnam', *Maritime Studies (MAST)*, **2**, 39–63.

Kleinsasser, Zachary C. (2005), 'Public and private property rights: Regulatory and physical takings and the public trust doctrine', *Boston College Environmental Affairs Law Review*, **32**, 421–458.

Klooster, Daniel (2000), 'Institutional choice, community, and struggle: A case study of forest co-management in Mexico', *World Development*, **28**, 1–20.

Knight, F. (1924), 'Some fallacies in the interpretation of social cost', *Quarterly Journal of Economics*, **38**, 582–606.
Kodoth, P. (2001), 'Gender, family and property rights: Questions from Kerala's land reforms', *Indian Journal of Gender Studies*, **8**, 291–306.
Kung, J.K.S. (2000), 'Common property rights and land reallocations in rural China: Evidence from a village survey', *World Development*, **28**, 701–719.
Kurian, Mathew and Ton Dietz (2007), *Hydro-Logic: Poverty, Heterogeneity and Cooperation on the Commons*, New Delhi: Macmillan India.
Lam, Wai Fung (1996), 'Institutional design of public agencies and coproduction: A study of irrigation associations in Taiwan', *World Development*, **24**, 1039–1054.
Lam, Wai Fung (1998), *Institutions, Engineering Infrastructure, and Performance in the Governance and Management of Irrigation Systems: The Case of Nepal*, San Francisco, CA: ICS Press.
Lanjouw, J.O. and P.I. Levy (2002), 'A study of formal and informal property rights in urban Ecuador', *Economic Journal*, **112**, 986–1019.
Larson, Bruce A. (ed.) (2003), *Property Rights and Environmental Problems*, Burlington, VT: Ashgate.
Larson, Bruce A. and Daniel W. Bromley (1990), 'Property rights, externalities, and resource degradation: Locating the tragedy', *Journal of Development Economics*, **33**, 235–262.
Laveleye, Emile de (1985), *Primitive Property; Translated from the French of Emile de Laveleye*, ed. G.R.L. Marriott, Littleton, CO: F.B. Rothman (reprint of 1878 ed.).
Leach, James (2003), 'Owning creativity: Cultural property and the efficacy of custom on the Rai Coast of Papua New Guinea', *Journal of Material Culture*, **8**, 123–143.
Leal, Donald (ed.) (2005), *Evolving Property Rights in Marine Fisheries*, Lanham, MD: Rowman & Littlefield.
Lenhart, L. and M.J. Casimir (2001), 'Environment, property resources and the state: An introduction', *Nomadic Peoples*, **5**, 6–20.
Lesorogol, C.K. (2003), 'Transforming institutions among pastoralists: Inequality and land privatization', *American Anthropologist*, **105**, 531–541.
Levasseur, A.A. (2006), 'The boundaries of property rights: La notion de biens', *American Journal of Comparative Law*, **54**, 145–166.
Levi, Margaret and Douglass C. North (1982), 'Toward a property rights theory of exploitation', *Politics and Society*, **11**, 315–320.
Levine, B.L. (1986), 'The tragedy of the commons and the comedy of community: The commons in history', *Journal of Community Psychology*, **14**, 81–99.
Levine, Ross (2005), 'Law, endowments and property rights', *Journal of Economic Perspectives*, **19**, 61–88.
Levmore, Saul (2002), 'Two stories about the evolution of property rights', *The Journal of Legal Studies*, **31**, 421–451.
Lewis, Tracy R. and James Cowens (1983), *Cooperation in the Commons: An Application of Repetitious Rivalry*, Vancouver: University of British Columbia Press.
Libecap, Gary D. (1989a), *Contracting for Property Rights*, New York: Cambridge University Press.
Libecap, Gary D. (1989b), 'Distributional issues in contracting for property rights', *Journal of Institutional and Theoretical Economics*, **145**, 6–24.
Libecap, Gary D. (1995), 'The conditions for successful collective action', in Robert O. Keohane and Elinor Ostrom (eds), *Local Commons and Global Interdependence: Heterogeneity and Cooperation in Two Domains*, London: Sage, pp. 161–190.
Libecap, Gary D. (2007), 'The assignment of property rights on the Western frontier: Lessons for contemporary environmental and resource policy', *Journal of Economic History*, **67**, 257–291.
Libecap, Gary D., and Steven N. Wiggins (1984), 'Contractual responses to the common pool: Prorationing of crude oil production', *American Economic Review*, **74**, 87–98.
Lichbach, Mark I. (1996), *The Cooperator's Dilemma*, Ann Arbor: University of Michigan Press.

Lienhoop, Nele and Douglas C. MacMillan (2007), 'Contingent valuation: Comparing participant performance in group-based approaches and personal interviews', *Environmental Values*, **16**, 209–232.
Lindner, Ines and Holger Strulik (2004), 'Why not Africa? Growth and welfare effects of secure property rights', *Public Choice*, **120**, 143–167.
Loehman, Edna and Nir Becker (2006), 'Cooperation in a hydro-geologic commons: New institutions and pricing to achieve sustainability and security', *International Journal of Water Resources Development*, **22**, 603–614.
Lotz, Marianne (2002), 'Colliding worlds: Indigenous rights, traditional knowledge, and plant intellectual property', *Business and Professional Ethics Journal*, **21**, 71–94.
Lu, F.E. (2001), 'The common property regime of the Huaorani Indians of Ecuador implications', *Human Ecology*, **29**, 425–447.
Lueck, Dean (1994), 'Common property as an egalitarian share contract', *Journal of Economic Behavior and Organization*, **25**, 93–108.
Lueck, Dean (1995), 'The rule of first possession and the design of the law', *Journal of Law and Economics*, **38**, 393–436.
Luoga, E.J., E.T.F. Witkowski, and K. Balkwill (2005), 'Land cover and use changes in relation to the institutional framework and tenure of land and resources in Eastern Tanzania Miombo woodlands', *Environment, Development and Sustainability*, **7**, 71–93.
Lynch, Owen J. and Emily Harwell (2002), *Whose Natural Resources? Whose Common Good? Towards a New Paradigm of Environmental Justice and the National Interest in Indonesia*, Jakarta: Center for International Environmental Law.
Maass, Arthur and Raymond L. Anderson (1986), . . . *and the Desert Shall Rejoice: Conflict, Growth, and Justice in Arid Environments*, Malabar, FL: R.E. Krieger.
Macinko, Seth and Daniel W. Bromley (2002), *Who Owns America's Fisheries?*, Covelo, CA: Center for Resource Economics.
Macintyre, Martha and Simon Foale (2007), 'Land and marine tenure, ownership, and new forms of entitlement on Lihir: Changing notions of property in the context of a goldmining project', *Human Organization*, **66**, 49–59.
Macpherson, C.B., Anthony Parel, and Thomas Flanagan (1979), *Theories of Property: Aristotle to the Present: Essays*, Waterloo, Ontario: Wilfred Laurier University Press for the Calgary Institute for the Humanities.
Madulu, Ndalahwa F. (2005), 'Impacts of population pressure and poverty alleviation strategies on common property resource availability in rural Tanzania', *African Journal of Environmental Assessment and Management*, **10**, 26–49.
Magrath, William B. (1989), 'The challenge of the commons: The allocation of nonexclusive resources', Washington, DC: The World Bank.
Maine, Henry Sumner (1890), *On Early Law and Custom*, London: J. Murray.
Maine, Henry Sumner (1963), *Ancient Law: Its Connection with the Early History of Society and its Relation to Modern Ideas; With Introduction and Notes by Frederick Pollack*, Boston: Beacon Press (reprint of 1861 ed.).
Majumdar, Sumit K. (2007), 'Institutions in transition: Property rights regime changes and the saga of foreign firms in India', *India Review*, **6**, 91–115.
Makdissi, P. (2001), 'Population, natural resources and property rights', *Annales d'Economie et de Statistique*, **61**, 91–104.
Mann, G. (2002), 'Class consciousness and common property: The international fishermen and allied workers of America', *International Labor and Working Class History*, **61**, 141–160.
Mansfield, Becky (2001), 'Property regime or development policy? Explaining growth in the U.S. Pacific groundfish fishery', *The Professional Geographer*, **53**, 384–397.
Mansfield, Becky (2004), 'Neoliberalism in the oceans: "Rationalization," property rights, and the commons question', *Geoforum*, **35**, 313–326.
Manzungu, Emmanuel, Godfrey Chikowore, Dorothy Mushayavanhu, and Dennis Shoko (eds) (2002), *Managing Common Property in an Age of Globalisation*, Harare, Zimbabwe: Weaver.

Marothia, Dinesh K. (ed.) (2002), *Institutionalizing Common Pool Resources*, New Delhi: Concept.

Marshall, Graham R. (2004), 'Farmers cooperating in the commons? A study of collective action in salinity management', *Ecological Economics*, **51**, 271–286.

Marshall, Graham R. (2005), *Economics for Collaborative Environmental Management: Renegotiating the Commons*, Bath, UK: Earthscan.

Marshall, Graham R., Simon J. Fritsch, and Robert V. Dulhunty (2005), 'Catalyzing common property farming for rural sustainability: Lessons from the Furracabad valley', *Australian Agribusiness Review*, 13, http://www.agrifood.info/review/2005/Marshall_et_al.html

Marshall, J. (2001), 'Landlords, leaseholders and sweat equity: Changing property regimes in aquaculture', *Marine Policy*, **25**, 335–352.

Martichuski, Diane K. and Paul A. Bell (1991), 'Reward, punishment, privatization, and moral suasion in a commons dilemma', *Journal of Applied Social Psychology*, **21**, 1356–1369.

Martin, Edward G. (1986), 'Resource mobilization, water allocation, and farmer organization in hill irrigation systems in Nepal', Ph.D. dissertation, Cornell University.

Marwell, Gerald, and Pamela Oliver (1993), *The Critical Mass in Collective Action: A Micro-Social Theory*, New York: Cambridge University Press.

Mason, C.F. and S. Polasky (2002), 'Strategic preemption in a common property resource: A continuous time approach', *Environmental and Resource Economics*, **23**, 255–278.

Mason, C.F., Todd Sandler, and Richard Cornes (1988), 'Expectations, the commons, and optimal group size', *Journal of Environmental Economics and Management*, **15**, 99–110.

Matthews, David Ralph (1993), *Controlling Common Property: Regulating Canada's East Coast Fishery*, Toronto: University of Toronto Press.

Maurer, Georg Ludwig von (1854), *Einleitung zur Geschichte der Mark-, Hof Dorf- und Stadtverfassung under der Öffentlichen Gewalt*, Munich: Verlag von Christian Kaiser.

Maurer, Georg Ludwig von (1856), *Geschichte der Markenverfassung in Deutschland*, Erlangen: F. Enke.

Maza, Arantza Murillas (2004), 'Common property under management flexibility: Valuation, optimal exploitation, and regulation', *Marine Resource Economics*, **19**, 173–194.

McCarthy, James (2006), 'Neoliberalism and the politics of alternatives: Community forestry in British Columbia and the United States', *Annals of the Association of American Geographers*, **96**, 84–104.

McCarthy, John F. (2000), 'The changing regime: Forest property and reformasi in Indonesia', *Development and Change*, **31**, 91–129.

McCay, Bonnie J. (1992), 'Everyone's concern, whose responsibility?: The problem of the commons', in S. Ortiz and S. Lees (eds), *Understanding Economic Process: Monographs in Economic Anthropology, no. 10*, Lanham, MD: University Press of America.

McCay, Bonnie J. (2000), 'Property rights, the commons, and natural resource management', in M.D. Kaplowitz (ed.), *Property Rights, Economics, and the Environment*, Stamford, CT: JAI Press, pp. 67–82.

McCay, Bonnie J. and James M. Acheson (eds) (1987), *The Question of the Commons: The Culture and Ecology of Communal Resources*, Tucson, AZ: University of Arizona Press.

McClellan, Traci L. (2001), 'The role of international law in protecting the traditional knowledge and plant life of indigenous peoples', *Wisconsin International Law Journal*, **19**, 249–266.

McCloskey, Donald N. (1976), 'English open fields as behavior towards risk', in Paul J. Uselding (ed.), *Research in Economic History 1*, Greenwich, CT: JAI Press.

McCloskey, Donald N. (1989), 'The open fields of England: Rent, risk, and the rate of interest, 1300–1815', in David W. Galenson (ed.), *Markets in History: Economic Studies of the Past*, Cambridge: Cambridge University Press.

McCusker, B. (2002), 'The impact of membership in communal property associations on livelihood in the northern province, South Africa', *Geojournal*, **56**, 113–122.

McKean, Margaret A. (1982), 'The Japanese experience with scarcity: Management of traditional common lands', *Environmental Review*, **6**, 63–88.

McKean, Margaret A. (1992a), 'Management of traditional common lands (*Iriaichi*) in Japan', in Daniel W. Bromley, et al. (eds), *Making the Commons Work: Theory, Practice, and Policy*, San Francisco, CA: ICS Press, pp. 63–98.
McKean, Margaret A. (1992b), 'Success on the commons: A comparative examination of institutions for common property resource management', *Journal of Theoretical Politics*, **4**, 247–282.
McKlevay, R. (1985), 'Decentralized regulation of a common property renewable resource industry with irreversible investment', *Journal of Environmental Economics and Management*, **12**, 287–307.
McMahon, Edward T. (2006), 'Sustainability and property rights', *Urban Land*, **65**, 30–33.
McPherson, M.A. and M.L. Nieswiadomy (2000), 'African elephants: The effect of property rights and political stability', *Contemporary Economic Policy*, **18**, 14–26.
Mearns, Robin (1996), 'Community, collective action and common grazing: The case of post-Socialist Mongolia', *Journal of Development Studies*, **32**, 297–339.
Meiners, Roger E. and Andrew P. Morriss (2001), 'Property rights in a complex world', *Contributions in Economics and Economic History*, **224**, 179–200.
Meinzen-Dick, Ruth (2007), 'Beyond panaceas in water institutions', *Proceedings of the National Academy of Sciences*, **104** (39), 15200–15205.
Meinzen-Dick, Ruth S. and Monica Di Gregorio (eds) (2004), *Collective Action and Property Rights for Sustainable Development*, Washington, DC: International Food Policy Research Institute.
Meinzen-Dick, Ruth, Anna Knox, Frank Place, and Brent Swallow (eds) (2000), *Property Rights, Collective Action, and Technologies for Natural Resource Management*, Washington, DC: Consultative Group on International Agricultural Research.
Meinzen-Dick, Ruth, Anna Knox, Frank Place, and Brent Swallow (eds) (2002), *Innovation in Natural Resource Management: The Role of Property Rights and Collective Action in Developing Countries*, Baltimore, MD: Johns Hopkins University Press.
Ménard, Claude (ed.) (2004), *Transaction Costs and Property Rights*, Cheltenham, UK: Edward Elgar.
Menon, Ajit and G. Ananda Vadivelu (2006), 'Common property resources in different agro-climatic landscapes in India', *Conservation and Society*, **4**, 132–154.
Merino, Leticia and Jim Robson (eds) (2005a), *Managing the Commons: Indigenous Rights, Economic Development and Identity*, Mexico: Consejo Civil Mexicano para la Silvicultura Sostenible A.C. et al.
Merino, Leticia and Jim Robson (eds) (2005b), *Managing the Commons: Markets, Commodity Chains and Certification*, Mexico: Consejo Civil Mexicano para la Silvicultura Sostenible A.C. et al.
Merlo, M., R. Morandini, A. Gabbrielli, and I. Novaco (eds) (1989), *Collective Forest Land Tenure and Rural Development in Italy*, Rome: Food and Agriculture Organization of the United Nations.
Messerschmidt, Donald A. (1986), 'People and resources in Nepal: Customary resource management systems of the Upper Kali Gandaki', in National Research Council, *Proceedings of the Conference on Common Property Resource Management*, Washington, DC: National Academies Press, pp. 455–480.
Messerschmidt, Donald A. (ed.) (1993), *Common Forest Resource Management: Annotated Bibliography of Asia, Africa, and Latin America*, Forests, Trees and People Programme, Rome: Food and Agriculture Organization of the United Nations.
Migot-Adholla, Shem E., Peter Hazell, Benoît Blarel, and Frank Place (1991), 'Indigenous land rights systems in sub-Saharan Africa: A constraint on productivity?', *World Bank Economic Review*, **5**, 155–175.
Miller, David (1989), 'The evolution of Mexico's spiny lobster fishery', in Fikret Berkes (ed.), *Common Property Resources: Ecology and Community-Based Sustainable Development*, London: Belhaven Press, pp. 185–198.
Mitchell, Ronald B. (1995), 'Heterogeneities at two levels: States, non-state actors and intentional oil pollution', in Robert O. Keohane and Elinor Ostrom (eds), *Local Commons and*

Global Interdependence: Heterogeneity and Cooperation in Two Domains, London: Sage, pp. 223–251.

Mixon, F.G. and L.J. Trevino (2003) 'Fugitives as fish: Bounty hunting and exploitation of the commons', *Social Science Journal*, **40**, 657–664.

Mobbs, C. and K. Moore (eds) (2002), *Property: Rights and Responsibilities: Current Australian Thinking*, Canberra: Land and Water Australia.

Montias, John Michael (1976), *The Structure of Economic Systems*, New Haven, CT: Yale University Press.

Moran, Emilio and Elinor Ostrom (eds) (2005), *Seeing the Forest and the Trees: Human-Environment Interactions in Forest Ecosystems*, Cambridge, MA: MIT Press.

Moser, C. (2004), 'Innovation in natural resource management: The role of property rights and collective action in developing countries', *Agricultural Systems*, **81**, 180–181.

Moyo, Sam (2005), 'Land and natural resource redistribution in Zimbabwe: Access, equity and conflict', *African and Asian Studies*, **4**, 187–224.

Mukhija, Vinit (2005), 'Collective action and property rights: A planner's critical look at the dogma of private property', *International Journal of Urban and Regional Research*, **29**, 972–983.

Muñoz Piña, Carlos, A. de Janvry, and E. Sadoulet (2003), 'Recrafting rights over common property resources in Mexico', *Economic Development and Cultural Change*, **52**, 129–158.

Murphy, Earl Finbar (1977), *Nature, Bureaucracy and the Rules of Property: Regulating the Renewing Environment*, Amsterdam: North-Holland.

Mutersbaugh, T. (2002), 'Migration, common property, and communal labor: Cultural politics and agency in a Mexican village', *Political Geography*, **21**, 473–494.

Mwangi, Esther (2006), 'The footprints of history: Path dependence in the transformation of property rights in Kenya's Maasailand', *Journal of Institutional Economics*, **2**, 157–180.

Mwangi, Esther (2007a), *Socioeconomic Change and Land Use in Africa: The Transformation of Property Rights in Maasiland*, New York: Palgrave Macmillan.

Mwangi, Esther (2007b), 'Subdividing the commons: Distributional conflict in the transition from collective to individual property rights in Kenya's Maasailand', *World Development*, **35**, 815–834.

Nabanoga, Gorettie Nsubuga (2005), *Transgressing Boundaries: Gendered Spaces, Species, and Indigenous Forest Management in Uganda*, Wageningen, Netherlands: Wageningen University and Research Centre.

Nabli, Mustapha K. and Jeffrey B. Nugent (1989), *The New Institutional Economics and Development: Theory and Tunisian Case Studies*, Amsterdam: North-Holland.

Nagendra, Harini (2007), 'Drivers of reforestation in human-dominated forests', *Proceedings of the National Academy of Sciences*, **104** (39), 15218–15223.

Nagendra, Harini, Mukunda Karmacharya, and Birendra Karna (2005), 'Evaluating forest management in Nepal: Views across space and time', *Ecology and Society*, **10**, http://www.ecologyandsociety.org/vol10/iss1/art24/

Nahrath, Stéphane (2000), '"Governing wildlife resources"? L'organisation de la chasse en Suisse comme exemple de régimes institutionnels de gestion d'une ressource naturelle', *Swiss Political Science Review*, **6**, 123–158.

National Research Council (2001), *Resolving Conflicts Arising from the Privatization of Environmental Data*, Washington, DC: National Academies Press.

National Research Council (2002), *The Drama of the Commons*, Committee on the Human Dimensions of Global Change, Elinor Ostrom, Thomas Dietz, Nives Dolšak, Paul Stern, Susan Stonich, and Elke Weber (eds), Washington, DC: National Academies Press.

Nelson, Gerald C., Virginia Harris, and Steven W. Stone (2001), 'Deforestation, land use, and property rights, empirical evidence from Darién, Panama', *Land Economics*, **77**, 187–205.

Nemarundwe, N. and W. Kozanayi (2003), 'Institutional arrangements for water resource use: A case study from southern Zimbabwe', *Journal of Southern African Studies*, **29**, 193–206.

Netting, Robert McC. (1976), 'What Alpine peasants have in common: Observations on communal tenure in a Swiss village', *Human Ecology*, **4**, 135–146.
Netting, Robert McC. (1981), *Balancing on an Alp: Ecological Change and Continuity in a Swiss Mountain Community*, New York: Cambridge University Press.
Netting, Robert McC. (1993), *Smallholders, Householders: Farm Families and the Ecology of Intensive, Sustainable Agriculture*, Stanford, CA: Stanford University Press.
Neuburger, M. (2001), 'Property rights in Brazil: The significance of institutional regulations for the vulnerability and survival strategies of smallholder groups', *Geographica Helvetica*, **56**, 34–47.
Newkirk, S.G. (2006), 'Property rights in fisheries', *Bulletin of Marine Science*, **78**, 563–574.
North, Douglass C. (1990), *Institutions, Institutional Change, and Economic Performance*, New York: Cambridge University Press.
North, Douglass C. (1993), 'Toward a theory of institutional change', in W.A. Barnett, M.J. Hinich, and N.J. Schofield (eds), *Political Economy: Institutions, Competition, and Representation*, New York: Cambridge University Press.
North, Douglass C. (2005), *Understanding the Process of Economic Change*, Princeton, NJ: Princeton University Press.
North, Douglass C., Terry L. Anderson, and Peter J. Hill (1983), *Growth and Welfare in the American Past: A New Economic History*, Englewood Cliffs, NJ: Prentice-Hall.
North, Douglass C. and Robert Paul Thomas (1976), *The Rise of the Western World: A New Economic History*, London: Cambridge University Press.
Nugent, Jeffrey B. and Nicolas Sanchez (1989), 'The efficiency of the mesta reconsidered: A parable', *Explorations in Economic History*, **26**, 261–284.
Nugent, Jeffrey B. and Nicolas Sanchez (1993), 'Tribes, chiefs, and transhumance: A comparative institutional analysis', *Economic Development and Cultural Change*, **42**, 87–113.
Oakerson, Ronald J. (1992), 'Analyzing the commons: A framework', in Daniel W. Bromley, et al. (eds), *Making the Commons Work: Theory, Practice, and Policy*, San Francisco, CA: ICS Press, pp. 41–59.
O'Flaherty, R.M. (2003), 'The tragedy of property: Ecology and land tenure in southeastern Zimbabwe', *Human Organization*, **62**, 178–190.
Okello, Moses (2005), 'Land use changes and human-wildlife conflicts in the Amboseli area, Kenya', *Human Dimensions of Wildlife*, **10**, 19–28.
Olson, Mancur (1965), *The Logic of Collective Action: Public Goods and the Theory of Groups*, Cambridge, MA: Harvard University Press.
Ørebech, Peter, Fred Bosselman, Jes Bjarup, David Callies, Martin Chanock, and Hanne Petersen (2005), *The Role of Customary Law in Sustainable Development*, Cambridge: Cambridge University Press.
Oses-Erasoa, Nuria and Montserrat Viladrich-Grau (2007), 'On the sustainability of common property resources', *Journal of Environmental Economics and Management*, **53**, 393–410.
Osmundsen, Petter (2002), 'Regulation of common property resources under private information about resource externalities', *Resource and Energy Economics*, **24**, 349–366.
Ostrom, Elinor (1990), *Governing the Commons: The Evolution of Institutions for Collective Action*, New York: Cambridge University Press.
Ostrom, Elinor (1992), 'The rudiments of a theory of the origins, survival, and performance of common-property institutions', in Daniel W. Bromley, et al. (eds), *Making the Commons Work: Theory, Practice, and Policy*, San Francisco, CA: ICS Press, pp. 293–318.
Ostrom, Elinor (1993), 'The evolution of norms, rules, and rights', Beijer International Institute of Ecological Economics Discussion Paper Series no. 39, The Digital Library of the Commons, http://dlc.dlib.indiana.edu/dlc/handle/10535/1733
Ostrom, Elinor (2003), 'How types of goods and property rights jointly affect collective action', *Journal of Theoretical Politics*, **15**, 239–270.
Ostrom, Elinor (2005), *Understanding Institutional Diversity*, Princeton, NJ: Princeton University Press.

Ostrom, Elinor (2007), 'A diagnostic approach for going beyond panaceas', *Proceedings of the National Academy of Sciences*, **104** (39), 15181–15187.
Ostrom, Elinor, Joanna Burger, Christopher Field, Richard Norgaard, and David Policansky (1999), 'Revisiting the commons: Local lessons, global challenges', *Science*, **284** (5412), 278–282.
Ostrom, Elinor, Roy Gardner, and James M. Walker (1994), *Rules, Games, and Common-Pool Resources*, Ann Arbor: University of Michigan Press.
Ostrom, Elinor, Marco Janssen, and John Anderies (2007), 'Going Beyond Panaceas' *Proceedings of the National Academy of Sciences*, **104** (39), 15176–15178.
Ostrom, Elinor and Harini Nagendra (2006), 'Insights on linking forests, trees, and people from the air, on the ground, and in the laboratory', *Proceedings of the National Academy of Sciences*, **103**, 19224–19231.
Ostrom, Elinor and Edella Schlager (1996), 'The formation of property rights', in Susan Hanna, Carl Folke, and Karl-Gorän Mäler (eds), *Rights to Nature: Ecological, Economic, Cultural, and Political Principles of Institutions for the Environment*, Washington, DC: Island Press, pp. 127–56.
Ostrom, Vincent (1975), 'Alternative approaches to the organization of public proprietary interests', *Natural Resources Journal*, **15**, 765–789.
Ostrom, Vincent (2007), 'Some developments in the study of market choice, public choice, and institutional choice', in J. Rabin, W.B. Hildreth, and G. Miller (eds), *Handbook of Public Administration*, New York: CRC Press.
Ostrom, Vincent (2008), *The Intellectual Crisis in American Public Administration*, 3rd ed., Tuscaloosa: University of Alabama Press.
Ostrom, Vincent and Elinor Ostrom (1977a), 'Public goods and public choices', in E.S. Savas (ed.), *Alternatives for Delivering Public Services: Toward Improved Performance*, Boulder, CO: Westview Press, pp. 7–49.
Ostrom, Vincent and Elinor Ostrom (1977b), 'A theory for institutional analysis of common pool problems', in Garrett Hardin and John Baden (eds), *Managing the Commons*, San Francisco, CA: W.H. Freeman, pp. 157–172.
Otsuka, Keijiro and Frank Place (eds) (2001), *Land Tenure and Natural Resource Management: A Comparative Study of Agrarian Communities in Asia and Africa*, Baltimore, MD: Johns Hopkins University Press.
Otsuki, T., I.W. Jardie, and E.J. Reis (2002), 'The implications of property rights for joint agriculture-timber productivity in the Brazilian Amazon', *Environment and Development Economics*, **7**, 299–324.
Oye, Kenneth A. and James H. Maxwell (1995), 'Self-interest and environmental management', in Robert O. Keohane and Elinor Ostrom (eds), *Local Commons and Global Interdependence: Heterogeneity and Cooperation in Two Domains*, London: Sage, pp. 191–221.
Palmer, Charles (2007), 'The role of leadership in the collective enforcement of community property rights in Indonesia', *Society and Natural Resources*, **20**, 397–413.
Panayotou, Theodore and Peter S. Ashton (1992), *Not by Timber Alone: Economics and Ecology for Sustaining Tropical Forests*, Washington, DC: Island Press.
Pandit, B.H. and G.B. Thapa (2003), 'A tragedy of non-timber forest resources in the mountain commons of Nepal', *Environmental Conservation*, **30**, 283–292.
Parlee, Brenda, Fikret Berkes, and Teetlit Gwichin Renewable Resources Council (2006), 'Indigenous knowledge of ecological variability and commons management: A case study on berry harvesting from northern Canada', *Human Ecology*, **34**, 515–528.
Pasqual, Joan and Guadalupe Souto (2003), 'Sustainability in natural resource management', *Ecological Economics*, **46**, 47–59.
Patel, Reena (2006), 'Hindu women's property rights in India: A critical appraisal', *Third World Quarterly*, **27**, 1255–1268.
Paul, Ellen Frankel, Fred D. Miller, and Jeffrey Paul (eds) (1994), *Property Rights*, New York: Cambridge University Press.
Payne, G. (2004), 'Land tenure and property rights: An introduction', *Habitat International*, **28**, 167–179.

Perrings, Charles (2007), 'Future challenges', *Proceedings of the National Academy of Sciences*, **104** (39), 15179–15180.
Peters, Pauline E. (1994), *Dividing the Commons: Politics, Policy, and Culture in Botswana*, Charlottesville: University Press of Virginia.
Petrzelka, Peggy and Michael M. Bell (2000), 'Rationality and solidarities: The social organization of common property resources in the Imdrhas valley of Morocco', *Human Organization*, **59**, 343–352.
Pickles, John (2006), 'Collectivism, universalism, and struggles over common property resources in the "new" Europe', *Social Analysis*, **50**, 178–186.
Pinkerton, Evelyn (ed.) (1989), *Co-Operative Management of Local Fisheries: New Directions for Improved Management and Community Development*, Vancouver: University of British Columbia.
Pinkerton, Evelyn (1994), 'Local fisheries co-management: A review of international experiences and their implications for salmon management in British Columbia', *Canadian Journal of Fisheries and Aquatic Sciences*, **51**, 2363–2378.
Pinto da Silva, Patricia (2004), 'From common property to co-management: Lessons from Brazil's first maritime extractive reserve', *Marine Policy*, **28**, 419–428.
Place, Frank and Peter Hazell (1993), 'Productivity effects of indigenous land tenure systems in sub-Saharan Africa', *American Journal of Agricultural Economics*, **75**, 10–19.
Platteau, Jean-Philippe (2000), *Institutions, Social Norms, and Economic Development*, Reading, UK: Harwood Academic.
Plourde, C.G. (1970), 'Exploitation of common property replenishable natural resources', *Western Economic Journal*, **9**, 256–266.
Polasky, Stephen, Nori Tarui, Gregory M. Ellis, and Charles F. Mason (2006), 'Cooperation in the commons', *Economic Theory*, **29**, 71–88.
Posner, Richard A. (1980), 'A theory of primitive society, with special reference to law', *Journal of Law and Economics*, **23**, 1–53.
Poteete, Amy R. (2003), 'Ideas, interests, and institutions: Challenging the property rights paradigm in Botswana', *Governance*, **16**, 527–557.
Poteete, Amy R. and Elinor Ostrom (2004), 'Heterogeneity, group size and collective action: The role of institutions in forest management', *Development and Change*, **35** (3), 435–461.
Poteete, Amy and Elinor Ostrom (2008), 'Fifteen years of empirical research on collective action in natural resource management: Struggling to build large-N databases based on qualitative research', *World Development*, **36** (1), 176–95.
Prasad, B.C. (2003), 'Institutional economics and economic development: The theory of property rights, economic development, good governance and the environment', *International Journal of Social Economics*, **30**, 741–762.
Prasad, B.C. and M. Reddy (2001), 'Coastal zone management and property rights: Issues for sustainable development in Fiji', *Global Environmental Research*, **5**, 55–62.
Putterman, Louis (1995), 'Markets, hierarchies, and information: On a paradox in the economics of organization', *Journal of Economic Behavior and Organization*, **26**, 373–390.
Quiggin, John (1988), 'Private and common property rights in the economics of the environment', *Journal of Economic Issues*, **22**, 1071–1087.
Quinn, Claire H., Meg Huby, Hilda Kiwasila, and Jon C. Lovett (2007), 'Design principles and common pool resource management: An institutional approach to evaluating community management in semi-arid Tanzania', *Journal of Environmental Management*, **84**, 100–113.
Rai, Arti and James Boyle (2007), 'Synthetic biology: Caught between property rights, the public domain, and the commons', *PLoS Biology*, **5**, 389–393.
Rai, M. (2002), 'Genetic resources and intellectual property rights in agricultural perspective', *Indian Journal of Pulses Research*, **15**, 1–18.
Randall, Alan (1975), 'Property rights and social microeconomics', *Natural Resources Journal*, **15**, 729–747.

Randall, Alan (1978), 'Property institutions and economic behavior', *Journal of Economic Issues*, **12**, 1–21.

Randeria, S. (2003), 'Cunning states and unaccountable international institutions: Legal plurality, social movements and rights of local communities to common property resources', *Archives Europeennes de Sociologie*, **44**, 27–60.

Rao, Nitya (2007), 'Custom and the courts: Ensuring women's rights to land, Jharkhand, India', *Development and Change*, **38**, 299–319.

Rao, K. Raja Mohan, M. Sabesh Manikandan, and Walter Leaf Filho (2005), 'An overview of the impacts of changes in common property resources management in the context of globalisation: A case study of India', *International Journal for Sustainable Development and World Ecology*, **12**, 471–478.

Rapoport, Anatol (1988), 'Experiments with N-person social traps: Tragedy of the commons', *Journal of Conflict Resolution*, **32**, 473–488.

Raychaudhuri, Bikash (1980), *The Moon and the Net: Study of a Transient Community of Fishermen at Jambudwip*, Calcutta: Government of India Press, Anthropological Survey of India.

Raymond, Leigh (2003), *Private Rights in Public Resources: Equity and Property Allocation in Market-Based Environmental Policy*, Washington, DC: Resources for the Future.

Reddy, S.P. (2002), 'Communal forests, political spaces: Territorial competition between common property institutions and the state in Guatemala', *Space and Polity*, **6**, 271–278.

Renard, V. (2007), 'Property rights and the "transfer of development rights": Questions of efficiency and equity', *Town Planning Review*, **78**, 41–60.

Repetto, Robert (1986), *Skimming the Water: Rent-Seeking and the Performance of Public Irrigation Systems*, Washington, DC: World Resources Institute.

Richard, Alan and Nirvikar Singh (2001), 'No easy exit: Property rights, markets, and negotiations over water', *International Journal of Water Resources Development*, **17**, 409–426.

Ricketts, Martin (2005), 'Poverty, institutions and economics: Hernando De Soto on property rights and economic development', *Economic Affairs*, **25**, 49–51.

Rifkin, Jeremy (2002), 'The treaty initiative to share the genetic commons', *Regulatory Affairs Journal*, **13**, 974–975.

Riley, Angela R. (2000), 'Recovering collectivity: Group rights to intellectual property in indigenous communities', *Cardozo Arts and Entertainment Law Journal*, **18**, 175–191.

Rose, Carol M. (1985), 'Possession as the origin of property', *University of Chicago Law Review*, **52**, 73–88.

Rose, Carol M. (1986), 'The comedy of the commons: Custom, commerce, and inherently public property', *University of Chicago Law Review*, **53**, 711–781.

Rose, Carol M. (1990), 'Property as storytelling: Perspectives from game theory, narrative theory, feminist theory', *Yale Journal of Law and the Humanities*, **2**, 37–57.

Rose, Carol M. (1994), *Property and Persuasion*, Boulder, CO: Westview Press.

Rose-Ackerman, Susan (1977), 'Market models for water pollution control: Their strengths and weaknesses', *Public Policy*, **25**, 383–406.

Rose-Ackerman, Susan (1985), 'Inalienability and the theory of property rights', *Columbia Law Review*, **85**, 931–969.

Ross, Michael L. (2001), *Timber Booms and Institutional Breakdown in Southeast Asia*, New York: Cambridge University Press.

Roux, Lani and Michael Barry (2001), 'Using video imagery in land tenure information systems: A study of a communal property association in the village of Algeria, South Africa', *Geomatica*, **55**, 47–55.

Roy, K.C. and C.A. Tisdell (2002), 'Property rights in women's empowerment in rural India: A review', *International Journal of Social Economics*, **29**, 315–334.

Ruddle, Kenneth (1989), 'Traditional sole property rights and modern inshore fisheries management in the Pacific basin', in H. Campbell, K. Menz, and G. Waugh (eds), *Economics of Fishery Management in the Pacific Islands Region*, Canberra: Australian Centre for International Agricultural Research.

Ruddle, Kenneth (1994), 'A guide to the literature on traditional community-based fishery management in the Asia-Pacific tropics', Rome: Food and Agriculture Organization of the United Nations.

Ruh, Michael A. and Matthew T. Lockaby (2005), 'Balancing private property rights with "public use": A survey of Kentucky courts' interpretation of the power of eminent domain', *Northern Kentucky Law Review*, **32**, 743–782.

Runge, C. Ford (1981), 'Common property externalities: Isolation, assurance and resource depletion in a traditional grazing context', *American Journal of Agriculture Economics*, **63**, 595–606.

Runge, C. Ford (1984), 'The fallacy of privatization', *Journal of Contemporary Studies*, **7**, 3–17.

Runge, C. Ford (1987), 'Common property and collective action in economic development', *World Development*, **14**, 623–635.

Runge, C. Ford and E. Defrancesco (2006), 'Exclusion, inclusion, and enclosure: Historical commons and modern intellectual property', *World Development*, **34**, 1713–1727.

Ruppert, Evelyn S. (2006), 'Rights to public space: Regulatory reconfigurations of liberty', *Urban Geography*, **27**, 271–292.

Rushton, Michael (2004), 'Contingent valuation and the public interest in privately owned cultural property', *Journal of Arts Management, Law, and Society*, **34**, 222–234.

Ryan, Alan (1984), *Property and Political Theory*, New York: Blackwell.

Safrin, Sabrina (2004), 'Hyperownership in a time of biotechnological promise: The international conflict to control the building blocks of life', *American Journal of International Law*, **98**, 641–685.

Sakurai, T. and K. Palanisami (2001), 'Tank irrigation management as a local common property: The case of Tamil Nadu, India', *Agricultural Economics*, **25**, 273–283.

Samuelson, Charles D. (1991), 'Perceived task difficulty, causal attributions, and preferences for structural change in resource dilemmas', *Personality and Social Psychology Bulletin*, **17**, 181–187.

Samuelson, Charles D., D.M. Messick, C.G. Rutte, and H. Wilke (1984), 'Individual and structural solutions to resource dilemmas in two cultures', *Journal of Personality and Social Psychology*, **47**, 94–104.

Sandberg, Audun (1998), 'The analytical importance of property rights to northern resources', in E. Berge and N.C. Stenseth (eds), *Law and the Governance of Renewable Resources: Studies from Northern Europe and Africa*, Oakland, CA: ICS Press.

Sandberg, Audun (2001), *Institutional Challenges for Common Property Resources in the Nordic Countries*, Stockholm: Nordregio.

Sandberg, Audun (2007), 'Property rights and ecosystem properties', *Land Use Policy*, **24**, 613–623.

Sandler, Todd (1992), *Collective Action: Theory and Applications*, Ann Arbor: University of Michigan Press.

Sandler, Todd and Keith Sargent (1995), 'Management of transnational commons: Coordination, publicness, and treaty formation', *Land Economics*, **68**, 249–262.

Sandler, Todd and Frederic P. Sterbenz (1990), 'Harvest uncertainty and the tragedy of the commons', *Journal of Environmental Economics and Management*, **18**, 155–167.

Saruchera, Munyaradzi (ed.) (2004), *Securing Land and Resource Rights in Africa: Pan-African Perspectives*, Cape Town, South Africa: Programme for Land and Agrarian Studies.

Sato, Kaori (1987), 'Distribution of the cost of maintaining common property resources', *Journal of Experimental Social Psychology*, **23**, 19–31.

Savas, E.S. (1987), *Privatization: The Key to Better Government*, Chatham, NJ: Chatham House Publishers.

Sax, Joseph L. (1971), 'Takings, private property, and public rights', *The Yale Law Journal*, **81**, 149–186.

Sax, Joseph L. (2002), 'Using property rights to attack environmental protection', *Pace Environmental Law Review*, **19**, 715–726.

Schaefer, Milner (1957), 'Some considerations of population dynamics and economics in

relation to the management of the commercial marine fisheries', *Journal of the Fisheries Research Board of Canada*, **14**, 669–681.
Schelling, Thomas C. (1978), *Micromotives and Macrobehavior*, New York: W.W. Norton.
Schlager, Edella (1994), 'Fishers' institutional responses to common-pool resource dilemmas', in Elinor Ostrom, Roy Gardner, and James M. Walker (eds), *Rules, Games, and Common-Pool Resources*, Ann Arbor: University of Michigan Press, pp. 247–265.
Schlager, Edella, William Blomquist, and Shui Yan Tang (1994), 'Mobile flows, storage, and self-organized institutions for governing common-pool resources', *Land Economics*, **70**, 294–317.
Schlager, Edella and Elinor Ostrom (1992), 'Property rights regimes and natural resources: A conceptual analysis', *Land Economics*, **68**, 249–262.
Schleyer, C. (2004), 'Economic and ecological transformation processes in East German water management regimes: The role of property rights and governance structures', *Environmental Management*, **34**, 281–290.
Schmidtz, David and Elizabeth Willott (2003), 'Reinventing the commons: An African case study', *U. C. Davis Law Review*, **37**, 203–232.
Schorr, D.B. (2005), 'Appropriation as agrarianism: Distributive justice in the creation of property rights', *Ecology Law Quarterly*, **32**, 3–72.
Schotter, Andrew (1981), *The Economic Theory of Social Institutions*, Cambridge, MA: Cambridge University Press.
Schulz, Ulrich, Wulf Albers, and Ulrich Mueller (eds) (1994), *Social Dilemmas and Cooperation*, Berlin: Springer-Verlag.
Schworm, William E. (1983), 'Monopsonistic control of a common property renewable resource', *Canadian Journal of Economics*, **16**, 275–287.
Scott, Anthony D. (1955), 'The fishery: The objectives of sole ownership', *Journal of Political Economy*, **63**, 116–124.
Scott, Anthony D. (1983), 'Property rights and property wrongs', *Canadian Journal of Economics*, **16**, 555–573.
Seabright, Paul (1993), 'Managing local commons: Theoretical issues in incentive design', *Journal of Economic Perspectives*, **7**, 113–134.
Sekar, C. (2001), 'Externality effects of common property resource degradation', *Indian Journal of Agricultural Economics*, **56**, 346–357.
Sened, Itai (1991), 'Contemporary theory of institutions in perspective', *Journal of Theoretical Politics*, **3**, 379–402.
Sengupta, Nirmal (1991), *Managing Common Property: Irrigation in India and the Philippines*, New Delhi: Sage.
Sengupta, Nirmal (1993), *User-Friendly Irrigation Designs*, New Delhi: Sage.
Sennlaub, Angelika (2005), 'Living with commons – between strain and opportunity: The sustainability of habitation through communal ownership', *GAIA: Ecological Perspectives for Science and Society*, **14**, 323–332.
Sethi, Rajiv and E. Somanathan (1996), 'The evolution of social norms in common property resource use', *American Economic Review*, **86**, 766–788.
Sgard, Jérôme (2004), 'Are there such things as international property rights?', *World Economy*, **27**, 387–401.
Shams, Numa and Mahfuzuddin Ahmed (2000), 'Common and private property linkages in the low-land forest-fishery-farming systems of Cambodia', *Journal of Sustainable Agriculture*, **15**, 59–88.
Sheehan, J. (2001), 'Indigenous property rights and river management', *Water Science and Technology*, **43**, 235–242.
Shivakoti, Ganesh P. and Elinor Ostrom (eds) (2002), *Improving Irrigation Governance and Management in Nepal*, Oakland, CA: ICS Press.
Shivakoti, Ganesh P., Douglas Vermillion, Wai-Fung Lam, Elinor Ostrom, Ujjwal Pradhan, and Robert Yoder (eds) (2005), *Asian Irrigation in Transition: Responding to Challenges*, Thousand Oaks, CA: Sage.

Shotton, Ross (ed.) (2001a), *Case Studies on the Allocation of Transferable Quota Rights in Fisheries*, Rome: Food and Agriculture Organization of the United Nations.
Shotton, Ross (ed.) (2001b), *Case Studies on the Effects of Transferable Fishing Rights on Fleet Capacity and Concentration of Quota Ownership*, Rome: Food and Agriculture Organization of the United Nations.
Sikor, Thomas (2001), 'The allocation of forestry land in Vietnam: Did it cause the expansion of forests in the northwest?', *Forest Policy and Economics*, **2**, 1–11.
Sikor, Thomas (2004a), 'The commons in transition: Agrarian and environmental change in Central and Eastern Europe', *Environmental Management*, **34**, 270–280.
Sikor, Thomas (2004b), 'Conflicting concepts: Contested land relations in north-western Vietnam', *Conservation and Society*, **2**, 75–95.
Singh, Chatrapati (1986), *Common Property and Common Poverty: India's Forests, Forest Dwellers, and the Law*, Oxford: Oxford University Press.
Singh, H. (2004), 'Intellectual property rights (IPR) issues in horticulture: An Indian scenario with particular reference to medicinal plants', *Acta Horticulturae*, **662**, 465–470.
Singh, J.P. (2001), 'From POTS to E-commerce: What have the developing countries learnt about property rights over the last 50 years?', *Prometheus*, **19**, 347–362.
Singh, Katar (1994), *Managing Common Pool Resources: Principles and Case Studies*, New Delhi: Oxford University Press.
Singh, Katar and Vishwa Ballabh (1996), *Cooperative Management of Natural Resources*, New Delhi: Sage.
Singh, Nandita (2006), 'Indigenous water management systems: Interpreting symbolic dimensions in common property resource regimes', *Society and Natural Resources*, **19**, 357–366.
Singh, V.K., A. Suresh, D.C. Gupta, and R.C. Jakhmola (2005), 'Common property resources, rural livelihood, and small ruminants in India: A review', *Indian Journal of Animal Sciences*, **75**, 1027–1036.
Singleton, Sara and Michael Taylor (1992), 'Common property, collective action and community', *Journal of Theoretical Politics*, **4**, 309–324.
Sinn, Hans-Werner (1984), 'Common property resources, storage facilities and ownership structures: A Cournot model of the oil market', *Economica*, **51**, 235–252.
Sipponen, M., K. Muje, T.J. Marjomaki, P. Valkeajarvi, and J. Karjalainen (2006), 'Interlocked use of inland fish resources: A new management strategy under private property rights', *Fisheries Management Ecology*, **13**, 299–307.
Siy, Robert Y., Jr. (1982), *Community Resource Management: Lessons from the Zanjera*, Quezon City: University of the Philippines Press.
Slaughter, R.A. and J.D. Wiener (2007), 'Water, adaptation, and property rights on the Snake and Klamath Rivers', *Journal of the American Water Resources Association*, **43** (2), 308–321.
Smajgl, Alex and Silva Larson (eds) (2007), *Sustainable Resource Use: Institutional Dynamics and Economics*, Sterling, VA: Earthscan.
Smets, Henri (2004), 'The right to water as an enforceable right', *Environmental Policy and Law*, **34**, 84–85.
Smith, Henry E. (2000), 'Semicommon property rights and scattering in the open fields', *Journal of Legal Studies*, **29**, 131–169.
Smith, R.J. (1981), 'Resolving the tragedy of the commons by creating private property rights in wildlife', *CATO Journal*, **1**, 439–468.
Smith, Vernon L. (1968), 'Economics of production from natural resources', *American Economic Review*, **58**, 409–431.
Snidal, Duncan (1985), 'Coordination versus prisoners dilemma: Implications for international cooperation and regimes', *American Political Science Review*, **79**, 923–947.
Sorger, Gerhard (2005), 'A dynamic common property resource problem with amenity value and extraction costs', *International Journal of Economic Theory*, **1**, 3–20.
Soroos, Marvin S. (2001), 'The evolution of global commons', in *Global Environmental Policies: Institutions and Procedures*, New York: Palgrave, pp. 39–65.
Sowerwine, Jennifer C. (2004), 'Territorialisation and the politics of highland landscapes in

Vietnam: Negotiating property relations in policy, meaning and practice', *Conservation and Society*, **2**, 97–136.
Spier, V.E. (2001), 'Finders' keepers: The dispute between developed and developing countries over ownership of property rights in genetic material', *Widener Law Symposium Journal*, **7**, 203–226.
Sproule-Jones, Mark (1982), 'Public choice theory and natural resources: Methodological explication and critique', *American Political Science Review*, **76**, 790–804.
Srinivas, Krishna Ravi (2006), 'Intellectual property rights and bio commons: Open source and beyond', *International Social Science Journal*, **188**, 319–334.
Sserunkuuma, Dick and Kent Olson (2001), 'Private property rights and overgrazing: An empirical assessment of pastoralists in Nyabushozi County, Western Uganda,' *Economic Development and Cultural Change*, **49**, 769–792.
Starrett, D.A. (2003), 'Property rights, public goods and the environment', *Handbook in Economics*, **20**, 97–123.
Steele, Scott R. (2001), 'Property regimes as information regimes: Efficiency and economies of joint production', *Environmental and Resource Economics*, **18**, 317–337.
Steelman, Toddi A. and Richard L. Wallace (2001), 'Property rights and property wrongs: Why context matters in fisheries management', *Policy Sciences*, **34**, 357–379.
Stern, P.C. (1978), 'When do people act to maintain common resources: A reformulated psychological question for our times', *International Journal of Psychology*, **13**, 149–158.
Stevenson, Glenn G. (1991), *Common Property Economics: A General Theory and Land Use Applications*, Cambridge: Cambridge University Press.
Stewart, James M. and Peter D. Callagher (2003), 'New Zealand fisheries management: Changes in property rights structure and implications for sustainability', *Sustainable Development*, **11**, 69–76.
Stolzenberg, Nomi Maya (2000), 'The culture of property', *Daedalus*, **129**, 169–192.
Strappazzon, Loris, et al. (2003), 'Efficiency of alternative property right allocations when farmers produce multiple environmental goods under the condition of economies of scope', *Australian Journal of Agricultural and Resource Economics*, **47** (1), 1–27.
Sugden, Robert (1986), *The Economics of Rights, Cooperation, and Welfare*, Oxford: Basil Blackwell.
Sugiah, Siti, Machfud Mugniesyah, and Mizuno Kosuke (2007), 'Access to land in Sundanese community: A case study of upland peasant households in Kemang village, West Java, Indonesia', *South East Asian Studies*, **44**, 519–544.
Sundberg, Jeffrey O. (2006), 'Private provision of a public good: Land trust membership', *Land Economics*, **82**, 353–366.
Suryanata, K. and K.N. Umemoto (2003), 'Tension at the nexus of the global and local: Culture, property, and marine aquaculture in Hawai'i', *Environment and Planning A*, **35**, 199–213.
Susilowati, Indah, Norman Bartoo, Ishak Haji Omar, Yongil Jeon, K. Kuperan, Dale Squires, and Niels Vestergaard (2005), 'Productive efficiency, property rights, and sustainable renewable resource development in the mini-purse seine fishery of the Java Sea', *Environment and Development Economics*, **10**, 837–859.
Svensson, Tom G. (2002), 'Indigenous rights and customary law discourse: Comparing the Nisga'a and the Sami', *Journal of Legal Pluralism and Unofficial Law*, **47**, 1–36.
Swallow, Brent M. and Daniel W. Bromley (1994), 'Co-management or no management: The prospects for internal governance of common property regimes through dynamic contracts', *Oxford Agrarian Studies*, **22**, 3–16.
Swallow, Brent M., Dennis P. Garrity, and Meine van Noordwijk (2002), 'The effects of scales, flows and filters on property rights and collective action in watershed management', *Water Policy*, **3**, 457–474.
Swaney, James A. (1990), 'Common property, reciprocity, and community', *Journal of Economic Issues*, **24**, 451–462.
Swaney, James A. (2003), 'Are democracy and common property possible on our small Earth?', *Journal of Economic Issues*, **37**, 259–288.

Swanson, Timothy and Timo Goschl (2000), 'Property rights issues involving plant genetic resources: Implications of ownership for economic efficiency', *Ecological Economics*, **32**, 75–92.

Swierzbinski, Joseph (1988), 'When more isn't better: Information and common-property resources', *Mathematical and Computational Modelling*, **11**, 899–902.

Tang, Shui Yan (1992), *Institutions and Collective Action: Self-Governance in Irrigation*, San Francisco, CA: ICS Press.

Tang, Shui Yan (1994), 'Building community organizations: Credible commitment and the new institutional economics', *Human Systems Management*, **13**, 221–232.

Tanner, Adrian (2007), 'On understanding too quickly: Colonial and postcolonial misrepresentation of indigenous Fijian land tenure', *Human Organization*, **66**, 69–77.

Tansey, Geoff (2002), 'Patenting our food future: Intellectual property rights and the global food system', *Social Policy and Administration*, **36**, 575–592.

Tarui, Nori (2007), 'Inequality and outside options in common-property resource use', *Journal of Development Economics*, **83**, 214–239.

Taylor, Michael and Sara Singleton (1995a), *Anarchy and Cooperation*, London: Wiley.

Taylor, Michael and Sara Singleton (1995b), 'The communal resource: Transaction costs and the solution of collective action problems', *Politics and Society*, **21**, 34–46.

Taylor, P.L. (2003), 'Reorganization or division? New strategies of community forestry in Durango, Mexico', *Society and Natural Resources*, **16**, 643–661.

Taylor, W.E. (2004), 'Property rights and responsibilities? The case of Kenya', *Habitat International*, **28**, 275–287.

Teng, Jimmy (2000), 'Endogenous authoritarian property rights', *Journal of Public Economies*, **77**, 81–95.

Thé, Ana Paula Glinfskoi and Nivaldo Nordi (2006), 'Common property resource system in a fishery of the Sao Francisco River, Minas Gerais, Brazil', *Human Ecology Review*, **13**, 1–10.

Thompson, Carol B. (2004), 'International law of the sea/seed: Public domain versus private commodity', *Natural Resources Journal*, **44**, 841–866.

Thompson, Dale B. (2006), 'Of rainbows and rivers: Lessons for telecommunications spectrum policy from transitions in property rights and commons in water law', *Buffalo Law Review*, **54**, 157–210.

Thomson, James T. (1977), 'Ecological deterioration: Local-level rule-making and enforcement problems in Niger', in Michael H. Glantz (ed.), *Desertification: Environmental Degradation in and around Arid Lands*, Boulder, CO: Westview Press, pp. 57–79.

Thomson, James T., David Feeny, and Ronald Oakerson (1992), 'Institutional dynamics: The evolution and dissolution of common-property resource management', in Daniel W. Bromley, et al. (eds), *Making the Commons Work: Theory, Practice, and Policy*, San Francisco, CA: ICS Press, pp. 129–160.

Tisdell, Clem (2004), 'Property rights in non-captive wildlife and biodiversity conservation', *International Journal of Global Environmental Issues*, **4**, 195–208.

Toly, Noah (2005), 'A tale of two regimes: Instrumentality and commons access', *Bulletin of Science, Technology and Society*, **25**, 26–36.

Tran, Thanh Ngoc (2005), *From Legal Acts to Village Institutions and Forest Use Practices: Effects of Devolution in the Central Highlands of Vietnam*, Aachen: Shaker Verlag.

Trommetter, Michel (2005), 'Biodiversity and international stakes: A question of access', *Ecological Economics*, **53**, 573–583.

Tubtim, Nattaya and Philip Hirsch (2005), 'Common property as enclosure: A case study of a backswamp in southern Laos', *Society and Natural Resources*, **18**, 41–60.

Tucker, Catherine, J.C. Randolph, and E. Castellanos (2007), 'Institutions, biophysical factors and history: An integrative analysis of private and common property forests in Guatemala and Honduras', *Human Ecology*, **35**, 259–274.

Tyer, C.B. (2000), 'Public needs vs. private loss: Land use regulation and property rights', *International Journal of Public Administration*, **23**, 479–505.

Ullmann-Margalit, Edna (1978), *The Emergence of Norms*, Oxford: Oxford University Press.

Umbeck, John R. (1981a), 'Might makes rights: A theory of the formation and initial distribution of property rights', *Economic Inquiry*, **20**, 38–59.

Umbeck, John R. (1981b), *A Theory of Property Rights: With Application to the California Gold Rush*, Ames: Iowa State University Press.

Unruh, Jon D. (2002), 'Poverty and property rights in the developing world: Not as simple as we would like', *Land Use Policy*, **19**, 275–276.

Unruh, Jon D. (2006), 'Land tenure and the "evidence landscape" in developing countries', *Annals of the Association of American Geographers*, **96**, 754–772.

Unruh, Jon, Lisa Cligget, and Ron Hay (2005), 'Migrant land rights reception and "clearing to claim" in sub-Saharan Africa: A deforestation example from southern Zambia', *Natural Resources Forum*, **29**, 190–198.

Vail, David and Lars Hultkrantz (2000), 'Property rights and sustainable nature tourism: Adaptation and mal-adaptation in Dalarna (Sweden) and Maine (USA)', *Ecological Economics*, **35**, 223–242.

vanderWalt, A.J. (2001), 'Dancing with codes: Protecting, developing and deconstructing property rights in a constitutional state', *South African Law Journal*, **118**, 258–311.

van Erp, S. (2003), 'Civil and common property law: Caveat comparator – the value of legal historical-comparative analysis', *European Review of Private Law*, **11**, 394–411.

Van Overwalle, Geertrui (2005), 'Protecting and sharing biodiversity and traditional knowledge: Holder and user tools', *Ecological Economics*, **53**, 585–607.

Varughese, George and Elinor Ostrom (2001), 'The contested role of heterogeneity in collective action: Some evidence from community forestry in Nepal', *World Development*, **29** (5), 747–765.

Veeman, T.S. and J. Politylo (2003), 'The role of institutions and policy in enhancing sustainable development and conserving natural capital', *Environment, Development and Sustainability*, **5**, 317–332.

Vincent, Linden (1995), *Hill Irrigation: Water and Development in Mountain Agriculture*, London: Overseas Development Institute.

Wade, Robert (1992), 'Common-property resource management in South Indian villages', in Daniel W. Bromley, et al. (eds), *Making the Commons Work: Theory, Practice, and Policy*, San Francisco, CA: ICS Press, pp. 207–228.

Wade, Robert (1994), *Village Republics: Economic Conditions for Collective Action in South India*, San Francisco, CA: ICS Press.

Waldron, Jeremy (1988), *The Right to Private Property*, Oxford: Clarendon.

Webb, Edward and Ganesh Shivakoti (eds) (2007), *Decentralization, Forests and Rural Communities: Policy Outcomes in South and Southeast Asia*, New Delhi: Sage.

Webster, Christopher J. (2002), 'Property rights and the public realm: Gates, green belts, and gemeinschaft', *Environment and Planning B*, **29**, 397–412.

Weinstein, Martin S. (2000), 'Pieces of the puzzle: Solutions for community-based fisheries management from native Canadians, Japanese cooperatives, and common property', *Georgetown International Environmental Law Review*, **12**, 375–412.

Weitzman, Martin (1974), 'Free access vs. private ownership as alternative systems for managing common property', *Journal of Economic Theory*, **8**, 225–234.

Welch, W.P. (1983), 'The political feasibility of full ownership property rights: The cases of pollution and fisheries', *Policy Sciences*, **16**, 165–180.

Westerland, K. 2007, 'Nepal's community forestry program: Another example of the tragedy of the commons or a realistic means of balancing indigenous needs with forestry conservation?', *Colorado Journal of International Environmental Law and Policy*, **18**, 189–216.

Whalley, John and Ben Zissimos (2001), 'What could a world environmental organization do?', *Global Environmental Politics*, **1**, 29–34.

Wiersma, Lindsey L. (2005), 'Indigenous lands as cultural property: A new approach to indigenous land claims', *Duke Law Journal*, **54**, 1061–1088.

Wiersum, K.F., R. Singhal, and C. Benneker (2004), 'Common property and collaborative forest management: Rural dynamics and evolution in community forestry regimes', *Forests, Trees and Livelihoods*, **14**, 281–294.

Wilke, Henk (1992), 'Greed, efficiency and fairness in resource management situations', *European Review of Social Psychology*, **2**, 165–187.
Williamson, Sima, David Brunckhorst, and Gerard Kelly (2003), *Reinventing the Common: Cross-Boundary Farming for a Sustainable Future*, Sydney: Federation.
Wilson, Douglas Clyde, Jesper Raakjaer Nielsen, and Poul Degnbol (eds) (2003), *The Fisheries Co-Management Experience: Accomplishments, Challenges and Prospects*, London: Kluwer.
Wilson, James A., James M. Acheson, Mark Metcalfe, and Peter Kleban (1994), 'Chaos, complexity, and community management of fisheries', *Marine Policy*, **18**, 291–305.
Wilson, James A. and Lloyd M. Dickie (1995), 'Parametric management of fisheries: An ecosystem-social approach', in Susan Hanna and Mohan Munasinghe (eds), *Property Rights in a Social and Ecological Context: Case Studies and Design Applications*, Stockholm and Washington, DC: The Beijer International Institute of Ecological Economics and The World Bank.
Wilson, James A., J. French, P. Kleban, S.R. Mckay, and R. Townsend (1991), 'Chaotic dynamics in a multiple species fishery: A model of community predation', *Ecological Modelling*, **58**, 303–322.
Wilson, James, Liying Yan, and Carl Wilson (2007), 'The precursors of governance in the Maine lobster fishery', *Proceedings of the National Academy of Sciences*, **104** (39), 15212–15217.
Wily, Liz Alden (2000), 'The democratization of forest management in eastern and southern Africa', *International Forestry Review*, **2**, 287–294.
Wily, Liz Alden (2002), 'The political economy of community forestry in Africa: Getting the power relations right', *Forests, Trees and People Newsletter*, **46**, 4–12.
Wily, Liz Alden and Sue Mbaya (2001), *Land, People, and Forests in Eastern and Southern Africa at the Beginning of the 21st Century: The Impact of Land Relations on the Role of Communities in Forest Future*, Nairobi, Kenya: IUCN-EARO.
Wollenberg, Eva, David Edmunds, and Jon Anderson (eds) (2001), *Accommodating Multiple Interests in Local Forest Management: Special Issue of the International Journal of Agricultural Resources, Governance and Ecology*, vol. 1, nos. 3/4, Oxford, UK: Inderscience Enterprises.
Wollenberg, Eva, Leticia Merino, Arun Agrawal, and Elinor Ostrom (2007), 'Fourteen years of monitoring community-managed forests: Learning from IFRI's experience', *International Forestry Review*, **9** (2), 670–684.
Wunderlich, Gene (1974), 'Property rights and information', *The Annals of American Academy of Political and Social Science*, **412**, 80–96.
Wunderlich, Gene and W.L. Gibson (eds) (1972), *Perspectives of Property*, College Station: Pennsylvania State University, Institute for Research on Land and Water Resources.
Yablon, M. (2004), 'Property rights and sacred sites: Federal regulatory responses to American Indian religious claims on public land', *Yale Law Journal*, **113**, 1623–1662.
Yandle, Bruce (ed.) (1995), *Land Rights: The 1990's Property Rights Rebellion*, Lanham, MD: Rowman & Littlefield.
Yandle, Tracy (2003), 'The challenge of building successful stakeholder organizations: New Zealand's experience in developing a fisheries co-management regime', *Marine Policy*, **27** (2), 179–192.
Young, Oran R. (1982), *Resource Regimes: Natural Resources and Social Institutions*, Berkeley: University of California Press.
Young, Oran R. (1989), *International Cooperation: Building Regimes for Natural Resources and the Environment*, Ithaca, NY: Cornell University Press.
Zwarteveen, Margreet and Ruth Meinzen-Dick (2001), 'Gender and property rights in the commons: Examples of water rights in South Asia', *Agriculture and Human Values*, **18**, 11–25.

5 Original assignment of private property

Boudewijn Bouckaert

1. Introduction

Property rights' systems, traditional as well as modern complex ones, have to cope with the problem of the assignment of non-owned, abandoned, lost or newly discovered goods. The origins of the assignment-problem are thus obvious: (1) either already known assets are not yet appropriated by members of the concerned community or are abandoned again by these members; (2) new types of scarce resources, not known or not regarded as scarce at the moment of the elaboration of the rules of the property system, may appear. Examples of (1) are: newly discovered acquired or conquered land such as the American West, wild animals, and water from seas, oceans and streams. Examples of (2) are: inventions and artistic creations, frequencies of the broadcast spectrum, subsurface minerals, and orbital spaces. The question arises by which rules or procedures goods without owner should be assigned and be put, provided transferability of such assets is allowed, within market circulation.

The choice of the rule of original assignment would not matter from an efficiency point of view when transaction costs are zero. Whomever the good is originally assigned to, the market would relocate it without friction to the most efficient user. As transaction costs may be prohibitively high for efficient relocation, it is possible that inefficiencies in the original assignment remain uncorrected through the market. This general remark, based on the Coase-theorem, applies also to the wider notion of political transaction costs. Libecap remarks that original assignment rules, once decided politically and made operational on the field, are often difficult to change as many constituencies develop a stake in the status quo and the distributional implications of any change in it can be both large and uncertain (Libecap, 2006).

In order to define the subject matter of this chapter more clearly we distinguish it from two other topics in the economic analysis of property law: the emergence of property systems as such and adverse possession.

The problem of emergence of property systems regards the economic rationale and the involved cost categories of setting up a property system and institutions as such. Under the heading of emergence of property rights the evolutionary process leading from an open access-situation without rules nor institutions towards an ordered system of rights and administrative, policing and adjudicative institutions is analyzed. In this chapter, however, a problem is discussed which necessarily emerges also within already established property systems. Most often the problem of the emergence of a property system also involves aspects of public choice and constitutional economics. In this chapter these aspects are not systematically but only occasionally discussed. Occasionally, when public choice aspects provide us with some explanation of the choice of an original assignment rule.

The problem of initial acquisition should also be distinguished from the problem of adverse possession. In the former case, assets non-owned in the terms of the concerned legal systems (for example lands of the American West in terms of the US legal system, not necessarily in terms of Native American tribal systems), are involved. In the latter case, assets are concerned which are, though still owned, not in actual possession of the owner but of another person, that is, the adverse possessor. The problem of adverse possession regards both the relationship of the adverse possessor with third parties and the real owner (see Chapter 8 in this volume). In both cases, however, the problem of the definition of possession arises. In the first case because first possession constitutes often the legal base of initial acquisition. In the second case, in order to determine who is entitled to claim the protection, the possessor enjoys against third parties, and to determine the start of prescription periods.

2. First appropriation, auction or contracts?

The rule of first appropriation ('first come, first served'; 'finders keepers') is firmly rooted in Western legal culture and social practice. Also in state of nature situations, such as the allocation of parking places on the street (Epstein, 2002) and seats in a restaurant, people spontaneously respect the position of the first occupant. Probably the possessive advantage, due to the fact that drive out-costs are on average higher than defence-costs, explains a lot of this spontaneous attitude.

Legal rules, endorsing first appropriation, are often considered as expressions of a democratic and egalitarian spirit. Everyone has an equal chance at the start, without regard to his class-status, race or religion. The *American Homestead Act* of 1862 is probably one of the most striking examples of this egalitarian philosophy (Allen, 1991; Lueck, 1995). The act allowed families to claim 160 acres of land, a surface considered as sufficient to feed a large farmer's family. At the payment of around 10 dollars and the uninterrupted occupation of the claimed land during five years, the claimants obtained a valid title. The Act was applicable to the vast federal territories, west of the Mississippi-Missouri. About 250,000,000 acres were patented under the Act.

Under *Roman law*, first appropriation (*occupatio*) was possible for goods not belonging to anybody (*quae antea nullius erant*), such as wild animals, for goods taken from enemies (*quae ex hostibus capiuntur*), for abandoned goods (*res derelictae*) (see Gaius 2, 66; see D. 41,1,1,1–7; D. 41,7,1. Van Oven, 1948). For *treasure trove* (*thesaurus*) finders keepers applied when the treasure was found in the finders land. When another found the treasure half of the treasure accrued to the finder, half to the owner (see I, 2, 1, 39). Van Oven 1948; see also art. 716 Belgian and French C.C.).

The *Common law* upholds also a rule of first appropriation concerning non-owned things such as wild animals, as is illustrated by the famous case of *Pierson v. Post* (3 Cai. R., 175, N.Y. Supreme Court, 1805 – see further). First appropriation is also deeply rooted in *liberal legal philosophy*. According to John Locke first appropriation through mixing labour with the land constituted the only way of initial acquisition in the state of nature. As Western colonists considered Native Americans as still living under a state of nature, Lockean philosophy provided them with an argument to homestead freely land in America (Grunebaum, 1987; Tully, 1994). While the first appropriation rule is firmly rooted in our legal tradition and social practices, many economic studies criticize this solution as an inefficient rule (Anderson and Hill, 1990; Barzel, 1968; Libecap and Wiggins, 1984; Merrill, 1986).

Before discussing the economic merits or shortcomings of the first appropriation rule, we have to make an important distinction between the possession of a *resource stock* and the possession of *resource flows* (Lueck, 1995). In the first case the possessor, able to control the stock in a stable way has the prospect to future flows of this stock. In the second case, the possessor, unable to control the stock as such, is only able to capture flows once they are generated by the stock.

Examples of the two categories are:

Table 5.1 Stock–flow distinction

Resource Stock	*Resource Flow*
– fields	crops
– cattle	meat, milk
– real estate	rents
– copyright	royalties
– money	interests
– ocean	fisheries
– streams, rivers	water
– aquifer	water
– woods	wild game
– oil wells	oil

The discussion about the efficiency of initial acquisition rules has another dimension in cases of stock possession than in cases allowing only flow capture. Consequently the case of stock possession is discussed first.

Several economic analyses point out that first appropriation rules concerning resource stock provoke a race among potential claimants, by which ownership is established *too early*. This may lead to *a full dissipation of the rental stream of the asset*. In order to show this source of inefficiency, a comparison is made with the situation in which only *a single claimant* is interested in establishing ownership of a stock resource. It is assumed also that the flow value *grows over time*, due to increases in the demand for the asset caused, for instance, by population growth (Lueck, 1995, 398).

Under these assumptions the optimal time *tx* to establish ownership for a single claimant is the point where the marginal return from waiting equals the marginal cost of waiting. The return from waiting consists of the returns of alternative activities, the single claimant can pursue by desisting temporarily from establishing stock possession. These returns are declining over time. The costs of waiting consist of the value of the stock flows missed during the waiting and as it was assumed that these flow values grow over time, marginal costs of waiting are increasing.

When a first appropriation rule opens an *unconstrained competition among many potential claimants* and these claimants are more or less homogeneous (more or less at an equal starting point in the race due to equality of physical strength, investments and information), rents will be entirely dissipated.

In case of a competitive rush between potential claimants to claim rights a claim is worth staking as long as the net value of the asset is positive. As a consequence the ownership will be established at *tR*, when the present value of the rental flow equals the present value of the entire costs of establishing ownership at *tR*. Rights are, compared with the single-claimant situation, established too early. The race equilibrium implies that the rental stream is fully dissipated. In addition, unconstrained competitive races involve also the costs of the not awarded claimants. Their efforts in the race are pointless *ex post*.

Homogeneity among potential claimants is, however, very unlikely. Several factors in the real world cause heterogeneity among claimants by which a full dissipation of rental streams of resource stock does not occur. Heterogeneity in this context does not refer to the variance of distribution of the costs of establishing ownership among potential claimants, but to the cost gaps between the lowest cost-contenders.

The distribution of costs in Figure 5.1b is at greater variance than in Figure 5.1a, yet heterogeneity, as understood in this context, is higher in the distribution of costs in Figure 5.1a because the differences between the

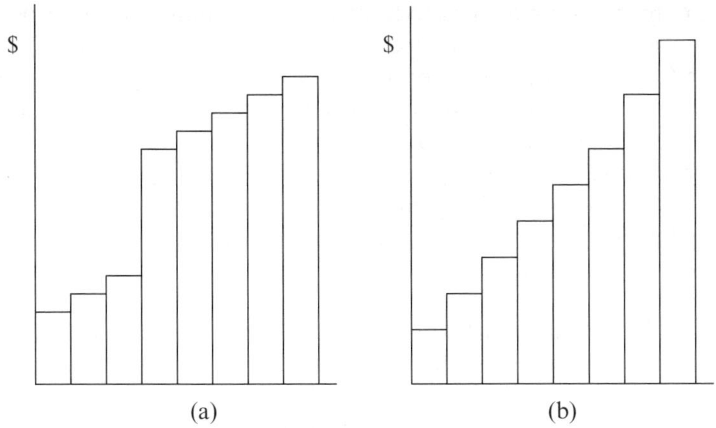

Figure 5.1 *Relevant cost-heterogeneity among race-contenders*

lowest cost-contenders, the ones most likely to participate to the race, and the higher cost-contenders, are larger.

In the case of relevant heterogeneity the lowest cost-contender may enjoy such an advantage to the next best contender that his appropriative behaviour becomes similar to that of a single claimant, by which appropriation at an efficient time may occur. Heterogeneity of potential claimants can be the result of different factors such as unequal distribution of talents and information, an historical advantage in investment, or random factors. It can be diminished by investments, for instance a company investing in research capacity in order to fill the gap with a competitor who had started already his rush to a patentable invention. The other factors are, however, important enough to preserve in most cases a decisive margin of heterogeneity.

Beside natural factors such as uneven distribution of talents and random factors, heterogeneity can also be preserved by an institutional factor. Possession can be defined in such way that competitive races are excluded. The finders keepers rule, for instance, attaches crucial legal importance to the random fact of finding, so that competitive rushes become impossible.

As a consequence, one must conclude that a first appropriation rule does not lead necessarily to full dissipation of rents. When heterogeneity among potential claimants is guaranteed, dissipation will be avoided and property rights will be established on the efficient point in time.

Auction is the most prominent alternative for a first appropriation rule. This procedure presupposes a pre-appropriation by a third party, such as public authorities, pretending to have a general claim on assets, especially land, on the basis of legal prerogatives such as eminent domain, or the right to the spoils of conquest or discovery. These pre-appropriated assets are then submitted to an auction procedure, through which the asset is allotted to the highest bidder. By this procedure, it is argued, assets are on average allotted to the most efficient users. The users expecting the highest return of the asset will consequently bid away with the highest offers. This market mimicking procedure implies, however, also some costs. Lueck considers three cost-categories (Lueck, 1995, 403):

(1) Defining the auctioned assets: an auction requires a definition of the auctioned assets; such a definition requires costly information (search costs, prospecting, and valuation) about the assets in order to avoid the so-called winners' curse. Bidders underestimating systematically the risks involved with the possession and exploitation of the asset, may win the auction. The bad bidders drive out the good bidders (Hansen and Thomas, 1999). Such costs can be prohibitively high, so that an auction procedure has to be written off for initial acquisition. An extreme example in this respect regards inventions. In order to auction them, the auctioneer has to invent them first, in order to define them. A first to invent policy, which allots the intellectual property to the inventor himself, is obviously much cheaper because it avoids the transaction costs between inventor and auctioneer, and auctioneer and bidders.

(2) Costs of the auction: auctions are costly, not only on the side of the auctioneer, but also on the side of potential bidders.

(3) Costs of protection of property rights: in order to auction, the auctioneer has to secure property rights on the auctioned assets.

According to Lueck a trade-off exists in the choice between the two main alternatives, that is, first appropriation or auction, between two categories of costs: the efficiency losses due to too early establishment of property rights in competitive races on one hand, and the different costs of auction procedures on the other hand. In particular two factors are decisive in this respect: the heterogeneity-homogeneity of potential claimants for the cost levels of first appropriation; and the possibilities to define and to evaluate *ex ante* the concerned assets for cost levels of auction (Lueck, 1995, 403).

Anderson and Hill perceive a third method of original assignment of property rights (Anderson and Hill, 2002). Races and auction are both the outcome of top-down procedures as they are exclusively driven by political processes. Anderson and Hill distinguish a bottom-up entrepreneurial alternative in which property rights are established by contracts.

This is possible either by specific or by general contracting. In case of specific contracting, i.e. between individuals, groups or corporations, the property establishing contract involves two aspects: a) a contract of the original holder with a new holder transferring the asset; b) a contract of the original and new holder and with all involved third parties in which the latter promise to respect the property right of the new holder. By general contracting the second aspect is embedded in a general law binding all members of a polity.

The establishment of property rights through contracting is driven by entrepreneurs, perceiving opportunities in a rearrangement or redefinition of property rights, allowing them to capture Ricardian rents from the scarcity of resources which cannot be replicated. The property rights' entrepreneur is alert to Ricardian rents, not perceived by others but derived from better-defined and better-enforced property rights.

The establishment of property rights on the Western frontier in the United States during the nineteenth century is the theatre par excellence of the contractual way. The customary range rights evolved from the simple priority principle and the claiming of land in an inexpensive way (e.g. by notification in newspapers) to refined systems of specific contracting. Cattlemen associations organized in the West a network of contracts aiming at preserving individual ownership on herds, affording protection of the herds, and controlling the grazing of the open range in order to avoid overcrowding. Roundup districts acted as exclusion systems towards interlopers. The system of specific contracts was gradually supplanted by the Washington-driven homestead laws. According to Anderson and Hill this law proved to be largely inefficient when applied to the big plains of the Midwest. The homesteading destroyed specific contracting networks, based on practical experience. The landholding units in the homestead laws were inappropriate because they were too small for more arid areas. This led to disasters such as the dust bowl in Oklahoma during the 1930s. Homesteading laws encouraged racing, thereby stimulating homogeneity of the participants. Settlements were premature and inappropriate investments were stimulated (Anderson and Hill, 2002). The belief in the sustainability of agriculture in arid zones on too small plots was stimulated by false folk wisdom such as the myth of 'rain follows the plow' or dry-farming-doctrine (Libecap and Hansen, 2001). The most dramatic episode of imposition of inefficient homesteading laws concerns the race on the Cherokee outlet, destroying an elaborated network of specific contracting, set up by the Cherokee Livestock Association (Anderson and Hill (2002), Lefebvre, 1992; Newsom, 1992). Anderson and Hill explain the inefficiency of the homestead laws by the lack of a residual claimant in the lawmaking process. This in contrast with the process of specific contracting, in which all involved parties were residual claimants (Anderson and Hill, 2002, 512).

3. Rules of capture

When the establishment of property rights on an entire stock is too costly, because exclusion costs are prohibitively high, property rights will only prevail on the flow of the stock (Lueck, 1995, 422). Sometimes property assignment is limited to flows of output because extraction is more easily measured than the stock itself (Libecap, 2006, 8). For instance, instead of establishing property rights on an entire oil well underground, property rights are only possible on pumped oil; instead of establishing property rights on herds of wild animals, property rights are only possible on captured and killed game; instead of establishing property rights on entire streams or rivers, property rights can only be established on water taken from them.

Capturing only flows creates risks of *an open access dissipation* (see also Chapter 4 in this volume). With an increasing number of users the marginal return to the effort of using declines. Due to the lack of any restriction, the number of users increases until the marginal return is equal to the marginal effort, which means that all rents from the flow of the resource are dissipated (Lueck, 1995, 403). Take, for instance, a river in an arid area, submitted to an open-access regime of capture. The evolution of returns is as follows:

Table 5.2

Number of Users	Effort Cost	Average Return	Total Profit
10	10	100	900
20	10	90	1600
30	10	80	2100
40	10	70	2400
50	**10**	**60**	**2500**
60	10	50	2400
70	10	35	1750
80	10	20	800
90	**10**	**10**	**0**
100	10	0	-1000

The optimal amount of users is 50 while under an open-access regime additional users will appear until the cost of effort is equal to the average return. Consequently, the number of users will increase up to the number of 90. At that number profits of water use are zero and rents are entirely dissipated.

This theory suggests that several institutions, legal as well as customary, which regulate flow capture, can be explained as attempts to solve or to alleviate this problem of overuse. We can distinguish the following ones:

3.1 Common property arrangements and regulations

The open access is restricted to some users. By this a kind of common property on the asset is introduced, the commoners being the ones entitled to capture. This can lead to more optimal use-levels. On the other hand exclusion costs may increase. Because there is an inverse relationship between exclusion costs and the number of included, the trade-off between exclusion costs and costs of rent dissipation may lead to a number of users, which is higher than the optimal amount (Lueck, 1995, 406). Examples of such a common-property arrangements are:

(1) Riparian rights: the system of riparian rights prevails in England and in the eastern American states. It is based on old common-law doctrine. Water rights are tied to ownership of land, bordering the water. Owners (or people with a derived right) of such land are entitled to correlative and reasonable use of the water. The water rights cannot be sold apart from the land (Lueck, 1995, 427; Rose, 1990). The system creates a common property regime of landowners adjacent to the water. Due to the restriction the users are able to control each other in order to prevent overuse and dissipation. The common property regime by the bordering landowners permits also a low-cost control. Downstream owners will suffer from overuse or pollution from upstream owners and will react quite swiftly. The setting up of expensive overarching control agencies can be avoided in this way. In the west of the United States the prior appropriation rule prevailed (Lueck, 1995; Libecap, 2006, 28). This rule allowed possession of a stock of water also for non-riparian owners. Lueck explains the difference with the Eastern rule by the extensive diversion of water away from riparian land, such as mining and irrigation (Lueck, 1995, 428)

(2) The commons: in most villages in Europe some land, such as wasteland and pasture-land, was held in commons. All families of the village were entitled to use this land for game keeping, for gathering dead wood and for grazing their cattle. Because the villages were involved in long-term and multiplex relationships, rules on overuse were easy to implement. In fact, most historical commons do not reflect the dramatic picture of the tragedy of the commons as depicted by Hardin (Ellickson, 1993; Lueck, 1995, 422). As far as arable land was concerned a semi-commons prevailed (Smith, 2000). Between the early spring and the time of harvesting private

property on the strips of arable land prevailed. During late autumn and winter the fields were used for grazing the cattle of the whole village. By rotating private and commons regimes the farmers were able to maximize the use of their land for crop growing as well as for cattle raising purposes. This semi-commons system collapsed with the development of large inter-regional markets for agricultural products. These markets allowed land being exclusively used either for crop growing or for cattle raising (Smith, 2000; Stahl-Rolf, 1998; Stahl-Rolf, 2000).

(3) Wild game: in feudal England, the right to capture game was a privilege enjoyed by feudal lords. This restriction, based on class origin, limited access and probably prevented inefficient over-hunting (Lueck, 1995, 424). It was expected that the collapse of this feudal privilege system would lead to overuse and rapidly declining populations of wild game. This was effectively the case at the beginning of the French Revolution, when all farmers suddenly started to hunt pigeons and rabbits, mainly in order to protect their crops (Shama, 1989). As a consequence, strict regulation had to be imposed to control the hunting of game in France. Also in England, game hunting privileges were abolished during the nineteenth century and ownership rights to wild game were granted to all landowners. The effect was, however, far less dramatic in England than in France. The enclosure movement had created large consolidated holdings. This permitted large wild game stocks to live on a few holdings. Agreements to control game capture remained as a consequence easy to reach and to implement. In America, with its scattered private landholdings (see also the Homestead Act) and its wide-ranging species, control of game capture by private owners was difficult, so states were granted extensive regulatory control over the access and use of wildlife.

(4) Unitization contracts: by contracts between those with surface access to oil and gas they coordinate their actions in order to mitigate rule of capture waste. Access to oil and gas underlying numerous surface holdings is limited through space-requirements limiting density of wells and prevent adjacent surface owners from drilling along their property lines to deplete their neighbours' reserves. States also compel the formation of reservoir units, if a supermajority of the surface owners agree (Lueck, 1995, 426).

3.2 Intensive and stable group interaction

As mentioned already in quoted examples, multiplex relationships between the members of the capturing community will stimulate spontaneous (that is, not imposed and not enforced by an external authority) restriction of the use of flows and the prevention of open-access dissipation. If some members of the same community care more than others about the common and the future wealth of it (moral entrepreneurs) they will be able to develop restrictive rules and practices, which can be enforced by second-party control (tit for tat, because multiplex relationships imply repeated games) and by third-party control, based on gossip and reputation (Ellickson, 1991). Historical examples of such close-knit societies, restricting spontaneously the capture of flows, are easy to find: the 'commons' of agricultural villages; hunting and fishing rights in tribal societies (Johnsen, 1986); customs of lobstermen in Maine (Acheson, 1989).

3.3 Maintaining homogeneous group membership by equal contingent rules

Often groups whose members are entitled to flow capture apply a rule following which each member is entitled to a same amount of capture. At first sight such a rule seems to be inefficient, as the highly productive capturer will spend too little effort, while the less productive too much. It is possible, however, that equal-contingent rules are maintained in order to stimulate homogeneity of group membership. These rules force a group to preserve homogeneity by screening potential members, by indoctrination and by limiting the transfer of membership rights (see below) (Lueck, 1995, 408).

By preserving homogeneity the group prevents the more efficient capturers from eliciting a race for capturing, which leads to overuse and open-access dissipation. As an historical example we can quote the equal access of English villagers to the common resources (pasture – grass, estover – wood, diggings – coal and stones, turbary – turf and peat, piscary – fish) (Lueck, 1995, 422).

3.4 Restriction of transfer of the right to capture

Restrictions of trade are usually inefficient as they hamper the allocation to the highest bidder, on average the most efficient user of the good. When property rights can be established on entire stocks, limits to transfer, which might have existed for religious and military reasons, tend to disappear. The gradual commodification of land in European legal history serves as an example. When rights can only be established on flows of stock, the restriction of transfer may find its economic rationale in the preservation of homogeneous membership and the avoiding of open-access dissipation (Lueck, 1995, 409). When rights of capture are transferable a rapid decline of homogeneity may be expected as rights will be always traded to more efficient users, offering a price which is higher than the expected capture returns of the present user. Consequently, trade of capture rights will lead to heterogeneity of users, possibly leading to a race for capturing.

Examples of such restrictions of trade are: the rights of English villagers to the commons, the right of riparian owners to use water for household consumption. Also the US/UK distinction concerning the trade of wildlife products can be explained by the different property situation of wildlife stocks. In the United States this trade is submitted to severe restrictions. Concerning wildlife stocks a rule of capture exists. Harvest pressure on the flow is limited by trade restrictions. In the UK rights on wildlife stocks are well defined and privately held. As a result trade serves only to generate wealth and does not dissipate the value of the stock (Lueck, 1995, 424).

4. Definition of possession as a title for initial acquisition

Under a rule of first appropriation the person who took the first control over the concerned asset becomes the owner. This apparently simple rule is, however, often difficult to apply to practical cases as questions may arise about the concrete acts and signs necessary to establish factual control. This is illustrated by the famous case *Pierson v. Post, 1805*. Post was hunting a fox on an unowned beach. He almost had the beast in his sights when an interloper appeared, killed the fox and ran off with the carcass. Post sued on the theory that his pursuit established his property right to the fox. The court, however, decided otherwise, arguing that only the one who killed or at least mortally wounded the animal and thereby bringing it under a certain control had a claim to ownership. One can find similar cases in all legal systems, about which long doctrinal debates developed. Does economics have to say anything in this debate? Can we develop an economic criterion for an efficient definition of possession in order either to apply the first appropriation rule or to fix the beginning of prescription in case of adverse possession? From an economic point of view the definition of possession should meet two criteria: clarity and stimulation of heterogeneity of potential claimants.

4.1 Clarity

The acts and circumstances which serve as a sign of possession should be clear and unambiguous to the members of the legal community. They must reveal in a clear way one's intent to appropriate. By linking ownership rights to unambiguous, visible signs of possession further inefficient racing for a specific asset and endless trials about possession are avoided. The preference for clarity is illustrated by the famous case *Brumagin v. Bradshaw* (39 Cal. 24 1870; Rose, 1985). The case concerned a considerable amount of land in the Potrero district of San Francisco. Before this land had become a residential and commercial area, it had been settled by a certain George Treat, who pastured livestock on the land. The party which claimed through Treat alleged that the latter had repaired a fence across the neck of the Potrero peninsula. The other party alleged that outsiders could still land in boats and that there was a gap in the fence. The court ruled that a jury should consider whether Treat's fences gave sufficient notice to the public that he had appropriated the property.

Also in the case *Pierson v. Post*, the court ruled in favour of Pierson, who killed the fox and took the carcass. The court decided in favour of the party which had put itself in the clearest position of possession and about which uninformed outsiders would most likely recognize the possession. The preference for clarity in the definition of possession implies also a trade-off between inefficient racing and litigation costs on one hand, and the impairing of incentives of efficient appropriation by saucy intruders on the other hand. In the case *Pierson v. Post*, Pierson free-rode on the efforts of Post. Such a ruling could stimulate free riders' attitudes in general, by which efficient appropriative behaviour would be hampered and suboptimal appropriation levels would prevail (Rose, 1985). Dharmapala and Pitchford analyze the dissenting opinion of Justice Livingstone in this case and reach some different conclusions. Flushing out foxes by hounds and killing the foxes are not substitutes but are fully complementary. The rule, adopted by the court, might have been socially suboptimal when killing foxes in order to protect farmers was the main social objective. As most foxes were not hunted in open access land, as was the case in *Pierson v. Post*, and as the case was driven by very personal concerns of honour, the social loss of the ruling of the court was probably minimal. According to the model of Dharmapala and Pitchford, however, the Livingstone rule seems to be the optimal one in other circumstances and not the rule of the court (Dharmapala and Pitchford, 2002).

4.2 Stimulation of heterogeneity among claimants

As mentioned already (see Section 2) the dissipation of rental streams is the highest when potential claimants are homogeneous. By defining possession in a certain way it is possible to influence the homogeneity-heterogeneity level of potential claimants and to prevent rent dissipation to a certain extent. As a consequence, some possession rules may find their economic rationale in the stimulation of claimants' heterogeneity. The following examples can be given:

(1) Finders keepers rule for finds: this rule applies often for treasure trove, abandoned property (voluntary parting) and lost property (involuntary parting). Salvage rules under maritime law, however, allow for a division of the spoils (sunken ship and their cargo) between finder and the former owner (Hallwood and Miceli, 2006). Art. 716 Code Civil (Belgium–France) also allows for a fifty–fifty division of treasure trove

between finder and owner, when the treasure is found on somebody else's land (see also art. 939 Code Civil Quebec) (Dukeminier and Krier, 1993; Lueck, 1995, 413). The finders keepers rule limits competition among potential claimants to time 'first come first served', by which appropriation becomes largely dependent on random factors. Consequently, other potential claimants than the finder are not able to eliminate heterogeneity by investments.

(2) Telepossession: in the case *Columbus-American Discovery Group Inc. v. Atlantic Mutual Ins. Co.*, 1992 [974, F. 2d 450–4th Cie 1992] (Lueck, 1995, 413) the court allowed the establishment of rights on a sunken treasure through the use of remote video cameras which produced live images. It did not require physical possession, but coined the term telepossession. By such a definition of possession in this case the court maximized heterogeneity among sea explorers and prevented costly duplication in exploration.

(3) The Homestead Act 1862: this already mentioned Act (see Section 2) seems to refute the thesis of efficient definition of possession. Rather, the procedures of this act concentrated on stimulating the homogeneity of potential claimants through publicly announcing and promoting the homesteading of the concerned areas. Further elements of the historical context of this act, however, offer an explanation of these procedures. On the one hand, auctioneering and land sale by the government, the most used procedure prior to the Homestead Act, proved to be too costly for the frontier (definition and division of land tracts). On the other hand, squatting on the land at the frontier increased rapidly, which created rising problems for protecting the squatters against Native American tribes and criminal gangs. By opening blocks of land tracts to the public, by organizing races among many potential claimants for these tracts, dense settlement of land was promoted, by which land enforcement costs were mitigated (Allen, 1991; Lueck, 1995, 414). This conclusion is, however, contested by Anderson and Hill, who contend that the Homestead Act was inefficient, certainly for the more arid lands in the West. The inefficiency of the Act can be explained by the lack of residual claimants (Anderson and Hill, 2002, 506)

(4) Hard rock mining: the American General Mining Law of 1872 establishes a first appropriation rule for mineral rights on public lands. The miner who discovers a valuable mineral deposit, locates the claim and does the assessment work, can apply for a patent. While prospecting, he is protected by the doctrine of *pedis possessio*. The law protects the possession

of the miner in order to obtain a patent eventually later on, at the moment when heterogeneity is the highest, that is, at the moment of the discovery (Lueck, 1995, 416).

(5) Intellectual property: for this type of property, mostly a first to invent policy is followed by applying the rule of acquisition by creation (Dukeminier and Krier, 1993).

The auction alternative would only be possible here after the invention or creation, which would impair incentives for research or artistic creativity a lot. Several studies point to the fact that the law tends to grant the invention ownership very early, when claimant heterogeneity is still large. Also courts tend to grant broad patent protection when a new invention signals room for many improvements, thus preventing a race for ownership. When an idea has limited room for improvement, only a narrow protection is granted (Grady and Alexander, 1992).

(6) Whaling norms: as for wild game the rule of first appropriation may pose a problem for whale fishing. Often whales are pursued by one ship, harpooned by another and, after breaking loose, killed and captured by a third ship. Customary rules were developed among whalers which reflect the avoidance of wasteful races by fixing possession at the moment of high heterogeneity. Such rules were sometimes upheld by court decision such as the rule that the first party to shoot the whale with a 'bomb-lance', gained rights over it (see *Gehn v. Rich* [8F.159 (1881)]; Dharmapala and Pitchford, 2002, 45). These rules differed, however, according to the kind of whale being fished. When the right whale, a docile kind of whale, was mostly fished, whalers applied the 'fast fish-loose fish' rule, that is, the whaling boat which kept the whale to the boat with the harpoon was the owner. If the whale got loose, it was open again for catching. This rule preserved maximum heterogeneity. When whale fishery turned more to the catching of sperm whales, a very energetic kind, whalers applied the 'iron holds the whale' rule, that is, even when the fish got loose but the boat whose harpoon was in the whale remained in fresh pursuit, this boat preserved its possession. The other rule became unpractical because sperm whales, once harpooned, could sink the boat by diving. As a consequence, a rule which preserved heterogeneity too, but was less dangerous, was applied (Ellickson, 1991, 195).

Bibliography

Acheson, James M. (1989), 'Where have all the Exploiters Gone? Co-management of the Maine Lobster Industry', in *Common Property Resources: Ecology and Community-Based Sustainable Development*, London, Belhaven, Fikret Berkes, 199–217.

Alexander, Larry and Wang, William K.S. (1984), 'Natural Advantages and Contractual Justice', **3** *Law and Philosophy*, 281–297. Reprinted in *Contract Law*, vol. 2, International Library in Law and Legal Theory, 1991, 453–469.

Allen, Douglas W. (1991), 'Homesteading and Property Rights; or "How the West Was Really Won"', **34** *Journal of Law and Economics*, 1–23.

Alston, Lee, Libecap, Gary D. and Schneider, Robert (1996) 'The Determinants and Impact of Property Rights: Land Titles on the Brazilian Frontier', **12** *Journal of Law, Economics and Organization*, 1, 25–61.

Anderson, Terry L. and Hill, Peter J. (1983), 'Privatizing the Commons: An Improvement?', **50** *Southern Economic Journal*, 438–450.

Anderson, Terry L. and Hill, Peter J. (1990), 'The Race for Property Rights', **33** *Journal of Law and Economics*, 177–197.

Anderson, Terry L. and Hill, Peter J. (2002), 'Cowboys and Contracts', **31** *Journal of Legal Studies*, 2, 489–514

Annen, Kurt (2006), 'Property rights assignment: conflict and the implementability of rules', **7** *Economics of Governance*, 155–166.

Bailey, Martin J. (1992), 'Approximate Optimality of Aboriginal Property Rights', **35** *Journal of Law and Economics*, 183–198.

Barnes, David W. and Stout, Lynn A. (1992), *Economics of Property Rights and Nuisance Law*, St Pauls, West Publishing.

Barzel, Yoram (1968), 'Optimal Timing of Innovations', **50** *Review of Economics and Statistics*, 348–355.

Benson, Bruce L. (1989), 'Enforcement of Private Property Rights in Primitive Societies: Law without Government', **9** *Journal of Libertarian Studies*, 1–26.

Benson, Bruce L. (1990), 'Customary Law with Private Means of Resolving Disputes and Dispensing Justice: A Description of a Modern System of Law and Order Without State Coercion', **9** *Journal of Libertarian Studies*, 25–42. Reprinted as 'Law and Order without State Coercion', in Veljanovski, Cento (ed.) (1991), *Regulation, Regulators and the Market*, London, Institute of Economic Affairs, 159–179.

Benson, Bruce L. (1991a), 'Reciprocal Exchange as the Basis for Recognition of Law: Examples from American History', **10** *Journal of Libertarian Studies*, 53–82.

Benson, Bruce L. (1991b), 'An Evolutionary Contractarian View of Primitive Law: The Institutions and Incentives Arising Under Customary American Indian Law', **5** *Review of Austrian Economics*, 65–89.

Benson, Bruce L. (1992), 'The Evolution of Values and Institutions in a Free Society: The Under-Pinnings of a Market Economy', **5** *International Journal on the Unity of Sciences*, 411–442. Reprinted in Radnitzky, Gerard and Bouillon, Hardy (eds) (1995), *Values and the Social Order Vol.I*, Aldershot, Ashgate, 87–125.

Benson, Bruce L. (1993), 'The Impetus for Recognizing Private Property and Adopting Ethical Behavior in a Market Economy: Natural Law, Government Law, or Evolving Self-Interest', **6** *Review of Austrian Economics*, 43–80.

Benson, Bruce L. (1994), 'Emerging from the Hobbesian Jungle: Might Takes and Makes Rights', **5** *Constitutional Political Economy*, 129–158. Translated into Spanish and republished (1995), *Las Instituciones y Los Derechos de Propiedad al Emerger de la Jungla Hobbesiana: La Fuerza Quita los Reprinted Derechos y los Crea Libertas*, 12, 35–75.

Benson, Bruce L. (1995), 'Competition Among Legal Institutions: Implications for the Evolution of Law', in Gerken, Luden (ed.), *Competition Among Institutions*, London, Macmillan, 153–175.

Braunstein, Michael (1985), 'Natural Environments and Natural Resources: An Economic Analysis and New Interpretation of the General Mining Law', **32** *UCLA Law Review*, 1133–1202.

Bulow, Jeremy and Klemperer, Paul, 'Why do Sellers (Usually) Prefer Auctions?', **99(4)** *American Economic Review*, 1544–1575.

Cooter, Robert D. (1991a), 'Economic Theories of Legal Liability', **5** *Journal of Economic Perspectives*, 11–30. Reprinted in Medema, Steven G. (ed.), *The Legacy of Ronald Coase in*

Economic Analysis, Cheltenham, Edward Elgar Publishing, forthcoming. Italian translation: 'Le Teorie Economiche della Risponsibilità Efficenza Produttiva: Alcuni Contributi su Noti Argomenti', published in Gianandrea Goisis.

Cooter, Robert D. (1991b), 'Inventing Market Property: The Land Courts of Papua New Guinea', **25** *Law and Society Review*, 759–801.

Cooter, Robert D. (1992), 'Organization as Property: Economic Analysis of Property Law and Privatization', in Clague, Christopher and Rausser, Gordon (eds), *The Emergence of Market Economies in Eastern Europe*, Oxford, Blackwell, 77–97.

Demsetz, Harold (1972), 'Wealth Distribution and the Ownership of Rights', **1** *Journal of Legal Studies*, 223–232.

Dennen, R. Taylor (1977), 'Some Efficiency Effects of Nineteenth-Century Federal Land Policy: A Dynamic Analysis', **44** *Agricultural History*, 718 ff.

Dharmapala, Dhamikka and Pitchford, Rohan (2002), 'An Economic Analysis of "Riding to Hounds": Pierson v. Post Revisited', **18** *The Journal of Law & Organisation*, N1, 39–65.

Dukeminier, Jesse and Krier, James E. (1993), *Property* (3rd edn), Boston, Little Brown.

Ellickson, Robert C. (1991), *Order without Law. How Neighbors Settle Disputes*, Cambridge, MA, Harvard University Press.

Ellickson, Robert C. (1993), 'Property in Land', **102** *Yale Law Journal*, 1315–1400.

Epstein, Richard A. (1986), 'Past and Future: The Temporal Dimension in the Law of Property', **64** *Washington University Law Quarterly*, 667–722.

Epstein, Richard A. (2001), 'Allocation of the Commons: Parking and Stopping on the Commons', *Olin Working Paper n° 134 and University of Chicago, Public Law Working Paper n° 15.*

Epstein, Richard A. (2002), 'The Allocation of the Commons: Parking on Public Roads', **31(2)** *Journal of Legal Studies*, 515–544.

Frech, H. Edward III (1970), 'Institutions for Allocating the Radio-TV Spectrum and the Vested Interests', **4(4)** *Journal of Economic Issues*, 23–37.

Frech, H. Edward III (1971), 'More on Efficiency in the Allocation on the Radio-TV Spectrum', **5(3)** *Journal of Economic Issues*, 100–104.

Frech, H. Edward III (1972), 'The Public Choice Theory of Murray N. Rothbard: A Modern Anarchist', **14** *Public Choice*, 143–154.

Frech, H. Edward III (1991), 'Review of Contracting for Property Rights, by Gary D. Libecap', **15** *Journal of Comparative Economics*, 536–538.

Furubotn, Eirik G. (1989), 'Distributional Issues in Contracting for Property Rights: Comment', **145** *Journal of Institutional and Theoretical Economics*, 25–31.

Gallastegui, M.C., Ibarra, E. and Macho-Stadler, I. (1993), 'Contratos de Pesca Desde la Perspectiva de la Teoría de la Agencia (Fishing Contracts from a Principal-Agency Viewpoint)', **20(2)** *Estudios de Economía, número especial sobre La Economía de la Incertidumbre y la Información*, 329–354.

Grady, Mark F. and Alexander, Jay I. (1992), 'Patent Law and Rent Dissipation', **78** *Virginia Law Review*, 305–350.

Grether, David M., Isaac, R. Mark and Plott, Charles R. (1989), *The Allocation of Scarce Resources. Experimental Economics and the Problem of Allocating Airport Slots*, Boulder, CO, Westview Press.

Grunebaum, James O. (1987), *Private Ownership*, London, Routledge and Kegan Paul, 53 ff.

Haddock, David D. (1986), 'First Possession versus Optimal Timing: Limiting the Dissipation of Economic Value', **64** *Washington University Law Quarterly*, 775 ff.

Hallwood, Paul and Miceli, J. Thomas (2006), 'Murky Waters: The Law and Economics of Salvaging Historic Shipwrecks', **35** *Journal of Legal Studies*, 285–303.

Hansen, Robert G. and Thomas, Randall S. (1999), 'The Efficiency of Sharing Liability for Hazardous Waste: Effects of Uncertainty over Damages', **19** *International Review of Law and Economics*, 135–157.

Haucap, Justus (2003), 'Telephone Number Allocation: A Property Rights Approach', **15** *European Journal of Law and Economics*, 91–109.

Hayhurst, William L. (1983), '"Dreamers" and the Patent System', *European Intellectual Property Review*, 263–265.
Hazlett, Thomas W. (1990), 'The Rationality of U.S. Regulation of the Broadcast Spectrum', **33** *Journal of Law and Economics*, 133–175.
Johnsen, D. Bruce (1986), 'The Formation and Protection of Property Rights among the Southern Kwakiutl Indians', **15** *Journal of Legal Studies*, 41–67.
Kaplow, Louis and Shavell, Steven (1996), 'Property Rules versus Liability Rules: An Economic Analysis', **109** *Harvard Law Review*, 713–790.
Laveleye, Emile De, 'De la Propriété et de ses Formes Primitives (Property and its Primitive Forms)', in Rottenberg, Simon (ed.), *Occupational Licensure and Regulation*, Washington, DC, American Enterprise Institute.
Lefebvre, Irene Sturm (1992), *Cherokee Strip in Transition: A Documentary*, Enid, Okla., Cherokee Strip Booster Club.
Levmore, Saul (1987), 'Variety and Uniformity in the Treatment of the Good-Faith Purchaser', **16** *Journal of Legal Studies*, 43–65.
Libecap, Gary D. (1989), 'Distributional Issues in Contracting for Property Rights', **145** *Journal of Institutional and Theoretical Economics*, 6–24.
Libecap, Gary D. (2006) 'The Assignment of Property Rights on the Western Frontier: Lessons for Contemporary Environmental and Resource Policy', *National Bureau of Economic Research*, Working Paper 12598.
Libecap, Gary D. and Wiggins, Steven (1984), 'Contractual Responses to the Common Pool: Prorationing of Crude Oil Production', **74** *American Economic Review*, 87–98.
Libecap, Gary D. and Hansen, Zeynep Kocabiyik (2001) '"Rain Follows the Plough" and Dryfarming Doctrine: The Climate Information Problem and Homestead Failure in the Upper Great Plains, 1890–1925', *National Bureau of Economic Research*, Working Paper 0127.
Lueck, Dean (1995), 'The Rule of First Possession and the Design of the Law', **38** *Journal of Law and Economics*, 393–436.
Lueck, Dean (1998), 'Auctions, Markets, and Spectrum Ownership: Comment on Moreton and Spiller', **41** *Journal of Law and Economics*, 717–724.
Lueck, Dean (1998), 'First Possession', in Newman, Peter (ed.), *The New Palgrave Dictionary of Economics and the Law*, London, Macmillan.
Mackaay, Ejan (1987), 'Le Paradoxe des Droits Acquis (The Paradox of Acquired Rights)', in X (ed.), *De 'l'Ancienne' à la 'Nouvelle' Economie. Essais à l'occasion de la dixième université d'été de la nouvelle économie*, Aix-en-Provence, Librairie de l'Université, 205–219.
Mackaay, Ejan (1990), 'Les Droits Intellectuels – Entre Propriété et Monopole (Intellectual Property Rights – Between Property and Monopoly)', **1** *Revue des Economistes et des Etudes Humaines*, 61–358.
McChesney, Fred S. (1990), 'Government as Definer of Property Rights: Indian Land Ownership, Ethnic Externalities, and Bureaucratic Budgets', **19** *Journal of Legal Studies*, 297–335.
Merrill, Thomas W. (1986), 'Roundtable Discussion: Symposium on Time, Property Rights and the Common Law', **64** *Washington University Law Quarterly*, 793–865.
Miceli, Thomas J. and Sirmans, C.F. (1995), 'An Economic Theory of Adverse Possession', **15** *International Review of Law and Economics*, 161–173.
Netter, Jeffrey M., Hersch, Philip L. and Manson, William D. (1986), 'An Economic Analysis of Adverse Possession Statutes', **6** *International Review of Law and Economics*, 217–228.
Newsom, D. Earl (1992), *The Cherokee Strip: Its History and Grand Opening*, Oklahoma, New Forums Press
Ramseyer, J. Mark (1989), 'Water Law in Imperial Japan: Public Goods, Private Claims, and Legal Convergence', **18** *Journal of Legal Studies*, 51–77.
Rolph, Elizabeth S. (1983), 'Government Allocation of Property Rights: Who Gets What?', **3** *Journal of Policy Analysis and Management*, 45–61.
Rose, Carol M. (1985), 'Possession as the Origin of Property', **52** *University of Chicago Law Review*, 73–88.

Rose Carol M. (1990), 'Energy and Efficiency in the Realignment of Common-Law Water Rights', **19** *Journal of Legal Studies*, 261 ff.

Rose-Ackerman, Susan (1985), 'Inalienability and the Theory of Property Rights', **85** *Columbia Law Review*, 931–969. Reprinted in Epstein, R. (ed.) (2007), *Economics of Property Law*, Cheltenham, Edward Elgar Publishing, 421–459.

Rouland, Norbert (1985), 'Lecture Anthropologique et Inter-culturelle des Systèmes Fonciers (Anthropology and Inter-cultural Reading of Systems of Property)', **1** *Destins du Droit de Propriété*, reprinted in Frech, H.E. (ed.), *Regulating Doctors' Fees: Competition, Benefits, and Controls under Medicare*, Washington, DC, American Enterprise Institute, 73 ff.

Rowe, Gerard C. (1992), 'Sachenrechtliche Ersitzungsregeln aus Okonomischer Sicht (An Economic Perspective on Limitations of Actions in Property Law)', **75** *Kritische Vierteljahresschrift der Gesetzgebung und Rechtswissenschaft*, 390–415.

Schanze, Erich (1989), 'Distributional Issues in Contracting for Property Rights: Comment', **145** *Journal of Institutional and Theoretical Economics*, 32–37.

Shama, Simon, (1989), *Citizens: a Chronicle of the French Revolution*, New York, Knopf.

Smith, Henry E. (2000), 'Semicommon Property Rights and Scattering in the Open Fields', **1** *Journal of Legal Studies*, 131–169.

Smith, Henry E. (2002), 'Exclusion versus Governance: Two Strategies for Delineating Property Rights', **31** *Journal of Legal Studies*, 2, 453–487.

Stahl-Rolf, Silke R. (1998), 'Transition Problems in the Russian Agricultural Sector: A Historical-Institutional Perspective', in Amin, Ash and Hausner, Jerzy (eds), *Beyond Market and Hierarchy: Interactive Governance and Social Complexity*, Cheltenham, Edward Elgar Publishing.

Stahl-Rolf, Silke R. (2000) 'Transition on the Spot. Historicity, Social Structure and Institutional Change', **28** *Atlantic Economic Journal*, 1–36

Stake, Jeffrey E. (1995), 'Loss Aversion and Involuntary Transfers of Title', in Malloy, Robin P. and Braun, Christopher K. (eds), *Law and Economics: New and Critical Perspectives*, New York, Peter Lang, 331–360.

Trebilcock, Michael J. (1988), 'The Role of Insurance Considerations in the Choice of Efficient Civil Liability Rules', **4** *Journal of Law, Economics, and Organization*, 243–265.

Tully, James (1994), 'Aboriginal Property and Western Theory: Recovering a Middle Ground', in Paul, Ellen Frankel, Miller, Fred D. Jr and Paul, Jeffrey (eds.), *Property Rights*, Social Philosophy and Policy Foundation, 158 ff.

Van Damme, E.E.C. (1997), 'Tien Misverstanden over Veilingen (Ten Misunderstandings about Auctions)', **82** *Economisch-Statistische Berichten*, 24–28.

Van Oven, J.C. (1948), *Leerboek van het Romeinsch Privaatrecht* (Roman Private Law Textbook), Leiden, Brill, 91 ff.

Wang, William K.S. (1982), 'Reflections on Contract Law and Distributive Justice: A Reply to Kronman', **34** *Hastings Law Journal*, 513–527.

Zimmerman, Martin B. (1988), 'Regulatory Treatment of Abandoned Property: Incentive Effects and Policy Issues', **31** *Journal of Law and Economics*, 127–144.

6 Decomposition of property rights

Jeffrey Evans Stake

1. Introduction

In light of the importance of property to the economic system and the tremendous attention to transaction costs since Coase (1960), it seems somewhat odd that the particular rules of English property law, which impose costs on land transactions, have received relatively little attention from economists. Perhaps this is because the English common-law system of property rules is both high enough in flexibility and generally low enough in administrative costs that it causes no large and obvious drag on commerce. Nevertheless, the rules governing subdivision or decomposition of property rights have received some attention from law and economics scholars (e.g., Shavell 2004, pp. 27–32). The purpose of this chapter is to review some of the literature relating to ways in which rights in land and other assets can be divided and suggest explanations for existing decompositions of property.

Economics and property law meet in at least two fundamentally different ways. In the standard analysis, researchers have attempted to determine the allocative and welfare effects of various legal rules and regimes. Both economists and lawyers have, in a positive vein, tried to explain and predict behavior of individuals and, in a normative vein, criticized the law and proposed reforms based on those predicted behaviors (e.g., Epstein 1982; Hirsch 1983). Second, economic analysis has occasionally (Posner 2007; Krier 1974) been used to explain the behavior of judges and, in so doing, to clarify vague legal rules and make the law more predictable. The latter is not an application of Public Choice theory, although the two have similar goals. It is instead an attempt to predict or explain the results of cases by developing specific hypotheses from the general proposition that the law leans toward efficient rules. This might be so because judges prefer efficient outcomes, or it might be the result of a Darwinian process of evolution toward efficient rules (Rubin 2007; Stake 2005).

Before an owner can divide her rights in land, she must both have some rights and have the right to transfer rights. One basic topic, therefore, in the decomposition of property is whether, and to what degree, private parties have the right to alienate their rights. In one sense, this is a definitional matter: is the right to transfer inherent in the bundle of sticks we call 'property'? The right of alienation is the first topic discussed below.

Once owners have the right to divide and transfer their interests, rights in land can be divided in at least four ways. First, and most obvious, land rights are divided spatially. In addition to the ordinary horizontal division of land by region, the common law allows vertical division into condominiums, useful for modern residential living, as well as surface estates and subsurface estates useful to mining firms. Although there are economic studies of the optimal size of landholdings for uses such as farming, the law and economics literature on spatial division of rights in land is not extensive. Perhaps this is because there is not much law to study. One major exception to this generalization is the substantial literature on takings law, within which one topic is whether geographic areas can be segmented by landowners hoping to establish an unconstitutional taking of a small part where the remaining portion has not been affected.

Second, land rights can be divided temporally. Indeed, under early English common law, a feudal tenant's land rights lasted no longer than he did. An obvious inefficiency of that system was that any lasting improvement made by the tenant to the land would redound to the benefit of the overlord. Perhaps in part to internalize these positive temporal externalities, the law soon allowed a tenant to acquire rights that would survive his death. This was accomplished by use of the ancient words 'and his heirs,' a phrase still found today. The literature on subdividing rights by time, including the substantial literature on landlord-tenant law, is discussed after alienation and tenurial systems.

Third, rights in land can be divided according to use. One person can enjoy nearly complete dominion over a piece of land while another person holds a right to put the land to some limited use, such as burying utility lines, harvesting timber, or driving across it to get to a landlocked parcel. The multiple and confusing common-law doctrines of covenants, equitable servitudes, easements and profits govern this area of law, along with more modern zoning rules imposed by legislative bodies. The common-law doctrines controlling private division of land by uses are discussed, jointly and severally, after temporal divisions.

Fourth, in the common law system, rights in land or any other asset can be divided by creating a trust. A trust divides ownership into rights to control, held by the trustee, and rights to enjoy, held by the beneficiaries. The trust is enjoying a resurgence of interest, in both financial and academic markets.

It is not hard to see the advantages of decomposing rights along some of these dimensions. An owner might have little use of some of his rights, and might find someone to whom they are worth more. The disadvantages of decomposition are sometimes harder to anticipate. Any subdivision raises possibilities of disputes along the line of division and, if that line is inadequately specified or monitored by the parties or their successors, externalities may flow from one subpart to another (Shavell 2004, p. 29). Another cost of dividing rights relates to the difficulty of reassembling them in the future when consolidated rights are more efficient.

A. 'Takings' doctrine

Decomposition of property rights has become an issue of constitutional importance in the United States. The Fifth Amendment prohibits the government from taking property without paying just compensation. One difficult issue is when to consider 'property' to have been 'taken'. If the government deprives an owner of all her rights in all her land, it has plainly taken property. It is also clear that the government cannot avoid a finding that it took property by decomposing the rights spatially or temporally and taking only a portion. If the government occupies half of the owner's land for ten years, that is just as surely a taking as a deprivation of all land forever. But the outcome of a takings claim becomes less predictable if the government decomposes the owner's rights along the dimension of use, prohibiting some uses and allowing others. Since the US Supreme Court's formula for resolving takings claims turns in part on the proportional degree of financial deprivation, aggrieved owners claiming compensation would like to decompose their rights, separating restricted uses from unrestricted uses in order to increase the percentage taken. Although owners have had little luck doing so, the US Supreme Court has said recently, in *Palazzolo v. Rhode Island* (2001), that the issue remains open.

In addition to percentage diminution, the US Supreme Court considers whether the regulation deprives the owner of distinct, investment-backed expectations. Thus the Court has decomposed uses according to how much the owner has invested in them. This uneconomic portion of takings doctrine has been defended by reference to the findings of experimental economics and psychology (Stake 1995). Depriving persons of longstanding uses carries especially high psychological costs, higher than would be recognized if the value of the loss were calculated by reference to the amount the owners would be willing to pay to acquire the rights taken. However, recent experiments by Zeiler and Plott (2005) have cast doubt on earlier conclusions.

B. Over-fractionalization

In addition to the specific doctrines discussed below, decomposition of property raises over-fractionalization issues that have recently received a good deal of attention. Productivity suffers when property is divided among too many owners (Dagan and Heller 2001). For example, land on Manhattan Island was cut up geographically into parcels that were presumably efficient for development in the nineteenth century. Larger parcels would be optimal today, but consolidating them is impeded by holdouts. One special case of over-divided rights is the anticommons, in which a number of people hold a right to exclude (Michelman 1982; Ellickson 1993; Heller 1998).

Fragmentation of intellectual property may prevent efficient use of knowledge (Heller and Eisenberg 1998) just as fragmentation of real estate may prevent efficient development of land. In both cases, holdouts may prevent assembly of the different rights into a package of the size most efficient for development in today's market. Depoorter and Parisi (2003) noted that if transaction costs are asymmetrical and dividing fragmented interests is easier than reconsolidating them, there will be a trend towards an ever increasing level of fractionalization in property. The *numerus clausus* principle has been heralded as a rule that helps limit decomposition to the efficient level (Heller 1999; Merrill and Smith 2000). There is an optimal standardization of rights that is determined by the trade off between utility of having more forms and the confusion they would engender (Merrill and Smith 2000). Hansmann and Kraakman (2002) argued that the law does not limit the forms of property so much as it regulates the types and degree of notice required to establish different sorts of property. These limitations aid verification of the ownership of rights offered for conveyance.

As technology has advanced, new land uses have created externalities more remote than those of land uses in the past. For example, chlorofluorocarbons, CFCs, degrade the ozone in the atmosphere, allowing greater penetration of ultraviolet radiation and increasing the risk of skin cancer in people far from the location at which the CFCs were released. Scientific advances have also increased our ability to detect remote effects of activities that were long thought to have only regional externalities. For example, the emission of carbon dioxide contributes to global climate change in ways that were not understood in the past and are not fully appreciated even at the present time. New technologies may create both commons and anticommons tragedies that are not easily solved using traditional rules of property law (Rose 1998 and 2002). New forms of property or decompositions of rights might, or might not, be useful in preventing the tragedies. Although the topic of governing a commons is closely related, its vast literature (e.g., Ostrom 1990) is outside the scope of this chapter.

2. Limited alienation of property – land tenure systems

The topic of land tenure systems sits between the general theory of property and the private subdivision of property rights. The question is what happens when private owners are not allowed to have full rights in land. A right sometimes missing from the property bundle is the right to alienate other rights.

By the Statute Quia Emptores in 1290, English landholders gained the right to transfer their interests to others without obtaining consent of the overlord, who in important ways played the role of the modern state. Prior to that time in England, and more recently in other places, landholders lacked complete freedom of alienation. From the date of statehood, all of the United States have allowed landowners to transfer their rights to others. So well ingrained is this right that it seems odd that it could be otherwise.

Despite a long heritage of free alienation, the United States government has not extended that right to many American Indians holding Reservation lands. As a result of various statutes and changes in policy, Indian Reservation lands are held in three types of tenure. Some Reservation lands are held in legal fee simple by individuals, both Native American and not, and are completely alienable. Some lands are held by Native American tribes, but legal title lies in the United States, so the tribes cannot alienate the lands. Similarly, some lands are held by individual Native Americans, with legal title resting in the United States, again with the result that the lands are inalienable.

Economic theory would predict that where rights cannot be transferred, productivity will suffer. Johnson (1972), applying the analysis of Coase (1960), Alchian (1963) and Demsetz (1964 and 1966) to land tenure, argued that restrictions on the sale of land reduce investment in land by making it difficult to borrow for improvements and by limiting an owner's ways of capturing his investment. He concluded that there must be freedom and legal enforcement of sale and rental contracts for a system of land tenure to facilitate wealth increases.

Rose-Ackerman (1985) argued that economic theory places too much confidence in private markets, and that restraints on alienation can efficiently exist as market corrections to externalities. Traditional economic remedies for externalities may be insufficient in the presence of high transaction costs. She concluded that in specific, enumerated instances restraints on alienation can advance efficiency.

The three types of land tenure existing on Indian Reservations presented Anderson and Lueck (1992) with an opportunity to study empirically the effects of tenure on land productivity. Where Native Americans cannot offer the land as security for a loan, costs of borrowing will be higher and capital investment will be lower. Where they cannot sell their interests, it becomes harder for an owner to gather parcels into a farm of optimum size. Difficulties in transfer during life increase the frequency of death-time transfers and thus the frequency of devolution by intestate succession which often divides ownership. Multiple ownership leads to decreased investment of labor by owners because the benefits of the effort will fall in part on other owners. Multiple ownership, which entails sharing of inputs and output, may also cause owners to avoid the most valuable use if the inputs to or outputs from such use are comparatively harder for multiple parties to monitor.

Anderson and Lueck found that per acre value of agricultural output is 85–90 percent lower on tribal-trust land than on fee-simple land and 30–40 percent lower on individual-trust land than on fee-simple land. Their study did not, however, eliminate the possibility that the lands held in individual or tribal trust were simply less productive lands than the average lands held in fee. They stated that the patterns of ownership appear random on the map, but untillable mountain peaks might also appear random on a map. They also argued that the determinants of value are probably different today than when the parcels were allotted, but that seems dubious for land in agricultural use today. The authors published data from the US Department of Agriculture relating to relative land quality. On average, trust land has a lower percentage of land in the top four land-capability categories, but the authors say that the difference is not sufficiently strong to reject the hypothesis that the land is equivalent. (Given the small number of observations on quality, N = 13, it would have taken a large difference in quality to reject the null hypothesis.) That the difference in rated capability is not strong enough to be significant does not mean that the difference might not indeed influence the actual land productivity. In addition, considering the obvious potential relationship between land quality and productivity, it is unfortunate that there were quality classification data for only 13 reservations.

Congress attempted to reduce the problems associated with divided ownership of American Indian lands by reducing the number of owners. The statute provided that, at the death of the owner, small fractional interests in individual trust lands would pass to the tribe instead of the intestate successors or devisees. This attempt to improve the productivity of Indian lands was struck down by the US Supreme Court (*Hodel v. Irving*, 1987), which held that depriving fractional interest holders of their ability to pass those interests at their death takes property without just compensation. Thus Congress's long history of failure in dealing with Indian lands continues.

Comparing the history of Congressional control of Indian ownership to English history shows the economic importance of a good fit between law and culture. In common-law England, when a landowner died his lands passed according to the rules of primogeniture, under which the eldest male child took full title. Primogeniture avoided fractional interests that could lead to ineffective use. By the time modern rules of intestate succession were adopted, hundreds of years of experience had created an English cultural expectation of individual ownership. The English tradition of individual ownership counteracted the tendency of the modern intestacy law to subdivide ownership; private transfers kept most lands from being shared by too many hands. The Native Americans, upon whom the US Government forced individual ownership and fractious laws of intestate succession, had a different cultural heritage, one of tribal ownership or no ownership at all. Native American culture, being less oriented toward individual control, did not counter the sterilizing tendency of the modern rules of heirship.

This relationship between culture and law is important for understanding third-world development. Demsetz (1967) contended that as resource values rise, individual property rights emerge to encourage more investment and better husbandry. However, Fitzpatrick (2006) argued that many developing regions still have open access and uncertain rights regimes because enforcement is unreliable. Other scholars have questioned whether Western individualized marketable property rights are optimal for development. Dixon (2007) argued for legitimation of tribal custom as a solution to the failure of governmental land mobilization. Banner (1999) argued that Maori use rights would not necessarily be inefficient, as use rights do not face the same collective action problems as open access. Although a commons can lead to overuse, the tragedy is not ineluctable as social norms and other informal regulations can constrain behavior (Fennell 2004). Serious problems arise when a government displaces social norms with a legal property regime that cannot be relied upon, effectively removing what rights there were (Fitzpatrick 2006).

The problem of alienability arises in a different way in connection with long-term leases. Historically, common-law courts have allowed landlords to impose restrictions on the alienability of leaseholds. By inserting the necessary terms in a lease, landlords could retain to themselves the legal power to prevent alienation without their consent. Courts upheld these clauses without concern for whether the landlord withheld consent unreasonably or arbitrarily. Recently, it has appeared to observers that some American courts will no longer let landlords prevent alienation by tenants. However, it is also possible to read some of the decisions as merely requiring landlords to express clearly their retention of an absolute veto, a requirement which would reduce tenants' information costs.

Johnson (1988) argues that restrictions on alienability serve legitimate purposes and, hence, the modern trend toward limiting the scope of restrictions will lead to inefficiency in the law. Landlords need to be able to keep tenants from leasing to new tenants whose occupancy might injure the value of the landlord's reversion. Because they cannot easily specify in advance all of the ways in which potential new tenants might injure their retained interest, landlords often need wide discretion to reject the transfer of the leasehold. Without that power, landlords will forsake the long-term lease in favor of otherwise less-efficient alternatives such as short-term leases. In addition, Johnson argues that requiring landlords to be more clear in their retention of unfettered discretion to veto transfers may be quite costly. He does not spell out in practical terms, however, why it would be ineffective or especially costly for landlords wanting to retain an unconstrained veto to do so by reserving 'sole, absolute, and unfettered discretion' in their leases.

3. Temporal division via the estate system

The English common-law system allows a number of different 'estates' in land, each estate varying in potential duration. A 'fee simple' lasts potentially forever. A 'life estate' lasts for the life of a person, usually the holder of the estate. A 'term of years' is measured by a period of time. All of these estates can be made 'defeasible', by attaching a condition specifying the circumstances in which the estate terminates prematurely. For example, a transfer 'to the City as long as the land is used for a public park' creates a fee simple determinable, an estate that could last forever but will terminate earlier if the land is not used for a public park. With the exception of the fee simple absolute, in which the owner holds perpetual rights, each of the estates above divides rights according to time or contingency or both, with the holder of the named estate holding the present possessory rights and at least one other person holding a 'future interest' which will become possessory when the present estate terminates.

It is plain that dividing rights temporally or contingently may increase the utility of land. A student may need a place to live for only a year and have no desire (or capital) to invest in ownership that lasts forever. A teacher taking sabbatical leave may have no interest in possession for that year, but a strong interest in the right to possession forever thereafter. A one-year lease with an early termination for non-payment of rent divides the risks and benefits associated with ownership of the land to accommodate both interests and maximize the value of the land.

Stake (1990) argued that some forms of divided ownership, those hinging on contingencies that might occur in the distant future, diminish rather than increase the utility of land to living persons. The empirical evidence for this proposition is that those temporal divisions of rights are made primarily in gifts (often testamentary gifts). Because such divisions are rarely, if ever, found in transactions in which two or more parties exchange rights to produce gains from trade, there is good reason to doubt that creating such interests increases value. Of course the act of dividing the ownership makes the donor happy, and that utility added to the values of the present and future interests will probably be greater than the value of a fee simple absolute. But after the donor dies, which is sometimes the instant the two interests are created, the donor's utility drops out of the sum and the remaining values are together less than the value of a fee simple. One economic function of the Rule against Perpetuities, which eliminates remote future interests, is to help reunite multiple interests into a more valuable fee simple.

Many courts and commentators have pointed out that the Rule against Perpetuities is often difficult to apply and the complexity of the Rule has led to various proposals for 'reform.' Hirsch and Wang (1992) argued that the Rule should be applied differently depending on the ways in which the dead hand attempts to control the land. The most popular reform is the wait-and-see approach, which saves interests that vest in a timely manner. Another popular 'reform' has been to eliminate whole categories of interests from the ambit of the Rule. At this point in time, it appears that the Rule against Perpetuities will itself be void within lives in being plus 21 years.

The possibility of negative externalities is created whenever land rights are divided according to time. A life tenant might fail to make repairs to existing buildings because the repair costs will fall solely on the tenant but the costs of not repairing will fall in part on the 'remainderman' holding the future interest. To the dismay of his landlord, a tenant with a one-year tenancy might cut down valuable trees to use for firewood despite the trees being worth more, in the long run, alive. The common law partially internalized negative temporal externalities by the doctrine of 'waste,' which makes the present estate holder liable to the holder of the future interest for actions that damage the land in a permanent way. Interestingly, the doctrine of waste also acknowledges the subjective value of land in its rule that merely changing the character of land can be waste even though the change increases market value. Posner (2007, p. 74) pointed out that present and future estate holders could in theory prevent inefficient maintenance by agreement, obviating the need for the doctrine of waste, but negotiations may bog down in bilateral monopoly problems. Furthermore, the future interest holders are often minors or unborns who lack the capacity to contract.

The converse of the waste problem is created by positive externalities. The present estate holder and future interest holder may both fail to make efficient improvements to the land because each bears the burden of the improvement while some of the benefits accrue to the other. With a nod to Coase, Posner (2007, p. 73) asked and answered why multiple owners cannot solve the problem of inadequate investment by contract. The possessory estate holder often lacks the endowment to make major capital improvements and the future interest holders may be hard to identify or lack the capacity to strike an enforceable bargain. The law plays an important role in regulating land use when ownership is divided.

4. Leaseholds

Landlord-tenant law is one topic in which there is a substantial literature that speaks to scholars from both the economics and the law perspectives. Limitations on the alienability of tenant interests and on landlords' rights to evict have been blamed for inadequate investment in improvements to land. Solow (1971) discussed the problem in connection with poverty in nineteenth century Ireland. Basu (1989) noted that landlords wanting to make an offer to share the costs of improvements face an adverse selection problem: only the tenants who expect to stay long enough for their investment to be repaid will accept the offer, leaving the landlord with inadequate return on his contribution.

Leases can have many functions, such as spreading risk (Cheung 1969) or creating appropriate incentives for development and husbandry (Allen and Lueck 1992a; Williams 1979a; see also Allen and Lueck 1996). In the context of leasing personalty, Flath (1980) discussed how leases can economize on transaction costs such as identifying, assuring, and maintaining quality. Those topics and many others in commercial leases are more a matter of contract law and are analyzed primarily with contractual analysis and thus are outside the scope of this chapter. One early use of leasehold estates may have been to avoid the ecclesiastical prohibition of usury. When the law prevented lending of money at market interest rates, a lender could avoid usury by transferring money in return for the borrower's (landlord's) transfer of an estate in land. The lease would be designed so that the periodic rents from the land during the term of the lease would be sufficient to pay off the principal and additional interest (see Simpson 1986, p. 72).

New developments in leases raise additional issues. Under the common law, landlords had few obligations with regard to the leased premises. To try to reduce the human misery due to squalid living conditions, some modern law reforms have attempted to force landlords to deliver habitable premises at an affordable price. The standard economic analysis of reforms designed to benefit residential tenants is presented entertainingly (that is, at the expense of lawyers) by Albon (1982). Assuming that supply decreases with price and shifts as landlords' costs increase and that such marginal costs exceed marginal benefits to tenants, the results of reform are not favorable to tenants. If rents are not controlled, rents will increase by more than the value of the increased housing services to tenants and the reforms end up forcing tenants to buy housing services they do not wish to buy. If rents are controlled, demand will exceed supply and a shortage will develop, housing search costs will increase for tenants, and landlords will discriminate more. Schwallie (1990) argued that, because investors are risk averse, increased uncertainties caused by law reform will reduce the attractiveness of the return from rental housing. In a neighborhood with declining values, the application of housing quality minima may hasten the withdrawal of units from the market and increase discrimination against riskier tenants. Some critics have pointed to reduced supply as a consequence of reforms, but a change in consumer preferences towards home ownership may have reduced new construction of rental housing (Rabin 1984, pp. 561–562).

Hirsch, Hirsch and Margolis (1975) stated that repair-and-deduct remedies may be an inefficient means of housing code enforcement for a number of reasons. Landlords, being specialists in housing, often have more experience than residential tenants in making repairs or finding an appropriate tradesman. Tenants have little reason to monitor the quality of the work, as long as it serves their temporary needs. Landlords have access to all portions of the building and can coordinate related repairs and improvements.

On the other hand, tenants, who often learn of problems before landlords, are more likely to make repairs before they become costly if they know they can deduct the cost. In addition, tenants might make more efficient repairs because they will make no more repair than they think is needed.

Nevertheless, landlords are repeat players. They are likely less transient than residential tenants and thus will know local repair tradespeople. More important, once landlords recognize that ignoring tenant requests for repairs leads to their paying for inefficient repairs, they will become more responsive to tenant requests. The inefficiency of repairs actually made by tenants can be analogized to the cost of incarcerating criminals which is justified if it deters wrongdoing. The repair-and-deduct remedy might be a low-cost way of getting landlords to pay attention to legitimate tenant complaints.

Markovits (1976) argued that the standard economic analysis is wrong in a number of ways. Some tenants, such as children, will value the mandated services more highly than their cost and those tenants will gain from law reform. Reform requirements can also be allocatively efficient if they require housing improvements that create benefits, such as reduced fire, disease and crime, that are external to the person who pays the rent.

Almost all reforms of landlord-tenant law were designed to improve the life of tenants by shifting rights from landlords to tenants. But empirical work indicates that the reforms have hurt many tenants (Hirsch, Hirsch and Margolis 1975; Hirsch 1980, 1981, 1983, 1984, and 1987; Rydell 1981; and Schafer 1979). If that is so, why have the habitability reforms been so popular? The passage of reforms increasing housing quality unaccompanied by rent controls might be explained as a rational attempt by tenants whose income has increased to increase their housing quality without incurring the costs of moving.

Vlatas (1994) argued for extension of habitability warranties to commercial leases on the basis of efficiency arguments like those used to support habitability in residential leases. However, Ashauer-Miller (1997) advised caution in adopting habitability in commercial settings, noting that efficiency arguments are weaker than they are in the residential setting.

5. Division of land by usage

This entry now shifts from division of land ownership by time to division by use, where one person holds the right to control one use while another holds the right to control remaining uses in the same land at the same time. These sorts of interests are not 'estates in land' but go by a number of other names such as easements, profits, covenants, and equitable servitudes. Examples include a utility company's easement to bury service lines under private lawns or a neighbor's equitable restriction preventing an owner from using his home for a business. A promise by an owner to keep his driveway cleared might be found by a court to be a covenant, a servitude, or an easement. Land-use doctrines govern the separation of such non-possessory rights from the rights of possession ordinarily thought of as ownership. The next sections address the enforceability, outside the landlord-tenant context, of easements, profits, licenses, covenants, and equitable servitudes.

The basic economic rationale for allowing an owner to divide the set of all rights to use a piece of land into smaller packages of use rights would appear to be the same as the rationale for allowing the owner of a farm to break it geographically into tracts for a subdivision, or allowing the owner of a house to slice it temporally into the rights of landlord and tenant. In all these cases, the sum of the parts can be worth more than the whole.

Assume that it is worth \$200 to Sara, who owns Blackacre, to be able to walk across her neighbor Ben's pasture on Whiteacre to get to town. Assume also that Ben feels a loss equal to \$100 from Sara's walking across the pasture. Ben and Sara could improve their positions by a contractual exchange, in this case Sara's \$150 for Ben's allowing her to walk across Whiteacre. The land-use situation differs from the ordinary contractual situation, however, in that Sara's real concern is not just with Ben's consent, but also the consent of all future owners of Whiteacre (see Dunham 1965). Sara's goal cannot be achieved by contract because Ben cannot bind his successors to perform his contractual promise.

Over the centuries, the tremendous gains to be had from exchanging rights to control the use of land have driven owners to seek legal mechanisms to accomplish those exchanges. And courts have obliged. The problem is solved by separating out the right to determine whether the owner of Blackacre can walk across Whiteacre to get to town from the other rights in Whiteacre. As Korngold (1990) put it, with servitudes people do not have to acquire more rights than they want.

The interesting economic issues relate not to why rights in Whiteacre can be subdivided according to usage, but rather why the law fetters the subdivision of rights, as it does, and whether there is any current utility to having multiple doctrines with differing rules by which rights are subdivided. Many of the restrictions have yet to be supported with an economic rationale. One concern, supporting constraints, is that subdivision of rights will lead to situations in which later purchasers think they are buying complete packages of rights when, in fact, they are not. During the initial development of the common law, England had no recording system to give purchasers notice of outstanding non-possessory interests in land. Without such a system, mistakes and fraud become likely, reducing the liquidity of land markets and undermining the basis for assuming that a voluntary exchange of rights is a Pareto improvement. Curtailing the number of non-possessory interests with restrictive doctrine, i.e., limiting the number of possible forms of rights, reduces the occasions for incomplete or false information.

In addition, peculiar restrictions and obligations impressed on land by a capricious or imprudent owner may continue to burden land in perpetuity. Indeed, if severe enough, such private restrictions could deprive the land of its productive power forever. In part for those reasons, judges and scholars have been quite reluctant to allow burdens placed on land to run to successors and have imposed the many limitations found in land-use doctrine.

As a means of controlling uses of land, servitudes of one form or another should be compared to and contrasted with zoning. Servitudes are created by private parties, whereas zoning is imposed by public entities, local governments. Following Siegan (1972) and Ellickson (1973), servitudes are often discussed as an alternative to zoning (see Speyrer 1989). As is obvious from thousands of modern developments, however, public and private controls are not mutually exclusive and often perform different functions.

Fischel (1990) noted that zoning is often easier to revise, at least compared to covenants requiring unanimous consent. Hughes and Turnbull (1996) contended that things that are inherently difficult to adjust, like lot configuration and basic type of use, are better candidates for regulation by zoning. By contrast, they said, activities that are easily adjusted by subsequent landowners, like yard plantings and automobile parking, require more rigid intertemporal regulation and would be better regulated by covenant. This led Korngold (2001) to conclude that it is most efficient to have a combination of both zoning and servitudes.

6. Easements, profits and licenses

When an easement is for the benefit of the owner of a particular parcel of land, the benefit is said to be 'appurtenant' to that 'dominant' parcel and may be exercised only for the benefit of that parcel. Suppose Ben, Sara, and Janet own lots 1, 2, and 3, respectively, and Ben grants to Sara an easement so that she and future owners of lot 2 can get from her dominant parcel to the road passing by Ben's servient parcel. Sara then buys Janet's lot and decides to build a new house on that lot instead of lot 2. Sara cannot use her easement for the benefit of lot 3 even though there is no more harm to Ben than he anticipated when he granted the easement (Bruce and Ely 2001, sec. 2.8). This rule obviously puts Ben and Sara in a bilateral monopoly situation, with the possible result that a Pareto-improving exchange of rights will not take place because of strategic bargaining. One justification for the rule is that in most situations, unlike the example above, the extension of an easement to benefit parcels other than the dominant tenement will indeed generate greater costs to the servient land, and it is administratively easier to lump all extensions together than to cull the harmless extensions from the bulk. The rule also creates an incentive for the holder of the easement to negotiate with the servient owner before extending or modifying her use of the easement in any way. It also creates an incentive for the party obtaining an easement to negotiate an agreement that it can be extended to his other parcels in the future. Nevertheless, it would seem a close case as to whether the rule is justified on efficiency grounds.

Easements can be created by express or implied grant or reservation and, unlike real covenants and equitable servitudes, can be created by prescription (longstanding use). Like real covenants and equitable servitudes, easements can be divided into negative (or restrictive) easements and positive (or affirmative) easements. Early English decisions recognized four types of negative easement: easements of light, air, building support, and flow of water in artificial streams. In most American states, a landowner has no right to sunlight coming across his neighbor's land. Because of increased interest in solar energy, some reformers have argued that either nuisance or prior appropriation rules should be applied to protect persons who install solar energy devices from being shaded by subsequent development (for a critical discussion, see Williams 1979b). However, private allocation of rights might suffice since current law defines solar rights clearly and allows for their alienation at low cost by restrictive covenant. Free-rider and holdout problems are minimal because it is rare for more than a few owners to be involved in the location of a particular solar collector, although bi-lateral monopoly could prevent the parties from reaching the efficient result.

For a number of reasons, courts cabined the development of negative easements with the rule that only four types could be created; no new forms were allowed. One economic rationale is that negative easements are harder for prospective purchasers of the servient parcel to discover than affirmative easements, such as shortcut footpaths. Limiting the number of unobservable easements reduces the frequency of inefficient transfers of the burdened parcel to unsuspecting purchasers.

A person who uses land of another in a particular way for a long time may gain an easement by prescription, which allows that person (and possibly her successors) to continue making that use of the land. In light of the ease of ex-ante contracting, it is unclear whether this ability to gain rights by wrongful act can be justified. It is some evidence of the questionable merits of the doctrine that in 1966 the Law Reform Committee debated total abolition of prescription in England. However, the closely related doctrine of adverse possession might be defended on the ground that depriving a longstanding user carries a higher cost than refusing to honor the meritorious claim of a non-user (Stake 2001). Perhaps prescription might be justified on a similar rationale.

The rules of prescription provide a good example of path-dependent evolution in the law. The possibility in England that negative easements could be created by prescription explains the English judicial reluctance to allow new types of negative easements. If new types of negative easements could be created by longstanding non-use, any new use of land could be met with a neighbor's objection that she had a prescriptive negative easement preventing such use. The law could not allow new sorts of negative easements to be created by prescription without creating great uncertainty about whether a parcel of land could be put to a new use without encroaching on prescriptive rights held by neighbors. In the United States, where most courts have held that negative easements cannot be created by prescription, allowing new sorts of negative easements is not similarly problematic and need not be proscribed.

Easements may terminate by their own terms, by express release, by adverse use, or by abandonment, though the latter is hard to prove. Easements terminate by the ancient doctrine of 'merger' if the servient tenement and the easement come into the same hands. In such cases the easement is not created anew when the once-dominant or once-servient parcel is transferred. This rule creates problems for future holders of the dominant parcel that wrongly assume the old easement still exists. However, the merger rule can be justified on the simple ground that it reduces the costs of selling the unencumbered fee in the future; the seller of the once-servient parcel need not specify that he is transferring both the previously encumbered fee and the right to be free of the encumbrance. On the reasonable assumption that sellers wish to transfer all their rights more often than they wish to transfer a previously divided subset of their rights, the rule reduces transaction costs.

A profit (or '*profit à prendre*') is a right to sever and remove some substance, like minerals, gravel, or timber, from land possessed by another. The common-law rules governing ownership of fugacious minerals were borrowed from the rules applied to the capture of wild animals. Because those rules created common-pool problems and led to massive waste, they have been superseded by statutory regimes.

7. Real covenants

Whereas easements and profits usually involve rights of the dominant owner to do something without interference from the servient owner, real covenants and equitable servitudes usually involve rights of the dominant owner to make the servient owner do something, such as maintain a wall, or to prevent the servient owner from doing something, such as making noise on Sundays. Servitudes and easements are not mutually exclusive, however. Equitable servitudes overlap with negative easements.

A real covenant is a promise. It is different from a contractual promise in that a real covenant is stuck to some interest in land and passes automatically to each owner of that interest rather than staying with the original party to the promise. The law of real covenants sets forth a number of 'elements' that must be met for a promise to 'run' with land: as covenants, they must be in writing; they must be intended to run; they must 'touch and concern' the land (rather than being irrelevant to the ownership of interests in land); there must be 'horizontal' and 'vertical' 'privity of estate' (abstruse requirements explained below); and, under modern recording acts, grantees of the affected interests in land must have notice of the covenants.

These requirements apply separately to the burden and the benefit of the covenant. Whether the burden (duty to perform) runs to future holders of the servient parcel and whether the benefit (right to performance) runs to holders of the dominant parcel are, for the most part, independent issues. The covenanting parties must intend, for example, that the burden of the promise run to the successors of the burdened party for the burden to run and must intend that the benefit run in order that the benefit run. An examination of the doctrinal elements follows next.

A. Intent

We can be reasonably confident that the parties to a real covenant will reap gains from their exchange only if the law enforces what the parties intended. If the law expands the rights exchanged, the chances that the outcome will be a Pareto improvement decrease dramatically. Furthermore, if promising parties think the law might increase the scope of their promise beyond what they intend, they might pass up a beneficial exchange. Therefore, it is essential that courts find that the parties intended for the promise to run before holding that it does so. However, Winokur (1989) contended that courts are all too willing to find intent, essentially dispensing with the requirement as an independent element. In order to assure more meaningful consent, he urged that courts require some explicit language expressing the parties' intention that the covenant run.

Although the running of the benefit and burden are usually independent, English (see *London County Council v. Allen*, 1914) and a few American authorities have linked the two. These authorities hold that the burden of a real covenant will not run with land if the benefit is 'in gross,' which means that the benefit is held by a person rather than being attached to a parcel of land. The cost of this rule is that it prevents many beneficial divisions of rights in land. Suppose, for example, a talented gardener has worked hard to make his house a showcase for his horticultural abilities. Suppose also that his family has outgrown this house, and he would like to sell if he could be assured that his successors would maintain his garden. He cares what happens to his garden no matter where he moves; he wants to hold 'in gross' the benefit of a promise that the subsequent owners will maintain the garden. If law does not allow the burden to run with the benefit is in gross, the gardener can assure that the garden will be maintained only by remaining the owner.

The advantage of this intent-frustrating rule is that it makes a real covenant easier to terminate by private negotiation because it will usually be possible to find the holder of the benefit since the benefit is tied to land and the owner of any given parcel of land can usually be identified. If the benefit is not tied to land, a successor willing to pay more than the gardener's price to convert the garden to another use might have a harder time finding the gardener. Thus, transaction costs could prevent the successor from buying his way free of the promise. The requirement that the benefit run with land helps keep down the costs of terminating promises. This justification seems to have failed to convince most American commentators, perhaps because the problem of locating benefit holders could be solved by requiring holders of benefits in gross to place their mailing address on record if they wish to keep the promise from lapsing.

B. Touch and concern

Courts require that the benefit of a real covenant touch and concern (sometimes 'touch or concern') the dominant parcel for the benefit to run to the successive owners and that the burden touch and concern the servient parcel for the burden to run successors to that parcel. Reichman (1978) pointed out that the touch and concern element is the only real barrier to the attachment of a promise to land. While it does not prohibit any particular agreement, it does shift the burden of negotiation once a parcel has been transferred. If the promise does touch and concern, the new neighbors have to negotiate if they want to terminate the covenant. If the promise does not touch and concern, the new neighbors have to negotiate if they want to reinstate the promise.

A promise to keep a party wall in good repair touches and concerns, as does a promise not to use for commercial purposes, but promises to pay money, promises enforcing ideologies, and promises for personal services usually do not. Some promises have proved hard for courts to categorize, and the touch and concern element has long been criticized as being indeterminate. Rarely, however, do the critics identify an actual case that has been decided badly because of the touch and concern element. Rather, Epstein (1982) said, the harm from indeterminacy is that it generates litigation, increases the costs of exchanges, or dissuades parties from using covenants.

The amount of litigation generated by the touch and concern requirement remains uncertain. The reported appellate cases in the United States in the twentieth century in which that element has played an important part number only in the hundreds. A Lexis search on 7 June 2007 for 'touch and concern and (covenant or servitude)' in the 'mega' file containing all US federal and state cases yielded 488 cases. Although the reported appellate cases are just the tip of the iceberg, this tip is so small that the whole might not be of huge concern. It is unknown to what degree the touch and concern element deflects parties from desirable transactions or raises the drafting costs of completed transactions.

The element may be less indeterminate than the critics suggest. According to one examination of American cases (Stake 1988), the element can be understood as a mechanism for efficiently allocating the burden and the benefit of the promise. If the benefit of the promise is likely to be enjoyed more by the successor than the original promisee, the court will find that the benefit touches and concerns. In other words, the benefits will be allocated to the person who would enjoy them most. On the burden side, courts act as if they assume the promise will be performed and the only question is whom to hold responsible for its performance. If placing the burden of performance on the successor to the promisor would avoid inefficiencies that would result from leaving the burden with the original promisor, the court will find that the covenant touches and concerns. In some cases it is a simple matter of allocating the burden to the party that can perform the obligation more easily. For example, the new owner of a barn is better able to perform a promise to keep the barn painted because he can monitor its condition and has easy physical access when it needs painting. In other cases the court improves the allocation of resources by avoiding situations having more subtle inefficiencies, such as when the court passes burdens to pay homeowners association dues on to those who will be spending those dues. If the court were to find that the covenant did not touch and concern, the homeowners in charge of the association would in theory have the power to make improvements and charge them to former homeowners, a group not represented in the decisions to purchase. The association might easily spend too much if it is spending other people's money.

There are other economic tests for determining whether a covenant touches and concerns land. Under one, a covenant touches and concerns if it was set up to regulate externalities generated by the use of one parcel (see Nelson, Stoebuck and Whitman 1996, p. 610). Another intuitive approach is to ask whether ownership of some particular land makes the burden easier to perform or the benefit more enjoyable.

Successful positive explanation of touch and concern does not as a normative matter justify the element's interference with the parties' intent that the covenant run. Krier (1974) developed a defense based on problems with successive bargaining. While it is possible for successive owners to re-bargain and contract for the original covenant, it is not hard to see that this is not probable. The purpose served by touch and concern is to continue those covenants which would have been agreed to by successive owners had they negotiated. Reichman (1978) defended the touch and concern element on the ground that tying to land the sorts of promises that do not touch and concern to land could reduce efficiency, democracy, or personal freedom.

Stake (1988) developed a justification of the touch and concern element that builds on the models suggested by Krier and Reichman by adding an observation about the low costs of renegotiating promises that do not touch and concern. First, the courts allow covenants to bind future owners when efficiency considerations support shifting the burden or benefit from the original party to his successor. Second, the touch and concern requirement distinguishes those situations in which it is difficult for the parties to re-create the promise from those in which it is not difficult. The cases in which the touch and concern element prevents the promise from running to successors are cases in which the successor parties can renegotiate the promise if it remains desirable to the successors. However, in situations where it would be hard to renegotiate the promise, the element allows the promise to continue without renegotiation. Thus the element serves as an efficiency check without undoing promises that would be hard to re-create.

Assume that a group of neighbors agreed that they and their successors would play poker together once a week. Assume that one of them sells to a new owner who refuses to play poker. If the group tries to enforce the covenant, the court will not enforce it because the burden fails to touch and concern his land. Assuming that this covenant as applied to the new owner is inefficient, generating less wealth than it costs to perform, the judicial refusal to enforce it against the new owner enhances efficiency. This freedom from enforcement might not be accomplished easily by the successor since each of the other parties is in a position to hold out. The touch and concern element beneficially prevents inefficient promises from running against parties that might find it hard to buy their way free of the obligations.

On the other hand, judicial refusal to enforce the covenant does not prevent new neighbors from negotiating a new covenant to play poker when it would be efficient. Transaction costs will rarely prevent the negotiation of that new covenant because no owner is necessary to the agreement; the group can simply get someone else to play. Therefore, private extension of the old covenant to new neighbors is unproblematic. The very fact that the covenant does not touch and concern land helps to assure that the unraveling of the promise will not be difficult to reverse.

The touch and concern element might be criticized for depriving some promisees of the benefit of their bargain. However, if the covenant fails to touch and concern it presumably remains enforceable against the original promisor. The mistaken promisee loses a remedy against the successor, but retains a remedy against the original promisor, a remedy that would have been lost if the burden had run. Thus, the distributional costs of the touch and concern element are mitigated.

The American Law Institute (ALI) (2000) urged courts to replace the touch and concern element with a judicial inquiry into whether the promise in question violates public policy. French (2003) applied the

ALI's recommended rule to three cases and concluded that the public-policy inquiry is superior to the touch and concern doctrine.

However, this approach will likely make the law less determinate and could interfere more with private intent, since the traditional touch and concern approach has prevented few covenants from running. In addition, this public-policy inquiry fails to distinguish between situations in which it is difficult to reinstate the promise and those in which it is not. Finally, the traditional touch and concern element in no way impedes enforcement of the promise between the original parties, as the ALI's validity test would do. The proposed reform fails to recognize that it could be useful to have a rule that allows a promise to be enforced between the original parties but not between their successors.

C. Notice

For the burden of a covenant to run, the promisor's successor must have had 'notice' before purchasing the land. The notice element requires that the successor to the promisor have some opportunity to find out about the obligations attached to the land. Requiring notice is often justified by lawyers on the ground that it would be unfair to hold successors to promises they did not know about, but there is also an efficiency rationale. Holding successors liable despite their lack of notice would create an opportunity for promisors to free themselves of promises by selling the burdened lands to unsuspecting buyers, who might place a lower value on the burdened lands. Thus, notice goes to the heart of voluntary consent. Without meaningful opportunity for parties to know of the burdens they assume, we cannot be sure that the exchange of an interest in land makes a Pareto improvement. Dilution of the notice requirement, as has occurred in some jurisdictions (see Winokur 1989), undermines the economic foundation of servitude doctrine.

D. Horizontal privity

According to many authorities, the original parties must have a special connection between them, called 'horizontal privity', for their covenant to run to either of their successors. Parties are in horizontal privity if they have simultaneous interests or successive interests, that is, at the time of the covenant one party conveys to the other an interest in the dominant or servient parcel. The horizontal privity requirement prevents neighbors from creating an enforceable, mutual, real covenant to keep their lawns mowed without their exchanging some interest in their lands at the same time. Thus, this element imposes substantial costs on parties attempting to create a real covenant. The legal world is still waiting for a convincing policy analysis explaining why courts should, by requiring horizontal privity, continue to impose costs on neighbors wishing to exchange running promises.

E. Vertical privity

A promisor and his successor are in 'vertical privity' if the promisor transfers his entire estate in land to the successor. Only in such cases is the successor bound by a real covenant. A possible rationale for the traditional requirement of vertical privity will be suggested in the section on equitable servitudes, below.

F. Termination

Real covenants terminate if all dominant and servient tenements come under the same ownership and also may terminate automatically by their own terms. Alternatively, judges will sometimes refuse to enforce a covenant on the ground that the holders of the dominant tenement have abandoned the covenant or acquiesced in its violation. In England there is a statutory procedure for discharging obsolete or destructive covenants. Additionally, real covenants can be terminated privately if the holders of the benefit waive their rights or release the burdened parties from their obligations. When real covenants involve a number of owners, holdouts will often prevent such private termination. For that reason, many modern covenants include a provision that the covenants can be terminated by the vote of a majority or supermajority of the parties.

Real covenants are also terminated if the government condemns the servient parcel and uses it in violation of the covenant. The issue arises as to whether the holder of the dominant parcel should obtain a portion of the condemnation award and, if so, how much that award should be. Cases limiting the total compensation awarded to the value of an unrestricted fee simple would seem to ignore the possibility that the value of the sum of the divided interests is higher than the value of the unencumbered, undivided fee. Such cases also undercut the allocative-efficiency rationale for requiring compensation, which is to make sure that the rights taken by the government are worth at least as much to the government as to the private land owners.

8. Equitable servitudes

Courts of equity, which have now merged with courts of law, have enforced promises stuck to land at least since *Tulk v. Moxhay* (1848). When a court sitting in equity enforces a promise attached to land, the promise is called an 'equitable servitude,' 'equitable restriction,' 'servitude,' or even 'restrictive covenant.' The court applies the requirements of intent, touch and concern, and notice in much the same manner as when it sits at law and analyzes the promise as a real covenant.

A. Changed conditions

Even when the holder of the benefit of an equitable servitude has established the elements above, the 'changed-conditions' (or 'changed-circumstances' or 'changed-neighborhood') doctrine, may prevent enforcement. This doctrine says that injunctive relief will be denied if conditions in the area affected by the covenant have so changed that the covenant can no longer achieve its purpose. Stake (1991) noted that the doctrine creates inefficient incentives. By destabilizing servitude law, it invites litigation and deters parties from beneficial exchanges of rights or shunts them to more reliable but clumsier legal mechanisms such as defeasible estates. If the clumsier forms of restriction are unsatisfactory, a seller may refuse to sell at all, in which case society loses the gains from trade that would have been possible had the seller been confident that the necessary restriction were enforceable.

On the other hand, there are other efficiency benefits from applying the changed-conditions doctrine. Reichman (1978) stated that there is a large difference between an interest expected to promote land utilization and a right having no value other than its negative capacity to prevent efficient land utilization. He said the changed-conditions doctrine applies only to promises of the latter sort. Krier's (1974) analysis suggests that judges might apply the changed-conditions doctrine so as to terminate specific performance when the current owners would not reconstruct the servitude if they were starting anew.

Judges can efficiently reallocate land-use rights in situations where strategic behavior would prevent the parties from privately terminating the servitude. The productivity of restricted land is improved by the changed-conditions doctrine so long as the doctrine is applied only if the challenged restriction generates no conceivable benefit to neighbors and is being asserted only to capture some of the gains from changing the use of the servient parcel.

It is not clear whether judges will extend this doctrine to real covenants. Stake (1991) argued that there is a reason not to do so. Adhering to the distinction between law and equity and allowing the holders of dominant tenements to assert rights only to damages reduces the distributional unfairness that would attend complete termination of the promise.

B. Privity

The primary difference between the requirements for real covenants and those for equitable servitudes is that courts sitting in equity require neither horizontal nor vertical privity, making it easier for a promisee's successor to assert the benefits of a promise in equity than at law. Any real covenant may also be enforced in equity as an equitable servitude, but some equitable servitudes cannot be enforced at law as real covenants. At first blush, this seems anomalous because the usual rule is that a court will grant equitable relief (an injunction) only if the legal remedy (damages) is inadequate.

The practical consequence of enforcement of a servitude in equity is that the court will issue an injunction against the covenantor's successor, requiring him to do, or not to do, an act, while it might not order him to pay damages. This distinction between legal and equitable enforcement of promises was attacked by Winokur (1989) as being indefensible. But there is an economic defense, which might be made clear by an example. Suppose Ben promises neighbor Sara that Whiteacre will not be used for a business, and then leases the land to Jake, who starts a business. If Sara brings an action against Jake to enforce Ben's promise, the court will order Jake not to operate the business on Whiteacre, but will not make him pay damages. If Sara sues Ben, the court will not enjoin Ben to do anything because the burden, in equity, has passed to Jake, but it will make him pay damages because the burden at law has not run to Jake and remains with Ben. Making Ben liable for any monetary damages caused by the business use of Whiteacre seems appropriate, especially if Ben failed to tell Jake about the covenant. Indeed, Ben's continuing liability on the covenant gives him an incentive to inform Jake. But Sara can enforce the equitable servitude directly against Jake, who is in possession, rather than having to find Ben and get him to control Jake's use of Whiteacre. Thus, it is possible that this division of responsibilities approximates what parties would choose for themselves if they thought about it. Moreover, when the vertical privity requirement does not yield results that fit the parties' needs, the parties can often privately mitigate the effect of the requirement. For example, if Ben wants Jake to be liable at law for damages for breach of the promise, Ben can put that term in his lease to Jake.

If the burdened owner passes his entire interest to a successor, the successor is bound by the promise in both law (in the US) and equity. Assuming that the original covenanting parties were not landlord and tenant (and assuming in England that the transferor is not the original covenantor), the transferor is released from any burden of the promise. It would unduly burden commerce in land if owners were to remain forever liable for breach of covenants attached to lands they once owned. But where the servient owner has not stepped out of the picture entirely by completely transferring his interest, it may be desirable to create an incentive for him to inform his tenant or other successor about the covenant.

Making him liable for damages at law upon a breach maintains that incentive for the transferor.

C. *Homeowners associations*

One of the many important uses of covenants and equitable servitudes is in the creation of homeowners associations or common interest communities. Thousands of such associations have been set up to regulate uses and provide for the maintenance of realty. They often operate on near-democratic principles, such as each house or condominium having one vote.

Because these organizations are geographically based and have powers to tax, spend, and regulate, homeowners associations are in many ways like private governments, as was noted by Epstein (1988). Fischel (1987) compared homeowners associations to local governments and found some advantages for private regulation of land use. The advantages of associations include unanimous consent and a contractual basis for development. The power to contract regarding uses to which lands may be put in the future is sometimes not available to municipalities because of judicial decisions invalidating attempts by municipalities to bind themselves by such agreements.

Winokur (1990) and Korngold (1990) disagreed as to whether the consent to be governed by community associations is voluntary or coerced. However, even if consent to association governance is initially and meaningfully unanimous by virtue of the fact that everyone governed has bought land within the area governed by the association, opportunities may subsequently arise for the majority to take unfair or inefficient advantage of the minority. To prevent this, courts sometimes impose a reasonableness requirement on the actions of the majority. Applying this requirement, courts have struck down rules that reduce the market value of minority interests or stop a minority member from doing something he has long been doing or cannot stop doing. In determining whether a majority has treated a minority unfairly, courts benefit from a natural advantage homeowners associations have over nearly all governments – they govern areas of land that are comparatively homogeneous in their use. For that reason, when the association attempts by majority rule to place unfair burdens on the minority it is often readily apparent to a court. Because characteristics and uses of land within the jurisdiction of a local government vary so widely, it is much more difficult for courts to identify situations in which the majority has increased its wealth at the expense of the minority.

Despite the potential gains from associating, common interest communities are not universally appreciated by their residents and a substantial number of persons would prefer to live outside their control. Winokur (1989 and 1990) argued that servitude regimes generate inefficiency, conflict, and excessive restraints on individual liberty and expression, and for those reasons the government should impose limits on the duration of the servitudes that form the legal basis for community associations. The legislative scheme Winokur proposed would reform the procedures for terminating or adjusting servitudes and would make servitudes unenforceable beyond 20 years unless, by the terms of the servitude, fewer than 11 parcels have the right to enforce the servitude. This would assure that any owner wishing to negotiate freedom from a 20-year-old servitude would not have to deal with too many other owners. On the other hand, such a law would, as Korngold points out, terminate beneficial servitudes and would do nothing to cure problems during the first 20 years of the covenant. In light of Winokur's concern for the difficulties of negotiations among multiple parties, it is somewhat odd that under his proposal servitudes could be modified after 20 years only by unanimous consent. Winokur does not provide a mechanism for protecting other neighbors outside the group from negative externalities of uses allowed by the 10 neighbors, externalities which are much more likely if the restricted party is allowed to buy his freedom with payments to the ten. Moreover, while his proposals might improve the private instruments used to establish associations, the case for legislative limitation is less compelling. Winokur's mix of temporal limitations and subsequent unanimous consent by a subgroup is not so obviously right for all developments that it should be imposed by law. As usual, this area of law calls for default rules rather than limiting rules.

9. Division of benefits from management via the trust

For centuries, English landowners used a special device called the 'use' to circumvent formal legal rules governing land. For example, Chris could transfer land 'to Laura for the use of Alison for life, and then whomever Alison appoints by will.' In this case, Chris has created in Alison a right to transfer Blackacre by will, which was not allowed at law before 1540. The courts of law would recognize Laura as the owner, but the courts of equity would compel Laura to manage the land for the benefit of Alison and then her appointee.

This ancient division of rights from responsibilities continues in common law countries today in the form of the 'trust.' The trustee holds legal title and the beneficiary holds equitable title. Strict fiduciary duties are imposed upon the trustee to protect the interests of the beneficiary, the *c'estui que* trust. The ubiquitous use of the trust today is a testament to the utility of decomposing rights into separate packages for management and enjoyment. Beyond the trust, the modern corporation might be seen as a variation on this ancient theme of placing control in the hands of professionals for the benefit of 'equity' stakeholders. Trusts offer an alternative to partnerships and corporations as a form for setting up a business.

Trusts are used in a variety of situations. Separating management duties from income benefits is important when a donor wishes to leave an asset to a group of beneficiaries. By leaving control in the hands of a single trustee, the donor can avoid the problems that would arise if all the beneficiaries were to attempt to manage it as a group. Separating management from enjoyment is also important when the donor wishes to make a gift to a person who has little ability to manage assets, such as an infant or a person lacking mental capacity. Even when the beneficiary is fully capable, the donor may wish to place control of an asset in the hands of a professional in order to benefit from his business and financial expertise or to ease the management burdens on the beneficiary.

In addition to employing trusts to assure prudent asset management, settlors settle trusts to protect the assets from the claims of creditors of the beneficiary. A trustee of a 'spendthrift' trust may continue to make payments to a beneficiary despite the fact that the beneficiary owes money to a creditor; ordinary creditors cannot reach the assets in the trust for payment of their claims. To protect against the claims of special creditors (spouses, children, suppliers of necessities) who can pierce through a spendthrift limitation, a settlor can create a 'discretionary' trust, the trustee of which may choose not to make a distribution from the trust rather than making a distribution that will wind up in the hands of a creditor. If the trustee chooses not to make a distribution to the debtor-beneficiary, that beneficiary gets nothing from the trust, but the trust assets are protected from his creditors. The result is something like a hostage standoff, with the creditor not able to gain control of the assets but able to prevent the trustee from making a distribution to the beneficiary.

Yet another important role for trusts appears when donors wish to make bequests to charities. By setting up a charitable trust, the settlor can specify the purpose to which the trust assets will be put for many years into the future. Indeed, if the trust is for a charitable purpose, the trust is exempt from the Rule against Perpetuities and may last forever.

Discretionary and charitable trusts are not without their worries, however. Posner (2007, p. 547) pointed out that charitable trustees may lack adequate incentives for efficient management of trust assets. He advocated a rule requiring charitable trusts to distribute all gifts within a period of years. He did not discuss the possibility that the trusts would then spend too much on advertising.

Another key concern falls within the broad category of agency costs (Sitkoff 2004). Whether the trustee is a friend or relative of the settlor or is a professional manager, there is some chance that the trustee will ignore the settlor's instructions and fail to make distributions in accordance with her wishes. If the terms of the trust make it difficult for outsiders to remove the trustee, the trustee may use his discretion to substitute goals of his own for goals of the settlor. If, on the other hand, the terms of the trust make it easy for outsiders to remove the trustee, the replacement trustee may be even less faithful to the goals of the settlor. To reduce the chances of mismanagement and misallocation of trust assets, to protect the interests of beneficiaries, and to guard against deviations from the settlor's intentions, settlors have recently and increasingly employed 'trust protectors' (Sterk 2006). Trust protectors have the power to oversee the actions of the trustee and to remove the trustee if necessary. The establishment of trust protectors may be viewed as a further decomposition of property rights in that legal control is subdivided into two parts, control of the asset and control of the person controlling the asset. Whether this additional decomposition increases social welfare is not yet clear (Stake 2006). Perhaps the next subdivision of control will occur when a settlor creates a trust that employs someone to oversee the trust protector.

10. Personalty

As seen above, the common law has developed an elaborate system for dividing rights in land, with numerous fine distinctions that make at least some economic sense. English and American law have not developed an equally extensive system for dividing rights in personal property. However, rights in personalty are not beyond decomposition. Personal property can be placed in a trust, which allows all of the divisions possible for realty, and can be divided temporally by lease, which for personalty is essentially a matter of contract law. Corporation and partnership laws can also be seen as sets of rules for decomposing personal property.

The law of wild animals was characterized by Lueck (1995) as divided ownership. The division of property in wild animals is, however, different from the decomposition of land property discussed above. The fundamental issue above was how private owners might decompose their rights. By contrast, a key issue in the law of living, uncaptured, wild animals is whether there is any owner at all. For many purposes, uncaptured wild animals are unowned. The federal government is not liable as an owner for damage done by wild animals (see *Sickman v. United States*, 1950). Moreover, the US refrained from asserting ownership of wild animals on federal land even in a Supreme Court case where doing so might have saved a federal statute from being declared unconstitutional, although the statute was upheld on other grounds (*Kleppe v. New Mexico*, 1976).

Lueck employed a transaction cost framework to examine the variation in the rules governing wild animals over time and geography. He confirmed that efficiency explains the development of the rules. His analysis does not justify complacency, however. Transaction costs, including strategic behavior, may prevent the creation of a system of property in wild animals. And, in the absence of a system of rights, it makes little sense for a person to refrain from capturing a wild animal worth more than the private costs of capture, which do not fully include depletion. For animals such as falcons and whales that roam or migrate in a range larger than the optimal (or actual) area of land ownership, the absence of a property system could result in extinction. The difference in remaining numbers of domesticated animals and endangered species suggests that the harvesting of some wild animals has been inefficiently high. Perhaps a rational whale would rather be owned.

Acknowledgements

The author thanks Indiana University School of Law-Bloomington for supporting the production of this entry and Adam Yowell, Sandra Owen, and Christopher Stake for research assistance. He also thanks Michael Alexeev, Ann Gellis, Val Nolan, the Encyclopedia editors, and two anonymous (to him) referees for their comments.

Bibliography

Ackerman, Bruce A. (1971), 'Regulating Slum Housing Markets on Behalf of the Poor: Of Housing Codes, Housing Subsidies and Income Redistribution Policy', *Yale Law Journal*, **80**, 1093–1197.

Ackerman, Bruce A. (1973), 'More on Slum Housing and Redistribution Policy: A Reply to Professor Komesar', *Yale Law Journal*, **82**, 1194–1207.

Albon, Robert P. (1982), 'Lawyers and the Rental Market for Housing: a Critical Appraisal or a Conversation Between two Academics in a Hotel Bar', in Ross Cranston and Anne Schick (eds), *Law and Economics*, Canberra: Australian National University, pp. 105–111.

Alchian, Armen A. (1963), 'Some Economics of Property Rights', *Il Politico*, **30**, 816–829.

Allen, Douglas and Dean Lueck (1992a), 'Contract Choice in Modern Agriculture: Cash Rent versus Cropshare', *Journal of Law and Economics*, **35**, 397–426.

Allen, Douglas W. and Dean Lueck (1992b), 'Farmland Leasing in Modern Agriculture', *Choices, The Magazine of Food, Farm, and Resource Issues*, **7**(1), 30–31.

Allen, Douglas W., and Dean Lueck (1993), 'Transaction Costs and the Design of Cropshare Contracts', *Rand Journal of Economics*, **24** (1), 78–100.

Allen, Douglas W. and Dean Lueck (1996), 'The Transaction Cost Approach to Agricultural Contracts', in David Martimort (ed.), *Agricultural Markets: Mechanisms, Failures, Regulations*, Amsterdam: North Holland Press, Elsevier Science B.V., pp. 31–64.

American Law Institute (2000), *Restatement Third, Property (Servitudes)*, St. Paul, Minnesota, US: American Law Institute.

Anas, Alex, Goran Cars, Joong Rae Cho, Bjorn Harsman, Ulf Jirlow, and Folke Snickars (1987), *The Economics of a Regulated Housing Market*, Stockholm: Swedish Council for Building Research.

Anderson, Terry L. and Dean Lueck (1992), 'Land Tenure and Agricultural Productivity on Indian Reservations', *Journal of Law and Economics*, **35**, 427–454.

Ashauer-Miller, Rena (1997), 'Dependent Covenants and Commercial Leases After Barton v. Tsern: Rhetoric of Reform Claims an Easy Victory in Utah', *Utah Law Review*, **1997**, 807–842.

Banner, Stuart (1999), 'Two Properties, One Land: Law and Space in Nineteenth-Century New Zealand', *Law and Social Inquiry*, **24**, 807–852.

Basu, Kaushik (1989), 'Technological Stagnation, Tenurial Laws, and Adverse Selection', *American Economic Review*, **79**, 251–255.

Bruce, Jon W. and James W. Ely (2001), *The Law of Easements and Licenses in Land*, Eagan, MN, US: West Group.

Cheung, Steven N.S. (1969), *The Theory of Share Tenancy*, Chicago, US: University of Chicago Press.

Coase, Ronald H. (1960), 'The Problem of Social Cost', *Journal of Law and Economics*, **3**, 1–44.

Coll Martin, Sebastián (1982), 'La Minería del Carbón en España a Finales del Antiguo Régimen (Coal Mining in Spain at the End of the Old Regime)', in Pedro Tedde (ed.), *La Economía Española al Final del Antiguo Régimen. II, Manofacturas*, Madrid: Alianza Editorial, pp. 240–335.

Cooter, Robert D. (1991), 'Inventing Market Property: The Land Courts of Papua New Guinea', *Law and Society Review*, **25**, 759–801.

Cooter, Robert D. (1992), 'Organization as Property: Economic Analysis of Property Law and Privatization', in Christopher Clague and Gordon Rausser (eds), *The Emergence of Market Economies in Eastern Europe*, Oxford: Blackwell, pp. 77–97.

Dagan, Hanoch and Michael A. Heller (2001), 'The Liberal Commons', *Yale Law Journal*, **110**, 549–624.

Demsetz, Harold (1964), 'The Exchange and Enforcement of Property Rights', *Journal of Law and Economics*, **7**, 11–26.

Demsetz, Harold (1966), 'Some Aspects of Property Rights', *Journal of Law and Economics*, **9**, 61–70.

Demsetz, Harold (1967), 'Toward a Theory of Property Rights', *American Economic Review*, **57**, 347–359.

Depoorter, Ben W.F. and Francesco Parisi (2003), 'Fragmentation of Property Rights: A Functional Interpretation of the Law of Servitudes', *Global Jurist Frontiers*, **3** (1) Art. 2.

Dixon, Kathrine (2007), 'Working with Mixed Commons/Anticommons Property: Mobilizing Customary Land in Papua New Guinea the Melanesian Way', *Harvard Environmental Law Review*, **31**, 219–277.

Dobris, Joel C. (1998), 'Changes in the Role and the Form of the Trust at the New Millennium, or, We Don't Have to Think of England Anymore', *Albany Law Review*, **62**, 543–578.

Dunham, Allison (1965), 'Promises Respecting the Use of Land', *Journal of Law and Economics*, **8**, 133–165.

Ellickson, Robert C. (1973), 'Alternatives to Zoning: Covenants, Nuisance Rules, and Fines as Land Use Controls', *University of Chicago Law Review*, **40**, 683–781. Reprinted in Bruce A. Ackerman (ed.) (1975), *Economic Foundations of Property Law*, Boston, US: Little Brown, pp. 265–301.

Ellickson, Robert C. (1982), 'Cities and Homeowners Associations', *University of Pennsylvania Law Review*, **130**, 1519–1580.

Ellickson, Robert C. (1991), 'Rent Control: A Comment on Olsen', *Chicago-Kent Law Review*, **67**, 947–954.

Ellickson, Robert C. (1993), 'Property in Land', *Yale Law Journal*, **102**, 1315–1400.

Epstein, Richard A. (1982), 'Notice and Freedom of Contract in the Law of Servitudes', *Southern California Law Review*, **55**, 1353–1368.

Epstein, Richard A. (1988), 'Covenants and Constitutions', *Cornell Law Review*, **73**, 906–927.

Fennell, Lee Anne (2004), 'Common Interest Tragedies', *Northwestern University Law Review*, **98**, 907–990.

Fischel, William A. (1987), 'The Economics of Land Use Exactions: A Property Rights Analysis', *Law and Contemporary Problems*, **50**, 101–113. Reprinted in Jay M. Stein (ed.) (1996), *Classic Readings in Real Estate and Development*, Washington, DC, US: ULI – the Urban Land Institute.

Fischel, William A. (1990), *Do Growth Controls Matter? A Review of the Empirical Evidence on the Effectiveness and Efficiency of Local Government Land Use Regulation*, Cambridge, MA, US: Lincoln Institute of Land Policy.

Fitzpatrick, Daniel (2006), 'Evolution and Chaos in Property Rights Systems: The Third World Tragedy of Contested Access', *Yale Law Journal*, **115**, 996–1048.

Flath, David J. (1980), 'The Economics of Short-Term Leasing', *Economic Inquiry*, **18**, 247–259.

Frankena, Mark (1975), 'Alternative Models of Rent Control', *Urban Studies*, **12**, 303–308.

French, Susan F. (2003), 'Can Covenants Not to Sue, Covenants Against Competition and Spite Covenants Run With Land? Comparing Results Under the Touch or Concern Doctrine and the Restatement Third, Property (Servitudes)', *Real Property, Probate, and Trust Journal*, **38**, 267–293.

García Sanz, Angel (1994), 'El Siglo XVIII: entre la Prosperidad de la Trashumancia y la Critica Antimestaña de la Ilustración (The Mesta in Spain, XVIIIth Century)', in Gonzalo A. Alvarez and Angel G. Sanz (eds), *Mesta, Trashumancia y vida Pastoril: exposición*, Madrid: Sociedad V Centenario del Tratado de Tordesillas, pp. 137–158.

Goldberg, Victor P., Thomas W. Merrill and Daniel Unumb (1987), 'Bargaining in the Shadow of Eminent Domain: Valuing and Apportioning Condemnation Awards Between Landlord and Tenant', *UCLA Law Review*, **34**, 1083–1137.

Grossman, Sanford J. and Oliver D. Hart (1986), 'The Costs and Benefits of Ownership: A Theory of Vertical and Lateral Integration', *Journal of Political Economy*, **94**, 691–719.

Hansmann, Henry and Reinier Kraakman (2002), 'Property, Contract, and Verification: The *Numerus Clausus* Problem and the Divisibility of Rights', *Journal of Legal Studies*, **31**, S373–S420.

Heady, Earl (1947), 'Economics of Farm Leasing', *Journal of Farm Economics*, **29**, 659–678.

Heller, Michael A. (1998), 'The Tragedy of the Anticommons: Property in the Transition from Marx to Markets', *Harvard Law Review*, **111**, 621–688.

Heller, Michael A. and Rebecca S. Eisenberg (1998), 'Can Patents Deter Innovation? The Anticommons in Biomedical Research', *Science*, **280**, 698–701.

Heller, Michael A. (1999), 'The Boundaries of Private Property', *Yale Law Journal*, **108**, 1163–1223.

Hirsch, Adam J. and William K.S. Wang (1992), 'A Qualitative Theory of the Dead Hand', *Indiana Law Journal*, **68**, 1–58.

Hirsch, Werner Z. (1980), 'Habitability Laws and the Welfare of Indigent Tenants', *Review of Economics and Statistics*, **63**, 263–274.

Hirsch, Werner Z. (1981), 'Landlord-Tenant Relations Law', in Paul Burrows and Cento G. Veljanovski (eds), *The Economic Approach to Law*, London, UK: Butterworths, pp. 277–306.

Hirsch, Werner Z. (1983), 'Effects of Habitability and Anti-Speedy Eviction Laws on Black and Aged Indigent Tenant Groups: An Economic Analysis', *International Review of Law and Economics*, **3**, 121–135.

Hirsch, Werner Z. (1984), 'Comment: From "Food for Thought" to "Empirical Evidence" About Consequences of Landlord-Tenant Laws', *Cornell Law Review*, **69**, 604–611.

Hirsch, Werner Z. (1987), 'Landlord-Tenant Laws and Indigent Black Tenants', *Research in Law and Economics*, **10**, 129–141.

Hirsch, Werner Z., Joel G. Hirsch and S. Margolis (1975), 'Regression Analysis of the Effects of Habitability Laws Upon Rent: An Empirical Observation on the Ackerman-Komesar Debate', *California Law Review*, **63**, 1095–1143.

Hughes, William T., Jr and Geoffrey K. Turnbull (1996), 'Restrictive Land Covenants', *Journal of Real Estate Finance and Economics*, **12**, 9–21.

Jaffe, Austin J. (1995), 'On the Role of Transaction Costs and Property Rights in Housing Markets', *Housing Studies*, **11**(3), 425–434.

Johnson, Alex M., Jr (1988), 'Correctly Interpreting Long-Term Leases Pursuant to Modern Contract Law: Toward a Theory of Relational Leases', *Virginia Law Review*, **74**, 751–808.

Johnson, Omotunde E.G. (1972), 'Economic Analysis: the Legal Framework and Land Tenure Systems', *Journal of Law and Economics*, **15**, 259–276.

Kennedy, Duncan (1987), 'The Effect of the Warranty of Habitability on Low Income Housing: "Milking" and Class Violence', *Florida State University Law Review*, **15**, 485–519.

Komesar, Neil K. (1973), 'Return to Slumville: A Critique of the Ackerman Analysis of Housing Code Enforcement and the Poor', *Yale Law Journal*, **82**, 1175–1193.

Korngold, Gerald (1984), 'Privately Held Conservation Servitudes: A Policy Analysis in the Context of Gross Real Covenants and Easements', *Texas Law Review*, **63**, 433–495.

Korngold, Gerald (1990), 'Resolving the Flaws of Residential Servitudes and Owners Association: for Reformation not Termination', *Wisconsin Law Review*, **1990**, 513–535.

Korngold, Gerald (2001), 'The Emergence of Private Land Use Controls in Large-Scale Subdivisions: The Companion Story to Village of Euclid v. Ambler Realty Co.', *Case Western Reserve Law Review*, **51**, 617–643.

Krier, James E. (1974), 'Book Review, reviewing Posner, Economic Analysis of Law (1972)', *University of Pennsylvania Law Review*, **122**, 1664–1705.

Lianos, Theodore P. and Despina Parliarou (1987), 'Land Tenure in Greek Agriculture', *Land Economics*, **63**, 237–248.

Livingston, Marie Leigh and Miller, Thomas A. (1986), 'A Framework for Analyzing the Impact of Western Instream Water Rights on Choice Domains: Transferability, Externalities, and Consumptive Use', *Land Economics*, **62**, 269–277.

Lueck, Dean (1989), 'The Economic Nature of Wildlife Law', *Journal of Legal Studies*, **18**, 291–324.

Lueck, Dean (1991), 'Ownership and the Regulation of Wildlife', *Economic Inquiry*, **29**, 249–260.

Lueck, Dean (1995), 'The Economic Organisation of Wildlife Institutions', in Terry L. Anderson and Peter J. Hill (eds), *Wildlife in the Market Place*, Lanham, MD, US: Rowman and Littlefield Press, Inc.

Lueck, Dean (1998), 'Wildlife Law', in Peter Newman (ed.), *The New Palgrave Dictionary of Economics and the Law*, London, UK: Macmillan.

Lueck, Dean and Philip Schenewerk (1996), 'An Economic Analysis of Unitized and Non-Unitized Reservoirs', Proceedings of the 1996 Society of Petroleum Engineers Annual Technical Conference, 67–76.

Lueck, Dean and Jonathan Yoder (1996), 'Federalism and Wildlife Conservation in the West', in Terry L. Anderson and Peter J. Hill (eds), *Environmental Federalism in the West*, Lanham, MD, US: Rowman and Littlefield Press.

Markovits, Richard S. (1976), 'The Distributive Impact, Allocative Efficiency, and Overall Desirability of Ideal Housing Codes: Some Theoretical Clarifications', *Harvard Law Review*, **89**, 1815–1846.

Merrill, Thomas W. and Henry E. Smith (2000), 'Optimal Standardization in the Law of Property: The *Numerus Clausus* Principle', *Yale Law Journal*, **110**, 1–70.

Miceli, Thomas J. and C.F. Sirmans (2000), Partition of Real Estate; or, Breaking Up Is (Not) Hard to Do, *Journal of Legal Studies*, **29** (2), 783.

Michelman, Frank I. (1982), 'Ethics, Economics and the Law of Property', *Nomos*, **24**, 3.

Moody, C.E., Jr and W.J. Kruvant (1990), 'OCS Leasing Policy and Lease Prices', *Land Economics*, **66**, 30–39.

Moorhouse, John C. (1972), 'Optimal Housing Maintenance Under Rent Control', *Southern Economic Journal*, **39**, 93–106.

Murray, Michael P., C. Peter Rydell, C. Lance Barnett, Carol E. Hillestad and Kevin Neels (1991), 'Analyzing Rent Control: The Case of Los Angeles', *Economic Inquiry*, **29**, 601–625.

Nelson, Grant S., William B. Stoebuck and Dale A. Whitman (1996), *Contemporary Property*, St. Paul, MN, US: West Publishing.
Nugent, Jeffrey B. and Nicolás Sanchez (1989), 'The Efficiency of the Mesta: A Parable', *Explorations in Economic History*, **26** (3), 261–284.
Olsen, Edgar O. (1972), 'An Econometric Analysis of Rent Control', *Journal of Political Economy*, **80**, 1081–1100.
Olsen, Edgar O. and David M. Barton (1983), 'The Benefits and Costs of Public Housing in New York City', *Journal of Public Economics*, **20**, 299–332.
Ostrom, Elinor (1990), *Governing the Commons: The Evolution of Institutions for Collective Action*, New York, US: Cambridge University Press.
Pardolesi, Roberto (1991), 'Energia (Energy)', *Digesto civile*, **VII**, 444–448.
Pigou, A.C. (1932), *The Economics of Welfare* (4th edn), London, UK: Macmillan, pp. 174–175, 178–183.
Posner, Richard A. (2007), *Economic Analysis of Law* (7th edn), New York, US: Aspen.
Rabin, Edward H. (1984), 'The Revolution in Residential Landlord-Tenant Law: Causes and Consequences', *Cornell Law Review*, **69**, 517–584.
Ramseyer, J. Mark (1989), 'Water Law in Imperial Japan: Public Goods, Private Claims, and Legal Convergence', *Journal of Legal Studies*, **18**, 51–77.
Ramseyer, J. Mark (1996), *Odd Markets In Japanese History: Law and Economic Growth*, New York, US: Cambridge University Press.
Reichman, Uriel (1978), 'Judicial Supervision of Servitudes', *Journal of Legal Studies*, **7**, 139–164.
Reichman, Uriel (1982), 'Toward a Unified Concept of Servitudes', *Southern California Law Review*, **55**, 1179–1260.
Robinson, Glen O. (1991), 'Explaining Contingent Rights: The Puzzle of "Obsolete Covenants"', *Columbia Law Review*, **91**, 546–580.
Rose, Carol M. (1998), 'The Several Futures of Property: Of Cyberspace and Folk Tales, Emission Trades and Ecosystems', *Minnesota Law Review*, **83**, 129–182.
Rose, Carol M. (2002), 'Common Property, Regulatory Property, and Environmental Protection: Comparing Community-Based Management to Tradable Environmental Allowances', in Elinor Ostrom, et al (eds), *The Drama of the Commons*, Washington, DC, US: National Academy Press, pp. 233–257.
Rose-Ackerman, Susan (1985), 'Inalienability and the Theory of Property Rights', *Columbia Law Review*, **85**, 931–969.
Rubin, Paul H. (ed.) (2007), *The Evolution of Efficient Common Law*, Cheltenham, UK and Northampton, MA, US: Edward Elgar.
Rydell, C. Peter et al. (1981), *The Impact of Rent Control on the Los Angeles Housing Market*, Santa Monica, CA, US: RAND Corporation.
Schafer, Robert (1979), 'Racial Discrimination in the Boston Housing Market', *Journal of Urban Economics*, **6**, 176–196.
Schwallie, Daniel P. (1990), 'Note: The Implied Warranty of Habitability as a Mechanism for Redistributing Income: Good Goal, Bad Policy', *Case Western Reserve Law Review*, **40**, 525–551.
Sevic, Zeljko (1996), *Law and Economics I: Ekonomska Analiza Prava Svojine u Tranziciji* (Law and Economics I: Economic Analysis of the Property Rights in Transition), Pravni Zivot, **45** (10), 964–977.
Shavell, Steven (2004), *Foundations of Economic Analysis of Law*, Cambridge, MA, US: Belknap Press of Harvard University Press.
Siegan, Bernard H. (1972), *Land Use without Zoning*, Lexington, MA, US: Lexington Books.
Simpson, A.W.B. (1961), *An Introduction to the History of the Land Law*, London, UK: Oxford University Press.
Simpson, A.W.B. (1986), *A History of the Land Law* (2nd edn), Oxford, UK: Clarendon Press. This is the second edition of Simpson (1961).
Sitkoff, Robert H. (2004), 'An Agency Costs Theory of Trust Law', *Cornell Law Review*, **89**, 621–684.

Solow, Barbara Lewis (1971), *The Land Question and the Irish Economy, 1870–1903*, Cambridge, MA, US: Harvard University Press.
Speyrer, Janet Furman (1989), 'The Effect of Land-Use Restrictions on Market Values of Single-Family Homes in Houston', *Journal of Real Estate Finance and Economics*, **2**, 117–130.
Stake, Jeffrey E. (1988), 'Toward an Economic Understanding of Touch and Concern', *Duke Law Journal*, **1988**, 925–974.
Stake, Jeffrey E. (1990), 'Darwin, Donations, and the Illusion of Dead Hand Control', *Tulane Law Review*, **64**, 705–781.
Stake, Jeffrey E. (1991), 'Status and Incentive Aspects of Judicial Decisions', *Georgetown Law Journal*, **79**, 1447–1497.
Stake, Jeffrey E. (1995), 'Loss Aversion and Involuntary Transfers of Title', in Robin P. Malloy and Christopher K. Braun (eds), *Law and Economics: New and Critical Perspectives*, New York, US: Peter Lang, pp. 331–360.
Stake, Jeffrey E. (2001), 'The Uneasy Case for Adverse Possession', *Georgetown Law Journal*, **89**, 2419–2474.
Stake, Jeffrey E. (2005), 'Evolution of Rules in a Common Law System: Differential Litigation of the Fee Tail and Other Perpetuities', *Florida State University Law Review*, **32**, 401–424. Reprinted in Paul H. Rubin (ed.) (2007), *The Evolution of Efficient Common Law*, Cheltenham, UK and Northampton, MA, US: Edward Elgar, pp. 460–483.
Stake, Jeffrey E. (2006), 'A Brief Comment on Trust Protectors', *Cardozo Law Review*, **27**, 2813–2819.
Sterk, Stewart E. (2006), 'Trust Protectors, Agency Costs, and Fiduciary Duty', *Cardozo Law Review*, **27**, 2761–2805.
Valdeon Buruque, Julio (1994), 'La Mesta y el Pastoreo en Castilla en la Baja Edad Media, 1273–1473 (The Mesta in the Low Medieval Age 1273–1473)', in Gonzalo A. Alvarez and Angel G. Sanz (eds), *Mestan Trashumancia y vida Pastoril: Exposición*, Madrid, Sociedad V Centenario del Tratado de Tordesillas, pp. 49–64.
Vlatas, Anthony J. (1994), 'An Economic Analysis of Implied Warranties of Fitness in Commercial Leases', *Columbia Law Review*, **94**, 658–709.
Vogel, Kenneth R. (1987), 'The Coase Theorem and California Animal Trespass Law', *Journal of Legal Studies*, **16**, 149–187.
Williams, Stephen F. (1973), 'Optimizing Water Use: The Return Flow Issue', *University of Colorado Law Review*, **44**, 301–321.
Williams, Stephen F. (1979a), 'Implied Covenants for Development and Exploration in Oil and Gas Leases – the Determination of Profitability', *Kansas Law Review*, **27**, 443–458.
Williams, Stephen F. (1979b), 'Solar Access and Property Rights: A Maverick Analysis', *Connecticut Law Review*, **11**, 430–458.
Williams, Stephen F. (1981), 'Implied Covenants in Oil and Gas Leases: Some General Principles', *Kansas Law Review*, **29**, 153–177.
Williams, Stephen F. (1983), 'The Requirement of Beneficial Use as a Cause of Waste in Water Resource Development', *Natural Resources Journal*, **23**, 7–23.
Williams, Stephen F. (1984), 'Free Trade in Water Resources: Sporhase v. Nebraska ex rel. Douglas', *Supreme Court Economic Review*, **2**, 89–110.
Williams, Stephen F. (1985), 'The Law of Prior Appropriation: Possible Lessons for Hawaii', *Natural Resources Journal*, **25**, 911–934.
Winokur, James L. (1989), 'The Mixed Blessings of Promissory Servitudes: Toward Optimizing Economic Utility, Individual Liberty, and Personal Identity', *Wisconsin Law Review*, **1989**, 1–97.
Winokur, James L. (1990), 'Rejoinder: Reforming Servitude Regimes: Toward Associational Federalism and Community', *Wisconsin Law Review*, **1990**, 537–552.
Yandle, Bruce and Andrew P. Morriss (2001), 'The Technologies of Property Rights: Choice Among Alternative Solutions to Tragedies of the Commons', *Ecology Law Quarterly*, **28**, 123–168.
Zeiler, Kathryn and Charles R. Plott (2005), 'The Willingness to Pay/Willingness to Accept

Gap, the "Endowment Effect," Subject Misconceptions and Experimental Procedures for Eliciting Valuations', *American Economic Review*, **95** (3), 530–545.

Cases

Hodel v. Irving (1987), 481 U.S. 704.
Kleppe v. New Mexico (1976), 426 U.S. 529.
London County Council v. Allen (1914), 3 KB 642.
Palazzolo v. Rhode Island (2001), 533 U.S. 606.
Sickman v. United States (1950), 184 F.2d 616 (7th Cir.), cert. denied, 341 U.S. 939, reh'g denied, 342 U.S. 874 (1951).
Tulk v. Moxhay (1848), Court of Chancery, 2 Phillips 774, 41 Eng Rep 1143.

7 Nuisance

Timothy Swanson and Andreas Kontoleon

1. Definition

The etymology of the term nuisance comes from the Latin *nocere* – to do harm, to inflict injury. In strict legal terms nuisance has been commonly defined as '. . . a condition or activity which unduly interferes with the use or enjoyment of land' (Clerk, 1989, p. 889). Fifoot (1949) notes that nuisance is one of the oldest branches of law dating back to the early assizes and that its 'very name – *nucumentum* – suggests the damage which he [i.e. the property owner] had suffered by conduct which nevertheless fell short of an actual dispossession'. The courts have identified nuisance disputes as involving a 'noxious' or 'offensive', 'unauthorised', and 'unreasonable' use of one's property that interferes, in a 'continuing way', with the use and/or enjoyment of another's property (Buckley, 1996). In economics terms, nuisance disputes may result when the choices of independent agents impact upon the outcomes affecting others, i.e. they are one of the possible legal consequences of externalities.

Nuisance can be of two kinds: private and public. A private nuisance occurs when the externality appears in the utility function of one consumer or the production function of one firm. If the externality affects many consumers or producers, then it is a public nuisance. Examples of such disputes include emissions from a factory that pollute a neighbouring property, noise that interferes with a person's sleep or unpleasant smells from one's use of his land. Generally, most cases of pollution and incompatible uses of land can be classified as nuisances, and could give rise to nuisance disputes.

2. Traditional legal approach to nuisance

Scholars have identified the traditional approach to nuisance law as originating in thirteenth century England (Fifoot, 1949; Buckley, 1996; Lewin, 1986; Ellickson, 1973; Brenner, 1974). In its English development, nuisance law was founded on property law and offered absolute protection to plaintiffs: either the nuisance existed and an injunction was granted or courts avoided granting an injunction by deciding that no nuisance existed.

The nineteenth century in the US brought about a significant change in the foundations of nuisance law. This re-formulation of nuisance law involved the introduction of the concept of 'reasonableness' that resulted in the abolition of the absolute rights enjoyed by property owners and the adoption of the 'reasonable use' criterion. The 'reasonableness test' was employed to determine whether a specific use of land constituted a nuisance in the particular context (Lewin, 1986, p. 780). It considered the nature of the activity that brought about the nuisance suit, the character of the neighbourhood, the frequency of the activity, the 'hypersensitivity' of the plaintiff, and the defendant's motive (Buckley, 1996). Thus the 'reasonableness test' limited the scope of the pre-existing nuisance doctrine since courts could now find that certain interferences with the use and enjoyment of land were not actionable. Yet, courts still retained an absolutist attitude in their decisions regarding remedies. If a nuisance was proven, an injunction was granted routinely.

Subsequently, however, this imbalance was gradually redressed by American courts, by incorporating the 'utility' of the defendant and society within the reasonableness test. In the first Restatement of Torts (1939) the American Law Institute (ALI) adopted the 'balancing of the equities or utilities' test.

Under the 'balancing of the equities' test a nuisance would be established 'only if its harmful consequences outweighed its benefits to society' (Lewin, 1986, p. 780). However, the test was soon found to be defective in that it rendered any activity with sufficient social value absolutely immune from liability for interference with the use and enjoyment of nearby land (Lewin, 1986, p. 781).

A less drastic judicial solution to the problem of the disproportionate impact of injunctive relief was to ignore the utility of the activity in determining liability and consider it only in determining the appropriate remedy after liability was established (Lewin, 1986, p. 781; Ellickson, 1973). Hence, the courts would first apply the reasonableness test to establish the nuisance and then apply the 'comparative hardship' or 'balancing of the conveniences test' to determine the nature of the relief. The court would then grant an injunction to the plaintiff only if the harm she experienced from the nuisance outweighed the social cost of abatement. This less drastic solution was also introduced in the first Restatement of Torts (1939). However, the co-existence of both the balancing of the equities test and the balancing of the conveniences test was found to be contradictory and confusing, and consequently judicial practice has been confined primarily to the use of injunctive relief (Lewin, 1986, p. 782).

Nevertheless, the ALI's approach to the law of nuisance as expressed in the Restatement (Second) of Torts (1969) was not radically different than that in the first Restatement (Ellickson, 1973; Lewin, 1986; Polinsky, 1980).

3. The law and economics approach to nuisance law

The new 'law and economics' paradigm as emerged in the 1960s recognised that traditional nuisance law faced several doctrinal and practical shortcomings. It had been characterised as 'unsystematic', 'neglected' and in a state of dismay and confusion (Coase, 1960; Ellickson, 1973; Newark, 1949; Epstein, 1979; Brenner, 1974). Prosser (1971) comments that '[t]here is perhaps no more impenetrable jungle in the entire law than that which surrounds the word "nuisance"' (p. 516). This new approach to nuisance law can be viewed as an attempt to reformulate and systematise the traditional approach to nuisance. It is also the field in which many of the first attempts to marry law with economics occurred.

A. General

The 'law and economics' paradigm analyses the nuisance dispute as a case of informal joint activity arising out of conflicting land uses (Coase, 1960; Posner, 1972; Calabresi and Melamed, 1972; Michelman, 1971; Polinsky, 1980; Kaplow and Shavell, 1996). Nuisance may also be viewed as a form of externality that interferes with the enjoyment or use of another's property. These externalities are a form of inefficiency which in turn can be corrected through the internalisation of these external effects. Hence, nuisance laws are the framework within which this cost internalisation occurs (Cooter and Ulen, 1988, p. 170). Equivalently, nuisance laws may be seen as the framework within which joint activities by independent agents are co-ordinated.

B. Coase (1960)

The literature acknowledges the beginning of the modern approach to nuisance law as being Ronald Coase's celebrated article 'The Problem of Social Cost.' The fundamental question raised by Coase was whether allocative efficiency was invariant to the initial assignment of property rights. The answer Coase gave to this problem has been referred to as the (simple) Coase Theorem (Polinsky, 1983, p. 12): In the absence of transaction costs, the efficient outcome will inhere irrespective of the assignment of rights.

Coase's article has been viewed as a reaction to the Pigouvean approach. This approach involved the identification of the agents imposing costs on others and then requiring these agents to compensate the injured parties in the amount of the full cost of their actions (i.e. to internalise the external costs). Coase emphasised the reciprocal nature of this problem – in that both of the parties to a nuisance cause the nuisance. In Coase's framework a nuisance dispute arises as the result of the interaction of two or more conflicting property uses, not as a cost inflicted by one onto another.

Coase's pioneering article dealt with a more general or fundamental issue in economics – the effect of the property right distribution on allocative efficiency. It was pure happenstance that many of the examples used to illustrate his innovative ideas involved nuisance and trespass disputes. In analysing these disputes under the assumption of zero transaction costs, Coase showed that the assignment of entitlements was irrelevant to the attainment of allocative efficiency. Under the zero transaction costs assumption, the party that incurs the costs from conflicting uses may acquire the entitlement to these uses from the other party at a price that is less than the costs she would suffer, if those uses of the resources are inefficient. Hence, where co-operation is not costly, the efficient allocation of resources will be achieved through private co-operation between the parties acting to maximise the value of their joint activities.

Obviously, much of the impact of this framework depends upon the usefulness of the assumption of zero transaction costs. The term 'transaction costs' includes the costs of identifying and assembling the parties involved in the negotiations, the costs of the actual negotiations and the costs of enforcing the outcome of the negotiations. Coase acknowledged that transaction costs are in reality positive. He used the examples involving nuisance disputes not to describe actual behaviour but to illustrate a point. Coase noted that in the presence of positive transaction costs the initial distribution of property rights does affect allocative efficiency, and that the courts may be in a position to assign property rights in such a way as to promote efficient outcomes. 'In a world in which there are costs of rearranging the rights established by the legal system, the courts, in cases relating to nuisance, are in effect, making a decision on the economic problem and determining how resources are to be employed'. And the 'economic problem' in cases of nuisances 'is how to maximise the value of production' (Coase, 1960, p. 15).

C. Calabresi and Melamed's Framework

Following Coase's pioneering work, Calabresi and Melamed (1972) offered the next notable contribution in the evolution of the modern approach to nuisance law. They furthered the Coasean ideas to construct a unified framework for the analysis of entitlements in property and torts. Their breakthrough was that they stressed that property and tort laws have a common objective: the protection of entitlements. However, the two systems differ in the rules used to enforce the entitlements: property rules for property entitlements and liability rules (negligence or strict liability) for torts. The novelty of their approach lies in that they recognised that these rules can be applied even in the cases where the entitlement is given to the defendant.

Calabresi and Melamed suggest that the resolution of a nuisance dispute involves two steps: first, a decision must be made to determine who should receive the entitlement (choice of entitlement) and second, a decision must be made on how to protect that entitlement (choice of remedies).

Within this general framework, Calabresi and Melamed noted that courts have traditionally considered the following rules or solutions in nuisance disputes:

i. the plaintiff is awarded the entitlement which is protected by a property rule (i.e. an injunction is awarded). The defendant must halt its nuisance-generating use of the property, unless the plaintiff agrees a price at which it will transfer its entitlement to the defendant;
ii. the plaintiff is awarded the entitlement which is protected by a liability rule. The defendant, on payment of the court-determined damages, may continue the use of his property in the manner that brought about the nuisance dispute. In effect, the court determines the price at which the entitlement may be transferred;
iii. the defendant is awarded the entitlement which is protected by a property rule (i.e. the defendant has thus the right to pollute and no injunction against its use will be granted). The defendant may continue its use of the property, unless the defendant agrees a price at which it will transfer its entitlement to the plaintiff.

However, for 'reasons of symmetry' they introduce an additional fourth rule:

iv. the defendant is awarded the entitlement which is protected by a liability rule. In this case, the plaintiff may acquire the entitlement from the defendant at a judicially determined price. Stated differently, the plaintiff may obtain an injunction against the defendant's activities only if he pays 'damages' to the defendant at a judicially determined price.

Lewin (1986) notes that this is the first explicit and thorough presentation of the concept of the 'compensated injunction', an injunction that the plaintiff could obtain only by paying damages to the defendant (p. 790). The fourth rule is also commonly referred to as the 'reverse liability rule' (e.g. Kaplow and Shavell, 1996) and has been the subject of extensive commentary and research (Ellickson, 1973; Rabin, 1977; Polinsky, 1983; Kaplow and Shavell, 1995; Ayres and Talley, 1995). Remarkably, the first judicial application of this rule appeared shortly after the time of the submission of their article, in the case of *Spur Industries, Inc. v. Del. E. Webb Development Co.* (Lewin, 1986, p. 790).

D. The importance of transaction costs

Within the framework established by Coase (1960) (i.e. assuming zero transaction costs), efficiency will result irrespective of which entitlement-remedy combination is chosen (i.e. no matter which of the four rules is chosen) (Posner, 1972; Polinsky, 1980, 1983). However, it is equally acknowledged that transaction costs are in reality not zero and, thus, the assignment of property rights must have serious implications for allocative efficiency (e.g. Calabresi, 1970; Calabresi and Melamed, 1972; Michelman, 1971). The subsequent literature has tried to analyse the impact of various forms of transaction costs on the efficiency of the outcome, and the implications of these impacts for the efficiency of various rules.

Echoing these lines, Polinsky (1983) notes that 'if there are positive transaction costs, the efficient outcome may not occur under every legal rule'. In these cases, 'the preferred legal rule is the rule that minimises the effects of transaction costs' (Polinsky, 1983, p. 13). The idea is to advance legal rules that work well in the world of the 'second-best': a world in which perfect bargaining in the context of perfect information is unlikely to occur.

The initial development of these ideas came from Calabresi (1970), Calabresi and Melamed (1972), and Michelman (1971), who put forth the criterion of 'the least cost abater' as a means for promoting allocative efficiency when transaction costs hinder (Coasean) bargaining between the parties. The rationale for this criterion is that, by assigning the responsibility for abatement to the party who can do so at the least cost, the need for Coasean bargaining is made redundant. Calabresi (1970) and Michelman (1971) show how allocative efficiency is promoted by the use of the 'least cost abater' criterion since it both eliminates the transaction costs of bargaining and also the risk of the failure of that bargaining process (i.e. its failure to reach the efficient solution).

A follow up to the 'least cost abater' criterion is what commentators have referred to as the 'best briber criterion' (Calabresi and Melamed, 1972; Lewin, 1986). This criterion has been proposed as a second best option when imperfect information and strategic behaviour do not allow the determination of the least cost abater. Under such circumstances, transaction costs might still be reduced and efficiency attained if the party who can least expensively bribe the other party is made liable (Calabresi, 1970; Calabresi and Melamed, 1972; Michelman, 1971).

In essence, the conclusion of the 'classical' literature on nuisance was that the design of legal rules does in fact matter. In a second-best world redolent with market imperfections and transaction costs, the best criterion for rule selection will be either to attempt to circumvent the (costly) bargaining process altogether (least cost abater criterion) or to attempt to reduce its costliness (least cost briber criterion). Much of the remainder of the literature in this area concerns the impacts of various forms of costliness on the choice of the legal rule.

4. The magnitude of transaction costs and the choice of remedies

The optimal choice of remedies (judically-set damages or assigned entitlement) will depend upon the relative costliness of using centralised (judicial) or decentralised (bargaining) methods for price determination. Kaplow and Shavell (1996) and Krier and Schwab (1995) observe that there is a trend in the literature that holds that 'property rules are best when transaction costs are low – assumedly because the use of property rules will induce parties to bargain and reach desirable outcomes – whereas liability rules are best when transaction costs are high – supposedly because the use of liability rules will induce injurers to act desirably, mimicking the outcomes that would otherwise have been reached through bargaining' (Kaplow and Shavell, 1995, p. 718).

A. High transaction costs

When the costs of bargaining are high, the implication is that the centralised approach to conflict resolution might be preferred; however, this must depend upon the nature and magnitude of the costs of centralised decision making. This will depend upon inter alia the availability of information to that decision maker, or the costs of resolving informational asymmetries (between the regulator and the regulated). The enquiry to the costs of centralised decision making in the context of informational asymmetries resulted in the development of an entirely distinct field of economics, known as the problems of 'principal-agent' theory. Within the nuisance literature, the issue has been focused on the question of the amount of information required by the judiciary in order to make an informed determination of the dispute.

High transaction costs with perfect knowledge of the level of damages In the presence of high transaction costs, liability rules (damages) are superior to property rules (injunctions) when courts have knowledge of the actual level of damages resulting from the conflict (Posner, 1972; Calabresi and Melamed, 1972; Barnes and Stout, 1992; Kaplow and Shavell, 1996). The argument is that if damages are assessed perfectly, then the defendant will stop the nuisance and abate only when it is more costly to pay the (correct level of) damages. If there was a property rule in effect (and high transactions costs prevented a negotiated resolution to the conflict) then the defendant would have to abate even if the abatement costs were greater than the damages (resulting in inefficiency).

High transaction costs with imperfect information Polinsky (1980, 1983) states that if the court lacks knowledge of both the damages to the plaintiff and the abatement costs to the defendant then no clear cut solution can be specified a priori. Kaplow and Shavell (1996), however, disagree with this view and demonstrate that 'even when courts are uncertain about the magnitude of harm, liability rules are superior to property rules' (p. 719). They demonstrate that courts faced with imperfect information when setting damages equal to an 'average' level of damages for cases characterised by similar facts, the outcome under the liability rule will be superior on average to that under the property rule (under the assumption that courts do not systematically underestimate or overestimate damages). This implies that courts do not require perfect information in order to establish an appropriate price for continuing nuisance, they only require sufficient information so as to allow them to determine an unbiased estimate of that price.

This criterion makes sense. It states that courts do not have to have perfect information in order to be a reasonable alternative to a costly decentralised price-setting mechanism; they will be as effective at price setting as the information that they have at their disposal. The more information that courts accumulate concerning a certain form of conflict, the more unbiased will be their estimate of its costliness and the more accurate will be their assessment of the appropriate price (damages). Talley (1994) also supports the proposition that liability rules with a 'properly' chosen level of damages are superior to property rules in the presence of high transactions costs. Therefore, the question of judicial efficiency as a regulator has to do with its unbiasedness as an estimator of damages, not the perfection of its information base.

B. Low transaction costs

Many commentators state that the decentralised mechanism (bargaining) is always the most efficient method for conflict resolution when transaction costs are low. Examples of this trend include Posner (1972), Calabresi and Melamed (1972).

For example, Merrill (1985) argues that trespass law should be used when transaction costs are low while the law of nuisance (implying payment of damages) should be used when transaction costs are high. However, several commentators (e.g. Polinsky, 1980; Kaplow and Shavell, 1996; Ayres and Talley, 1995) believe that this tendency is ill-founded. The general theme in this criticism is that even when transaction costs are low, both property rules and liability rules can induce bargaining and in fact in certain cases more efficient solutions can be attained under liability rules.

Very low transaction costs Polinsky (1980) applies the Coase Theorem and shows that under zero transaction costs both property rules and liability rules lead to equally efficient outcomes. This reasoning is followed by several subsequent commentators (e.g. Kaplow and Shavell, 1996). The reasoning is that, if bargaining is virtually costless, then the parties will be able to resolve the conflict irrespective of the process within which the bargaining is embedded. In short, institutional questions only become interesting when private cooperation is faltering as a coordination mechanism, i.e. when the costs of private transactions are significant.

Low transaction costs and imperfect information The invariance result of the Coase Theorem is not robust over a very wide range of institutional costliness. Once there are at least some transactions costs and information costs, the optimal choice of rule or criterion is more complicated. Polinsky (1980) argues that under imperfect information it is uncertain whether liability rules or property rules are superior.

Kaplow and Shavell (1996) state that liability rules may not be better than property rules under conditions of imperfect information but that (if constructed in an unbiased manner) they tend to be better. They base their argument on the idea of the court's unbiased estimation of damages set forth above, and the court's capacity to use accumulated information to resolve current conflicts. Ayres and Talley (1995) also argue that liability rules may be superior to property rules under imperfect information but offer a different basis for their argument. They argue that in cases of imperfect information and costly bargaining 'liability rules possess an "information-forcing" quality' that may induce and facilitate more efficient bargaining (pp. 1032–33). In their approach the price announced by the court separates the pool of all plaintiffs into those adequately-compensated and those inadequately-compensated. This separation is the information-forcing characteristic of liability rules that facilitates bargaining (whereas such bargaining is not induced under property rules). In effect the plantiff's response to the judicial price initiates the bargaining process by providing information on that party's bargaining position.

Therefore, judicial intervention has been portrayed as a potentially useful form of centralised activity, even when the costs of decentralised conflict resolution are low. It can be an efficient method for accumulating and applying information on previous similar conflicts to current ones (informational efficiency gains). Or, it can be an effective approach to initiating bargaining between parties where asymmetric information creates bargaining costliness (bargaining efficiency gains).

5. Other important factors in determining the appropriate remedy

The comparative costliness of centralised solutions (judicially determined prices) versus decentralised solutions (negotiation determined prices) depends upon factors other than simply the costs of bargaining. There are also the costs of the institution, the costs of implementation and enforcement, and the impacts on other legitimate societal objectives. A substantial literature surveys the range of costs that must be considered when the resolution of a nuisance conflict is being undertaken.

A. Enforcement

When the defendant cannot pay assessed damages then Kaplow and Shavell (1996) show that the liability-related incentives to take precautions [to reduce or avoid nuisance] will be compromised. Hence, a property rule solution protecting victims would be preferable. Alternatively, it may be possible to retain the advantages of the liability rule in some contexts by requiring injurers to pay in advance for expected harm rather than to pay for actual harm after it occurs. Finally, another way to overcome the judgement proof problem is to require potential injurers to offer proof that they have the ability to pay the damages before any damage has occurred (e.g. by purchasing insurance) (Kaplow and Shavell, 1996, pp. 740–741).

B. Numbers: public versus private nuisances

The principal reason public nuisances are dealt with separately is because they involve 'free-rider' and 'hold out' problems. Regarding remedies, Calabresi and Melamed (1972) imply that injunctions are more efficient than damages when there is only one victim and one injurer. When there is a public nuisance (i.e. many victims) Calabresi and Melamed argue that damage remedies tend to be more efficient. Ellickson (1973) has disputed this argument. Posner (1972) argues that damages should be awarded when transaction costs are high and injunctions should be assigned in the opposite case. Yet, Posner states that transaction costs could be high in both the public nuisance and private nuisance disputes (in the latter case due to strategic behaviour). Michelman (1971) also suggests that the damages remedies should be used in the case of one injurer and many victims unless the injurer is the 'cheapest cost avoider'. For other commentators, however, the public nuisance case is seen as a less serious theoretical challenging since, it can be reduced to a private nuisance analysis by aggregating the parties in a class action (e.g. Polinsky, 1980, 1983).

C. Institutional costs

Institutional costs mean the costs of the chosen approach to governance. In the context of nuisance disputes, the institutional costs are the costs to the judiciary of its involvement in the resolution of the dispute. Clearly, one of the most significant advantages to property-based resolutions is that the judiciary's involvement is minimised. It needs only identify which party to the dispute holds the entitlement. This is the reason that any movement toward increased judicial intervention must be justified by balancing the benefits of that intervention against the costs that they entail.

This is the essence of the approach taken by Calabresi and Melamed (1972) who argued in favour of injunctions when administrative costs were low (p. 1118). They argued that a property-based resolution avoided two costs: (a) the administrative costs of judicially valuing the damages and (b) the costs of enforcing the judgment against plaintiffs who have to exchange their right at prices to which they may not consent. But Ellickson (1973) argues that Calabresi and Melamed fail to see that a combination of rules may entail lower administrative costs than a simple injunction (even when administrative costs are low). He argues that injunctions may involve three additional administrative costs: 'the costs of difficult searches for subjective values, delays in initiation of cost-justified nuisance activities, and added administrative costs in determining what remedies are in a specific case' (p. 747).

D. *Entitlements and wealth effects*

Much of the analysis thus far has assumed that the externality was unilateral in nature, whereas Coase had pointed out that most nuisances are best conceived of as situations of reciprocal externality. If plaintiffs are able to elect behaviour that exposes themselves to a nuisance (as in cases of 'coming to the nuisance') or able to mitigate the effects of a nuisance (e.g. through the use of an air purifier), then the externality is best thought of as a joint cost determined by the joint activities of the two parties. In this case, it is probably inappropriate to think of the remedy as simply the framework for determining the price at which a unilateral transfer is effected. It is more appropriate to think of it as the framework within which the parties must work to move away from the non-cooperative outcome and toward the cooperative outcome. In this light, the important issue becomes the differential wealth effects of different entitlement rules. That is, irrespective of the remedy used to enforce the rule and the ultimate achievement of allocative efficiency, the choice of entitlements will effectively endow one party rather than the other with the wealth represented by the joint use. These wealth effects may have many other impacts within society, and on society's goals other than allocative efficiency. This is the essence of the bonus payment argument in favour of damages remedies, summarised by Polinsky (1980) as follows: once damages have been awarded then 'it is possible to pursue additional distributional goals by making the defendant's liability more or less than the plaintiff's actual damages'. (e.g. Calabresi and Melamed, 1972; Ellickson, 1973). For example, if the plaintiff is less well off than the defendant and a more equitable distribution is desired, then the damage awarded could be augmented by a bonus payment by the amount that will bring about the distribution preferred. 'Under the injunctive remedy, on the other hand, distributional outcomes are uncertain' (Polinsky, 1980, p. 1078).

Property-based rules disallow any consideration of these other objectives, i.e. the distributional effects of the entitlement. The court only decides which party will receive the entitlement, and leaves it at that. A liability-based system of remedies allows the court to balance these other objectives, when determining the price at which the entitlement may be transferred. In effect, the court is better able to 'balance the equities' of the situation in determining both issues of entitlement and its price.

6. Determining entitlements: the 'coming to the nuisance' doctrine

Most often the allocation of an entitlement within a nuisance dispute rests on the relative impact of one use of land on the other, i.e. on the degree of interference with the reasonable uses of another parcel of land. When a specific use of one parcel of land disqualifies many other reasonable uses of another parcel, then the offending use is deemed to be the 'nuisance'. Equivalently, the other landowner is deemed to hold an entitlement to pursue a reasonable range of uses on its land without interference. The exception to this rule has been where the landowner is deemed to have 'come to the nuisance'. This doctrine involves a defendant who has used his property in a specified way for a prolonged period of time without complaint, and then receives a complaint when the plaintiff introduces a new use on a neighbouring parcel of land. In this case, the defendant may claim that it is entitled to its use by reason of prior appropriation, while the plaintiff is not entitled to its new use of the neighbouring land.

'Coming to the nuisance' has been considered as a defence in nuisance disputes. The doctrine of coming to the nuisance has very old roots in the general ancient maxim of *volenti non fit injuria* (no legal wrong is done to him who consents). 'The person coming to the nuisance implicitly consents by his voluntary choice of establishing a residence or business in the neighbourhood of a pre-existing producer of negative externalities' (Wittman, 1980). Yet, it is considered that the influence of the 'coming to the nuisance' principle has gradually diminished in modern judicial decision making (Epstein, 1979; Tromans, 1982; Wittman, 1980).

Several proponents of the law and economic paradigm argue that the weight of 'being first' ought to be considered in judicial practices since it has implications for allocative efficiency (Posner, 1972; Wittman, 1980;

Rob, 1986). If entitlements are allocated on the basis of being first, there is an efficiency cost associated with establishing oneself 'there' first. For example, unnecessary or inappropriate timing of investment may occur in order to establish prior rights (Posner, 1972; Wittman, 1980).

A notable contribution on the issue is that by Wittman (1980). Wittman suggests that in order to avoid such strategic behaviour a two-staged procedure must be followed in cases of 'coming to the nuisance': first, the court must establish, based on efficiency criteria, who should have been first instead of who was first and then, once the efficient sequence is determined, the court must 'determine the liability or property rule that promotes the efficient sequence' (p. 559). In searching for the most efficient sequence the court must take under consideration the costs and benefits of the two parties involved (the 'first party' and the 'newcomer'). Wittman (1980, p. 561) points out that no efficient sequence would allow for the compensation of relocating the 'first' party if that party should not have been first.

Another concept related to issue of coming to the nuisance is that of 'foreseeability': In certain cases, the party that is first can, based on the characteristics of the location, foresee that the location is prone to generate a nuisance dispute. Consequently, that party should not have been there first and their prior appropriation should not give rise to an entitlement (Wittman, 1980).

7. Impacts of rules on bargaining outcomes and investment

The most recent piece on nuisance considers how various rules and remedies impact upon investment efficiency via their impacts upon threat points in bargaining outcomes (Pitchford and Snyder, 2003) They incorporate the bargaining problem explicitly into their analysis, and examine how different forms of property rules (injunction, damages, first mover, second mover) impact upon the decision to invest prior to the existence of the externality. In their analysis, the bargaining problem occurs after the fact, and the issues regarding nuisance have to do with the impact of various property rules on the threat points in that bargaining. The more that court rules favour the first-mover (in terms of right and remedy), the more that the first mover will invest in its particular use of the property, and irrespective of the potential for externalities from that use. This is because the remedy available moves the threat points, as does the level of investment undertaken by the first-mover.

Pitchford and Snyder (2003) find unambiguously that the first-best rule in nuisance is to vest the second mover with the property right but only when protected by a damages remedy. As mentioned, any right or remedy that favours the first-mover provides incentives to overinvestment in the use, given the prospect of full compensation *ex post*. They show that a right given to the second mover but protected by an injunction will result in underinvestment.

The bargaining approach of Pitchford and Snyder (2003) brings the nuisance literature into line with many other parts of the literature dealing with property rights problems. It incorporates the issues of bargaining, transactions costs, threat points and *ex ante* investment incentives. The framework is very similar to that used to examine other property rights problems, such as government takings (Blume and Rubinfeld, 1984) and multiple-property right investment problems in industry (Scotchmer, 1996). The problem of nuisance becomes one more example of how different forms of rules shape the bargaining environment between uncoordinated agents.

8. Alternative approaches to the resolution of nuisance disputes

The law and economics literature on nuisance has focused on a fairly limited (but fundamentally important) institutional choice, between judicially-determined remedies (damages, injunctions) and party-negotiated outcomes. There are – of course – an entire range of possible institutions, ranging from free markets in all sorts of securitised property rights to wholly centralised regulatory institutions. A few commentators have pointed to these alternatives, and the overall limitations of the classic approach to nuisance disputes.

A. More decentralised approaches

Knetsh (1983, ch.10) argues that the case-by-case approach adhered to by the law and economics literature to resolving nuisance disputes increases the uncertainty associated with investment in property since the maximisation-efficiency doctrine may grant an entitlement or choose a remedy 'depending on the circumstances' (Polinsky, 1983) that maximise efficiency.

Uncertainty of these 'circumstances' and of how the court will react to these, reduces the security in investment in property. Knetsh (1983) proposes an alternative market-based approach that aims to reconcile security in investment with allocative efficiency whereby the nuisance-causing party would be required to buy off the 'easements' from neighbouring landowners so as to compensate them. Future purchasers of land would have to 'buy back' the easement if they required the termination of the nuisance. Such a system, Knetsh argues, brings about certain and unambiguous entitlements. Another example of a private mechanism for the resolution of nuisance disputes is the use of restrictive covenants (e.g. Ellickson, 1973).

B. More centralised approaches

Burrows (1981) offers a more general attack on the mainstream framework developed from Coase (1960) and Calabresi and Melamed (1972). Burrows argues that more centralised methods of intervention are required in nuisance disputes, such as pollution control (see Burrows, 1981, 1985). He argues that (a) it is contradictory to resort to the best briber when by assumption bargaining is difficult and (b) (in the case of imperfect information regarding the efficient level of nuisance), identifying the least cost abater is an insufficient criterion. Burrows further argues that the Calabresian criteria are irrelevant if transaction costs are considerably low. In fact, under such a situation there is no need for any criteria since the 'efficient decentralised process will ensure that the least cost avoider does the abating, and that he does so to an efficient level' (Burrows, 1981, p. 156). If transaction costs are high (or other obstacles to bargaining exists) then Burrows argues that the criteria are ambiguous. In this case, the transaction costs are 'too high to allow decentralised transactions whichever of the four legal rules is selected' (Burrows, 1981, p. 156). Burrows concludes that 'if progress is to be made in the direction of efficiency and justice in the pollution context, we must look to more centralised policies of pollution evaluation and control' (p. 163) and proposes that future research should focus on the development of a 'systematic statutory approach' to nuisance control (p. 164).

C. Ellickson on zoning

Influenced by Coase (1960) and Calabresi and Melamed (1972), Ellickson (1973) argued for decentralised mechanisms to deal with conflicts among neighbouring landowners. Ellickson criticised the system of zoning 'as an ideal model for highlighting the economic consequences of all mandatory [centralised] regulation' (p. 691). Other notable contributions that critically examine centralised mechanisms for resolving conflicting land uses in the manner of Ellickson (1973) include Siegan (1970, 1972), Note (1969), Davis (1963), and Crecine et al (1967).

Ellickson (1973) notes that the usual practice in traditional nuisance law (to resort to the property rule solution) resulted in the belief that zoning was necessary. In his view zoning is not desirable on efficiency grounds since it fails to reduce the costs of the nuisance, but also increases the preventive and administrative costs associated with it. With respect to equity, zoning does not correct the changes in the wealth distribution it causes (p. 699). Hence zoning as a means of controlling nuisance is seen as neither efficient nor equitable as compared to other alternatives. Ellickson thus concludes that other less centralised remedies must be used.

Ellickson (1973) proposes the use of covenants (consensual agreements among landlords that limit the uses of one's property) as a means to deal with nuisance disputes. Again, he argues on efficiency grounds: 'Covenants negotiated between landowners will tend to optimise resource allocation among them. In other words, the reduction in future nuisance costs to each party will exceed the sum of the prevention and administrative costs each agrees to bear, with all costs discounted to present value' (p. 713). Though Ellickson acknowledges that '[n]ot all conflicts between neighbours can be solved by covenants', covenants 'generated by market forces will tend to promote efficiency' (p. 714) and that 'assuming equal bargaining power and information, consensual covenants will not involve inequitable gains or losses to any party' (p. 714). Covenants are problematic 'when they impose external costs on third parties, creating suboptimal resource allocation and unfairness' (p. 714) (e.g. when certain racial minorities are excluded from specific zones). Though old judicial practices and high transaction costs of the past have limited the use of covenants, Ellickson urges that the new emerging judicial attitude (influenced by the new 'law and economics' school) and the standardisation of legal procedures can bring about the reduction of transaction costs and thus facilitate the use of covenants.

More recently, Ellickson (1991) has advanced these ideas and has further argued for the use of informal mechanisms as effective means for resolving nuisance disputes. He shows how non-legal-informal social controls are likely to supplant legal rules when transaction costs are high. He argues that in certain cases of conflicting uses of property, individuals often resort to such informal means of settlement not only because they tend to be administratively cheaper but also because they are more likely to promote efficiency (social wealth maximisation).

Where the application of covenants or other non-formal legal mechanisms are not feasible, due to high administrative and information costs, then a remedy for nuisance dispute can be found by altering the property rights amongst landowners. Ellickson (1973) held that a remedy settling a nuisance dispute will be efficient to a party if its preventive costs (the costs to avoid the nuisance) and administrative costs (the costs of litigation and bargaining) are less than the costs from reduction in nuisance. Legal rules cannot affect preventive costs, since the latter are affected only by technological innovations. Legal rules, however, can affect administrative costs involved in the execution of a specific measure and thus property rights ought to be assigned so as to minimise administrative costs that will lead to the increase in the number of preventive measures that the parties perceive to be in their self interest. Ellickson (1973) developed a framework comprising of four guidelines for the choice of a nuisance remedy: (a) assign the entitlement to the party with the greater knowledge of the risks involved; (b) assign the entitlement to the party with the better organisation for dealing with the risk; (c) assign the entitlement to the party with the better control over implementing the most efficiency preventive measures; and (d) use the most simple rules of liability since they are less costly than complex rules.

Using these guidelines, Ellickson (1973) proceeds to generate efficient remedies for nuisance dispute. He strongly advocates the use of damages over injunction. He proposed the elimination of traditional injunctive relief in nuisance disputes. In the context of the framework established by Calabresi and Melamed (1972) he proposed that only rule ii (i.e. damages) and rule iv (compensated injunction) were granted (Ellickson, 1973, p. 115–122). Ellickson argued against the use of injunctive relief on the basis that the balancing of equities or conveniences tests were uncertain and costly and hence allow the possibility of inefficiency arising from granting an injunction that poses costs to the defendant greater than the benefits gained from the plaintiff. A novelty in Ellickson's (1973) work is that it implies that compensated injunctions could be granted to a plaintiff that would not have been entitled to damages. For example, in the cases where the plaintiff would not be entitled to damages on the grounds that they were 'hypersensitive to injury' or had 'come to the nuisance', the plaintiff could nevertheless purchase a compensated injunction in cases 'involving personal safety or fundamental freedoms' (Ellickson, 1973, p. 740). What is more, a plaintiff that has been protected by a liability rule could also purchase a compensated injunction (rule iv) if they were not satisfied with the damages awarded (rule ii) (Ellickson, 1973, pp. 745–746). Ellickson is thus seen by commentators as proposing a remedy that is a 'hybrid of Rule Two and Rule Four remedies' (Lewin, 1986, p. 796).

D. Merrill on Trespass

Merrill (1985) discusses trespass and nuisance law and how they differ in the remedies that can be effective. He considers trespass and nuisance law in the context of the right to exclude intrusions by others. He argues that this right is not one right but a 'bundle' of rights. In case of intrusion in the form of trespass the strict liability rule readily applies. Intrusion as a nuisance, however, is more complex in both establishing the nuisance (actionability) and to decide on the appropriate remedy. Whereas in nuisance law deciding on actionability and remedy involves weighing cost and benefits, this is not required in the case of trespass. Merrill further develops the 'mechanical – judgmental' distinction: trespass law as entailing limited judicial discretion in the determination of remedies (they are determined 'mechanically'). Nuisance law involves discretion and entitlements are established judgmentally. Merrill further analyses the economic underpinnings of the difference between nuisance and trespass law. His main thesis is that 'when the costs of transacting are low, the legal system will gravitate towards rule that determine entitlements at a low cost – such as the strict liability rule of trespass . . . In contrast, when the costs of transacting are apt to be high, the legal system will incline toward rules for the determination of entitlement that are more expensive – such as the balancing or cost-benefit approach of nuisance'. That is, in the presence of high transaction costs market transactions are more prone to fail and thus 'these more expensive entitlement-determination rules are necessary in order to give judges the needed discretion to adopt what they perceive as the best "compromise" solution (the efficient solution) to land use disputes' (Merrill, 1985, p. 14).

9. Comparative nuisance: differing systems in different jurisdictions

Regarding the relative trends in the application of injunction and damages remedies, most commentators hold that damage remedies have been used increasingly by American courts (Ellickson, 1973; Note, 1979; Rabin, 1977; Polinsky, 1980) over the past four decades. On the other hand, courts in England have traditionally shown a preference for injunctive relief based on the high esteem they have held for private property, despite the fact English law prescribes that injunction is a discretionary remedy (Tromans, 1982; Atiyah, 1980; Brenner, 1974). Yet, it has been argued that there may be '[s]ome easing in the judicial attitude' regarding this preference (Ogus and Richardson, 1977, p. 310).

For comparison of English and UK judicial treatments of nuisance see Stephen (1988), while Lang (1979) offers a comparative discussion of the development and application of private law in cases of harmful externalities in England, France and Germany. Ogus and Richardson (1977) examine certain judicial practices in the area of nuisance law and how they compare to the economic models developed by the law and economics tradition.

10. Conclusion

Many of the most important issues of law and economics arose out of the article by Coase, and hence by happenstance they arose within the context of the nuisance dispute. The problems of legal frameworks, property right allocations, bargaining costs, information costs and asymmetries, institutional costs, endowments and invariance results – all of these issues were raised first by Coase in his landmark article 'The Problem of Social Cost' (1960). For good reason each of these issues now constitutes a field of research in itself. Some of it could continue to occur within the confines of the nuisance dispute, but most of the issues are far more fundamental and far-reaching than this one context. For this reason the law and economics literature on nuisance is incredibly rich at its outset. It is a field of research far more notable for its past than it could ever be for its future.

Nevertheless nuisance disputes continue to provide a context for substantial analysis and academic interest. The fundamental nature of the nuisance dispute – individual activities with joint outputs by reason of physical proximity – raises many of the interesting issues involved in the coordination of society.

The alternative approaches to their resolution – centralised or decentralised pricing and bargaining – raises many of the most fundamental questions of governance. The field will continue to provide an interesting context for the consideration of these fundamental issues.

Acknowledgements

The authors gratefully acknowledge the helpful comments of two anonymous referees.

Bibliography

Ackerman, Bruce A. (1975), *Economic Foundations of Property Law*, Boston, Little Brown.

Adams, Michael (1990), 'Warum das "Verursacherprinzip" eine leere Worthülse darstellt und von feinsinnigen Juristen bei Haftungslastentscheidungen im Umweltrecht als ungeeignetes Kriterium verworfen werden sollte (Why the "Polluter Pays Principle" Is an Empty Formula and Should Be Disregarded by Sensitive Lawyers when Making Decisions on Liability in Environment Law)', in Haller, M., Hauser, H. and Zäch, R. (eds.), *Ergängzungen, Festschrift Erweiterungsbau der Hochschule St. Gallen*, Haupt, 605–612.

Adelstein, Richard P. and Edelson, Noel (1976), 'Subdivision Exactions and Congestion Externalities', 5 *Journal of Legal Studies*, 147–163.

Atiyah, Patrick S. (1970), *Accidents Compensation and the Law*, London, Weidenfeld and Nicolson.

Atiyah, Patrick S. (1980), 'Liability for Railway Nuisance in the English Common Law: A Historical Footnote', 23 *Journal of Law and Economics*, 191–196.

Ayres, Ian and Talley, Eric (1995), 'Solomonic Bargaining: Dividing a Legal Entitlement to Facilitate Coasean Trade', 104 *Yale Law Journal*, 1027–1117.

Barnes, David W. and Stout, Lynn A. (1992), *Economics of Property Rights and Nuisance Law*, Minneapolis, West Publishing.

Bergstrom, John C. and Centner, Terence J. (1989), 'Agricultural Nuisances and Right to Farm Laws', 19 *Review of Regional Studies*, 23–30.

Blume, Larry and Rubinfeld, Daniel (1984), 'Compensation for Takings: An Economic Analysis', 72 *California Law Review*, 569–628.

Brenner, Joel Franklin (1974), 'Nuisance Law and the Industrial Revolution', 3 *Journal of Legal Studies*, 403–433.

Buckley, R.A. (1996), *The Law of Nuisance*, London, Butterworths.

Burrows, Paul (1981), 'Nuisance, Legal Rules and Decentralised Decisions: a Different View from the Cathedral Crypt', in Borrows, P. and Veljanovski, C.G. (eds.), *The Economic Approach to Law*, London, Butterworths, 151–166.

Burrows, Paul (1985), 'Efficiency Levels, Efficiency Gains and Alternative Nuisance Remedies', 5 *International Review of Law and Economics*, 59–71.

Calabresi, Guido (1970), *The Costs of Accidents: A Legal and Economic Analysis*, New Haven (CT), Yale University Press.

Calabresi, Guido and Melamed, A. Douglas (1972), 'Property Rules, Liability Rules and Inalienability: One View of the Cathedral', 85 *Harvard Law Review*, 1089–1128.

Centner, Terence J. (1986), 'Agricultural Nuisances and the Georgia Right to Farm Law', 22 *Georgia State Bar Journal*, 19–26.
Centner, Terence J. (1988), 'Agricultural Nuisances Under the Amended Georgia "Right-to-Farm" Law', 25 *Georgia State Bar Journal*, 36–41.
Clerk, John Frederic (1989), *Clerk and Lindsell on Torts* (16th ed), London: Sweet & Maxwell.
Coase, Ronald H. (1960), 'The Problem of Social Cost', 3(1) *Journal of Law and Economics*, 1–44.
Coleman, Jules L. (1982), 'The Economic Analysis of Law', in Pennock, J. Roland and Chapman, John W. (eds.), *Ethics, Economics and the Law* (Nomos 24), New York, New York University Press.
Coleman, Jules L. (1992), *Risks and Wrongs*, Cambridge, Cambridge University Press.
Comment (1970), 'Equity and the Eco-System: Can Injunctions Clear the Air?', *Michigan Law Review*.
Cooter, Robert (1976), *The Cost of Believing Coase Theorem*, Working Paper No 84, Department of Economics, University of California.
Cooter, Robert and Ulen, Thomas S. (1988), *Law and Economics*, Glenview (IL), Scott Foresman.
Cosentino, Fabrizio (1996), 'Neil Komesar, il danno da immissioni e la responsabilità civile: una storia di alternative imperfette? (Neil Komesar, damage from nuisance and tort law: a story of imperfect alternatives?)', *Politica del diritto*, 321–329.
Crecine, John P., Davis, Otto A. and Jackson, John E. (1967), 'Urban Property Markets: Some Empirical Results and Their Implications for Municipal Zoning', 10 *Journal of Law and Economics*, 79–99.
Davis, Otto A. (1963), 'Economic Elements in Municipal Zoning Decisions', 39 *Land Economics*, 375–386.
Dworkin, Ronald M. (1975), 'Hard Cases', 88 *Harvard Law Review*, 1057–1109.
Dworkin, Ronald M. (1980), 'Why Efficiency? A Response to Professors Calabresi and Posner', 8 *Hofstra Law Review*.
Ellickson, Robert C. (1973), 'Alternatives to Zoning: Convenants, Nuisance Rules, and Fines as Land Use Controls', 40 *University of Chicago Law Review*, 683–781. Reprinted in Ackerman, Bruce A., *Economic Foundations of Property Law*, Boston, Little Brown, 1975, 265–301.
Ellickson, R.C. (1991), *Order Without Law*, Cambridge (MA), Harvard University Press.
Epstein, Richard (1979), 'Nuisance Law: Corrective Justice and Its Utilitarian Constraints', 8 *Journal of Legal Studies*, 49–102.
Fifoot, C.H.S. (1949), *History and Sources of the Common Law*, Cambridge (MA), Harvard University Press.
Finsinger, Jörg and Von Randow, Philip (1991), 'Neue Aktivitäten und Haftungsregeln – Zugleich ein Beitrag zur ökonomischen Analyse des privaten Nachbarrechts (New Activities and Liability Rules – Also a Contribution)', in Ott, Claus and Schäfer, Hans-Bernd (eds.), *Ökonomische Probleme des Zivilrechts*, Berlin, Springer, 87–108.
Fiss, Owen M. (1978), *The Civil Rights Injunction*, Bloomington (IN), Indiana University Press.
Fletcher, George P. (1972), 'Fairness and Utility in Tort Theory', 85 *Harvard Law Review*, 537–573.
Freeman (1976), 'Give and Take: Distributing Local and Environmental Control Through Land-Use Regulation', 60 *Minnesota Law Review*.
Gallo, Paolo (1995), 'Immissioni, usi Incompatibili e Problemi di Allocazione di Risorse Scarse (Nuisance, Incompatible Uses and Problems of Allocation of Scarce Resources)', 1 *Rivista di Diritto Civile*, 657–693.
Hirsch, Werner Z. (1979), *Law and Economics: An Introductory Analysis*, London, Academic Press.
Kaplow, Louis and Shavell, Steven (1994), 'Why the Legal System is Less Efficient than the Income Tax in Redistributing Income', 23 *Journal of Legal Studies*, 667–681.

Kaplow, Louis and Shavell, Steven (1995), 'Do Liability Rules Facilitate Bargaining? A Reply to Ayres and Talley', 105 *Yale Law Journal*, 221–233.

Kaplow, Louis and Shavell, Steven (1996), 'Property Rules Versus Liability Rules: An Economic Analysis', 109 *Harvard Law Review*, 713–790.

Keeton and Morris (1940), 'Notes on "Balancing the Equities"', 18 *Texas Law Review*, 412 ff.

Knetsh, J. (1983), *Property Rights and Compensation-Compulsory Acquisitions and Other Losses*, Toronto, Butterworths.

Krier, James E. and Schwab, Stewart J. (1995), 'Property Rules and Liability Rules: The Cathedral in Another Light', 70 *New York University Law Review*, 440–483.

Kuperberg, Mark and Beitz, Charles R. (1983), *Law, Economics, and Philosophy*, New Jersey, Rowman and Allanheld.

Lang (1979), 'Grundfragendes privatrechtlichen Immissioschutzes in Rechtvergleichender Sicht', 174 *Archiv für die civilistische Praxis*, 381 ff.

Lewin, Jeff L. (1986), 'Compensated Injunctions and the Evolution of Nuisance Law', 71 *Iowa Law Review*, 777–832.

Manson, William D. (1985), 'A Re-examination of Nuisance Law', *Harvard Journal of Law and Public Policy*, 185 ff.

Merrill, Thomas W. (1985), 'Trespass, Nuisance, and the Costs of Determining Property Rights', 14 *Journal of Legal Studies*, 13–48.

Miceli, Thomas J. (1993), 'Optimal Deterrence of Nuisance Suits by Repeat Defendants', 13 *International Review of Law and Economics*, 135–144.

Michelman, Frank I. (1967), 'Property, Utility and Fairness: Comments on the Ethical Foundations of "Just Compensation" Law', 80 *Harvard Law Review*, 1165–1258.

Michelman, Frank I. (1971), 'Pollution as a Tort: A Non-Accidental Perspective on Calabresi's Costs', 50(3) *Yale Law Journal*, 647–686.

Newark, F.H. (1949), 'The Boundaries of Nuisance', 65 *Law Quarterly Review*, 480–490.

Note (1969), 'An Economic Analysis of Land Use Conflicts', 21 *Stanford Law Review*, 293 ff.

Note (1975), 'Injunction Negotiations: An Economic, Moral, and Legal Analysis', 27 *Stanford Law Review*.

Note (1978), 'Internalising Externalities: Nuisance Law and Economic Efficiency', 53 *New York University Law Review*, 219–240.

Note (1979), 'Efficiency Land Use and the Internalisation of Beneficial Spillovers: An Economic and Legal Analysis', 31 *Stanford Law Review*, 457 ff.

O'Driscoll, L. (1980), 'Justice, Efficiency, and Economic Analysis of Law: A Comment on Fried', 9 *Journal of Legal Studies*, 355–366.

Ogus, Anthony I. and Richardson, G. (1977), 'Economics and the Environment: A Study of Private Nuisance', 36 *Cambridge Law Journal*, 284–325.

Ogus, Anthony I. and Veljanovski, Cento G. (1984), *Reading in the Economics of Law and Regulation*, Oxford, Oxford University Press.

Panella, Giorgio (1994), 'Responsabilità Civile ed "Effetti esterni": un'Applicazione ai Problemi dell'Inquinamento (Tortious Liability and "External Effects": an Application to the Problems of Pollution)', *Economia e Diritto del Terziario*, 631–653.

Pardolesi, Roberto (1977), 'Azione Reale E Azione Di Danni Nell Art. 844 C.C. Logica Economica E Logica Giuridica Nella Composizione Del Conflitto Tra Usi Incompatibili Delle Proprietà Vicine (Property Rule and Liability Rule in Article 844 Codice Civile: Economic Arguments, Legal Arguments and Litigation for Inconsistent Uses of Neighbours Lands)', 1 *Foro Italiano*, 1144–1154.

Pejovich, Svetozar (1972), 'The Economic Basis of Property', *Review of Social Economics*, 309 ff.

Pigou, A.C. (1932), *The Economics of Welfare*, London, Macmillan.

Pitchford, R. and Snyder, C. (2003), 'Coming to the Nuisance: An Economic Analysis from an Incomplete Contracts Perspective', *Journal of Law, Economics And Organisation*, 19(2), 491–516.

Polinsky, A. Mitchell (1974), 'Economic Analysis as a Potentially Defective Product', 87 *Harvard Law Review*, 1655–1681.

Polinsky, A. Mitchell (1979), 'Controlling Externalities and Protecting Entitlements: Property Right, Liability Rule, and Tax-Subsidy Approaches', 8 *Journal of Legal Studies*, 1–48.
Polinsky, A. Mitchell (1980), 'Resolving Nuisance Disputes: The Simple Economics of Injunctive and Damage Remedies', 33 *Stanford Law Review*, 1075–1112.
Polinsky, A. Mitchell (1983), *An Introduction to Law and Economics*, Boston, Little Brown.
Posner, Richard A. (1972), *Economic Analysis of Law*, Boston, Little Brown.
Posner, Richard A. (1979a), 'Utilitarianism, Economics and Legal Theory', 8 *Journal of Legal Studies*, 103–140.
Posner, Richard A. (1979b), 'Epstein's Tort Theory: A Critique', 8 *Journal of Legal Studies*, 457–475.
Posner, Richard A. (1980), 'The Ethical and Political Basis of the Efficiency Norm in Common Law Adjudication', 8 *Hofstra Law Review*.
Pozzo, Barbara (1996), *Danno Ambientale ed Imputazione della Responsabilità. Esperienze Giuridiche a Confronto (Environmental Damage and Charge of Liability. Legal Experiences Compared)*, Milano, Giuffrè.
Prosser, William Lloyd (1971), *Handbook of Torts*, St. Paul, West Publishing Company.
Rabin, Edward H. (1977), 'Nuisance Law: Rethinking Fundamental Assumptions', 63 *Virginia Law Review*, 1299–1348.
Ramseyer, J. Mark (1996), *Odd Markets In Japanese History: Law and Economic Growth*, New York, Cambridge University Press.
Regan, Donald H. (1972), 'The Problem of Social Cost Revisited', 15 *Journal of Law and Economics*, 428–432.
Rizzo, Mario J. (1980), 'Law Amid Flux: The Economics of Negligence and Strict Liability in Tort', 9 *Journal of Legal Studies*, 291–318.
Rob, Rafael (1986), *Coming to the Nuisance: An Efficiency Analysis*, University of Pennsylvania Center for the Study of Organizational Innovation Working Paper, 20.
Schmid, A. Allan (1978), *Property, Power and Public Choice*, New York, Praeger.
Scotchmer, Suzanne (1996), 'Protecting Early Innovators: Should Second Generations Innovations be Patentable?', 27 *Rand Journal of Economics*, 322–331.
Shavell, Steven (1981), 'A Note on Efficiency vs. Distributional Equity in Legal Rulemaking: Should Distributional Equity Matter Given Optimal Income Taxation?', 71(2) *American Economic Review*, 414–418.
Shavell, Steven (1986), 'The Judgement Proof Problem', 6 *International Review of Law and Economics*, 45–58.
Siegan, Bernard H. (1970), 'Non-Zoning in Houston', 13 *Journal of Law and Economics*, 71–147.
Siegan, Bernard H. (1972), *Land Use Without Zoning*, Lexington, Mass., Lexington Books.
Spittje, Petra J. (1991), 'De hinderwetgeving (Nuisance Legislation)', in Coljee, P.D., Franken, H., Heertje, A. and Kanning, W. (eds.), *Law and Welfare Economics*, Amsterdam, VU Amsterdam, 115–132.
Stephen, Frank H. (1988), *The Economics of the Law*, Hemel Hempstead, Harvester Wheatsheaf.
Talley, Eric (1994), *Property Rights, Liability Rules, and Coasean Bargaining Under Incomplete Information*, Working Paper, Stanford Law School, 114.
Trimarchi, Pietro (ed.) (1994), *Per una Riforma della Responsabilité Civile per Danno all'Ambiente (The Reform of Tort Law for Environmental Damage)*, Milano, Giuffrè.
Tromans, Stephen (1982), 'Nuisance-Prevention or Payment?', 41 *Cambridge Law Journal*, 87–109.
Weinrib, Ernest J. (1994), 'The Gains and Losses of Corrective Justice', 44 *Duke Law Journal*, 277 ff.
White, Lawrence H. (1985), 'Economics and Nuisance Law: Comment on Manson', 8 *Harvard Journal of Law and Public Policy*, 213–223.
Winfield, P.H. (1931), 'Nuisance as a Tort', 4 *Cambridge Law Journal*, 189–206.
Wittman, Donald A. (1980), 'First Come, First Served: An Economic Analysis of "Coming to the Nuisance"', 9 *Journal of Legal Studies*, 557–568.
Wittman, Donald A. (1998), 'Coming to the Nuisance', in Newman, Peter (ed.), *The New Palgrave Dictionary of Economics and the Law*, London, Macmillan.

8 Adverse possession

Ben Depoorter

A. The concept of adverse possession

The doctrine of adverse possession allows an occupier of a parcel of land who is not the true owner to acquire title to the land without consent from or compensation to the 'true' owner. This legal rule, firmly established in both civil and common law legal systems, specifies that after a certain period of time, termed the limitation or statutory period, not even the true owner of the property can bring action to eject an unauthorized possessor.

Adverse possession was formalized in English common law in 1632 in the Statute of Limitations. It fits within the framework of the general doctrine of limitations, which fixes the time within which parties must follow suit to bring an action. After a certain period of time a person, whether he had acquired the possession of property rightfully or wrongfully is to be protected from actions to recover possession of the property (Callahan, 1961). Under the Statutes of Limitation which were in force in England prior to 1833 the effect of remaining in possession for the prescribed period was to bar only the remedy of the person dispossessed, not his rights. His title remained intact. If he were to obtain possession of the land in a lawful manner his title would prevail against the possessor. Under the statutes that have been in force since 1833 the right as well as the remedy of the dispossessed owner is extinguished. The *usucapio* of Roman law, as adopted in civil law systems, represents what is often called acquisitive prescription in the sense that adverse possession conferred a positive title upon the occupier, who had remained in possession for a certain time.

Although the doctrine of adverse possession was adopted as a rule in all states of the United States, statutory rules and judicial interpretations vary across states (see Netter, Hersch and Manson, 1986). Similarly, differences in the implementation of adverse possession exist across countries around the world.

The remainder of this chapter will focus on the various economic explanations of adverse possession, the various conditions of adverse possession, the optimal length of the prescription period, and the distinction between good and bad faith possessors.

B. The economic foundations of adverse possession

Various economic explanations of the doctrine of adverse possession have been forwarded in the literature.

First, adverse possession is presumed to reduce evidence costs. With the passage of time, it is increasingly difficult to keep track of facts that occurred a long time ago. As a result, adverse possession serves the dual purpose of litigation and uncertainty costs. By limiting the amount of (more complex) cases that can be tried after a substantial amount of time has passed, adverse possession may reduce litigation costs in the long run. Also, by quieting old title claims, the doctrine of adverse possession reduces uncertainty to adverse possessors and third party purchasers. To the latter, adverse possession reduces the risks associated with title transfer (Baird and Jackson, 1984; Netter, Hersch and Manson, 1986). Search costs and verification costs are reduced as the potential purchaser is assured of the validity of the title presented. A potential purchaser who knows that the current possessor has occupied the property for the requisite statutory period is assured that the title he acquires is good. In this sense, adverse possession reduces transaction costs and uncertainty with regard to the title of the property concerned. On the other hand, adverse possession increases the costs of landowners who, with the possibility of losing title through adverse, will likely incur more monitoring costs over their land (Ellickson, 1986).

A second justification of adverse possession holds that the doctrine seeks to reward adverse possessors for making productive use of land. A related explanation focuses on the true owner, suggesting that adverse possession serves the purpose imposing a penalty on punishing dormant owners for sitting on their rights. In this sense, adverse possession promotes the productive use of property. Both the reward and penalty explanations of adverse possession presume that the original owner has failed to maximize the value of the property by not using it. A potential objection to this conception of adverse possession relates to the difficulty with assessing the most valuable use of the property. Often, the value maximizing use of certain property at a certain time might be to wait until one develops or uses the land.

Third, adverse possession can be regarded as an incentive mechanism to reduce both the occurrence and costs of boundary mistakes. Prior to the running of the prescription period, the possibility of ejection encourages adverse possessors to avoid boundary errors (the first-best solution). At the same time, the possibility of adverse possession maintains the incentives for true owners to mitigate errors in a timely fashion (the second best solution). Additionally, adverse possession reduces the ability of a true owner to extract rents from a possessor who has started to rely on an error, for instance by improving the property or development (Miceli, 1997). Without a limitation period, a true owner would indefinitely be in a position to exercise his or her property rule protection in order to extract payments while the reliance costs of the adverse possessor increase over time with his or her investments in the property. Accordingly, by imposing a time-limited property rule, the doctrine of adverse possession provides owners incentives to correct errors in a timely manner and limits the ability to appropriate quasi-rent from adverse possessors that have relied in good faith on a boundary mistake (Miceli, 1997).

C. The requirements of adverse possession

For the rules of adverse possession to apply, a few interrelated conditions have to be met. The possessor must hold the property actually, exclusively, continuously, in open and notorious manner, and adversely to the owner, with a claim of right. The interpretation of these conditions has been the subject of debate and the interpretation differs between states (see Netter, Hersch and Manson, 1986). Generally, it is required that the possessor holds the possession exclusive from others for a period at least as long as the statutory period, without being dispossessed (continuously), in an open and visual manner that is inconsistent with the title of the owner (adverse) and without the owner's permission (hostile). With the exception of variations in time periods and some minor differences the doctrine of adverse possession under common law does not differ much from that found in most civil law systems.

The above conditions comport quite naturally with the purposes of adverse possessions set out in the previous section. Especially the reward/punishment explanation of adverse possession seems to justify the legal requirements of adverse possession. For instance, if adverse possession is to punish land owners that fail to act and alert good faith possessors before the latter rely on the use of land that they do not own, it is within reasonable expectations that such duty is imposed only if the acts of adverse possession are reasonably visible (open and notorious) and provide sufficient signal to the outside world that the adverse use is premised on an ownership claim (exclusive possession, claim of right). Similarly, the protection of any reliance interest on behalf of the adverse possessor is warranted only if the possessor has made sufficient use of the property (continuous) in a manner that would traditionally be associated with ownership (exclusive, with claim of right). Similarly, the legal conditions of adverse possession fit well the purpose of reducing the occurrence and costs of boundary mistakes. The requirements that possession during the statutory period must be actual, open, notorious and exclusive ensure to the true owner an opportunity to discover boundary errors prior to investment by the encroacher (Miceli and Sirmans, 1995b).

One notable difference between the rule of adverse possession within civil law and common law systems is the significance of the state of mind of the adverse possessor ('does the adverse possessor realize that the property is not his/hers?'). In the United States there is a debate whether the intention of the possessor matters for the applicability of the adverse possession doctrine. The so-called Maine rule (mistaken possession is not found to be sufficiently hostile to the owner's right) has generally been abandoned in favor of the newer Connecticut rule which emphasizes that the possessor's state of mind is irrelevant. While this represents a formal legal shift from the favorable treatment of bad faith possessors – which is more in line with the punishment theory of adverse possession – to include also good faith possessors as potential benefactors of adverse possession – corresponding with the reward and incentive theories – judicial practice has traditionally favored good faith possessors, often by manipulating the application of the conditions to the facts so that good faith possessors may acquire ownership through adverse possession (Helmholz, 1983). By contrast, most civil law systems more explicitly distinguish between good and bad faith adverse possessors. Generally, prescription periods are longer for bad faith possessors than for good faith possessors.

Distinctions between good and bad faith possessors are difficult to justify from the perspective of the evidence costs-reducing justification of adverse possession. Good faith errors are difficult, often impossible, to distinguish from intentional errors, for instance with regard to real property issues such as boundary encroachments (Bouckaert and De Geest, 1998). Any attempt to prove bad faith might significantly increase high litigation costs, notably if the plaintiff must reverse the presumption of good faith against the defendant possessor. Also, the current, differing treatment of good and bad faith possession does not sit comfortably with the reward and punishment explanations of adverse possession. If the focus of adverse possession is on preventing good faith mistakes and preventing strategic behavior on behalf of the true owner, adverse possession can simply be limited to good faith possession. By contrast, the adverse possession suggest to reward productive use of property that is held by dormant land owners, especially bad faith possessors should be awarded for making productive use of resources, provided that sufficient notice is provided to landowners (see for example Fennell, 2006, suggesting bad faith oriented system of adverse possession).

On the other hand, there are economic arguments in favor of extending the prescription period of bad faith possessors. Prolonging the prescription period likely reduces the incidence of preying by squatters and the consequences demoralization costs on behalf of surprised landowners that are faced with a completed adverse possession period (Ellickson, 1986). In this vein, Thomas Merrill has argued in favor of adjusting the rule of adverse possession to provide liability rule protection against bad faith possession (Merill, 1985). Such remedial shift, from property rule to liability rule protection, on behalf of a true owner at the end of the prescription period of a bad faith possession, reduces the incentives of a true owner to be vigilant, but likely reduces the lure of preying on behalf of bad faith adverse possessors (in this manner it has a similar effect as a lengthening of the prescription period, see below).

D. The Optimal Prescription Period

Adverse possession essentially involves the following efficiency trade-off between the adverse possessor and the true owner: a shorter statutory period reduces uncertainty as to the title in subsequent transfers, while a longer statutory period reduces the costs to property owners to protect their land from potential adverse possessors.

On the other hand, there are costs to the application of the adverse possession doctrine. With the risk of losing title, owners must monitor their land. When they are not using the property they need to be careful not to lose ownership to a possessor. By reducing the costs of mistakes of encroachments, adverse possession introduces a moral hazard problem, in the sense that there is less incentive to make sure mistakes are not made in the first place (Netter, 1998).

Figure 8.1 illustrates this trade-off. At point *e*, where the time of occupation (on the vertical X-axis) required to obtain title is set optimally, a balance is found between prevention and uncertainty costs. As the

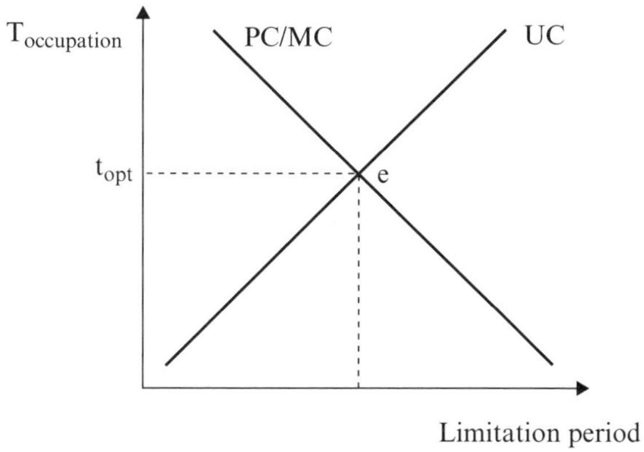

Figure 8.1 Optimal prescription period

limitation period is set beyond point *e*, the uncertainty costs, represented by the UC curve, increase further. The longer the statutory period is set, the lower the monitoring costs of owners. If the limitation period is set below *e*, the prevention and monitoring costs, as represented by the PC/MC curve. increase while uncertainty costs reduce.

Economic theory holds that the greater the benefit from reducing uncertainty with regard to the ownership of a good, the shorter should be the time period required of adverse possession.

A fairly recent study of prescription statutes in the different North American states (Netter, Hersch and Manson, 1986) provides empirical evidence on the various differences and examines the determinants of the length of the occupation period in the statutes of limitations of states' adverse possession at the time of statehood.

First, a negative relationship between property value in a state and statute length was observed. When the property has great value, there is simply a higher return to be obtained from ending potential disputes about ownership that arise from mistakes. Also, the costs of mistakes are higher when property value is high. In such circumstances it is recommendable that adverse possession requirements (length, type of possession) are less demanding. However, it should be acknowledged that if property values are high, owners have more to lose from adverse possession.

Secondly, a positive relationship between population density and statute length was found. As population density increases more property transfers take place, which raises the probability that errors (in determination of boundaries, identification of the title holder, registration, and so on) will occur. The length of the prescription period will affect incentives in various ways.

Protection costs will be lower when protection periods are relatively long. The shorter the prescription time period, the more theft or deceit is encouraged. Stolen, lost and fraudulently acquired goods will have a higher market price when potential buyers know that the possibility of claims and other repossession actions are restricted to only a limited period of time. Thus, the introduction of a prescription period will affect criminality and tortuous acquisition rates. The possibility of becoming a true owner through mere adverse possession increases the value of an adversely possessed good. A thief who wants to resell the stolen good will be able to charge a higher price to the buyer under a system where the latter can become the legally unchallenged owner after the elapse of a short period of time. As theft, fraudulent and deceptive acquisition will become more profitable, property owners will need to invest more into protection of the property.

Also, short prescription periods force owners of lost, stolen or fraudulently divested goods to concentrate their search and repossession acts within a short period of time, which leads to higher opportunity costs of search (Bouckaert and De Geest, 1998). On the other hand, short prescription periods provide the possessor with efficient incentives with regard to investment decisions.

Bibliography

Anderson, Terry L. and Lueck, Dean (1992), 'Land Tenure and Agricultural Productivity on Indian Reservations', **35** *Journal of Law and Economics*, 427–454.

Baird, Douglas G. (1983), 'Notice Filing and the Problem of Ostensible Ownership', **12** *Journal of Legal Studies*, 53–67.

Baird, Douglas G. and Jackson, Thomas H. (1984), 'Information, Uncertainty, and the Transfer of Property', **13** *Journal of Legal Studies*, 299–320.

Bouckaert, B. and De Geest, G. (1998), 'The Economic Functions of Possession and Limitation Statutes', in Ott, C. and von Wagenheim, G., *Essays in Law and Economics IV*, Antwerpen and Apeldoorn, Maklu, 151–168.

Bowles, Roger A. and Phillips, Jennifer (1977), 'Solicitors' Remuneration: A Critique of Recent Developments in Conveyancing', **40** *Modern Law Review*, 639–650.

Callahan, C. (1961), *Adverse Possession*, Columbus, Ohio State University Press.

Cooter, Robert D. (1991), 'Inventing Market Property: The Land Courts of Papua New Guinea', **25** *Law and Society Review*, 759–801.

Cooter, Robert D. (1992), 'Organization as Property: Economic Analysis of Property Law and Privatization', in Clague, Christopher and Rausser, Gordon (eds), *The Emergence of Market Economies in Eastern Europe*, Oxford, Blackwell, 77–97.

Crawford, Robert G., Klein, Benjamin and Alchian, Armand A. (1978), 'Vertical Integration, Appropriable Rents, and the Competitive Contracting Process', **21** *Journal of Law and Economics*, 297–326.

Ellickson, R. (1986), 'Adverse Possession and Perpetuities Law: Two Dents in the Libertarian Model of Property Rights', **64** *Washington University Law Quarterly*, 723–737.

Epstein, Richard A. (1979), 'Possession as the Root of Title', **13** *Georgia Law Review*, 1221 ff.

Fennell, Lee Anne (2006), 'Efficient Trespass: The Case for "Bad Faith" Adverse Possession', **1037**, *Northwestern University Law Review*, 1073–1075.

Frech, H. Edward III (1991), 'Review of Contracting for Property Rights, by Gary D. Libecap', **15** *Journal of Comparative Economics*, 536–538.

Goldberg, Michael A. and Horwood, Peter J. (1987), 'The Costs of Buying and Selling Houses: Some Canadian Evidence', **10** *Research in Law and Economics*, 143–159.

Helmholz, Richard H. (1983), 'Adverse Possession and Subjective Intent', **61** *Washington University Law Quarterly*, 331–358.

Janczyk, Joseph T. (1977), 'An Economic Analysis of the Land Title Systems for Transferring Real Property', **6** *Journal of Legal Studies*, 213–233.

Janczyk, Joseph T. (1979), 'Land Title Systems, Scale of Operations, and Operating and Conversion Costs', **8** *Journal of Legal Studies*, 569–583.

Kennedy, Duncan (1981), 'Cost-Benefit of Entitlement Problems: A Critique', **33** *Stanford Law Review*, 387–445.

Lueck, Dean and Anderson, Terry L. (1992), 'Agricultural Development and Land Tenure on Indian Country', in Anderson, Terry L. (ed.), *Property Rights and Indian Economics*, Lanham, MD, Rowman and Littlefield Press.

Mascolo, E. (1992), 'A Primer on Adverse Possession', **21** *Connecticut Bar Journal*, 297–326.

Merrill, T. (1985), 'Property Rules, Liability Rules, and Adverse Possession', **79** *Northwestern University Law Review*, 1122–1154.

Miceli, Thomas J. (1997), *Economics of the Law*, New York and Oxford, Oxford University Press, 1997.

Miceli, Thomas J. and Sirmans, C.F. (1995a), 'The Economics of Land Transfer and Title Insurance', **10** *Journal of Real Estate Finance and Economics*, 81–88.
Miceli, Thomas J. and Sirmans, C.F. (1995b), 'An Economic Theory of Adverse Possession', **15** *International Review of Law and Economics*, 162–173.
Miceli, Thomas J. and Turnbull, G.K. (1997), 'Land Title System and Incentives for Development', 14th Annual Conference of the European Association of Law and Economics, University of Pompeu Fabra, Barcelona, Spain.
Miceli, Thomas J., Sirmans, C.F. and Turnbull, G.K. (1998), 'Title Assurance and Incentives for Efficient Land Use', **6(3)** *European Journal of Law and Economics*, 305–322.
Netter, J.M. (1998), 'Adverse Possession', in *The New Palgrave Dictionary of Economics*, London, Macmillan.
Netter, J.M., Hersch, P.H. and Manson, W.D. (1986), 'An Economic Analysis of Adverse Possession Statutes', **6** *International Review of Law and Economics*, 217–227.
Schechter, Dan S. (1988), 'Judicial Lien Creditors Versus Prior Unrecorded Transferees of Real Property: Rethinking the Goals of the Recording System and Their Consequences', **62** *Southern California Law Review*, 105–186.
Williams, Philip L. (1993), 'Mabo and Inalienable Rights to Property', **103** *Australian Economic Review*, 35–38.

9 Title systems and recordation of interests

Boudewijn Bouckaert

1. Title systems. Definition, history and types

A title system is a legal institution by which written evidence on the legal status of assets is systematically recorded. The written evidence mostly concerns acts of conveyances, providing data on the transfer of the asset, or on the vesting of partial rights, various interests or security rights on the asset. Their most prominent aim is to facilitate market circulation of assets by providing to potential buyers certainty about the legal status of the traded good. Often title systems serve also fiscal aims as they provide tax collectors with information on the wealth of taxpayers. The legal consequences of recordation can vary. Sometimes recordation is limited to the passive collection of conveyances and merely consists of a systematisation of already existing written evidence. Sometimes recordation has a deeper legal impact as the recordation implies also a procedure of checking the validity of written evidence and the rights and interests mentioned in it. In this case invalid rights and interests are purged from the asset (see further 4. Registration or recording system). In modern nation states title systems are most often organized by the government. They are a vital part of civil administration. As shown further, this was not always the case. Also nowadays recordation of rights and interests is often provided through private initiative. Major examples here are the registers of the title insurance companies in the USA and the Art Loss Register set up by major business from both the insurance and art industries.

As soon as trade expanded across the boundaries of small and informal groups, institutions, generating public knowledge on the legal status of the transferred assets emerged. The Athenians, for instance, posted a slab known as *horos* on land in order to signal that the land was under the charge of a security interest (Arrunadã, 2003, 6). In Roman law the transfer of land was sometimes operated through a court procedure in which the purchaser stated that the land was his. Because there was no opposition he was awarded ownership (*in iure cessio*). The simulated trial provided public knowledge on the transfer (Kaser, 1971). Also the other legal form of transfer, the *mancipatio*, involved ceremonies providing some publicity to the transfer (Garro, 2004, 13; Kaser, 1971). In Hellenistic Egypt recordation was particularly well developed. In each district a book, entering all transactions affecting land and slaves (*diastromata*) was kept. Certificates on the legal status of land (*katagraphé*) were enacted by a public officer (*agronomos*) (Garro, 2004, 14). In feudal Europe land tenures were mostly transferred by a ceremony held in a public place such as a market, church or court (Garro, 2004, 18). After the Middle Ages attempts were made by the central state to organize title systems covering the whole country. The customary law of the most northern part of France (*pays de nantissement*) provided already a system of recordation of titles. By an Edict of Colbert this recordation system was introduced in the whole country. Fierce opposition by the nobility and the notaries forced Colbert to repeal the Edict in 1674. The former did not like disclosing the highly encumbered status of their land. The latter feared the loss of absolute control exercised in dealings with immovable property (Garro, 2004, 19). After the French Revolution title systems were introduced for the recordation of mortgages (*Code Hypothécaire of 1795*). These were, however, again abolished by the enactment of the Code Civil. The drafters of the Code, inspired by the natural law consensualistic doctrine on transfers, considered transfers as an exchange, merely affecting the legal position of the contracting parties and in which the wider public had no business at all. The negative impact of this was felt quite soon in the financing sector and credit financing supported by immovable property was grossly impaired (Garro, 2004, 22). To repair this deplorable situation the law on transcription of mortgages, providing also for the recordation of all transfers of land and the vesting of all property rights and interests (rights *in rem*) on land, was enacted in 1855.

Also in Germany recordation of land transactions was part of customary law in some regions. In 1783 Prussia enacted a General Ordinance on Mortgages and Bankruptcy, establishing land records giving public notice to land transfers and the creation of mortgages. This ordinance was the forerunner of the current Grundbuch-system, regulated by the BGB of 1900, art. 873–902 (Garro, 2004, 24).

Also in medieval England the transfer of rights in land occurred through a ceremony providing public knowledge to third parties. The transfer of a freehold estate, called feoffment, included the ceremony of livery of seisin, in which the transferor (feoffor) took the transferee (feoffee) to the concerned piece of land. There a stick, a piece of turf or a handful of soil were handed over (Garro, 2004, 28). A first attempt to establish a title system was the advent of 'uses', an equitable interest, recognized by the Lord Chancellor. In order to convert this equitable title into a legal one, registration of the deed of conveyance in a court of record of Westminster was required. However, this system failed. During the nineteenth century recordation initiatives were taken by the Parliament with the Land Registry Act of 1862. Among other reasons, the fact that the recordation had not been made compulsory but depended on the will of the purchaser, resulted in a failure of the law. Together with a thorough simplification of land law in England a system of recordation was set up in 1925 (the Law of Property Act, the Land Registration Act). It is estimated that about 80 per cent of the land in England and Wales is recorded under this system (Garro, 2004, 34).

The early colonists in the English colonies of North America continued to practice the common law-transfer of livery of seisin. Quite soon, however, towns and states developed recordation practices which gradually supplanted the livery of seisin. The title systems in the US vary widely from state to state as concerning what has to be recorded, the way it is recorded, the legal consequences of it. Attempts to introduce more uniformity, such as the Uniform Simplification of Land Transfer Act of 1976 (USOLTA), failed (Garro, 2004, 38). Due to the archaic and incomplete character of many official recordation institutions, the private insurance sector developed title insurance, providing purchasers with additional certainty in return for a premium. The introduction of the so-called Torrens system provided an alternative to this combination of an official recording system with title insurance. The Englishman Robert Richard Torrens developed in Australia a registration system, in which the registrar acquired conclusive competences to check and validate evidence on title and to purge a title from apparent but, after checking, invalid rights and interests. Such a system, provided it was operated by able personnel, would make additional title insurance redundant. The system was introduced in Australia, the Canadian provinces Alberta, British Columbia, Manitoba and Saskatchewan, many African countries such as Tanzania, Uganda, Ethiopia, Kenya, Asian countries such as the United Arab Republic, Nepal, India, Sri Lanka, Malaysia, Thailand, Turkey and Iran (Garro, 2004, 44). The Torrens system became popular in the United States during the late nineteenth century. More than 20 states passed enabling acts for a Torrens system during the period 1895–1915. Prompted by the failure of three of four title insurance companies in the state of New York during the 1930s, the New York Law Society engaged R. Powell of Columbia University in order to study an eventual introduction of the Torrens system in the state of New York. His report was highly critical about such an introduction stating that the recordation system, then prevailing in the state of New York and in 16 other states, operated at lower cost than the Torrens system. His report gave a fatal blow to the hopes that the Torrens system would be generally accepted in the United States. Many states which had adopted the system repealed the statutes (Garro, 2004, 47). The discussion about the effectiveness and efficiency of both systems still looms in legal literature, also in the law-and-economics-literature (see further 4. Registration or recording system).

2. Title systems as a critical factor of economic development

Functional analysis of title systems, in classical legal doctrine as well as in law-and-economics, focuses on the provision of certainty in market transactions and the lowering of information costs (see further sections 3 and 4). De Soto (2000) lifted the economic function of a recordation system on the wider level of macro-economics and development economics. Recordation systems are considered as critical factors for the success of capitalist economies. While mere possession of an asset provides the holder with the immediate benefits of physical use, recordation converts the assets into genuine capital, allowing to the holder a much wider range of economic use. This conversion operates through six so-called property effects of recordation (De Soto, 2000, 49–62): 1) by recordation abstraction is made from the physical characteristics of the asset while the asset becomes represented within the conceptual universe of capital; 2) by recordation dispersed information on the potentialities of capital is integrated into one system; 3) recordation makes people accountable: individuals do not have to rely anymore on local arrangements to protect their property rights; 4) recordation makes assets fungible, i.e. assets are made able, to be fashioned to suit any transaction (for instance a single factory can be held by multiple owners); 5) recordation allows for the networking of people: by recordation assets such as buildings are legally attached to their owners which facilitates the integration into networks such as electricity provision, Internet, radio, TV and telephone cable networks; and 6) recordation protects transaction. Only the latter effect is taken into consideration by the current analysis of title systems. The larger and the poorer portion of the world population remains cut off from the benefits of the expansion of markets throughout the world because of the lack of an operational title system. The poorer urban masses within less developed countries (LDCs) dispose of a lot of entrepreneurial energy and also control many physical assets. Due to the lack of a title systems and the ensuing lack of formal protection of property rights, these poor are not able to integrate their potential into the wider network of the world market economy. They remain locked into large social pockets of economic stagnation, corruption and violence (De Soto, 2000, 18–28). Concerning the impact of De Soto's analysis Calderon points out that the issuing of titles in Peru has increased and peaked at 400 000 in 2000, slowing down considerably since then (Calderon, 2003, 289–300). Field found that housing investment was 68 per cent higher in households with a title than in households without one (Field, 2003b, 281). Also prices increased considerably by the recordation of the property rights on housing. The Institute for Liberty and Democracy (ILD) and the Commission para la formalizaçion de la Propriedad Informal (COFOPRI) estimated the price effect of titling at 25 per cent (ILD, 2006). The predicted effect concerning the use of recorded property as collateral, resulting in a better access to the credit market, remained, however, disappointing in the first years after the titling (ILD, 2006). Morris Guerinoni observes, however, a considerable increase of mortgages and loans during later years (Morris Guerinoni, 2004, 26). Jansen and Roquas perceive only a weak link between titling of land and access to the credit market in Honduras (Jansen and Roquas, 1998, 88). Field and Torero found that people with a title are more inclined to apply for loans and that such applicants enjoy also a higher approval rate from the public banks or a lower interest rate from private banks (Field and Torero, 2003, 5–11). Finally Field found that titling led to higher labour participation as people have to spend less time in protecting their property (Field, 2003a, 34; Field, 2003b, 19).

3. Security in transaction: the rule of possession or a title system

We have seen above that uncertainty plays an important role as one of the dominant cost factors in the transfer of assets and rights and these assets. In order to diminish uncertainty in markets legal systems develop what Hansmann and Kraakman call verification rules (Hansmann and Kraakman, 2002, 384). A possession rule is a common example of a verification rule. A simple possession rule establishes an absolute link between possession and ownership. To be certain the potential purchaser has only to check whether the vendor is in actual possession. Possession rules are often more sophisticated as they combine with a prescription rule (or limitation statute in the common law tradition). In this case certainty is only provided when the vendor is in possession of a good during the required prescription term. The elapse of this term avoids all possible other claims on the assets which might have been established prior to the acquisition by the vendor. In this case the potential purchaser has only to check whether the purchaser was in effective possession during the required prescription term. Recordation and title system are a different verification rule. In this case relevant information about the legal status of the asset is stored in a public register, so that potential purchasers are able to check about the rights' situation of the asset they are envisaging to acquire. In legal systems both verification rules operate side by side but on other categories of goods. A very common distinction is the chattel-real estate one, whereby the possession rule rather prevails for chattel and title systems for real estate (Bouckaert and De Geest, 1998).

A cost-minimizing efficiency model should focus on the comparison between the costs of a possession-based property system and a title system. According to Baird and Jackson the latter is more costly to administer but reduces the likelihood of non-consensual transfer, while the former facilitates transactions but not without raising the possibility of fraud and theft (Baird and Jackson, 1984).

Hansmann and Kraakman develop an efficiency model in order to explain the choice of the verification rule. Each verification rule has its user costs, i.e. the costs for the ones establishing the right (the purchaser, the mortgagee), nonuser costs, i.e. the costs for third persons not submitted to the established right (e.g. a purchaser checking whether there are no encumbrances on land he envisages to acquire), system costs, i.e. general, relatively fixed costs of establishing and maintaining a given verification rule for a particular right (e.g. the costs of establishing and maintaining a registry) (Hansmann and Kraakman, 2002, 396). A system is efficient when it maximizes the aggregate value of assets to right holders less the aggregate user, nonuser and system costs. According to Miceli the choice between a possession-based property system and a title system will depend on the magnitude of the different cost categories, which will be in turn determined by the characteristics of property (Miceli, 1997). Bouckaert and De Geest perceive the following determinants for the choice between a possession rule and the development of a title system: 1) durability of the good in question: as the costs of title systems are rather fixed, the more durable the good the lower the cost of a filing; 2) frequency of transfer: when goods are frequently transferred, the costs of filing is relatively higher; 3) the heterogeneity of a good: items with unique characteristics are cheaper to file than homogeneous goods for which an artificial uniqueness is necessary; and 4) the value of the good: as costs of filing are fixed filing is relatively cheaper for high-value goods than low-value ones. These determinants explain why title systems prevail for real estate and why possession systems prevail for low-value mobile goods. Path dependencies may explain why many legal systems did not develop title systems for high value, not too frequently transferred, and relatively durable mobile goods (e.g. cars) (Bouckaert and De Geest, 1998). Miceli perceives another determinant for the choice for a filing system. A possession rule cannot signal shared ownership and other multiple rights on one asset. Such rights cannot be visualised by possession (Miceli, 1997). Arruñada has a similar view concerning abstract rights, i.e. rights which exist only conceptually but are not actually practiced in a visually perceivable way. Only a title system allows such rights to be operational (Arruñada, 2003, 4). Arrunãda perceives another cost of title systems. Such systems are often set up for, or at least allow, closer control on the wealth of citizens and will ease fiscal collection. In how far this might lead to predatory taxation depends on the people's capacity to control their government and impede excessive taxation (Arruñada, 2003, 5). Moreover, publicity about the wealth of citizens might attract rent seekers and criminals in low security countries (Arruñada, 2003, 5).

Arruñada also raises the question whether title systems and recordation require a territorial monopoly. As far as the certainty of the transaction between the parties is concerned, there is no need for such a monopoly. Parties should be able to choose on open markets by which instance and through which type of evidence they are willing to give their transaction more certainty. The costs of their choice are fully internalized. For this reason the oligopoly of the notaries public in many countries should be contested from efficiency concerns. The transaction between parties can, however, involve rights and interests of third parties. As they are not involved in the choice of the drafter of the conveyance and the way it is drafted, externalisation of costs is possible in this case. For this reason the established territorial monopolies of recording and registration systems, recording data on the transactions on real estate, mortgages and other security rights, even on mobile goods, can be defended on efficiency grounds. Also systems, which allow free choice at first sight and seem to contradict this argument, rely on single authorities when rights of third parties are involved. For the registers of financial assets the best practice seems to consist of having a single clearing agency and depository. For Internet Domains there is only one register for each top-level domain. The users can, however, freely choose among 'registrars'. Protection for third parties *ex post* is provided by enforcing the Uniform Domain-Name Dispute-Resolution Policy (UDRP) that applicants have to accept *ex ante*. According to UDRP disputes are not decided by 'registrars' but by a panel of arbitrators approved by The Internet Corporation for Assigned Names and Numbers (ICANN) (Arruñada, 2003, 15–16).

4. Registration or recording system

As mentioned before title systems belong either to the type of a recording system or to the type of a registration system.

Under a recording system the only aim of recordation in the registers is to give public notice of a transfer or to the vesting of a right or an interest, by which the transfer or the vested right can be given effect to third parties. The transfer or the vesting of the right occurs through a contract, either made up by the parties themselves or drafted by an official, such as a notary public. Suppose A is the mortgagor and B the mortgagee. The mortgage is vested by an act, drafted by a notary public, as required in many civil law countries. Suppose A sells the mortgaged asset to C. Does C have to tolerate the mortgage on his asset and eventually be submitted to foreclosure when A, the former owner, defaults on his loan? The answer depends on the recordation. When the mortgage is recorded at the moment of the transfer from A to C, C has to tolerate the mortgage for he was able to check its existence at the registry. When not, the mortgage has no effect for him. The 'opposability' towards third parties, effectuated by registry, does not entail anything about the validity of the recorded rights or interests. The recordation is not constitutive but merely declaratory. The recordation merely signals that parties expressed their will to transfer a right or to vest a right or interest. The recordation does not provide exclusive evidence about the validity of title. The registrar in a recording system has a merely passive role. The registry accepts the conveyances, drafted by the parties or by other officials without effectuating a search of possible legal defects. As a consequence the recordation does not result in a purge of possible defects of the title. Suppose A conveys a real estate to B and the act of conveyance is registered within a recording system. C, however, claims to be the true owner and files a successful claim to the court. C will obtain a valid title while B can obtain, depending on circumstances (e.g. good faith) damages from A. For C a property rule applies, for B only a liability rule (Arruñada, 2003, 13). As mentioned before the recording system prevails in most civil law countries, influenced by the French civil code (France, Belgium, Spain, Italy, Portugal and most Latin American countries) but also in most states of the USA (Garro, 2004, 55).

Under a registration system the aim of recordation is more thorough: recordation results in the constitution of a valid title. This means that a transfer or vesting of a right has only full legal effect at the moment of the recordation. In Germany for instance the sale of land occurs through the phases of consent ('Einigung'), official conveyance by a notary public ('Grundstückskaufvertrag') and registration in the 'Grundbuch' ('Eintragung') (Garro, 2004, 53). Unlike recording systems the recordation results in a constitutive effect. The registrar is supposed to make a search into possible defects of the title. In case such defects are not found the title is purged and a valid title is awarded. Suppose A transfers land to B and the transfer is duly recorded under a registration system. C, though, files a claim against A and B. Even when the right of the seller (A) is overruled by the court the buyers' right (B) is protected by the certificate of the registrar. B enjoys the protection of a property rule while C can eventually claim damages either against A or against the registrar. C is at most protected only by a liability rule.

The registration system operates in Germany and countries influenced by German civil law (Austria, Switzerland), in England and Wales since 1925, in the states under the Torrens system (Australia, western Canadian provinces, some states in the USA, several African and Asian countries) (Garro, 2004, 44, 55).

As the difference has serious legal consequences, law-and-economics literature spent some attention to the efficiency of the choice between the two types.

Miceli and Sirmans argue that an efficient title system should create proper incentives for landowners to invest in capital improvements prior to the appearance of adverse claims and provide compensation for wrongfully injured parties. A registration system satisfies this requirement as it stimulates *ex post*-efficiency by allocating the land to the highest valuing user. One may assume that land tenure involves an increase of subjective valuation of land above market value. By awarding the land to the current holder and compensating the claims of the legitimate holder at market value the value of land is maximized with regard to the enhancements that have been made previously by the holder. Registration also provides incentives for efficient investment in land *ex ante* by the landowner (Miceli and Sirmans, 1995a; Miceli and Turnbull, 1997).

A recording system on the other hand seems more likely to meet the requirements of *ex ante* efficiency as the risk of future expropriation will provide landowners with an incentive to optimalize information on the validity of the title prior to investment. Owners, faced with the risk of expropriation will desire protection of their reliance interests through insurance. *Ex ante* efficiency is enhanced under a recording system by title insurance. Profit incentives of these companies will enforce efficiency in the title examination process, which extends beyond the reach of a governmentally administered registration indemnity fund, where the profit incentive is lacking. Miceli and Turnbull conclude that the recording system may have an advantage over the registration system (Miceli and Turnbull, 1997).

Arruñada researched the relationship between the number of rights *in rem*, allowed by the *numerus clausus* of the property right system and the prevailing title system. The prediction is that the number will be relatively low under a registration system as many rights *in rem* would render the task of the registrar, the final judge on possible claims, very complex. The number will be higher under a recording system as the costs of the complexity, following from this, will be shared between the recording instances and the courts, deciding *ex post* on the validity of titles. This prediction seems to be confirmed by an econometric model, involving data of 42 jurisdictions (Arruñada, 2003, 8–10). This conclusion could be challenged by the analysis of Hansmann and Kraakman, arguing that the *numerus clausus* does not reduce as such the complexity in the legal system, as the *numerus clausus* consists of abstract categories of rights, of which the concrete elements may vary considerably (Hansmann and Kraakman, 2002, 399).

In his cost-comparison of the two systems Arruñada starts from the classical position that the recording system is more cost-efficient while the registration system is more effective.

Concerning the higher cost-efficiency of the recording system Arruñada admits that many minor defects of title, which are not worth being purged, are insured either by the user or by his title insurer. Under a registration system these minor defects can result in hold-out situations. This efficiency advantage should, however, be nuanced, because competing title insurance systems trigger duplicate efforts of registering, and yield less economics of scale. On the suppliers' side, also the efficiency advantages, linked with the profit incentive of the private title insurance companies should be nuanced as this sector is submitted to strong regulation concerning prices and entry barriers, which endangers the competitive level.

Concerning the higher effectiveness of the registration system, Arruñada admits that it provides a strong protection of title for the good faith-acquirers. Registration systems can nevertheless be highly inadequate. This depends on a variety of factors. Sometimes their performance is weak due to fixed salary bureaucracy (e.g. Cook County, Puerto Rico). When staff is paid out by the profits of his office performance seems to be higher. The slowness of the search by the registration office may create additional uncertainty and necessitate again title insurance. Finally, incompleteness of the scope of registration can undermine the credibility of the registration system. When some rights *in re* are not within this scope, the effectiveness of the system is undermined as users have to rely on additional searches. The incompleteness may be due to opposition by the conveyance market and by the courts. The latter may be tempted to deny the conclusiveness of the registration in order to protect their own competence. The latter is the case in the USA but not in Germany as judges are involved in the Gründbuchsystem (Arruñada, 2003, 18–20).

Baker, Miceli, Sirmans and Turnbull developed research on the optimal title search under recording systems in the USA (Baker et al., 2002). Although the aim of their research is not on efficiency comparison between recording and registration systems, the results of their research strengthen the efficiency argument in favour of the recording system. Under recording systems rules are developed on optimal search length. When this optimal search is matched and chain of title is established, claims stretching beyond the required search period are considered as extinguished, so that the optimal search period has an effect similar to a limitation statute. Guidelines on optimal search are provided statutorily by Marketable Title Acts or practically by local bars and insurers. In the model agents pursue title search until the marginal costs of search become higher than the benefits in terms of reduction of uncertainty. The model involves determinants such as the value of land, the next best investment in land, the land development rate. The empirical analysis carried out about the optimal search of title rules in 47 states, points to the efficiency of the search length. As a consequence such rules act as substantive palliatives for the apparent defects of recording systems.

Bibliography

Arruñada, Benito (2003) 'Property Enforcement as Organized Consent', **19** *Journal of Law, Economics and Organization,* 401.

Arruñada, Benito and Garoupa, Nuno (2005), 'The Choice of Titling System in Land', **48** *Journal of Law and Economics,* 709.

Baird, Douglas G. (1983), 'Notice Filing and the Problem of Ostensible Ownership', **12** *Journal of Legal Studies*, 53–67.

Baird, Douglas G. and Jackson, Thomas H. (1984), 'Information, Uncertainty, and the Transfer of Property', **13** *Journal of Legal Studies*, 299–320.

Baker, M., Miceli, Thomas J., Sirmans, C.F., Turnbull, Geoffrey K. (2002), 'Optimal Title Search', **30** *Journal of Legal Studies*, 139–158.

Bouckaert, B. and De Geest, G. (1998), 'The Economic Functions of Possession and Limitation Statutes', in Ott., C. and von Wangenheim, G., *Essays in Law and Economics IV*, Antwerpen and Apeldoorn, Maklu, 151–168.

Bowles, Roger A. and Phillips, Jennifer (1977), 'Solicitors' Remuneration: A Critique of Recent Developments in Conveyancing', **40** *Modern Law Review*, 639–650.

Calderon, J, (2003), 'The Formalization of Property in Peru 2001–2002: the case of Lima', **28** *Habitat International,* 289–300.

Cooter, Robert D. (1991), 'Inventing Market Property: The Land Courts of Papua New Guinea', **25** *Law and Society Review*, 759–801.

Cooter, Robert D. (1992), 'Organization as Property: Economic Analysis of Property Law and Privatization', in Clague, Christopher and Rausser, Gordon (eds), *The Emergence of Market Economies in Eastern Europe*, Oxford, Blackwell, 77–97.

De Soto, Hernando (2000), *The Mystery of Capital. Why Capitalism Triumphs in the West and Fails Everywhere Else*, New York, Basic Books.

Ellickson, R. (1986), 'Adverse Possession and Perpetuities Law: Two Dents in the Libertarian Model of Property Rights', **64** *Washington University Law Quarterly*, 723–737.

Epstein, Richard A. (1979), 'Possession as the Root of Title', **13** *Georgia Law Review*, 1221 ff.

Field, E. (2003a), 'Entitled to Work: Urban Property Rights and Labor Supply in Peru', Research Program in Development Studies, Princeton University, Working Paper no. 220.

Field, E. (2003b), 'Property Rights and Household Time Allocation in Urban Squatter Communities: Evidence from Peru', Harvard University, Working Paper.

Field, E. and Torero, M. (2003), 'Do Property Titles Increase Access to Credit? Evidence from Peru', Harvard University, Working paper.

Garro, A.M. (2004), 'Recordation of Interests in Land', *International Encyclopedia of Comparative Law, Volume VI: Property and Trust*, Tübingen, Mohr Siebeck.

Goldberg, Michael A. and Horwood, Peter J. (1987), 'The Costs of Buying and Selling Houses: Some Canadian Evidence', **10** *Research in Law and Economics*, 143–159.

Hansmann, H. and Kraakman, R. (2002), 'Property, Contract, and Verification: The *Numerus Clausus* Problem and the Divisibility of Rights', **31** *Journal of Legal Studies*, 373–420.

Helmholz, Richard H. (1983), 'Adverse Possession and Subjective Intent', **61** *Washington University Law Quarterly*, 331–358.

Janczyk, Joseph T. (1977), 'An Economic Analysis of the Land Title Systems for Transferring Real Property', **6** *Journal of Legal Studies*, 213–233.

Janczyk, Joseph T. (1979), 'Land Title Systems, Scale of Operations, and Operating and Conversion Costs', **8** *Journal of Legal Studies*, 569–583.

Jansen, K. and Roquas, E. (1998), 'Modernizing Insecurity: The Land Titling Project in Honduras', *Development and Exchange,* Vol. 29, 81–106.

ILD (2006), 'Dead capital in 12 Latin American Countries', www.ild.org.pe.

Kaser, Max, *Das Römische Privatrecht* (2 vol.: I, 2nd ed., München 1971; II: 2e ed., München 1975).
Kennedy, Duncan (1981), 'Cost-Benefit of Entitlement Problems: A Critique', **33** *Stanford Law Review*, 387–445.
Merrill, T. (1986), 'Property Rules, Liability Rules, and Adverse Possession', **79** *Northwestern University Law Review*, 1122–1154.
Miceli, Thomas J. (1997), *Economics of the Law*, New York and Oxford, Oxford University Press.
Miceli, Thomas J. and Sirmans, C.F. (1995a), 'The Economics of Land Transfer and Title Insurance', **10** *Journal of Real Estate Finance and Economics*, 81–88.
Miceli, Thomas J. and Sirmans, C.F. (1995b), 'An Economic Theory of Adverse Possession', **15** *International Review of Law and Economics*, 162–173.
Miceli, Thomas J. and Turnbull, G.K. (1997), 'Land Title System and Incentives for Development', 14th Annual Conference of the European Association of Law and Economics, University of Pompeu Fabra, Barcelona, Spain.
Miceli, Thomas, J., Sirmans, C.F. and Turnbull, G.K. (1998), 'Title Assurance and Incentives for Efficient Land Use', **6(3)** *European Journal of Law and Economics*, 305–322.
Morris Guerinoni, F. (2004), 'La Formalizaçion de propriedad en el Peru: develando el misterio', Commision para la formalizaçion de la Propriedad Informal (COFOPRI).
Schechter, Dan S. (1988), 'Judicial Lien Creditors versus Prior Unrecorded Transferees of Real Property: Rethinking the Goals of the Recording System and Their Consequences', **62** *Southern California Law Review*, 105–186.

10 The economics of slavery

Jenny Wahl

Overview

Slavery exists where it is economically worthwhile to those in power – that is, where masters derive either market profits or other sorts of net benefits from owning slaves. Certain conditions enhance the likelihood that any given society might hold slaves – cheaply obtained supplies of foreigners (especially ones with features distinct from those of the reigning class), division of production processes into a series of simple and easily monitored tasks, and well-developed markets that sell specialized commodities for specie – but slavery has flourished in many places, regardless of religion, climate, or cultural attainments.

Central to the economic success of slavery are political and legal institutions that validate the ownership of other persons. Some slave societies have considered slavery a part of the natural order of things; others have viewed slavery as established only by positive law. Regardless of underlying philosophy, slave societies typically craft finely nuanced legal rules that govern the ownership of other human beings.

In many instances, these laws reveal economic principles at work. Consider manumission rules. Allowing masters to free slaves at will would create incentives to manumit unproductive slaves – those for whom no one would pay a positive price. Consequently, the community at large would bear the costs of young, old, and disabled former slaves. The public might also run the risk of having rebellious former slaves in its midst. Roman emperor Augustus worried considerably about this adverse selection problem and eventually enacted restrictions on the age at which slaves could go free, the number freed by any one master, and the number manumitted by last will (Watson, 1987; Finley, 1987). Antebellum US Southern states passed similar laws (Finkelman, 1988, 1989a; Morris, 1996; Wahl, 1998).

Aside from these sorts of restrictions, societies that permit ownership of slaves typically confer upon masters the usual rights of property ownership. The law generally considers slaves as personal chattels, although late Roman law (and Louisiana law) sometimes classified slaves as chattels real, precluding their sale separate from land (Schafer, 1994; Wahl, 1998). Like other chattels, slaves and their offspring can typically be bought, sold, hired, exchanged, given, bequeathed, seized for debts, and put up as collateral. Unlike other property, however, slaves sometimes bear responsibility for their behavior, receive an education, and buy their own freedom.

Slavery has features in common with other forms of coerced labor, such as debt bondage, indenture, peonage, serfdom, and corveé (statute) labor (Domar, 1970; Bloch, 1975; Kolchin, 1987; Bush, 1996). Yet slavery is a species of servitude set apart: slaves typically have been aliens with minimal freedom of action, permanently deprived of the title to their own human capital and of the right to raise their own children, and often with no higher authority than their masters. Orlando Patterson put it plainly (1982, p. 5): the slave is a socially dead person.

The early history of slavery

Slavery probably developed after civilization turned from hunting to pastoral societies: agriculture brought specialization of tasks and opportunities for exploiting another's labor. Ancient Sumerian, Phoenician, Hebrew, Babylonian, and Egyptian societies used slaves to tend flocks, work fields and mines, and help with domestic chores (Jones, 1956). Moses Finley (1961) made the provocative argument, however, that the pre-classical world actually was one without any 'free' men: just as the Greeks invented individual freedom, so too did they invent chattel slavery.

Slavery flourished in the classical period, predominantly in cities open to commercial exchange (Westermann, 1943; Finley, 1961 and 1987). Rarely was the Greek a slave in his own city. Greek slaves worked in mines, quarries, fields, handicrafts, and domestic, police, and secretarial work; skilled slaves often lived apart from their masters. A unique feature of Greek society was benefit clubs that lent slaves money to buy their freedom.

Rome inherited the slave trade; slaves comprised about 30 per cent of the population in Rome's heyday. Roman slaves enjoyed limited freedoms – they could acquire property, schooling, and, unlike Greek slaves, citizenship upon manumission (Phillips, 1985; Watson, 1987).

Slavery declined – but did not end – with the decline of Rome (Meltzer, 1993). The word 'slave' itself derived from the most numerous ethnic group in the medieval trade in human beings – Slavs. The Germanic tribes held slaves, sometimes using long hair as an identifying mark. With the emergence of Islam along the Arabian peninsula, religious wars generated large slave populations, mostly used for domestic and military service. William the Conqueror ended the export of English slaves, but serfdom did not replace domestic slavery in England until about 1200. Scandinavians held and traded thralls until the Swedish king declared all offspring of Christian slaves free in 1335. But slavery continued unabated in Italy and the Iberian peninsula: Genoa and Venice had active slave markets in the thirteenth century, Seville and Lisbon two centuries later. Ship captains reporting to Prince Henry the Navigator brought the first black slaves to Portugal in the 1440s. This act was a portent of things to come, as the Portuguese helped instigate the cross-Atlantic trade in Africans shortly thereafter.

The African slave trade

Perhaps the most highly developed market of its time was the lucrative African slave trade. From 1500 to 1900, an estimated 12 million Africans left their homes to go west to the New World, with about 10 million of them completing the journey. The first African slaves in North America arrived in Virginia in 1619 on a Dutch ship. Yet very few imported slaves ended up in the British colonies and the young American republic. By 1808, when the trans-Atlantic slave trade to the US officially ended, only about 6 per cent of African slaves landing in the New World had come to North America (Anstey, 1975; Manning, 1990 and 2006; Evans and Richardson, 1995; Blackburn, 1997; Eltis et al., 1999).

Africans were sold east as well as west: millions of them made the long trek across their own continent to Arab, Asian, and even some European countries. Some 6 million African slaves were sent from sub-Saharan Africa eastward; another 8 million remained enslaved on their own soil (Lovejoy, 1983).

One feature particularly distinguished New World slavery: its association with race. Early Spanish settlers enslaved native Americans, who soon perished in droves from smallpox and punishingly hard work. Via licensing arrangements, Portugal and Spain began importing African slaves into their colonies in the early 1500s to replace the dying native population. In 1517, Charles I began to import Africans, first to the West Indies, then to the Spanish-controlled mainland. Brazil commenced legal importation of black slaves in 1549. Traders could acquire slaves in specific African zones, then sell them in America – up to 120 per year per Brazilian planter, for example. Because prices for Brazilian licenses were cheaper than other licenses, traders applied for these, then rerouted their vessels in search of extra profits (Anstey, 1975; Blackburn, 1997).

The evils of the trade expanded when Britain replaced Spain and Portugal as the major trafficker in African slaves. Elizabethan-era captain Sir John Hawkins had transported slaves, but England did not figure large in the African trade until the seventeenth-century Royal African Company became the biggest slaver in the world (Galenson, 1982; Watson, 1989).

Many parties were involved in the infamous 'trading triangle': European captains plied the chieftains of West Africa with liquor, guns, cotton goods, and trinkets. In exchange, Africans supplied slaves to suffer through the arduous middle passage across the Atlantic Ocean. Over

40 per cent went to Brazil. Slaves worked on sugar plantations in the West Indies, grew coffee and mined precious metals in Brazil, and grew tobacco, sugar, rice, and eventually cotton in North America. These goods, along with molasses and rum, went back to England (Sheridan, 1947; Solow and Engerman, 1987). One innovative study even links the rise in tooth decay in Britain to the slave trade (Austen and Smith, 1990). It suggests that sugar in one's tea increasingly signified respectability, so even working-class folks could enjoy rotting teeth in their quest for social standing as sugar flowed freely and cheaply back to England.

Profitability of the Atlantic slave trade

Commanders of slave vessels and their financial backers made fortunes from the Atlantic trade. Transporting slaves was a major industry in the seventeenth and eighteenth centuries, with the Royal African Company a principal player for at least five decades. David Galenson (1982), in his study of the Company, unveiled a picture of closely connected competitive economic markets in Africa and America that responded quickly to economic incentives.

Despite its size, the Company was hardly a monopoly – hordes of small ship captains found the trade worthwhile, with the principal costs being those associated with capturing and transporting Africans, and the prospective profits at least comparable to returns on other sorts of ventures. Many researchers have devoted themselves to ascertaining the exact rate of return that these captain-traders earned, with the most plausible estimates being about 9 to 10 per cent. Among these scholars are David Eltis (1987, 2000), Seymour Drescher (1999), David Richardson (1987, 1989), William Darity (1985, 1989), Joseph Inikori (1981), Roger Anstey (1975), and E.W. Evans (with Richardson, 1995).

But other interests also made much from the Atlantic trade. European banks and merchant houses helped develop the New World plantation system through complicated credit and insurance mechanisms, enjoying substantial returns as part of the bargain (Engerman, 1972; Menard, 2006). Well-placed African dealers also benefited. In sickening cycles, Sudanic tribes of the fifteenth and sixteenth centuries sold slaves for horses, then used the horses to obtain more slaves. Tribes of the seventeenth and eighteenth centuries similarly traded slaves for guns, then used guns to hunt down more slaves (Lovejoy, 1983).

But of all who reaped rewards from the Atlantic trade, British and US citizens stand out. In the 1940s, West Indian scholar Eric Williams (1944) went so far as to suggest that British industrialization was intimately linked to slavery. Without the slave trade to fuel growth in her colonies, Williams claimed, Great Britain could not have become the industrial superpower of the eighteenth and nineteenth centuries that she was. Although Williams's thesis has since largely been discarded, other scholars nevertheless agree that the slave trade benefited England (Dunn, 1972; Engerman, 1972; Engerman and Genovese, 1975; Eltis and Engerman, 2000). Even Elizabeth I made money by investing in slaving ships and captains. David Eltis (1987) speculates, in fact, that Britain would have enjoyed higher living standards by continuing as a slave trader rather than becoming an abolitionist power. Early industry in New England – cotton textiles, shipbuilding, and the like – also had strong connections to the slave trade and slavery (Bailey, 1986 and 1990). Among those who benefited were the New England families of Browns, Cabots, and Faneuils.

Internal slave markets

Several early societies set up thriving internal markets for trade in slaves. Greek slaves sold like other commodities, in the agora (Westermann, 1943; Finley, 1961). Many Roman slaves started out as prisoners of war; because field commanders could dispose of prisoners as they wished, Roman slave dealers simply began traveling along with the army to snap up likely specimens (Phillips, 1985; Watson, 1987). Judging from the distribution of Italian wine jars in Gaul, wine evidently exchanged for Gallic slaves in the first and second centuries BC. The slave trade generated so much gold for Western Europe – necessary for trade with the East – that the early ninth-century Church made little headway in its abolition campaign. In his writings, Hernando Cortés left a description of the large number of slaves brought to auction at the great marketplace near Tenochtítlan (present-day Mexico City) (Watson, 1989; Meltzer, 1993).

Slave markets also existed across the antebellum US South. Even today, one can find stone markers like the one next to the Antietam battlefield, which reads: 'From 1800 to 1865 This Stone Was Used as a Slave Auction Block. It has been a famous landmark at this original location for over 150 years.' Private auctions, estate sales, and professional traders facilitated easy exchange. Established dealers like Franklin and Armfield in Virginia, Woolfolk, Saunders, and Overly in Maryland, and Nathan Bedford Forrest in Tennessee prospered alongside itinerant traders who operated in a few counties, buying slaves for cash from their owners, then moving them overland in coffles to the lower South (Bancroft, 1931; Pritchett, 1997). Over a million slaves were taken across state lines between 1790 and 1860 with many more moving within states. Some of these slaves went with their owners; some were sold to new owners. In his monumental study, Michael Tadman (1990) found that slaves who lived in the upper South faced a very real chance of being sold by their owners for speculative profits. Along with US slave sale markets came farseeing methods for coping with risk, such as explicit – and even implicit – warranties of title, fitness, and merchantability (Wahl, 1998).

Slave prices

Scholars have gathered slave prices from a variety of sources, including censuses, probate records, plantation and slave-trader accounts, and proceedings of slave auctions. The largest source of information is a New Orleans data set compiled by Robert Fogel and Stanley Engerman (1974), but people have analyzed the structure of slave prices for many societies.

The exchange prices for slaves – often substantial – reflect their economic value. Healthy male slaves sold for an entire date plantation grove in Sumeria in 2000 BC. Eight oxen bought a slave among the Anglo-Saxon tribes in the mid-400s (Jones, 1956). Prime field hands went for four to six hundred dollars in the US in 1800, thirteen to fifteen hundred dollars in 1850, and up to three thousand dollars on the eve of the Civil War. Even controlling for inflation, slave prices rose significantly in the six decades before secession. Slavery remained a thriving business on the eve of the Civil War: by some estimates, average slave prices by 1890 would have increased more than 50 per cent over their 1860 levels (Fogel and Engerman, 1974; Schmitz and Schaefer, 1981; Fogel, 1989; Mancall et al., 2001). No wonder the South rose in armed resistance to protect its enormous investment.

Individual characteristics

Prices reflect the characteristics of particular slaves. Studies of ancient Rome, fifteenth-century Spain and Portugal, and the antebellum US South all reveal that the prices of slaves varied by their sex, age, skill level, and physical condition (Fogel and Engerman, 1974; Schmitz and Schaefer, 1981; Phillips, 1985; Fogel, 1989; Friedman and Manning, 1992; Newland and San Segundo, 1996). Important individual features also included temperament and childbearing capacity for females. In addition, the supply of slaves, demand for products produced by slaves, and seasonal factors helped determine market conditions and therefore prices.

Prices for both male and female slaves tended to follow similar life-cycle patterns. Infant slaves sold for a positive price in the antebellum South because masters expected them to live long enough to make the initial costs of raising them worthwhile. Prices rose through puberty as productivity and experience increased. In nineteenth-century New Orleans, for example, prices peaked at about age 22 for females and age 25 for males (Kotlikoff, 1979). In the Old South, boys aged 14 sold for 71 per cent of the price of 27-year-old men, whereas girls aged 14 sold for 65 per cent of the price of 27-year-old men. After the peak age, prices declined slowly for a time, then fell off rapidly as slaves' ability to work disappeared. Girls cost more than boys, up to age 16 in Brazil, Cuba, and the US and up to age 20 in Peru. The genders then switched places in terms of value. Compared to men, women were worth 90 to 95 per cent as much in Cuba, 80 to 90 per cent as much in the US and West Indies, and 70 to 80 per cent as much in Brazil (Mintz, 1974; Engerman and Genovese, 1975; Margo and Steckel, 1982; Fogel, 1989; Moreno Fraginals et al., 1993; Newland and San Segundo, 1996).

One characteristic in particular set females apart: their ability to bear children. In the US, fertile females commanded a premium. But, in medieval Italy, men who impregnated slaves had to pay their masters compensation because of the high likelihood of childbed death. Genoan men could even buy indemnification insurance against this possibility. The mother-child link also proved important in a different way: people sometimes paid premiums for intact families (Wahl, 1998).

Besides age and sex, skills helped determine a slave's price. Premiums paid for skilled workers interacted with mortality rates and rates of depreciation for different characteristics. The US had a relatively low slave mortality rate and skilled workers sold for premiums of 40 to 55 per cent. Slaveowners in areas with higher death rates could not reap as large a benefit from their skilled workers, due to shorter life spans. In Peru, the skill premium was about 35 per cent; in Cuba, about 10 to 20 per cent. Because the human capital associated with strength drops off more quickly as people age than the human capital associated with skills and training, prices for unskilled slaves in the Spanish colonies fell more rapidly with a slave's age than prices for skilled slaves (Fogel and Engerman, 1974; Engerman and Genovese, 1975; Newland and San Segundo, 1996).

Physical traits, mental capabilities, and other qualities contributed to price differentials as well. Crippled and chronically ill slaves sold for deep discounts. Slaves who proved troublesome – runaways, thieves, layabouts, drunks, slow learners, and the like – also sold for lower prices. Taller slaves cost more, perhaps because height acts as a proxy for nutritional status. In New Orleans, light-skinned females (who enjoyed greater popularity as concubines) sold for a 5 per cent premium (Kotlikoff, 1979; Fogel, 1989; Wahl, 1998).

One pricing variant appeared in the West Indian 'scramble.' Here, owners and agents devised a fixed-price system, dividing slaves into four categories, penning them up accordingly, and assigning a single price per pen. Potential buyers then jumped into the pens, attempting to pick off the best prospects for the given price (Dunn, 1972).

Market conditions

Slave prices fluctuated with market conditions as well as with individual characteristics. Supply factors mattered, for example. Slave prices dropped dramatically in fourth-century Egypt when the sale of babies became legal. In the Old World, slave prices rose sharply after the Black Death decimated the population, particularly the servile portion (Meltzer, 1993). US slave prices fell around 1800 as the Haitian revolution sparked the movement of slaves into the Southern states. Less than a decade later, slave prices climbed when the international slave trade was abolished, cutting off legal external supplies.

Many Southern slaveholders actually supported closing the Atlantic trade because the resulting reduction in supply drove up prices of slaves already living in the US and, hence, their masters' wealth. US slaves had high enough fertility rates and low enough mortality rates to reproduce themselves, so Southerners did not worry about having too few slaves to go around. Unlike elsewhere in the New World, the South did not require constant infusions of immigrants to keep its slave population intact. In fact, by 1825, 36 per cent of the slaves in the Western hemisphere lived in the US (Fogel, 1989).

Demand helped determine prices as well. In most slave societies, the demand for slaves derived from the demand for the commodities and services that slaves provided. Changes in slave occupations and variability in prices for slave-produced goods therefore created movements in slave prices. For example, a slave cost about a year's keep in early Athens, but prices rose significantly as the use of slaves expanded to include managerial and civil-service work (Westermann, 1943). As slaves replaced increasingly expensive indentured servants in the New World, their prices went up. In the period 1748 to 1775, slave prices in British America rose nearly 30 per cent (Menard, 1977; Galenson, 1984; Grubb, 1994). As cotton prices fell in the 1840s, Southern slave prices also fell. But, as the demand for cotton and tobacco grew after about 1850, the prices of slaves increased as well (Fogel and Engerman, 1974). The connection between commodity and slave prices is not confined to the US South. Some scholars have speculated that abolition in Cuba occurred because sugar prices had fallen too low to make slavery worthwhile (Moreno Fraginals et al., 1993).

Demand sometimes had to do with the time of year a sale took place. For example, slave prices in the New Orleans market were 10–20 per cent higher in January than in September (Kotlikoff, 1979). Why? September was a busy time of year for planters: the opportunity cost of their time was relatively high. Prices had to be relatively low for them to be willing to travel to New Orleans during the harvest.

Differences in demand across regions led to transient regional price differences, which in turn meant large movements of slaves. Yet because planters experienced greater stability among their workforce when entire plantations moved, 84 per cent of slaves were taken to the lower South in this way rather than being sold piecemeal (Tadman, 1990; Pritchett, 1997).

One additional demand factor loomed large in determining slave prices: the expectation of continued legal slavery. As the American Civil War progressed, slave prices dropped dramatically because people could not be sure that the peculiar institution would survive. In New Orleans, prime male slaves sold on average for $1381 in 1861 and for $1116 in 1862. Burgeoning inflation meant that real prices fell considerably more. Not surprisingly, by war's end slaves sold for a small fraction of their 1860 price (Kotlikoff, 1979; Wahl, 1998).

Profitability of ancient and antebellum slavery

Slavery was a profitable enterprise, at least in antiquity and in the New World. As classical scholar Moses Finley (1961) put it, Greek and Roman slaveowners went on for centuries believing they were making profits – and spending them. Americans and West Indians found slaveowning lucrative as well (Dunn, 1972; Fogel and Engerman, 1974; Higman, 1976; Solow and Engerman, 1987). Slavery never generated superprofits, because people always had the option of putting their money elsewhere. Nevertheless, investment in slaves offered a rate of return – about 10 per cent – that was comparable to returns on other assets (Fogel, 1989).

That slavery in the American South was profitable seems almost obvious. Yet scholars have argued furiously about this matter. On one side stand antebellum writers such as Hinton Rowan Helper (1857) and Frederick Law Olmstead (1861), and contemporary scholars like Eugene Genovese (at least in his early writings), who speculated that American slavery was unprofitable, inefficient, and incompatible with urban life. On the other side are those who contend that slavery was profitable and efficient relative to free labor and that slavery suited cities as well as farms, industry as well as agriculture (Yasuba, 1961; Starobin, 1970; Aitken, 1971; Fogel and Engerman, 1974; Goldin, 1976; Barzel, 1977; Dew, 1991 and 1994). These researchers stress the similarity between slave markets and markets for other sorts of capital.

The significance of Time on the Cross

Perhaps the most controversial book ever written about American slavery is Robert Fogel's and Stanley Engerman's *Time on the Cross* (1974). These men were among the first to use modern statistical methods, high-speed computers, and large datasets to answer a series of empirical questions about the economics of slavery. Building on earlier work by Alfred Conrad and John Meyer (1958 and 1964), Fogel and Engerman used data from probate and plantation records, invoices from the New Orleans slave-sale market, coastwise manifests for shipped slaves, and manuscript census schedules to find profit levels and rates of return. Fogel and Engerman pioneered the use of an index they called 'total factor productivity,' which measures the ratio of output per average unit of all inputs.

Among Fogel's and Engerman's findings are these: antebellum Southern farms were 35 per cent more efficient overall than Northern ones and slave farms in the cotton South were 28.5 per cent more efficient than free farms. Moreover, slavery generated a rate of economic growth in the US South comparable to that of many European countries. Fogel and Engerman also discovered that, because slaves constituted a considerable portion of individual wealth, masters fed and treated their slaves reasonably well. Although some evidence indicates that infant slaves suffered much worse conditions than their freeborn counterparts, juvenile and adult slaves lived in conditions similar to – sometimes better than – those enjoyed by many free laborers of the same period (see also Steckel, 1986a and 1986b).

Despite criticism (notably a collection of articles entitled *Reckoning with Slavery* edited by Paul David and others, 1976), *Time on the Cross* and Fogel's subsequent *Without Consent or Contract* (1989) have solidified the economic view of Southern slavery. Even Eugene Genovese (1989), long an ardent proponent of the belief that Southern planters held slaves for prestige value, finally acknowledged that slavery was probably a profitable enterprise. Much like any businessmen, New World slaveowners responded to market signals – adjusting crop mixes, reallocating slaves to more profitable tasks, hiring out idle slaves, and sometimes selling slaves for profit. One instance well-known to labor historians shows that contemporaneous free labor thought that urban slavery may even have worked too well: workers at the Tredegar Iron Works in Richmond, Virginia, went out on their first strike in 1847 to protest the use of slave labor at the Works (Fogel, 1989).

Labor practices contributing to profitability

The value of Southern slaves arose in part from the value of labor generally in the antebellum US. Scarce factors of production command economic rent, and labor was by far the scarcest available input in America.

But a large proportion of the reward to owning and working slaves results from innovative labor practices (Fogel and Engerman, 1974; Metzer, 1975; Licht, 1983). Certainly, the use of the 'gang' system in agriculture contributed to profits in Roman times as well as in later time periods. Treating people like machines pays off handsomely. In the West

Indies, for instance, sugar slaves worked in three separate gangs: one harvesting the crop, a second cleaning up after the first, and a third bringing water and food to the others (Sheridan, 1947; Dunn, 1972; Higman, 1976; Menard, 2006). Planters in the US South also used the gang system to their advantage.

Integral to many gang-oriented operations across the Americas were plantation overseers, who served as agents for oft-absent plantation owners. Overseers certainly had some authority so they could elicit work from their charges (Scarborough, 1966). Yet law and custom alike circumscribed overseers' abilities to administer correction, because slaves represented such a large chunk of their masters' wealth (Wahl, 1998). This balance between authority and accountability worked well enough to turn handsome profits for many planters, particularly those who entrusted reliable slave drivers as liaisons. By the mid-1820s, slave managers actually took over much of the day-to-day operations in the West Indies (Dunn, 1972; Higman, 1976).

Antebellum slaveowners experimented with a variety of other methods to increase productivity. Masters developed an elaborate system of 'hand ratings' in order to improve the match between the slave worker and the job. Slaves could sometimes earn bonuses in cash or in kind, or quit early if they finished tasks quickly. Slaves – in contrast to free workers – often had Sundays off. Some masters allowed slaves to keep part of the harvest or to work their own small plots. In places, slaves could even sell their own crops and produce. To prevent stealing, however, many masters limited the crops that slaves could raise and sell, confining them to corn or brown cotton, for example (Wahl, 1998).

Masters capitalized on the native intelligence of slaves by using them as agents to receive goods, keep books, and the like (Wahl, 1998). In some societies – for example, ancient Rome and her offspring, antebellum Louisiana – slaves even had under their control a sum of money called a peculium. This served as a sort of working capital, enabling slaves to establish thriving businesses that often benefited their masters as well (Schafer, 1994). Yet these practices may have helped lead to the downfall of slavery, for they gave slaves a taste of freedom that left them longing for more.

The potential profits from reproduction

In the US, masters profited from reproduction as well as production. Southern planters encouraged slaves to have large families because US slaves lived long enough (past about age 27) to generate more revenue than cost over their lifetimes. But researchers have found little evidence of slave breeding; instead, masters encouraged slaves to live in nuclear or extended families for stability (Fogel and Engerman, 1974). Lest one think sentimentality triumphed on the Southern plantation, one need only recall the willingness of most masters to break up families by sale if the bottom line was big enough.

In contrast to US slaves, the average West Indian slave did not live past his or her mid-twenties. Masters in Jamaica, Haiti, Barbados, and Trinidad therefore behaved differently, establishing much longer periods of breastfeeding (which helped provide natural protection against subsequent pregnancy). As a result, birth rates among West Indian slaves were relatively much lower (Sheridan, 1947; Dunn, 1972; Engerman and Genovese, 1975; Higman, 1976; Solow and Engerman, 1987).

Society's role in the profitability of antebellum slavery

The great sugar plantations in the eighteenth century and cotton plantations in the nineteenth were the largest privately owned enterprises of their time, and their owners among the richest men in the world. During the three centuries of New World slavery, slave-produced goods – especially sugar – dominated world trade. Accordingly, slaveowners were not the only ones to reap rewards. French, Spanish, Portuguese, Dutch, and Danish citizens also thrived on buying from or selling to slave colonies. So too did cotton consumers who enjoyed low prices and Northern entrepreneurs who helped finance plantation operations (Fogel, 1989; Menard, 2006). As James de Bow said in reply to a query by the *London Times* in 1860, without slavery 'ships would rot at [the New York] docks; grass would grow in Wall Street and Broadway, and the glory of New York . . . would be numbered with the things of the past' (quoted in Foner, 1941, p. 4).

Society at large shared in maintaining the machinery of slavery as well as enjoying its yields (Wheeler, 1837; Goodell, 1853; Stroud, 1856; Hurd, 1858; Wiecek, 1977; Finkelman, 1988, 1989a; Wahl, 1998). All Southern states save Delaware passed laws to establish citizen slave patrols that had the authority to round up suspicious-looking or escaped slaves, for example. Patrollers were a necessary enforcement mechanism in a time before standing police forces were customary. Essentially, Southern citizens agreed to take it upon themselves to protect their neighbors' interests as well as their own so as to preserve slavery as an institution.

Northern citizens often worked hand-in-hand with their Southern counterparts, returning fugitive slaves to masters either with or without the prompting of national and state law. Yet not everyone was so civic-minded. As a result, the profession of 'slave-catching' evolved – often highly risky (enough so that insurance companies denied such men life insurance coverage) and just as often highly lucrative (Campbell, 1968; Wahl, 1998).

Labor-force transitions and profits from slavery

One potent piece of evidence supporting the notion that slavery provides pecuniary benefits is this: slavery often gives way to other forms of organizing the labor force when the costs and risks of maintaining slaves become too large. In Europe, for example, serfdom evolved in part as a way of shifting some of the risks of poor crop yields away from masters (Bloch, 1975; Bush, 1996). A similar system arose within Africa in the nineteenth century. Slaves paid their masters for the right to work on their own; in exchange, masters no longer paid for the slaves' upkeep (Watson, 1980). The Spanish Crown for a time favored a system of forced labor called encomienda, whereby the indigenous population could not be bought, sold, rented, bequeathed, or removed from the area. Scholars have speculated that this form of coercion, relative to outright slavery, reduced threats to the security of the Crown's interest (Yeager, 1995). Thus, other types of labor take the place of slaves when slavery costs too much.

In like fashion, slavery replaces other labor when it becomes relatively cheaper. In the early US colonies, for example, indentured servitude was common. As the demand for skilled servants (and therefore their wages) rose in England, the cost of indentured servants went up in the colonies. At the same time, second-generation slaves became more productive than their forebears because they spoke English and did not have to adjust to life in a strange new world. Consequently, the balance of labor shifted away from indentured servitude and toward slavery (Galenson, 1982, 1984, and 1986; Grubb, 1985 and 1994; Engerman, 1992). Georgia offers a compelling example. Its original 1732 charter prohibited ownership of black slaves. Yet by 1750 the trustees of the new colony had to relax the prohibition because Georgia growers simply could not compete with producers elsewhere who utilized lower-cost slave labor (Grindle, 1990).

Profitability and race

One element that contributed to the profitability of New World slavery was, for several reasons, the African heritage of the slaves. Africans, more than native people, were accustomed to the discipline of agricultural practices and knew metalworking. Some scholars surmise that Africans, relative to Europeans, could better withstand tropical diseases and, unlike native Americans, also had some exposure to the European disease pool (Coelho and McGuire, 1997).

Perhaps the most distinctive feature of Africans, however, was their skin color. Because they looked different from their masters, their movements were easy to monitor. Denying slaves education, property ownership, contractual rights, and other things enjoyed by those in power was simple: one need only look at people to ascertain their likely status. Using color was a low-cost way of distinguishing slaves from free persons. For this reason, perhaps, early colonial practices that freed slaves who converted to Christianity quickly faded away. Deciphering true religious beliefs is far more difficult than establishing skin color. Other slave societies have used distinguishing marks like brands or long hair to denote slaves, yet color is far more immutable and therefore better as a cheap way of keeping slaves separate.

Among those who profited from slavery were men who worked as slave catchers and received fees for returning escaped slaves to their masters. Because skin color was the principal identifying mark, however, free blacks also faced the horrifying possibility of capture and sale.

Efficiency of antebellum slavery

So New World slavery was profitable; was it an efficient way of organizing the workforce? On this question, considerable controversy remains. Slavery might well profit masters, but only because they exploit their chattel. What is more, slavery could have locked people into a method of production and way of life that might later have proven burdensome.

Fogel and Engerman (1974) claim that slaves kept about 90 per cent of what they produced. Because these scholars also found that agricultural slavery was 35 per cent more efficient than family farming in the North, they argue that slaves actually may have shared in the overall benefits resulting from the gang system. Other scholars contend that slaves in fact kept less than half of what they produced and that slavery, while profitable, certainly was not efficient (Vedder, 1975; Ransom and Sutch, 1977, 1988).

Gavin Wright (1978, 2006) critiques the work of Fogel and Engerman by focusing on the exceptional nature of the crop year they used to calculate their statistics and by using alternative data to attack their estimates of total factor productivity. Wright calls attention as well to the difference between the short run and the long run. He notes that slaves accounted for a very large proportion of most masters' portfolios of assets. Although slavery might seem an efficient means of production at a point in time, it ties masters to a certain system of labor that may not adapt quickly to changed economic circumstances.

Wright's argument has some merit. Although the South's growth rate compared favorably with that of the North in the antebellum period, a considerable portion of wealth was held in the hands of planters – and much of that 'wealth' depended upon the accounting convention of treating the human capital embodied by slaves as personal property owned by slaveholders. The consequence was a far different portfolio from that of the North, where immobile land was the largest investment. Consequently, commercial and service industries lagged in the South. The region also had far less rail transportation and internal improvements than the North (Wahl, 2007).

Yet many plantations used the most advanced technologies of the day, and certain innovative commercial and insurance practices appeared first in transactions involving slaves (Wahl, 1998). In Cuba, planters were behind the move to construct railroads (Moreno Fraginals et al., 1993). Slaveowners led in using new inventions, such as the circular saw (Wahl, 1998). What is more, although the South fell behind the North and Great Britain in its level of manufacturing, it compared favorably to other advanced countries of the time. In sum, no clear consensus emerges as to whether the antebellum South created a standard of living comparable to that of the North or, if it did, whether it could have sustained it.

Profitability and efficiency of slavery elsewhere

What of the profitability and efficiency of slavery in places and times other than the ancient world and the antebellum Americas? Much less empirical economic work exists on slavery elsewhere, although Orlando Patterson (1982) and Eugene Genovese (1974) portray slavery in Islamic societies as nonproductive.

Yet to the extent that slaves perform domestic and other chores, they free masters from drudgery and therefore confer some benefits, though not necessarily market profits. Even slaves who appear merely ornamental must provide some pleasure to the masters, or else they would go free. We can still consider slavery an economic enterprise simply because it provides more benefits to their owners – pecuniary or otherwise – than costs.

Slavery in modern times

Rising British sentiment against slavery culminated in the *Somerset* case, which outlawed slavery in England in 1772.[1] Britain and the US abolished the international slave trade in 1807–8; Britain freed slaves in its colonies (except India) in 1833, with full emancipation in 1838. Slavery in the US officially disappeared by the end of the American Civil War in 1865.

Abolition came later elsewhere, often accompanied by a rise in other forms of servitude (Watson, 1991). Eastern Europe and Russia kept slavery alive into the late nineteenth century. In 1890, all major European countries, the US, Turkey, Persia, and Zanzibar signed the General Act of Brussels in an attempt to suppress slavery. Forty years later, an international labor convention acted to outlaw forced labor in the former Ottoman and German colonies. In 1948, the UN General Assembly declared that all forms of slavery and servitude should be abolished (Bush, 1996).

Yet slavery in Southeast Asia, the Arabian peninsula, and parts of Africa continued well into the twentieth century (Watson, 1980; Lovejoy, 1983; Klein, 1990 and 1993). Perhaps the saddest legacy of American slavery is that the system established to supply the New World with slaves also shaped society at home. Some scholars believe that slavery was endemic to Africa, others date its origins to medieval Muslim society or the later European infiltration. Regardless of beginnings, slavery within Africa burgeoned along with the Atlantic trade – in 1600 Africa had a minority of the world's slaves, in 1800 the overwhelming majority. The Great Scramble for Africa spread slavery further. Regrettably, the tragedy continues: Angolan slaves fought bloodily for freedom in 1961, Mauritania kept slavery legal until 1980, Nigeria still had slave concubinage in the late 1980s; and numerous African regions actively practice slavery today.

Some of the harshest forms of slavery have arrived only recently. Modern weaponry, increased population density, and mass communication and transportation technology have made it that much easier to capture and move purported enemies as well as to incite one's allies to do the same. The classic mechanism of modern slavery, patterned after the practices of Nazi Germany and the Soviet Union, is this: Officials in power arrest suspected opponents of the current political regime, or those considered racially or nationally unfit, and throw them into forced-labor camps to work under terrible conditions.

Unlike slaves in earlier societies, the unfortunates who landed in Nazi and Soviet concentration camps were not privately owned and traded in open markets. Rather, they served as property of the state, sometimes to be rented out to private interests.

Modern slaves consequently represent something far different than their historic counterparts. From pre-classical times through the nineteenth century, masters – including public entities – typically viewed their slaves as productive investments, as bookkeeping entries in their wealth portfolios, as forms of valuable capital. Slaves in these circumstances could often count on minimal food, shelter, and clothing, and time for rest and sleep. This was true even for government-owned slaves, because these slaves were typically used in money-making enterprises that just happened to be government-run, and they could potentially be sold to private owners. Not so for the 'publicly owned' slaves of the twentieth century. Because these people were 'acquired' at very low cost with public money and served primarily as political symbols, their masters had little incentive to care for them as assets.

To be sure, when Nazi Germany needed labor to fuel production of her war machinery, the country turned to the inmates of concentration camps. Likewise, the Soviets rounded up peasants to work on public projects and mineral extraction. Various regions across Africa, Asia, America, and Europe have done the same. Yet these sorts of 'slaves' are often worth more dead than alive. Killing one's political adversaries makes the state that much easier to run. Exterminating those labeled as unfit 'cleanses' society – in a truly twisted sense of the word – and binds together the 'chosen.' Accordingly, modern forms of mass slavery seem far different institutions than those of earlier times.

Re-examining the economics of slavery

Despite differences between modern slavery and its earlier counterparts, slavery in any time and place cannot be thought of as benign. In terms of material conditions, diet, and treatment, slaves in some societies may have fared as well as the poorest class of free citizens. Yet the root of slavery is coercion. By its very nature, slavery involves involuntary transactions. Slaves are property, whereas free laborers are persons who make choices (at times constrained, of course) about the sort of work they do and the number of hours they work.

The behavior of American ex-slaves after abolition clearly reveals that they cared strongly about the manner of their work and valued their non-work time more highly than masters did. Even the most benevolent former masters in the US South, for instance, found it impossible to entice their former chattels back into gang work, even with large wage premiums. Nor could they persuade women back into the labor force: many female ex-slaves simply chose to stay at home (Fogel and Engerman, 1974).

So is slavery an economic phenomenon? Yes, but only because slave societies fail to account for the incalculable costs borne by the slaves themselves.

Note

1. *Somerset v. Stewart*, Loftt 1–18; 11 Herg. State Trials 339; 20 Howell's State Trials 1, 79–82; 98 Eng Rep 499–510 (King's Bench, 22 June 1772).

Bibliography

Aitken, Hugh (ed) (1971), *Did Slavery Pay? Readings in the Economics of Black Slavery in the United States*, Boston: Houghton-Mifflin.

Anstey, Roger (1975), *The Atlantic Slave Trade and British Abolition, 1760–1810*, London: Macmillan.

Austen, Ralph, and Woodruff Smith (1990), 'Private Tooth Decay as Public Economic Virtue: The Slave-Sugar Triangle, Consumerism, and European Industrialization,' *Social Science History* **14** (1): 95–115.

Bailey, Ronald W. (1986), 'Africa, The Slave Trade, and the rise of industrial capitalism in Europe and the US: A historiographic review,' *American History: A Bibliographic Review*, vol. 2, pp. 1–91.

Bailey, Ronald W. (1990), 'The Slave(ry) Trade and the Development of Capitalism in the United States: The Textile Industry in New England,' *Social Science History* **14** (3): 373–414.

Bancroft, Frederic (1931), *Slave Trading in the Old South*, New York: Ungar.

Barzel, Yoram (1977), 'An Economic Analysis of Slavery,' *Journal of Law and Economics* **20** (1): 87–110.

Berlin, Ira, and Herbert Gutman (1983), 'Natives and Immigrants, Free Men and Slaves: Urban Workingmen in the Antebellum American South,' *American Historical Review* **88** (5): 1175–1200.

Berlin, Ira, and Philip Morgan (eds) (1991), *The Slave's Economy: Independent Production by Slaves in the Americas*, London: Frank Cass.

Berlin, Ira, and Philip Morgan (eds) (1993), *Cultivation and Culture: Labor and the Shaping of Slave Life in the Americas*, Charlottesville: University Press of Virginia.

Blackburn, Robin (1997), *The Making of New World Slavery: From the Baroque to the Modern*, London and New York: Verso.

Bloch, Marc (1975), *Slavery and Serfdom in the Middle Ages*, Berkeley, University of California Press.

Bush, Michael (ed) (1996), *Serfdom and Slavery: Studies in Legal Bondage*, New York: Addison Wesley Longman.

Campbell, Stanley W. (1968), *The Slave Catchers*, Chapel Hill: University of North Carolina Press.

Coelho, Philip, and Robert A. McGuire (1997), 'African and European Bound Labor in the British New World: The Biological Consequences of Economic Choices,' *Journal of Economic History* **57** (1): 83–117.

Conrad, Alfred H., and John R. Meyer (1958), 'The Economics of Slavery in the Antebellum South,' *Journal of Political Economy* **66** (2): 95–130.

Conrad, Alfred H., and John R. Meyer (1964), *The Economics of Slavery and Other Studies*, Chicago: Aldine.

Darity, William, A., Jr. (1985), 'The Numbers Game and the Profitability of the British Trade in Slaves,' *Journal of Economic History* **45** (3): 693–703.

Darity, William A., Jr. (1989), 'Comment: Profitability of the British Trade in Slaves Once Again,' *Explorations in Economic History* **26** (3): 380–4.

David, Paul A., Herbert G. Gutman, Richard Sutch, Peter Temin, and Gavin Wright (1976), *Reckoning with Slavery: A Critical Study in the Quantitative History of American Negro Slavery*, New York: Oxford University Press.

Dew, Charles B. (1991), *Slavery in the Antebellum Southern Industries*, Bethesda: University Publications of America.

Dew, Charles B. (1994), *Bond of Iron: Master and Slave at Buffalo Forge*, New York: Norton.

Domar, Evsey (1970), 'The Causes of Slavery or Serfdom: A Hypothesis,' *Journal of Economic History* **30** (1): 18–32.

Drescher, Seymour (1999), *From Slavery to Freedom: Comparative Studies in the Rise and Fall of Atlantic Slavery*, London: Macmillan Press.

Drescher, Seymour and Stanley Engerman (eds) (1998), *A Historical Guide to World Slavery*, New York: Oxford University Press.

Dunn, Richard S. (1972), *Sugar and Slaves: The Rise of the Planter Class in the English West Indies, 1624–1713*, Chapel Hill: University of North Carolina Press.

Elkins, Stanley M. (1976), *Slavery: A Problem in American Institutional and Intellectual Life*, Chicago: University of Chicago Press.

Eltis, David (1987), *Economic Growth and the Ending of the Transatlantic Slave Trade*, New York: Oxford University Press.

Eltis, David (2000), *The Rise of African Slavery in the Americas*, New York: Cambridge University Press.

Eltis, David, and Stanley Engerman (2000), 'The Importance of Slavery and the Slaver Trade to Industrializing Britain,' *Journal of Economic History* **60** (1): 123–44.

Eltis, David, and David Richardson (1995), 'Productivity in the Transatlantic Slave Trade,' *Explorations in Economic History* **32** (4): 465–84.

Eltis, David, Stephen Behrendt, and David Richardson (1999), *The Atlantic Slave Trade: A Database on CD-Rom*, New York: Cambridge University Press.
Engerman, Stanley (1972), 'The Slave Trade and British Capital Formation in the 18th Century: A comment on the Williams thesis,' *Business History Review* **46** (4): 430–43.
Engerman, Stanley (1992), 'Coerced and Free Labor: Property Rights and the Development of the Labor Force,' *Explorations in Economic History* **29** (1): 1–29.
Engerman, Stanley, and Eugene Genovese (1975), *Race and Slavery in the Western Hemisphere: Quantitative Studies*, Princeton: Princeton University Press, 1975.
Evans, E.W., and David Richardson (1995), 'Hunting for Rents: The Economics of Slaving in Pre-colonial Africa,' *Economic History Review* **48** (4): 665–86.
Fehrenbacher, Don (1981), *Slavery, Law, and Politics*, New York: Oxford University Press.
Finkelman, Paul (1988), *Slavery, Race, and the American Legal System, 1700–1872*, 16 vol., New York: Garland.
Finkelman, Paul (1989a), *State Slavery Statutes*, Frederick, MD: University Publications of America (microfiche).
Finkelman, Paul (1989b), *Articles on American Slavery*, 18 vol., New York: Garland.
Finley, Moses (ed.) (1961), *Slavery in Classical Antiquity*, New York: Barnes and Noble.
Finley, Moses (ed) (1987), *Classical Slavery*, London: Frank Cass.
Fogel, Robert W. (1989), *Without Consent or Contract*, New York: Norton.
Fogel, Robert W., and Stanley L. Engerman (1974), *Time on the Cross: The Economics of American Negro Slavery*, Boston: Little, Brown.
Foner, Laura, and Eugene Genovese (eds) (1969), *Slavery in the New World: A Reader in Comparative History*, Englewood Cliffs, NJ: Prentice-Hall.
Foner, Philip (1941), *Business and Slavery*, Chapel Hill: North Carolina Press.
Franklin, John H. (1988), *From Slavery to Freedom*, New York: Knopf.
Friedman, Gerald, and Richard Manning (1992), 'The Rent and Hire of Slaves,' in Robert Fogel, Ralph Galantine, and Richard Manning (eds), *Without Consent or Contract: Evidence and Methods*, New York: Norton, pp. 77–78.
Galenson, David (1981), *White Servitude in Colonial America: An Economic Analysis*, New York: Cambridge University Press.
Galenson, David (1982), 'The Atlantic Slave Trade and the Barbados Market, 1673–1723,' *Journal of Economic History* **42** (3): 491–511.
Galenson, David (1984), 'Rise and Fall of Indentured Servitude in the Americas: An Economic Analysis,' *Journal of Economic History* **44** (1): 1–26.
Galenson, David W. (1986), *Traders, Planters, and Slaves: Market Behavior in Early English America*, New York: Cambridge University Press.
Genovese, Eugene D. (1974), *Roll, Jordan, Roll*, New York: Pantheon.
Genovese, Eugene D. (1989), *The Political Economy of Slavery: Studies in the Economy and Society of the Slave South*, Middletown, CT: Wesleyan.
Goldin, Claudia D. (1976), *Urban Slavery in the American South, 1820–1860: A Quantitative History*, Chicago: University of Chicago Press.
Goodell, William (1853), *The American Slave Code*, New York: Antislavery Society.
Grindle, David J. (1990), 'Manumission: The Weak Link in Georgia's Law of Slavery,' *Mercer Law Review* **41** (2): 701–22.
Grubb, Farley (1985), 'Immigrant Servant Labor: Their Occupational and Geographic Distribution in the Late Eighteenth Century Mid-Atlantic Economy,' *Social Science History* **9** (3): 249–75.
Grubb, Farley (1994), 'The End of European Immigrant Servitude in the US: An Economic Analysis of Market Collapse, 1772–1835,' *Journal of Economic History* **54** (4): 794–824.
Helper, Hinton Rowan (1857), *The Impending Crisis of the South*, New York: Burdick Brothers.
Higman, Barry (1976), *Slave Population and Economy in Jamaica, 1807–34*, New York: Cambridge University Press.
Hindus, Michael S. (1980), *Prison and Plantation*, Chapel Hill: University of North Carolina Press.

Hurd, John (1858), *Law of Freedom and Bondage in the United States*, Boston: Little, Brown.
Inikori, Joseph (1981), 'Market Structure and the Profits of the British African Trade in the Late 18th Century,' *Journal of Economic History* **41** (4): 745–76.
Jones, A.H.M. (1956), 'Slavery in the Ancient World,' *Economic History Review* **9** (2): 185–99.
Klein, Martin (1990), 'The Impact of the Atlantic Slave Trade on the Societies of the Western Sudan,' *Social Science History* **14** (2): 231–54.
Klein, Martin (1993), *Breaking the Chains: Slavery, Bondage, and Emancipation in Modern Africa and Asia*, Madison: University of Wisconsin Press.
Kolchin, Peter (1987), *Unfree Labor: American Slavery and Russian Serfdom*, Cambridge, MA: Harvard University Press.
Kotlikoff, Laurence (1979), 'The Structure of Slave Prices in New Orleans, 1804–1862,' *Economic Inquiry* **17** (4): 496–518.
Licht, Walter (1983), *Working for the Railroad: The Organization of Work in the Nineteenth Century*, Princeton: Princeton University Press.
Lovejoy, Paul (1983), *Transformations in Slavery: A History of Slavery in Africa*, New York: Cambridge University Press.
Mancall, Peter, Joshua Rosenbloom, and Thomas Weiss (2001), 'Slave Prices and the South Carolina Economy, 1722–1809,' *Journal of Economic History* **61** (3): 616–39.
Manning, Patrick (1990), 'The Slave Trade: Formal Demography of a Global System,' *Social Science History* **14** (2): 255–79.
Manning, Patrick (2006), *Slavery and African Life: Occidental, Oriental, and African Slave Trades*, Cambridge: Cambridge University Press.
Margo, Robert, and Richard Steckel (1982), 'The Heights of American Slaves: New Evidence on Slave Nutrition and Health.' *Social Science History* **6** (4): 516–38.
Meltzer, Milton (ed) (1993), *Slavery: A World History*, New York: Da Capo Press.
Menard, Russell R. (1977), 'From Servants to Slaves: The Transformation of the Chesapeake Labor System,' *Southern Studies* **16**: 355–90.
Menard, Russell R. (2006), *Sweet Negotiations*, Charlottesville: University of Virginia Press.
Metzer, Jacob (1975), 'Rational Management, Modern Business Practices and Economies of Scale in the Ante-Bellum Southern Plantations,' *Explorations in Economic History* **12** (2): 123–50.
Mintz, Sidney (1974), *Caribbean Transformations*, New York: Columbia University Press.
Moreno Fraginals, Manuel, Herbert Klein, and Stanley Engerman (1993), 'The Level and Structure of Slave Prices on Cuban Plantations in the Mid Nineteenth Century: Some Comparative Perspectives,' *American Historical Review* **88** (5): 1201–18.
Morris, Thomas D. (1996), *Southern Slavery and the Law: 1619–1860*, Chapel Hill: University of North Carolina Press.
Newland, Carlos, and Maria Jesus San Segundo (1996), 'Human Capital and Other Determinants of the Price Life Cycle of a Slave,' *Journal of Economic History* **56** (3): 694–701.
Oakes, James (1982), *The Ruling Race: A History of American Slaveholders*, New York: Knopf.
Olmstead, Frederick Law (1861, rep. 1953), *The Cotton Kingdom: A Traveler's Observation on Cotton and Slavery in the American Slave States*, ed. A.M. Schlesinger, New York: Knopf.
Parish, Peter (1989), *Slavery: History and Historians*, New York: Westview Press.
Patterson, Orlando (1982), *Slavery and Social Death: A Comparative Study*, Cambridge, MA: Harvard University Press.
Phillips, Ulrich B. (1918) *American Negro Slavery: A Survey of the Supply, Employment and Control of Negro Labor as Determined by the Plantation Regime*, New York: Appleton.
Phillips, Ulrich B. (1927), *Life and Labor in the Old South*, Boston: Little, Brown.
Phillips, William, Jr. (1985), *Slavery from Roman Times to the Early Transatlantic Trade*, Minneapolis: University of Minnesota Press.

Pritchett, Jonathan (1997), 'The Interregional Slave Trade and the Selection of Slaves for the New Orleans Market,' *Journal of Interdisciplinary History* **28** (1): 57–85.
Ramsdell, Charles W. (1929), 'The Natural Limits of Slavery Expansion,' *Mississippi Valley Historical Review* **16** (2): 151–71.
Ransom, Roger L. (1989), *Conflict and Compromise*, New York: Cambridge University Press.
Ransom, Roger L., and Richard Sutch (1977), *One Kind of Freedom: The Economic Consequences of Emancipation*, New York: Cambridge University Press.
Ransom, Roger L., and Richard Sutch (1988), 'Capitalists Without Capital: The Burden of Slavery and the Impact of Emancipation,' *Agricultural History* **62** (3): 133–60.
Richardson, David (1987), 'The Costs of Survival: The Transport of Slaves in the Middle Passage and the Profitability of the 18th Century British Slave Trade,' *Explorations in Economic History* **24** (2): 178–96.
Richardson, David (1989), 'Accounting for Profits in the British Trade in Slaves: A Reply to Darity,' *Explorations in Economic History* **26** (4): 492–9.
Roark, James L. (1977), *Masters Without Slaves*, New York: Norton.
Scarborough, William K. (1966), *The Overseer: Plantation Management in the Old South*, Baton Rouge, Louisiana State University Press.
Schafer, Judith K. (1994), *Slavery, The Civil Law, and the Supreme Court of Louisiana*, Baton Rouge: Louisiana State University Press.
Schmitz, Mark, and Donald Schaefer (1981), 'Paradox Lost: Westward Expansion and Slave Prices Before the Civil War,' *Journal of Economic History* **41** (2): 402–7.
Sheridan, Richard B. (1947), *Sugar and Slavery: An Economic History of the British West Indies, 1607–1776*, Barbados: Caribbean University Press.
Solow, Barbara, and Stanley Engerman (1987), *Capitalism and Caribbean Slavery: The Legacy of Eric Williams*, New York: Cambridge University Press.
Stampp, Kenneth M. (1956), *The Peculiar Institution: Slavery in the Antebellum South*, New York: Knopf.
Starobin, Robert (1970), *Industrial Slavery in the Old South,* New York: Oxford University Press.
Steckel, Richard (1986a), 'Birth Weights and Infant Mortality Among American Slaves,' *Explorations in Economic History* **23** (2): 173–98.
Steckel, Richard (1986b), 'A Peculiar Population: The Nutrition, Health, and Mortality of American Slaves from Childhood to Maturity,' *Journal of Economic History* **46** (3): 721–41.
Steinfeld, Robert J. (1991), *The Invention of Free Labor: The Employment Relation in English and American Law and Culture, 1350–1870*, Chapel Hill: University of North Carolina Press.
Stroud, George (1856), *A Sketch of the Laws Relating to Slavery in the Several States of the USA*, New York: Negro University Press.
Tadman, Michael (1990), *Speculators and Slaves*, Madison: University of Wisconsin Press.
Tushnet, Mark V. (1981), *The American Law of Slavery, 1810–60: Considerations of Humanity and Interest*, Princeton: Princeton University Press.
Vedder, Richard K. (1975), 'The Slave Exploitation (Expropriation) Rate,' *Explorations in Economic History* **12** (4): 453–7.
Wahl, Jenny B. (1998), *The Bondsman's Burden: An Economic Analysis of the Common Law of Southern Slavery*, New York: Cambridge University Press.
Wahl, Jenny B. (2007), 'Stay East, Young Man? Market Repercussions of the *Dred Scott* decision,' *Chicago-Kent Law Review* **82** (1): 361–91.
Walvin, James (1992), *Black Ivory: A History of British Slavery*, Washington, DC: Howard University Press.
Watson, Alan (1987), *Roman Slave Law*, Baltimore: Johns Hopkins Press.
Watson, Alan (1989), *Slave Law in the Americas*, Athens, GA: University of Georgia Press.
Watson, Alan (1991), *Roman Law and Comparative Law*, Athens, GA: University of Georgia Press.

Watson, James (ed) (1980), *Asian and African Systems of Slavery*, Berkeley and Los Angeles: University of California Press.
Westermann, William (1943), 'Slavery and the Elements of Freedom in Ancient Greece,' *Quarterly Bulletin of the Polish Institute of Arts and Sciences in America* **1** (January): 1–16.
Wheeler, Jacob (1837), *A Practical Treatise on the Law of Slavery*, New York: Allan Pollack, Jr.
Wiecek, William M. (1977), 'The Statutory Law of Slavery and Race in the Thirteen Mainland Colonies of British America,' *William and Mary Quarterly* **34** (2): 258–80.
Williams, Eric (1944), *Capitalism and Slavery*, Chapel Hill: University of North Carolina Press.
Wright, Gavin (1978), *The Political Economy of the Cotton South: Households, Markets, and Wealth in the Nineteenth Century*, New York: Norton.
Wright, Gavin (2006), *Slavery and American Economic Development*, Baton Rouge: Louisiana State University Press.
Yasuba, Yasukichi (1961), 'The Profitability and Viability of Slavery in the US,' *Economic Studies Quarterly* **12** (September): 60–7.
Yeager, Timothy J. (1995), 'Encomienda or Slavery? The Spanish Crown's Choice of Labor Organization in Sixteenth Century Spanish America,' *Journal of Economic History* **55** (4): 842–59.

11 New forms of private property: property rights in environmental goods

Daniel H. Cole

1. Introduction

A property right is a form of power – as Denman (1978, p. 3) puts it, 'a sanction and authority for decision-making' – over resources. Dasgupta (1982, p. 38) refers to property as 'a set of rights to control assets,' including environmental goods. Scholars have long recognized that the nature, extent, and allocation of property rights can significantly affect the rate of resource depletion and degradation. In the 4th century B.C.E., Aristotle (1941, sec. 1262b34–35) wrote, 'that which is common to the greatest number has the least care bestowed on it.' His observation has resonated throughout history, and today is understood (after Hardin, 1968) as 'the tragedy of the commons.'

Despite Aristotle's early warning, many environmental goods never have been subject to private ownership, for a variety of economic, technological, political and cultural reasons. Writing 350 years after Aristotle, the Roman poet Ovid (1992, p. 111) put these words in the mouth of Daedalus: 'Though he may possess everything, Minos does not possess the air.' Indeed, according to Roman Law, it was against natural law for any individual, even the emperor, to own the air or other important environmental goods. The Institutes of Justinian (Grapel, 1994, p. 50), compiled one thousand years after Aristotle, decreed, '[b]y the law of nature these things are common to mankind – the air, running water, the sea and consequently the shores of the sea.' In most countries, for most purposes, these environmental goods have ever since remained off limits to private ownership.

If we were to construct a syllogism, positing Aristotle's observation as a major premise and the rule from Justinian's Institutes as a minor premise, the conclusion would be that the commonly owned air, running water, sea, and seashore have the least care bestowed upon them. History, unfortunately, has only too often confirmed this. In the absence of property rights to protect them, environmental goods have been abused, sometimes to the point of destruction. As Hardin (1968, p. 1245) puts it, we have been 'locked into a system of "fouling our own nest."' In more technical terms, environmental degradation has resulted from 'incomplete and asymmetric information combined with incomplete, inconsistent, or unenforced property rights.' See Hanna, Folke and Mäler (1996, p. 3).

Two general solutions typically are offered for resolving environmental problems: (1) specify property rights in environmental goods by 'privatizing' them, or (2) control access to and use of environmental goods through government regulation. See Hardin (1968, p. 1245). This entry concerns the role of property rights in both solutions. More specifically, it concerns the utility of property rights for resolving environmental problems in tandem with, or in place of, regulation.

In recent years regulators have begun replacing command-and-control environmental regulations with 'market-mechanisms,' including property 'rights'-based programs, such as tradeable pollution 'rights,' in order to improve regulatory efficiency. This shift in regulatory approach, which amounts to a limited reallocation of environmental goods from public to private control, has been completely uncontroversial among law and economics scholars, such as Dales (1968), who have advocated the use of 'rights'-based approaches for decades. More controversial is the suggestion, issuing from certain quarters of the law and economics literature, including Anderson and Leal (1991) and Block (1990), that governmental environmental regulation should be completely replaced (with the exception of the common law and its courts) by a regime of well-defined, private (meaning individual, corporate or communal) property rights in environmental goods. This recommendation is premised on the belief that some form of non-public ownership of environmental goods is both necessary and sufficient for optimal environmental protection. Property rights are necessary, according to this theory, because state regulation cannot provide adequate environmental protection; and they are sufficient because they obviate the need for any state regulation beyond traditional common law protections. These assertions and the policy recommendations of self-described 'free market environmentalists' are highly controversial. This chapter does not purport to resolve the issue, but merely reports its treatment in the law and economics literature. For a broader critique of 'free market environmentalism,' see Cole (2002).

Before examining how property rights apply to environmental goods, we need to clarify some concepts. The next two sections attempt, respectively, to unpack the notion of 'environmental goods' and explain the conventional typology of property regimes that apply to environmental goods.

2. What is an 'environmental good'?

The term 'good' is used here in its basic economic sense to mean some thing or amenity to which individuals assign a positive value, whether out of simple desire or because it is necessary to life. But what is an 'environmental good,' as distinguished from other goods? While the phrase is not commonly used in the economic literature, we ordinarily think of environmental goods in basic elemental terms such as air, land, and water. Economists often use the word 'land' as a proxy representing all natural resources used in production (along with capital and labor). But environmental goods are in reality incredibly diverse, and their diversity is reflected in their treatment as property.

Environmental goods are not one kind of thing, but many kinds of various things that come in all shapes and sizes, from the minute probiotic bacteria that aid our digestion of food (but not the 'bad' bacteria that would kill us) to the warming (but not *too* warm) light of the sun. A single blade of grass is an environmental good; so too is the world's largest rainforest. Differences in the physical scale of environmental goods matters for property regime choice.

Environmental goods are also differentiated according to their relative subtractibility, congestibility, and substitutability. A good is subtractible if one person's use necessarily leaves less available for someone else to use. A good is congestible if subtractibility is a non-problem up to a certain level of demand, but becomes a problem once that level is passed. Substitutability refers to alternative environmental or human-made goods that might be substituted for an environmental good, without causing any loss in utility or social welfare.

An example of a nonsubtractible environmental good is sunlight, which cannot be depleted by human use no matter how high the level of demand. Occasionally one person's use of sunlight may block the use of another. See, e.g., *Fountainbleu Hotel Corp. v. Forty-five Twenty-five, Inc.*, 114 So.2d 357 (Fla.App. 1959). And property-related legal rules may regulate the obstruction of sunlight. See, e.g., *Prah v. Maretti*, 321 N.W.2d 182 (Wis. 1982). As a general rule, however, no one's use of sunlight leaves less sunlight available for anyone else to use. Very few environmental goods are of this type, however. Most environmental goods are subtractible or congestible. For instance, a small pristine park may provide undiminished utility for up to 20 users, who may never discover one another's presence there. But if another 20, 30, or more users should begin to use the park – as the park grows more congested – the utility for each individual user may be diminished, and the park itself could at some point become degraded.

Perceptions of environmental goods may change over time as circumstances change. What was once thought to be a nonsubtractible public good may be understood now as a subtractible good. So, for example, the atmosphere was once thought to be a pure (nonsubtractible) public good. But that was before air pollution became a significant problem, and before civil aviation congested the skies. Today, the atmosphere – or, more precisely, clean air – is understood to be subtractible.

As perceptions of a particular environmental good's subtractibility and congestibility change over time, those perceptions may precipitate changes in the good's legal treatment as property. Thus, where roman law and common law once presumed land boundaries to extend upwards to the heavens, ownership of the atmosphere is limited to the practically useable area immediately above the surface of the land. *See United States v. Causby*, 328 US 256 (1946).

Likewise, the excludability of environmental goods can change over time as a result of technological innovations. Thousands upon thousands of acres of rangelands in the Western United States were converted from public to private ownership after the invention of barbed wire in the 1870s dramatically reduced exclusion costs. See Anderson and Hill (1975).

Technological innovations can also alter the perceived substitutability of some (though not all) environmental goods. Oxygen and water are two environmental goods that are absolutely necessary for human existence; they are simply not substitutable. Most other environmental goods have substantial non-economic values, which raise substitution costs. Thus, for most people (with inevitable exceptions, such as Krieger (1973)), plastic trees would be no substitute for the real things. But what if scientists perfected artificial trees to a point where people couldn't tell any difference from 'natural' trees? Some environmental goods, such as fossil fuels, have few, if any non-economic values – no one values crude oil for its 'existence value' or for aesthetic reasons. Today, fossil fuels have great economic value, and the property regime governing them is important. But what if scientists perfected a less-costly, less-polluting, safer, and more reliable, alternative energy source? What would happen to the economic value of fossil fuels? And what would become of the elaborate property system governing fossil fuel extraction and ownership? One thing is certain, no one would worry much about it.

Non-physical attributes of environmental goods can also affect property regime choice. A river is an environmental good, as are the fish that swim in it. Less obviously, the recreational opportunities the river affords humans are environmental goods. In fact, the phrase 'recreational opportunities' may describe various, possibly competing, environmental goods. Consider, for example, a fast, free-flowing river that provides habitat for certain fish species, recreational opportunities for fishers and white water rafters (but not water-skiers), and satisfaction for preservationists. That river could be dammed up and used to provide hydroelectric power, habitat for different fish, and recreational opportunities for the same or different fishers and water-skiers (but not white water rafters). Either way, the river provides a basket of environmental goods, but at the opportunity cost of some other environmental goods. Similarly, a high mountain can be preserved as habitat to protect an endangered species of mountain goat or developed as a ski resort, but not both. Used for either purpose, it provides environmental goods. The mountain's use or non-use for a certain purpose will reflect social choices that may, but will not necessarily, maximize social welfare; and those choices will likewise be reflected in the choice of property regime that governs the mountain.

3. Typology of property regimes

According to the conventional typology, there are four property regimes: private, common, state and nonproperty (or open access). In the law and economics literature, 'private property' (*res privatae*) typically denotes property owned by individuals holding rights to use (in socially acceptable, i.e., non-nuisance-causing, ways), dispose of, and exclude others from resources. 'Common property' (*res communes*) refers to collective ownership situations, in which the owners cannot exclude each other, but can exclude outsiders. 'Public' or 'state' property (*res publicae*) is a special form of common property supposedly owned by all the citizens, but typically controlled by elected officials or bureaucrats, who are free to determine the parameters for use and exclusion. Finally, 'nonproperty' or 'open access' (*res nullius*) denotes a situation in which a resource has no owner; all are at liberty to use it; no one has the right to exclude anyone else. See, e.g., Bromley (1991, p. 31). Some scholars have elaborated more extensive typologies of property rights regimes. See, e.g., Hanna, Folke, and Mäler (1996) and McCay (1997).

These conventional property categories are idealizations. In the real world, property regimes inevitably combine features from various ownership categories. See, e.g., Feeny, Hanna and McEvoy (1996). Moreover, *de facto* property regimes sometimes trump *de jure* property rights. See, e.g., Ellickson (1991). The academic typology also differs significantly from the ways in which most people distinguish property regimes. For example, in common parlance 'private' property is not counterpoised to 'common' property as it is in much of the academic literature. Co-owned property, including joint tenancy, partnership, and corporate property, is usually considered 'private', so long as it is not owned by the state or some other public entity. See, e.g., Denman (1978, p. 102). Indeed, were the term 'private' strictly limited to describing property owned by individuals, there would be precious little 'private' ownership of land in the United States or in any other country. From another point of view, however, co-ownership simply denotes multiple individual ownership, with each co-owner possessing individual rights in (or attributes of) the property.

See Bromley (1991, pp. 25–6), and Barzel (1990). Eggertsson (1996, p. 161) suggests that the distinction between private and common (or, in his terms, 'communal') ownership has less to do with the number of owners than with the comparatively free transferability of private property rights.

A more problematic terminological issue in the academic literature is the conflation of 'common' property with 'nonproperty' or 'open access.' Hardin (1968), North and Thomas (1973) and others have been criticized for this. See, e.g., Cox (1985) and Bromley (1991, pp. 22, 137). However, the conflation of 'common' with 'open access' is somewhat understandable because, in the vernacular, nonproperty resources are often described as 'commonses' or 'common pool' resources. Indeed, they *are* 'commonses' in that they are common to all. Frank Michaelman (1982, p. 9), for example, defines a 'commons' as 'a scheme of universally distributed, all-encompassing privilege' (where 'privilege' is defined in its Hohfeldian sense of 'no duty not to use,' see Hohfeld, 1913).

What really distinguishes 'open access' resources from 'common property,' as that phrase is defined in the law and economics literature, is the unlimited size of the group capable of accessing and using the resources. See, e.g., Seabright (1993, p. 114, n. 1). In order for property to be 'common' (*res communes*) rather than 'open access' (*res nullius*) there must be at least two groups, one of which collectively controls the resource and excludes the other from access and control. See Ciriacy-Wantrup and Bishop (1975, p. 715). Daniel Bromley (1991, p. 149) claims that '[a] common property regime for the group becomes an open access regime for the individuals within the group.' In reality, however, in most (if not all) common property regimes individual members of the common ownership group do not possess rights to unfettered access and use; rather, the ownership group regulates the access and use of individual members. Still, Bromley (1991, pp. 25–6) is right to note that 'common property represents *private property for the group of co-owners* because all others are excluded from use and decision making.' In sum, common property is more like 'private' (individual) property than like 'open access,' which is characterized by universal access and the utter absence of legal rights and duties with respect to the resource.

'Common' property is also sometimes confused or conflated with 'state' property. The state could be viewed, of course, as just another group of co-owners, like partnerships, collectives or villages. But those, such as Elinor Ostrom (1990), who write about 'common' property resources distinguish 'state' from 'common' ownership based on the size of the ownership group and its location vis-à-vis the resource (see chapter 2000). When a group of self-governing villagers controls access to a fishery, for example, that is considered 'common' ownership. But when non-users, far removed from the village, control access and use, that is 'state' or 'public' ownership. Moreover, depending on the political circumstances and management practices, 'state' or 'public' property may more closely resemble individually- or corporately-owned 'private' property than 'common' property. See, e.g., Eggertsson (1990, p. 37); Rose (1994, pp. 116–7); and Denman (1978, pp. 3–4).

One final conceptual problem concerns the general neglect of a crucial question: Just what specific rights and corresponding duties do the various property regimes entail? As Bromley (1989, p. 187) notes, those who write about 'property' or 'property rights' rarely are 'specific about the content of those terms.' They often assume facilely that 'private' property means Blackstonian absolute dominion (which has always been a myth). But as Demsetz (1988, p. 19) explains, 'full private rights, full state rights, full communal rights are notions that are very elastic with respect to the substantive bundle of entitlements involved.'

Honoré (1961) lists 11 distinct 'sticks' in the *complete* bundle of property rights – the right to exclusively possess, the right to use, the right to manage, the right to the income, the right to the capital, the right to security, transmissibility, absence of term, the prohibition of harmful use, liability to execution, and the right to residuary character – but none of these rights is strictly necessary in the sense that one cannot be considered an owner of property without it. Even if one or more 'sticks' are missing from a particular bundle, someone may still meaningfully be said to 'own' property. It is not good enough, therefore, to recommend a certain property regime for environmental goods; one must also specify just what rights and corresponding duties that regime would entail. See Ostrom (1990, p. 22). Those rights and duties may well vary from one environmental good to another, or, with respect to any particular environmental good, from one institutional context to another.

In view of these terminological confusions, which arguably reflect ideological issues more than real distinctions between property rights regimes, Dales (1968, p. 61) sensibly abandons the conventional typology. Rather than opposing 'private' to 'common' property, he merely refers to 'property rights, by whomever exercised.' Depending on the circumstances, property rights may be vested in individuals, groups (collectives or firms), or the state. The implication is that distinctions between individual, group and state property tend to be more informative and less ideologically loaded than the conventional distinction between 'private' and 'common' property. See also Goetze (1987, p. 187).

Although the problems arising from the ideal typologies of property rights regimes are troublesome, especially when they are neglected, they do not go to the ultimate concern of law and economics scholars, which is not the ownership regime *per se* but the costs of transacting (or refraining from transacting) over resources. The ownership and management regime is important only in so far as it impacts on externalities and transaction costs. See, e.g., Coase (1960), Demsetz (1967), Dahlman (1979), and Terrebonne (1993).

4. The allegory of 'the tragedy of the commons' (which is really about open access)

The relationship between property rights and resource depletion – specifically, Aristotle's observation that goods held in common receive the least care – has been a subject of extensive economic research throughout the twentieth century. Warming (1911), Gordon (1954), and Scott (1955) each elaborated on Aristotle's observation in the context of unowned and over-exploited fisheries. In the late 1960s Hardin (1968) and Demsetz (1967) provided the classic accounts of, respectively, the depletion of open-access resources, including many environmental goods, and the historical evolution of property institutions to avert the over-exploitation of such goods by reducing externalities and transaction costs.

Hardin's 'The Tragedy of the Commons' provides a particularly useful framework for the analysis of property rights in environmental goods. Its thesis is that resource depletion and pollution problems both stem from the incentives created by 'open access' regimes (*not* common-property regimes), in which no one can exclude anyone else from using a given resource. Unless property rights are imposed, these incentives lead inexorably (assuming a significant level of demand for the resource) to what Hardin calls 'the tragedy of the commons' – the despoliation and ultimate destruction of environmental goods. Hardin would have avoided a great deal of confusion had he more accurately titled his article, 'The Tragedy of Open Access,' which is how the problem will be described from this point on. See Cole (2002, pp. 5–6).

Hardin suggests two means of averting the 'tragedy', which he combines under the heading, 'mutual coercion, mutually agreed upon.' The first is privatization: convert the open-access pasture to private (but not necessarily individual) ownership. On a privately owned pasture, the costs of any decision to add an extra animal would be internalized by the pasture owner(s). They would continue to use the pasture but not to the point of destruction because, Hardin assumes, such over-exploitation would generate net costs for the presumptively rational pasture owner(s). Hardin's second means of averting the tragedy of open access is government regulation (loosely defined). Under this regime, economic incentives toward overexploitation might be reduced or eliminated through (self-) imposed restrictions on all herders. Assuming enforceability and sufficient penalties for noncompliance, entry and use restrictions would raise the (internal) cost of adding animals to the common, but no longer 'open-access' pasture.

Each of Hardin's proffered solutions to the tragedy of open access involves the conversion of the resource from nonproperty to some form of property ownership – private, common, or state. However, contrary to the claims of critics such as Cox (1985), Berkes, Feeny, McCay and Acheson (1989), Feeny, Berkes, McCay and Acheson (1990), and Feeny, Hanna, and McEvoy (1996), Hardin's analysis provides no basis for preferring private ownership over common or state ownership (as those regimes are conventionally defined). In other words, his analysis calls for the creation of property rights where none previously existed, but does not suggest in whom (individuals, groups or the state) those property rights should be vested. In a subsequent writing, Hardin (1978) lists private and state ownership (or 'private enterprise' and 'socialism') as the only two viable solutions to the tragedy of open access, implying that 'common' property regimes (as defined in Section 2) would not suffice. But nothing in Hardin (1968) supports such a claim; and numerous empirical and theoretical studies dispute it. See, e.g., Ostrom (1990), Bromley (1992), Hanna and Munasinghe (1995b), and Anderson and Hill (2002).

A more legitimate criticism of Hardin concerns his assumption that rational private owners would never knowingly exploit their resources to destruction. This assumption is empirically and theoretically dubious. Empirically, individual private owners have often done exactly what Hardin assumes they would not do. Bromley (1991, p. 171) reminds us of the Dust Bowls created when supposedly 'omniscient private entrepreneurs' plowed up the prairies against the advice of agricultural experts (but see Hansen and Libecap 2004, arguing that the Dust Bowls were primarily the result of institutional limitations on farm size). Even as a matter of economic theory, it is sometimes economically rational for resource users to extinguish rather than conserve resources in some circumstances. See Gordon (1958, pp. 117, 119–20). Clark (1973a, pp. 950–51) has shown, for example, that 'extermination of an entire [animal] population may appear as the most attractive policy, even to an individual resource owner,' when '(a) the discount (or time preference) rate sufficiently exceeds the maximum reproductive potential of the population, and (b) an immediate profit can be made from harvesting the last remaining animals.' The outcome may not be socially optimal, but private property owners make decisions to maximize private, not social, benefits. See also Clark (1973b); Larson and Bromley (1990); and Schlager and Ostrom (1992). We will revisit this point later in Section 12, when reviewing claims that the complete privatization of environmental goods would necessarily result in their optimal conservation.

Despite these criticisms, Hardin's chief insight remains nonetheless valid: 'open access' resources will be unsustainably exploited unless *some* property-rights regime is imposed for their protection. But which property-rights regime? 'Open access' may be replaced by a traditionally-conceived 'private' property regime, in which units of the resource are allotted to individual owners. Or the resource may be kept intact as 'common' property, with entry and use restrictions imposed by some governing body. This governing body may be private – collective self-government by the group of resource users *cum* 'owners' – or public–state ownership or regulation.

An adequate theory of property rights on environmental goods must consider the full range of possible property-rights and regulatory solutions to 'the tragedy of the commons,' and recognize that no single regime is likely to work for every resource and in every institutional and ecological setting. As Noll (1989), Komesar (1994), and Eggertsson (1996, p. 166) have pointed out, each circumstance requires a comparative assessment of the costs of production, exclusion and administration. A private property regime based on individual ownership may be appropriate in cases where the costs of governance are relatively high, but exclusion costs are relatively low. Some form of (private or public) 'common' or state ownership may be preferable, however, in the converse situation of high exclusion costs and relatively low costs of administration. Finally, where the costs of either exclusion or governance would be extraordinarily high (reflecting, perhaps, the technological infeasibility of exclusion) or the resource itself is 'superabundant' (see Demsetz, 1964, p. 20), 'open access' may be inevitable, maximally efficient or both. See Coase (1960, p. 39) and Libecap (1989, pp. 13–14). Stated as a rule: that property regime is best (i.e., most efficient) which, in the circumstances, would achieve social goals at the lowest social cost (or greatest net social benefit).

Stating a decision rule is one thing; implementing it is quite another. As Libecap (1989, p. 5) points out, society will not always (and perhaps never) select the 'best' property regime for conserving environmental goods: 'examination of the preferences of individual bargaining parties and consideration of the details of the political bargaining underlying property rights institutions are necessary for understanding why particular property rights institutions are developed and maintained, despite imaginable alternatives that would appear to be more rational.' This has public choice implications that are explored briefly, as they relate to 'Free Market Environmentalism', in Sections 10 and 11.

5. Regulatory solutions to 'the tragedy of open access'

In most countries environmental goods have been subject to multiple property rights regimes. Some environmental goods, such as land, have been protected primarily (though not exclusively, and not at all in socialist economies) through the allocation of private property rights. Many other environmental goods, such as the upper atmosphere, have, for various reasons, never been allotted to private owners. At Roman law and common law, the property rights of landowners supposedly extended down to the center of the earth and up to the heavens. But, of course, that was purely theoretical with respect to the upper atmosphere before the advent of civil aviation, at which point the common law rule was summarily displaced. See *United States v. Causby*, 328 US 256 (1946). Today, the atmosphere (above the area immediately useful for landowners) is treated as a publicly owned resource, and the government regulates private uses, including civil aviation and pollution. Thus, societies have relied on both of Hardin's proffered solutions – privatization and public ownership/regulation – to avert the tragedy of open access.

Most property regimes governing environmental goods are admixtures of individual private ownership, private (non-state) common property management, state ownership and management (i.e., regulation). These actually-existing systems of property rights on environmental goods hardly resemble the idealized versions presented above in Section 3. Some law and economics scholars maintain, however, that a 'private' property regime of the ideal type would offer more effective *and* efficient environmental protection than any other ownership/management regime. Their arguments are reviewed in Sections 11 and 12. Sections 6 through 10 focus on the theory and practice of environmental regulation using property or quasi-property mechanisms. The balance of this section, meanwhile, merely identifies different types of environmental regulation.

The law and economics literature distinguishes between regulatory approaches in a number of different ways. Many scholars recognize two categories of regulation: command-and-control and 'market-based'. See, e.g., Stavins and Whitehead (1992). The second category actually encompasses (at least) two distinct regulatory approaches: taxes and trading systems. See, e.g., Baumol and Oates (1988) and Opschoor and Vos (1989). Percival et al. (1996, pp. 154–158) derive a more expansive list of 12 distinct approaches, including (1) design standards or technology specifications, (2) performance standards or emissions limits, (3) ambient or harm-based standards, (4) product bans or use limitations, (5) marketable allowances, (6) challenge regulation or environmental contracting, (7) pollution taxes or emissions charges, (8) subsidies, (9) deposit-refund schemes, (10) liability rules and insurance requirements, (11) planning or analysis requirements, and (12) information disclosure (e.g., labeling) requirements. The regulatory approaches in this more expansive typology combine varying amounts of commands, controls, and economic incentives.

From the perspective of regulated industries, these typologies are misleading because, at bottom, all regulatory approaches are economic; the only meaningful difference between one approach and another lies in their differential costs of compliance and administration. As a practical matter, then, the key to choosing between different regulatory approaches to achieve certain environmental protection goals is cost-effectiveness or regulatory efficiency: In any given situation, how much pollution control or resource conservation would alternative regulatory regimes buy for the buck? This is the question that law and economics scholars have been addressing in their theoretical modeling and empirical investigations of environmental protection regimes. See, e.g., Cole and Grossman (1999 and 2002).

6. The theory of property rights-based environmental regulation

All forms of environmental regulation constitute, in effect, property-based solutions to the 'tragedy' of open-access environmental goods. See Barnes (1982–3); Cole (2002). Whenever the state regulates air pollution, for example, it imposes a system of rights and obligations with respect to the atmosphere. Whether it employs technology-based standards or market-based incentives, the state imposes on polluters a legally enforceable duty to comply with all restrictions on use of (what amounts to) the public's atmosphere. Alternatively, the state may choose not to assert public rights on the environmental goods themselves, but on privately-generated information respecting those goods, e.g., through the use of public disclosure requirements. See, e.g., Hamilton (1995) and Konar and Cohen (1997). Such state regulations may be characterized as exercises in sovereignty (*imperium*) rather than ownership (*dominium*). See Denman (1978, pp. 25, 29–30). But this makes little practical difference. Whether the state is purporting to act as sovereign or owner, the rights it asserts are in the nature of property.

By viewing the state as 'owner' (in some meaningful sense) of the environmental goods it regulates, it becomes clear that the choice in regulating is not *whether* to adopt a property-based approach in environmental regulation, but *which* property-based approach to adopt. To what extent should the state assert public rights (as owner or sovereign), as opposed to vesting (limited) property rights in individual users or groups of users? The answer to this question requires the same comparative assessment of production, exclusion and administrative costs discussed at the end of the preceding section.

Since the advent of federal pollution-control regulation in the late 1960s and early 1970s, economists have advocated the allocation of transferable property (or quasi-property) rights in wastes, as less costly alternatives to command-and-control environmental regulations. See Dales (1968). The idea is simple enough in theory. The government sets a pollution control goal and determines the extent of emissions reduction necessary to attain it. Necessary reductions are then subtracted from current emissions levels to derive total allowable emissions. Next, the government unitizes and allocates those allowable emissions, in the form of transferable pollution rights or allowances among regulated firms. The total number of 'rights' in circulation should match the emissions level the government deemed appropriate to achieve its pollution-control goal. Assuming the government's calculations were accurate, its pollution control goal should be achieved, regardless of whether the firms can trade 'rights' to pollute. The primary purpose of allowing trading, therefore, is not to reduce emissions (though, depending on market conditions, allowing trading may create incentives for emissions reductions beyond government-mandated levels) but to minimize the costs of reducing emissions. By making pollution 'rights' transferable, the government 'automatically ensures that the required reduction in waste discharge will be achieved at the smallest possible total cost to society' Dales (1968, p. 107). It does so by creating markets that efficiently allocate the costs of pollution control among regulated firms. Firms with low pollution-control costs may find it worthwhile to reduce their emissions below mandated levels, leaving them with excess 'rights' to sell to firms with higher pollution-control costs. In theory, exchanges of pollution 'rights' should occur at any price below the marginal pollution-reduction costs of some firms and above the marginal pollution-control costs of others.

The great advantage of this system over traditional command-and-control regulations is that it takes account of the different cost structures individual firms have for pollution control. Command-and-control regulations disregard differential compliance costs, forcing all regulated firms to reduce emissions by the same amount. The market-based system of transferable pollution 'rights,' by contrast, allocates the bulk of the pollution-control burden to those firms that can reduce emissions at lower cost. Firms that cannot reduce emissions so cheaply are allowed to pollute more, though they must pay for the privilege by purchasing pollution 'rights' on the open market.

In addition to lowering the total cost of achieving administratively determined environmental goals, there is evidence that property rights-based trading systems encourage the development of new abatement technologies, leading to even greater emissions reductions. See Jung, Krutilla, and Boyd (1996); Burtraw (2000). Empirically, however, the relative merits of tradable permitting on technological innovation remain questionable (at least). See Taylor, Rubin, and Hounshell (2005). Some proponents of emissions trading, such as Ackerman and Stewart (1985), further contend that it is a more democratic approach to regulation than command-and-control because it focuses public attention on the fundamental question of how much pollution is acceptable, supposedly leading to more meaningful public participation in the political process and more reasoned deliberation over environmental policy by elected representatives. Heinzerling (1995) disputes such claims, however, pointing to actual legislative deliberations over pollution trading programs, in which the public and their elected representatives avoided entirely the fundamental questions of environmental policy.

Property rights-based approaches to environmental regulation place a premium on a government's ability to calculate current waste levels and necessary waste reductions to achieve environmental goals. If the government fails to accurately measure current emissions or necessary reductions, its environmental goals may not be met. This is similar to the problem of getting the prices right in a tax-based pollution control regime. See, e.g., Baumol and Oates (1971). Of course, in a tax-based system the government can adjust the tax rate up or down until it achieves the desired incentive effects. Dales (1968) recommends something similar for transferrable pollution 'rights': The 'rights' may be limited in duration (one-year, five-year, etc.), so that the government can make occasional adjustments to ensure the attainment of existing or newly-adopted pollution-control goals. Although this makes good sense from a regulatory perspective, it may seem problematic from a property rights perspective, and has not been incorporated into any existing tradable permitting system.

Holders of 'property rights' typically cannot be defeased involuntarily. When a person holds property 'rights' in something, that means that everyone else has a corresponding duty not to interfere. See Hohfeld (1920). The government may 'take' the property pursuant to Eminent Domain, but only upon payment of just compensation. What, then, is the status under property law of 'rights' to pollute that can be confiscated by the government without compensation? Are they *really* property rights?

As noted earlier, whenever the government regulates for environmental protection, it is (if only implicitly) asserting public rights in environmental goods. And when the government creates a market in transferable pollution 'rights,' this can be viewed as a conveyance of some of the public's property rights in the atmosphere to market participants. What the private firms receive is something akin to a usufruct, a leasehold, or a defeasible fee on the environmental goods. These are certainly valuable property 'rights,' though they amount to something less than fee simple ownership. To say they are not 'property rights' simply because they are neither absolute nor perpetual would be akin to saying that fee simple is the only legitimate estate in land.

From an economic point of view, the legal characterization of property rights is less important than their incentive effects for market participants. The less secure property rights are, the less likely potential buyers will be to invest in them (assuming alternative investment possibilities). See Posner (1992, p. 32). Leaseholds certainly are less valuable than freeholds precisely because of their more limited tenure and security. And there is every reason to suspect that defeasible pollution 'rights' would have lower market value than absolute pollution 'rights.' Of course, if the market value of the 'rights' falls too low, the market for them will simply disappear.

7. The development of property rights-based environmental regulations: netting, offsets, bubbles, and banking

The theory of property 'rights' to pollute has been implemented at various times, in various ways, in various environmental goods, and with varying degrees of success. This section and the two that follow focus on the American experience with tradeable pollution 'rights' because it has been the most extensive. See Opschoor and Vos (1989, p. 99). And most of the American experience with emissions trading has occurred under the Clean Air Act (42 U.S.C. §§ 7401 to 7671q).

The first generation of federal pollution control regulations, adopted in the early 1970s, took a predominantly command-and-control approach to regulation. Federal regulators not only set environmental goals (or pollution reduction targets), but imposed industry-wide, health- or technology-based performance standards that applied to all plants, regardless of their differential costs of compliance. The Clean Air Act of 1970 included nothing like the transferable pollution 'rights' system that Dales (1968) had envisioned.

In the early days of federal environmental regulation, the command-and-control approach made some sense. The Environmental Protection Agency (EPA), at its inception in 1970, may not have possessed the 'technical capability' or economic expertise needed to design and implement transferable pollution rights programs. See Tripp and Dudek (1989, p. 375). According to some analysts, such as Latin (1985), command-and-control air pollution regulations were easier and less costly for a new and inexperienced administrative agency like the EPA to design and implement. It was almost certainly cheaper and easier for the fledgling agency to require firms to install and operate specified air pollution-control devices, which would reduce emissions by known amounts, than to monitor and enforce individualized output levels at thousands of sources. See Maloney and McCormick (1982, p. 106); Cole and Grossman (1999, 920–22).

Moreover, in the early days of federal environmental regulation improvements came cheap, so that even a relatively expensive system of command-and-control regulations provided substantial net social benefits. Indeed, the Clean Air Act may have provided its greatest net social benefits at the very time it was most heavily dominated by expensive command-and-control regulations. According to best estimates, the total social cost of Clean Air Act regulations between 1970 and 1981 amounted to \$13.7 billion, while the easily quantifiable benefits from those regulations in 1978 amounted to \$37.3 billion, yielding a net social profit of almost \$24 billion (not including the more difficult to quantify health, aesthetic and ecosystem benefits of pollution control). See Portney (1990, p. 69). Still, many have argued that the net social benefits of air pollution control would have been far higher had the government adopted less costly approaches to regulation than command-and-control. According to various studies, federal air pollution regulations in the 1970s and early 1980s were between 7 and 400 percent more expensive than 'least-cost' solutions. See Ackerman and Stewart (1985, p. 1338), and Tietenberg (1985, pp. 39–56).

Even in its early years, however, the EPA was not oblivious to alternative approaches to regulation. It began experimenting with emissions trading programs as early as 1974. See Hahn and Hester (1989a, p. 109). By 1980 the agency had approved four different types of emissions trading schemes: netting, offsets, bubbles, and banking. See Liroff (1986).

Netting

First, in 1974 EPA adopted 'netting,' a policy that allows firms to avoid the application of expensive 'New Source Performance Standards' by netting increased emissions from modernized or expanded existing sources with emissions decreases from other existing sources at the same facility. See Hahn and Hester (1989a, pp. 132–3). So long as the net increase in plant-wide emissions does not equal the minimal requirement for a 'major' source, as defined in the Clean Air Act, the modernization or expansion will not be treated as a 'new' source for purposes of the Clean Air Act. Netting can occur in all areas of the country, whether or not they have attained the National Ambient Air Quality Standards. But netting obviously applies only to internal trades, i.e., trades between sources located at the same facility. See EPA (1986a). Nevertheless, according to Hahn and Hester (1989a, p. 133), it 'is the most commonly used emissions trading activity by a wide margin.' Between 1974 and 1984, as many as 12,000 sources used netting to avoid more onerous regulatory burdens under the Clean Air Act. The result has been estimated cost savings of between \$525 million and \$12 billion. Hahn and Hester (1989b, p. 374).

Offsets

'Offsets' were the second form of emissions trading created by the EPA. By the mid-1970s, the agency had become concerned that many of the country's Air Quality Control Regions would fail to attain the National Ambient Air Quality Standards by the 1977 deadline. The question arose whether the Clean Air Act would permit the construction of new air pollution sources in nonattainment areas. A construction ban obviously would have entailed great economic costs for nonattainment areas, as well as political fall-out for state and federal regulators. To avoid this prospect, the EPA in late 1976 promulgated 'offset' regulations that permitted the construction of new stationary sources in nonattainment areas, provided that their new emissions were offset by reductions at existing sources. Under this offset rule '[e]xisting sources are, in effect, given pollution rights equal to their existing emissions, which can then be sold to new sources or to existing sources that wish to increase their emissions.' See Stewart and Krier (1978, p. 593).

Offsets are different from netting in several respects: they apply only in nonattainment regions (and in certain attainment regions where emissions contribute to nonattainment in other regions); they are mandatory; and they cannot result in a net increase in emissions. EPA's original offset rule was codified in §178 of the 1977 Amendments to the Clean Air Act, which additionally required that all new emissions in nonattainment regions be *more than offset* by reductions from existing sources. The purpose was to ensure that new economic development in nonattainment regions would contribute to the attainment of the National Ambient Air Quality Standards. Subsequently, the 1990 Clean Air Act Amendments established precise offset ratios, ranging from 1.1:1 to 1.5:1, that apply depending on the region's level of nonattainment. For example, in Los Angeles, which is the only 'extreme' nonattainment area in the country, 1.5 tons of Volatile Organic Compound (VOC) emissions must be retired from existing sources for every ton to be emitted from a new source. As of about 1988, some 2,000 offset transactions had taken place, though only about 10 percent of these were external, i.e., involving more than a single facility (Hahn and Hester, 1989b, p. 373). The economic effects of these transactions are difficult to estimate. Offsets are not designed to yield direct regulatory cost savings. However, the fact that offset transactions occur at all suggests that they must provide some economic benefits both for firms seeking to locate in nonattainment regions and for the nonattainment regions themselves. See Hahn and Hester (1989b, p. 375).

Bubbles

In 1979, EPA permitted regulated firms to use 'bubbles' to avoid more burdensome regulations. A single plant may contain many individual sources of pollution. The 'bubble' policy allows existing plants (or groups of plants) under common management to place all their individual smokestacks under a bubble, as it were, with a single opening at the top. By treating the entire plant or group of plants as a single source with a single emissions target (for each pollutant), plant managers are free to allocate necessary reductions to those smokestacks with the lowest control costs. Instead of having to reduce emissions by a certain amount at each and every smokestack, the plant (or plants) can reduce emissions more at some smokestacks and less (or not at all) at others. 'In effect, emissions credits are created by some sources within the plant and used by others' (Hahn and Hester, 1989b, p. 372). By the mid-1980s the EPA had approved 42 bubbles for firms and various states with EPA-delegated authority had approved another 89; but only two of them involved external trades. See Hahn and Hester (1989a, pp. 123–5, and 1989b, p. 373). The total cost savings from bubbling have been significant. Federally-approved and state-approved bubbles have saved an estimated $435 million in regulatory costs. While this total is lower than the total cost savings from netting, it reflects a higher average savings per transaction. See Hahn and Hester (1989b, p. 374).

Banking
Also in 1979, EPA began allowing regulated firms to bank emissions credits for future use, sale or lease. This banking system is not so much a separate emissions trading scheme as a mechanism to facilitate the use of other emissions trading schemes, notably bubbles and offsets. The EPA delegated authority to the states to administer their own emissions credit banks. But, according to Hahn and Hester (1989b, p. 373), banking has not been well-received by either state administrators or regulated firms. As of September 1986, firms had withdrawn credits from banks for sale, lease or use only 100 times. Thus, the cost savings realized through banking were 'necessarily small' (Hahn and Hester, 1989b, p. 374). One possible reason for the reluctance of firms to use the banking system for emissions reduction credits is the lack of secure property rights in the credits, which can be confiscated by state or federal regulators at any time in order to further environmental protection goals (Hahn and Hester, 1989a, p. 130).

Indeed, none of the four pollution trading programs discussed in this Section – netting, offsets, bubbles, and banking – provide secure property rights in emissions reduction credits (ERCs). According to the EPA (Oct. 1980, p. 2), '*an ERC cannot be an absolute property right.*' Because of its continuing statutory obligation to attain National Ambient Air Quality Standards, the agency reserves the right to impose new emissions controls that could, in effect, confiscate saved or purchased emissions reduction credits. See Hahn and Hester (1989a, p. 117). As noted earlier, the lack of secure property rights on ERCs is not necessarily a fatal flaw in the system; the market will discount their economic value based on the risk of confiscation. But, according to Hahn and Hester (1989b, p. 379), the lack of secure property rights on ERCs has served 'as a disincentive for engaging in trading in nonattainment areas, and especially for external trading in those areas.' The lack of secure property rights raises similar issues with respect to the most ambitious emissions trading program to date: the sulfur dioxide allowance trading program under the 1990 Clean Air Act Amendments.

8. The Clean Air Act's sulfur dioxide allowance trading program

Program design

When the federal government took over primary responsibility from the states for air pollution control in 1970, one of its main justifications was the problem of interstate air pollution. See Revesz (1996, p. 2341). Since then, ironically, interstate air pollution problems have been among the 'thorniest' problems for federal regulators (Squillace, 1992, p. 301). Acid rain is a prime example. It is created when sulfur dioxide (SO_2) and nitrogen oxide (NO_x) emissions, primarily from midwestern power plants, combine with constituent elements in the atmosphere to produce sulfuric and nitric acids that precipitate back to earth, acidifying lakes, burning forests, and corroding structures. The biggest regulatory problem with acid rain is that most of it falls far from its midwestern emissions sources in the northeastern United States and in Canada. In 1990, after more than a decade of political wrangling, Congress enacted an innovative new program to control acid rain. The 'acid deposition control' program established in Title IV of the 1990 Clean Air Act Amendments (42 U.S.C. § 7651) sought to cut SO_2 emissions by 10 million tons and NO_x emissions by two million tons by the year 2000. To reduce NO_x emissions, Congress relied primarily on traditional technology-based standards, i.e., command-and-control: regulated utilities were required to retrofit controls on existing boilers. The SO_2 reduction effort, by contrast, relied on a new, two-phase (quasi-) property-based approach utilizing transferrable emissions allowances.

The different regulatory approaches may reflect the fact that NO_x controls are significantly cheaper than SO_2 controls. See, e.g., State Utility Forecasting Group (1991, p. 45) (estimating the capital cost for NO_x control retrofits at less than \$100 million, compared to \$0.9 billion for SO_2 control retrofits). Consequently, the marginal benefits of an emissions trading program for NO_x would be lower, perhaps so low as to be outweighed by the higher administrative costs of such a program.

In Phase I of the SO_2 program, Congress issued emissions

'allowances' – with each allowance equalling one ton of SO_2 emissions – for the 240 dirtiest generators at 110 power plants in 21 states. Sixty-three percent of regulated generators were located in just six states: Illinois (17), Indiana (37), Kentucky (17), Ohio (41), Pennsylvania (21), and Tennessee (19). The total number of allowances issued equalled approximately one-half of the total emissions of all 240 generators, in order to achieve a 3.5 million ton reduction in aggregate SO_2 emissions before the second phase of emissions reductions begins in the year 2000. The allowances were allocated to individual generating units based on their average quantity of fossil fuel consumed during the three-year period 1985–1987, assuming 2.5 lbs SO_2 per each million BTUs of fuel input. In Phase II, the goal is to reduce SO_2 emissions from all but the smallest generating units by an additional 6.5 million tons, based on a formula of 1.2 pounds per million BTUs of fossil fuel input during the 1985–1987 period.

Congress' pollution reduction targets really are not as stringent as they appear because the Act provides extra allowances for plants in 'high growth' states, including the six states that produce the lion's share of the country's SO_2 emissions. The Act also provides that deadlines may be extended for plants that take early steps to reduce emissions beyond the Act's requirements. However, the Act sets a fast 8.7 million pound cap on utility SO_2 emissions after 2000. Moreover, the Act does not hold in reserve any emissions allowances for new sources entering the market; new sources must obtain allowances from existing ones.

All the pollution reduction realized under the Clean Air Act's acid rain program will result from these administratively set quotas. They are 'commands,' but they have been issued without attendant 'controls.' The Act does not specify *how* sources are to meet emissions reduction requirements. In fact, the law does not even require sources to reduce emissions to the levels set by Congress but only to possess allowances equal to their actual emissions. Congress designed the Act to utilize market forces by expressly authorizing the nationwide buying and selling of emissions 'allowances.' Sources that can economically reduce their emissions below required levels can sell their excess allowances. Sources with higher costs of controlling emissions can purchase extra allowances, i.e., increase their quota, rather than reduce emissions to Phase I or Phase II levels. Congress even provided for the creation of a futures market in emissions allowances, authorizing generating units to buy and sell allowances for future years. See Mazurek (1994).

The goal of this trading system is primarily to minimize the total costs of achieving the legislatively commanded reductions in SO_2 emissions. According to some estimates, it could reduce the total cost of achieving a 10 million ton reduction in SO_2 emissions by 20 percent, from \$5 to \$4 billion or less. Menell and Stewart (1994, p. 410).

Not everything about the program is market-driven, however. The program places a premium on monitoring trades and emissions. When a generating unit buys or sells an allowance, that alters its emissions quota. The EPA has to keep track of the trades to know, at any given moment, how much SO_2 each generating unit is permitted to emit. To that end, the agency created a central accounting system to which firms must report all allowance transactions. And to ensure that sources are complying with their emissions quotas, they must install continuous emissions monitoring systems and report their actual emissions to the EPA. Sources that violate their emissions limitations are subject to a penalty of \$2,000 per ton. This penalty is significant, amounting approximately to 20 times the price of one ton of SO_2 at the March 1997 auction.

The key to the design of the acid rain program is the development of a well-functioning emissions market. But certain aspects of the program's design initially caused some to doubt that a market would develop. One major concern was the lack of property rights in emissions 'allowances.' Congress expressly provided in § 403(f) of the 1990 Clean Air Act Amendments (42 U.S.C. § 7651(f)) that an 'allowance is not a property right.' And it expressly authorized the EPA 'to terminate or limit' allowances, when necessary to achieve environmental goals, without having to pay just compensation for taking property under the 5th Amendment to the U.S. Constitution. See Dennis (1993, pp. 1118–22). This provision may serve to placate environmentalists, who are repulsed by the very notion of a right to pollute, as well as the idea that firms might profit from trading in pollution. See Percival et al. (1996, pp. 829, 832). However, § 403(f) is premised on a typical confusion between property rights on something and the thing itself. An emissions 'allowance' is not a property right, but there certainly are property rights in allowances. A utility that holds an allowance to emit SO_2 cannot prevent the government from confiscating it but certainly can exclude all others from interfering with it. The rights to possess and exclude (within limits) certainly are property rights on the allowance. Indeed, disputes over property interests in emissions allowances have led to civil litigation. See *Ormet Corporation v. Ohio Power Company*, 98 F.3d 799 (4th Cir. 1996).

In addition to property rights concerns, some analysts expected allowances to be priced beyond any potential market. See Squillace (1992, p. 302). However, the performance of the SO_2 emissions trading system to date has allayed this concern.

The SO_2 market in operation

By November 1995, 23 million allowances worth \$2 billion had been transferred in more than 600 transactions under the acid rain program. In addition to external transfers, many sources had reduced their emissions and banked the excess allowances for future use after Phase II emissions restrictions took effect in the year 2000. The result was a greater than expected reduction in SO_2 emissions and a 10 to 25 percent reduction in acid precipitation in the Northeast. See Swift (1997, p. 17). The cost savings as against an alternative command-and-control approach, such as technology-based standards, were significant. During Phase I, trading saved an estimated $250 million annually. See Carlson et al. (2000).

Since Phase II of the trading program took effect in 2000, the scale and scope of the trading program has grown. By 2005, more than 3,400 electricity generating units were operating under tradable emissions quotas. That year, more than 5,700 private transfers of emissions allowances took place. By the end of 2005 (the eleventh year of the program), total power sector SO_2 emissions had been reduced by 35 percent or more than 5.5 million tons from 1990 levels. Those emissions reductions led to a substantial decline in acid deposition – up to 36 percent in the northeastern United States – and annual net social benefits estimated at $119 billion. See Environmental Protection Agency (2006); Chestnut and Mills (2005).

Perceived problems and unresolved issues

The lack of secure and perpetual property rights in emissions 'allowances' apparently has not impeded trading. As noted earlier, markets compensate for the risk of confiscation by discounting prices. So, if SO_2 allowances were perceived to be highly insecure, their value would fall, perhaps so low as to completely wipe out the market. But the EPA is well aware of this potential threat, which it encountered in earlier emissions trading programs. See EPA (1986b, p. 43,847, n. 48). In order to preserve the market, the EPA decided to treat emissions allowances as if they were property rights, except in unusual circumstances. See Dennis (1993, p. 1137). Thus, the risk of confiscation has been remote. See Rosenberg (1994, p. 508, n. 54).

The acid rain program is not completely without problems, however. In creating a nationwide market in SO_2 emissions, Congress ignored distributional considerations related to emissions of SO_2 and acid deposition. As noted earlier, the states that suffer the most from acid rain are located in the Northeast, while the states that produce most of the SO_2 emissions that cause the acid rain are located in the Midwest. The emissions trading program does not guarantee that midwestern power plants will reduce their emissions sufficiently to resolve acid rain problems in northeastern states. Imagine if power plants in Indiana purchased emissions allowances from plants in New York. This would permit Indiana plants to continue emitting high levels of SO_2, creating further acid rain problems for the State of New York, while power plants in New York profited from the transactions. This prospect has led to some political and legal skirmishes between northeastern states and the EPA. But, in fact, the problem never materialized. Power plants upwind of New York have actually reduced their emissions more than required by their Phase I quotas. See US General Accounting Office (GAO) (1994, p. 56). On state and regional responses to this and other perceived problems with the Clean Air Act's acid rain program, see Mostaghel (1995) and Rosenberg (1994).

A 1994 report by the GAO (1994, pp. 43–58) identified other potential impediments to a more vibrant market in SO_2 emissions allowances, including the fact that Phase I reductions apply to only about 14 percent of the country's power plants. More trading was expected, and has materialized, during Phase II, as the program has broadened to cover thousands more power plants. The GAO also pointed out that potential traders might feel insecure about how state legislatures, public utility commissions and the Federal Energy Regulatory Commission will treat SO_2 allowances. Finally, the GAO suggested that the tax treatment of allowance trading under the Internal Revenue Code could discourage trades because sales of allowances are taxed as ordinary capital gains with zero basis. However, utilities incur tax liability only when they sell allowances; meanwhile, utilities that purchase allowances realize equivalent tax savings. The tax treatment of trades therefore should be revenue neutral for the federal government. (See Revenue Procedure 92–91, October 29, 1992, 92 Fed. Reg. ¶ 46,595.) If taxes on emissions allowance transactions created a disincentive for traders, we should expect to see evidence of it on the supply side. Yet, the price and availability of SO_2 allowances on the market suggests that supplies have been more than adequate; any lack of trading appears to be more a problem of demand, which cannot be explained by federal tax policy.

Uncertainties about the SO_2 emissions trading program may have complicated the compliance strategies of regulated utilities. But trading volume is not the only or even the most important measure of the acid rain program's success. See Burtraw (1996). Allowance trading is but a means to the end of attaining administratively set emissions reduction targets at the lowest possible cost. And on that measure, the program has proven to be a great success. Meanwhile, compliance has been at or near 100 percent throughout the history of the acid rain program. See BNA Daily Environment Report, Aug. 12, 1996; Environmental Protection Agency (2006). In sum, the Clean Air Act's acid rain program is achieving both pollution reductions and cost savings beyond all expectations.

9. Other pollution 'rights' trading schemes

Although the Clean Air Act's acid rain program constitutes the most extensive use to date of pollution 'rights' trading, there are several other examples worth mentioning. In the mid-1980s, the EPA introduced a short-lived but highly successful program for trading rights to use lead in gasoline. This program is discussed extensively in Hahn and Hester (1989b, pp. 380–91). Another largely successful program, described in Tripp and Dudek (1989, pp. 378–82), concerned the use of tradeable development permits to conserve the New Jersey Pinelands, the world's largest pineland forest. Less successful efforts include tradeable water pollution rights programs on Wisconsin's Fox River and Colorado's Dillon Reservoir, both of which are discussed in Hahn and Hester (1989b, pp. 391–6).

In 1993 California's South Coast Air Quality Management District (SCAQMD), the agency responsible for implementing federal and state clean air legislation in Los Angeles, established a new allowance trading model, to help the country's most polluted city attain the National Ambient Air Quality Standards. The goal of its Regional Clean Air Incentives Market (RECLAIM) was to reduce stationary source emissions of nitrogen oxides (NO_x) and sulfur dioxide (SO_2) at average annual rates of 8.3 percent and 6.8 percent, respectively, between 1994 and 2003. Polesetsky (1995) provides a complete description of the RECLAIM program. Unfortunately, the RECLAIM experiment failed for reasons having to do primarily with a faulty institutional design. The administrative body responsible for RECLAIM initially flooded the market with an abundance of too many emissions allowances, which meant high-cost compliers had little incentive to purchase additional allowances and low-cost compliers had little incentive to reduce emissions below quota limits to generate excess allowances that could not be sold. Subsequently, when credits became more scarce, administrators failed to act against noncompliers, which once again reduced the value of emissions allowances on the market to approximately zero by giving emitters the option simply emitting more for free. See Bakken (2001, p. 183).

Other states also began to experiment with pollution trading systems in the late 1990s in their efforts to attain the Clean Air Act's National Ambient Air Quality Standards. See, for example, Schroder and Johnson (1997), on Michigan's trading program, which applies to all 'criteria' pollutants. And beyond US borders, several other countries have been experimenting with property 'rights'-based approaches to environmental protection. Denmark's 1991 Environmental Protection Act, for example, relies heavily on contractual agreements between polluting industries and the government. Polluters receive permits that embody the contract terms, but, as with emissions allowances under the American acid rain program, Danish pollution contracts create only 'quasi-rights,' so that the government can, if necessary to attain environmental goals, amend permits without expropriating property. See Ercmann (1996, pp. 1226–7).

Finally, emissions trading has become the mechanism of choice for reducing emissions of greenhouse gases under the Kyoto Protocol to the United Nations Framework Convention on Climate Change. See, e.g., Stewart and Wiener (2003).

10. Assessing pollution rights trading schemes as a method of environmental regulation

Based on the various early experiences with pollution 'rights' trading, analysts have derived certain lessons for designing successful trading systems. Tripp and Dudek (1989), for example, identify eight 'institutional guidelines': The responsible administrative agency must have (1) 'clear legal authority' and (2) the 'technical capability' to design, implement and enforce the program; (3) the program must be 'evasion proof,' meaning that regulated sources have no way (through loopholes, waivers, etc.) to avoid either reducing emissions or purchasing additional allowances; (4) the program should have 'clearly specified objectives' based on sound science and with strong political backing; (5) trading programs work best when applied to pollution problems with 'regional significance,' as opposed to those with only local impacts; (6) the tradeable 'rights must have economic value'; (7) the program should provide an 'equitable and administratively simple method for allocating' tradeable rights, although there may be 'trade-offs between fairness and administrative simplicity'; and (8) the institutional structure for buying and selling rights should be designed so as to minimize transaction costs. This last guideline ties in with the sixth: the higher the transaction costs involved in trading – '[t]he greater the administrative or public hassle confronting a prospective buyer or seller of rights' – the less economic value rights will have.

Interestingly, Tripp and Dudek do not list security of property rights as a distinct guideline for a successful pollution trading program, though it implicitly factors into their sixth guideline, concerning the economic value of the rights to be traded. Their decision not to focus on the lack of secure property rights is supported by the success of trading schemes, such as the Clean Air Act's acid rain program and the EPA's earlier lead trading program, both of which involved 'rights' that could be confiscated by the government.

Other analysts, however, consider the lack of secure property rights in pollution as a potentially major hindrance to trading. Hahn and Hester (1989a, p. 149), for example, maintain that trading systems would operate more efficiently, creating greater cost savings, if 'uncertainties over the definition of property rights' in pollution were eliminated. But even they would not recommend absolutely secure property rights in pollution emissions, in recognition that the government might need to reduce emissions further in order to meet environmental quality goals (Hahn and Hester, 1989a, p. 150). And in comparing various emissions trading programs it appears that the transaction costs associated with variable administrative rules governing trading systems can exert a far greater negative influence on trading than the lack of protection against governmental confiscation of pollution 'rights.' See Foster and Hahn (1995, pp. 38–40), and Hahn and Hester (1989b, pp. 396, 401–406).

The few successful experiments with pollution trading have encouraged scholars to innovate new applications for conserving ocean resources (see Tipton, 1995), endangered species habitat (see Sohn and Cohen, 1996), and wetlands (see Sapp, 1995). Although these schemes could all work, it is doubtful that pollution-rights trading would be both effective and efficient for all environmental goods in every ecological and institutional context. See, e.g., Miller (1996) and Thompson (1993) (both identifying institutional impediments to successful trading programs in water pollution rights).

11. Beyond the regulatory model: a complete property rights solution to environmental problems

Somewhat surprisingly, the most hostile critics of pollution 'rights' trading schemes have not been environmentalists but certain law and economics scholars, including McGee and Block (1994) and Anderson and Leal (1991, pp. 158–9), who contend that such schemes really amount to nothing more than 'market socialism.' These self-described 'free market environmentalists' do not doubt that so-called 'market-based' environmental regulations are an improvement over traditional command-and-control – just as market socialism would constitute an improvement over 'feudalism' (see Yandle, 1992) – but they reject the assumed need for *any* form of government environmental regulation. Instead, they promote a complete property rights solution to environmental problems. This Section reviews and Section 12 critiques their arguments.

The worldwide trend toward privatization

Privatization has swept the globe. Spurred by the Reagan–Thatcher Revolution of the 1980s, governments around the world have been selling off public assets to private owners in order to improve efficiency and increase production. In the ten-year period from 1985 to 1994, some $468 billion worth of state enterprises were sold off to private investors (see Poole, 1996, p. 1). Interestingly, those sales were limited to economic enterprises. States have not, with a few notable and controversial exceptions, shed much of their vast natural resource holdings, including forest lands, parks, waterways and the atmosphere. Free market environmentalists argue that they should do so, pointing out that the same economic theories that favor private ownership of economic producers also support the private ownership of environmental goods. As Stroup and Goodman (1992, p. 427) put it, 'government ownership and control works just as badly with environmental resources as with all other resources.'

What constitutes 'privatization'

The word 'privatization,' as it is used throughout the law and economics literature, encompasses a wide variety of activities by which some public entity conveys property rights to a private entity or entities – everything from outright giveaways or sales of public lands to licenses or concessions under which private firms finance, construct and manage hotels, airports, wastewater treatment plants, highways, prisons, and schools (see Poole, 1996, p. 1). On this broad definition, 'privatization' can but need not be total. One could sensibly maintain that government allocations of transferable pollution permits, for example, constitute partial privatization. But many of privatization's most vociferous advocates would reject this broad understanding of 'privatization.' They (often implicitly) adopt a narrower definition which requires *total* government relinquishment of property rights through the outright sale or gift of public resources. See, e.g., Anderson and Leal (1991).

'Free market environmentalism'

Conventional welfare economics explains environmental problems as symptoms of market failure, caused by externalities, which justifies corrective government intervention in the marketplace. See, e.g., Samuelson (1980, p. 450), Royal Commission on Environmental Pollution (1971, pp. 4–6). Government intervention can take various forms. Davis and Kamien (1969), for instance, list six distinct governmental means of resolving environmental problems: (1) by prohibition; (2) by directive; (3) by taxes and subsidies; (4) by regulation; (5) by payment; and (6) by action. They also list one nongovernmental means: by voluntary action. Stewart and Krier (1978, pp. 109–111, 116) provide just four categories of governmental action for environmental protection: (1) redefinition of property rights; (2) subsidies or payments; (3) coercive commands; and (4) financial penalties or fees.

Free market environmentalists do not dispute that environmental problems arise from market failures; nor do they take issue with the need for responsive government action (though they often sound as if they do). But they challenge the conventional welfare economics story concerning the cause(s) of market failure and the appropriate governmental response(s).

According to free market environmentalism, environmental market failures occur only because property rights are incompletely specified. Government remedies that ignore that root cause are, at best, palliative; they may treat the symptoms of environmental externalities, but they do not cure the underlying cause of the market failure. The only way to do that – and, thus, the only truly appropriate and effective remedy to environmental problems – is to completely specify property rights in environmental goods, i.e., privatize them. Free market environmentalists claim that a system of completely specified and protected property rights should prevent inefficient externalities and, therefore, market failures. And in the absence of market failures government regulatory intervention is neither necessary nor justifiable.

It is important to note that the theory of free market environmentalism does not necessarily support individual ownership over group or communal ownership. See Anderson and Leal (1991, p. 3). The important distinction under this theory is between 'public' property (*res publicae*) and 'private' property, where 'private' is defined to include both individual property (*res individuales*) and common property (*res communes*). Free Market Environmentalists contend that there should be no 'public' property rights in environmental goods for reasons that derive largely from the public choice writings of Downs (1957), Buchanan and Tullock (1962), Olson (1965), and Niskanen (1971).

Public environmental goods, bureaucratic management, and government failure

Free market environmentalists, in essence, deny the very possibility of 'public' property, claiming that private individuals, whether politicians, bureaucrats or members of favored interest groups, inevitably will assert what amounts to *dominium* over so-called 'public' assets. As Huffman (1994) puts it, there will always be 'private rights in public lands.' Like private owners, the politicians and bureaucrats who are *de facto* owners of *de jure* 'public' property presumably manage resources so as to maximize their self-interests. See, e.g., Anderson and Leal (1991, p. 4), and Stroup and Baden (1983, p. 43). But their incentives turn out to be quite different from those of private owners for two main reasons. First, bureaucrats and politicians do not bear all the costs of their management decisions because they are not personally invested in the resources. If they manage resources poorly, they do not bear the economic losses. Thus, as Anderson and Leal (1991, p. 14) put it, the '*political sector operates by externalizing costs.*' This is also true for private property owners in many circumstances, but only because property rights on some resources are insufficiently specified. See Anderson and Leal (1991, p. 20).

The second main difference between the incentives of public resource managers and private owners is their relative myopia. Many environmental management issues include significant time-preference aspects – an old growth forest harvested today will not be available to future generations of users or viewers. All resource owners, whether public or private, implicitly or explicitly weigh present use values against expected future benefits, if current use is foregone. They do so by discounting the expected future benefits, reducing them to present day dollars, which can then be compared directly with current use values. If the discounted expected future value is greater than the present use value, the resource will be conserved (i.e., invested for future use); otherwise, it will be presently used or consumed. The comparison of present and future values depends predominantly on two variables: the estimation of future value and the owner's subjective discount rate, i.e., the interest rate at which they reduce future values to present dollars. A low discount rate favors longer-term investments or conservation; a higher discount rate tends to favor current usage or consumption.

One common justification for 'public' control of environmental goods is that the discount rates of private owners exceed the social rate of discount, resulting in too rapid resource use and depletion. See, e.g., Hotelling (1931), and Howe (1979, p. 103). But free market environmentalists counter that private property owners can be expected to have lower discount rates and longer time horizons than public resource managers, i.e., politicians and bureaucrats. See, e.g., Stroup and Goodman (1992). As Stroup and Baden (1983, p. 24) put it, 'there is no "voice of the future" in government equivalent to the rising market price of an increasingly valuable resource. The wise public resource manager who forgoes current benefits cannot personally profit from doing so.' For politicians facing re-election in two-, four- or six-year cycles, the choice between preserving natural resources for unborn generations of voters and developing them for living generations of voters is a no-brainer. Indeed, studies of congressional voting patterns on environmental legislation indicate that legislators do not vote for or against policies based on abstract conceptions of inter-generational public welfare but on the estimated costs and benefits to living constituents. See Pashigian (1985).

Bureaucrats do not face re-election of course, but they are dependent on the legislative authorizations and annual budget decisions of politicians who do. Bureaucrats are not driven to maximize profits, as are private resource owners, but to maximize budget allocations and administrative turf. See, e.g., Orzechowski (1977) and Stroup and Baden (1983). 'Accordingly,' writes Gary Libecap (1981, p. 9), 'they do not have the same incentive that profit-maximizing firms do to increase the discounted net value of the resources under their control.' Their actions respond not to market conditions but to political conditions, 'even though it reduces the total value of production.' Given their incentives, bureaucrats are likely to favor, and therefore to subsidize, resource uses that increase (or protect) their budgets and political influence, regardless of economic waste or environmental degradation. Even if this were not true and public agencies endeavored to maximize both economic and environmental values in resource management, it remains doubtful, especially in light of the demise of socialism, that any government agency could 'accurately measure, simulate, predict, and plan for both ecological and economic outcomes.' Rasker (1994, p. 392).

The usual result of bureaucratic management, according to free market environmentalists, is government failure to allocate environmental goods efficiently. In many, if not all, cases, 'public' ownership does not protect the environment from market failure, but itself becomes 'the cause of environmental problems' (Baden and Stroup, 1990, p. 132). And because governments fail too, market failure cannot automatically justify government intervention. See Castle (1965, p. 552).

Evidence of government failure in the management of 'public' natural resources

The free market environmentalism literature is chock-full of anecdotes about government mismanagement of publicly owned natural resources, where 'mismanagement' is defined (if only implicitly) as economically inefficient and/or environmentally harmful management. See generally Anderson and Leal (1991), Stroup and Baden (1983), Nelson (1995), and Klyza (1996). Libecap (1981) explains how government rangeland management practices have led to overgrazing on, and even desertification of, rangeland resources. Stroup and Baden (1973) and Hyde (1981), among many others, identify 'social failures' (inefficiencies and environmental harm) resulting from federal timber management policies, such as below-cost timber sales in National Forests. Anderson (1994, p. 36) discusses just one of many uneconomic and environmentally harmful water projects promoted by the Federal Bureau of Reclamation. And Epstein (1995, pp. 291–6) and Anderson and Leal (1992, pp. 306–308) explain the perverse incentives created by well-meaning but misguided federal wildlife preservation policies. The entire history of 'public' resource management is presented as an immense tragedy of the 'political commons.' See Borcherding (1990, p. 99). And the only solution to this tragedy, according to free market environmentalists, is complete privatization.

The privatization 'solution'

Free market environmentalists claim that 'privatization,' i.e., the complete specification of 'private' property rights in environmental goods, would avert both market failures and misguided government efforts to correct them, resolving problems ranging from the mismanagement of timber resources to global warming. See Anderson and Leal (1991). Their argument is a logical (though unwarranted) extension from Demsetz (1967), who established that private property rights in land evolve at a certain stage of socio-economic development (i.e., when resource scarcity relative to the rate of demand becomes problematic) in order to reduce the externalities that impede effective investment, i.e., resource conservation. If property rights reduce externalities, the logic goes, then more completely specified property rights should more completely reduce externalities. But see Demsetz (1968) (noting that efficiency is sometimes maximized through government action rather than market transactions of private property rights).

Privatization replaces the decisionmaking of bureaucrats and politicians with the decisionmaking of private owners whose incentive structures, according to free market environmentalists, are more conducive to economically and environmentally sound resource management. Unlike 'public' resource owners, who make management decisions – present use versus conservation – without the benefit of market prices to guide their valuations, private owners operate within the marketplace where prices can accurately measure an asset's value. Stroup and Goodman (1992, pp. 431–2) explain how the information provided by market prices induces private resource owners to take a longer-term perspective in resource management decisionmaking:

> The current market price reflects the present, discounted value of all future revenue flows that are expected to stem from the asset.
>
> The ability to capitalize future value into an asset's present value induces property owners to consider the long-term implications of their asset-use decisions. It creates a strong incentive for owners to consider fully the effects of deferring consumption of their asset returns. Furthermore, it implies that property owners will be responsible to future users. Any activity that reduces the future benefits or increases the future costs stemming from an asset results in a reduction of that asset's current value. As soon as an appraiser or potential buyer anticipates future problems, his assessment of a property's value falls, and the owner's wealth declines immediately.

Thus, '[p]otential buyers interact with owners to maximize asset value over time.' And this logic holds for both individual and corporate resource owners. See Stroup and Goodman (1992, p. 432). But, as we have already seen, it does not hold for 'public' resource owners, who make their management decisions outside the marketplace, without benefit of the information market prices provide. Free market environmentalists conclude, therefore, that the privatization of publicly owned resources would promote better-informed and longer-view management of environmental goods.

Of course, some publicly owned environmental goods are easier (i.e., less costly) to privatize than others. National parks and forests, like other land areas, could easily be parcelized and allotted to private owners. But other environmental goods, such as the atmosphere, are notoriously difficult (i.e., costly) to privatize. Clean air traditionally has been considered a subtractible public good – a good from which no one can be excluded, but which can be depleted by use. See, e.g., Goetze (1987, pp. 188–9). But free market environmentalists point out that neither clean air, nor any other natural resource, is inevitably a *public* good. It is not strictly impossible to impose private property rights on the atmosphere, only too costly so long as the supply of clean air remains plentiful relative to the rate of demand. Under these circumstances, the costs of developing the technologies necessary to create enforceable boundaries and, hence, property rights, are not economically justifiable; the transaction costs would outweigh the benefits to be gained from privatization. But this situation is not immutable. It is quite possible for clean air to become scarce enough relative to the rate of demand to justify the costs of privatization. Alternatively, the supply of clean air might remain constant relative to the rate of demand, but the costs of imposing property rights could drop because of technological innovations. See Anderson and Leal (1991, pp. 165–7). The innovation of barbed wire in the 1870s, for example, greatly reduced the cost of enclosing land, which facilitated settlement and private ownership of formerly public lands. See Anderson and Hill (1975, p. 172). What counts as a 'public good,' then, is determined economically by reference to the rates of supply and demand and the costs of privatization, given technological capabilities. Under the right circumstances, property rights can be imposed on all environmental goods.

Privatization in action

Free market environmentalists point to many cases where private property rights and markets have combined to conserve or produce environmental goods. Private environmental organizations, such as the Nature Conservancy, pay market prices for lands they dedicate for conservation. See Anderson and Leal (1991, pp. 3, 70–71). Of course, the Nature Conservancy is a non-profit organization, but many for-profit companies also find that good resource stewardship enhances profits. The International Paper Company, for example, finds it profitable to manage its forest resources for wildlife as well as for timber. See Anderson and Leal (1991, p. 68). This and other examples, free market environmentalists contend, prove the power of private property to protect and promote environmental values.

12. The critique of free market environmentalism

The property rights prescriptions of free market environmentalists have not greatly influenced policy, though they have been widely disseminated.

The Reagan Administration tentatively proposed to privatize public lands in the early 1980s, but rapidly retreated for (at least) two reasons. First, certain interest groups – including extractive industries and environmentalists – that benefit from current public land ownership and management policies exercised their political clout to protect their 'investments.' See Nelson (1995, p. 181). This explanation conforms to the Public Choice view of 'public' resource ownership. However, Public Choice theory itself has been criticized for not capturing the full flavor of public decisionmaking. Critics claim that it is inaccurate as a positive theory of political and bureaucratic behavior because it fails to account (among other things) for ideology, the role of culture, and the endogeneity of preferences. See generally Green and Shapiro (1994); Farber and Frickey (1991); Wittman (1995); and Menell (1992). And these same criticisms apply, by association, to free market environmentalism. Indeed, studies of the environmental regulatory process have shown that although political interests certainly influence (perhaps not inappropriately) the process, the results often conform to implicit or explicit benefit-cost analyses. See, e.g., Cropper et al. (1992).

In any case, there certainly was more to the policy failure of free market environmentalism than simple interest-group politics. Efforts to privatize public lands and resources proved to be highly unpopular with both the public-at-large and economists; those who advocated privatization were 'a clear minority even in their own profession.' See Leman (1984, p. 113). Indeed, many economists and legal scholars have criticized both the policy prescriptions and basic assumptions of free market environmentalism. See generally Cole (2002, Ch. 5).

In the first place, it is inherently improbable that a single human-created institution – private property – would be the first-best solution in all economic, social, technological, and ecological circumstances. See Cole (1999, p. 117); Cole (2002); Ostrom (2007). But criticisms of free market environmentalism do not rely solely on the inherent implausibility of its policy recommendations.

One common criticism is that the advocates of privatization rely too heavily on anecdotal evidence of poor public management and superior private management of environmental goods, while ignoring a wealth of contrary evidence. See, e.g., Bromley (1991, p. 171). As we saw earlier (in Section 3), private owners cannot always be relied on to conserve environmental goods because they too often possess high discount rates and short time horizons. See Clark (1973a and 1973b). Consider, as just one example, private timberland owners in the Pacific Northwest, who accelerated harvests beyond sustainable levels during the late 1980s either to avert or to pay for junk bond-financed hostile take-overs. See

Power (1996, p. 138). That this should be an acceptable practice simply because the economic costs are internalized to private owners is questionable, even assuming the idealized circumstances of complete privatization of all environmental goods. See Menell (1992, pp. 495–6) (discussing reasons for, at least sometimes, preferring the 'expression of preferences through democratic processes').

While free-market environmentalists presume that privatization would lead to improved environmental management, they ignore real-world cases where the poor economic and environmental consequences of private ownership have been poor. For example, after privatization of pasture lands in Botswana in the mid-1970s, output per head of cattle remained constant, cost per head was higher for privatized ranches than for ranches that remained under tribal governance, and the return on capital was 61 percent lower for privatized ranches. See Carl Bro International (1984). In both Africa and Indonesia, 'the introduction of European methods of cultivation and systems of landholding is now seen to reduce, not increase, the productivity of local agriculture.' See Toulmin (2001, pp. 104–5). Similarly, in nineteenth-century Europe privatization sometimes led to 'environmental tragedies.' See McNeill (2002, p. 223). By 1919, for example, the UK had the smallest percentage of forested land (3 percent) in Europe. That year, Parliament created a Forestry Commission to purchase and reforest land. Twenty years later, the UK's total acreage of forests had grown to 25 percent. See Cole (2002, pp. 97–8). Apparently, the system of land tenure is not the only significant determinant of resource use or abuse. See McCay (2000, p. 75).

Free market environmentalists have also been criticized for their background assumptions, including the assumption that market prices capture all relevant values. See, e.g., Randall and Castle (1985, pp. 613–14) (providing reasons 'to be suspicious of normative uses of land market theory in support of privatization proposals'). After criticizing government management agencies for trying to value environmental goods without prices, they simply presume that market prices would incorporate all values worth considering. See, e.g., Menell (1992, pp. 493–4). Free market environmentalists also assume that private resource owners would possess environmental information superior to that possessed by public resource managers. See Anderson and Leal (1991, pp. 4–6, 170–172). But critics point out that environmental regulation itself was largely a response to inadequate environmental information provided by the market. See Blumm (1992, p. 379) and Hines (1966, pp. 197–201). Menell (1992, p. 502) argues that '[e]conomies of scale in research and difficulties in appropriating returns to innovation may enable even highly imperfect public institutions to outperform private entrepreneurs in some technological fields.'

There is little reason, therefore, to presume that private owners would possess better environmental information on the basis of which to manage environmental goods.

Economies of scale are important not only in the provision of environmental information but also, in many cases, for the provision of environmental goods themselves. For example, a recent study found that 'farms with larger acreage have a higher probability of making [soil] conservation expenditures' (Featherstone and Goodwin, 1993). And the scale economies involved in soil conservation are minuscule compared to those involved in the provision of many other environmental goods, such as wilderness or species habitat, which can require land masses larger than entire states. See Cole (2002, pp. 25–9). Anderson and Leal (1991, p. 69) provide a lone anecdote about a group of private landowners who contracted with one another to provide a 2.8 million acre recreation area in the North Main Woods in upper New England. But this may be the exception that proves the rule. According to Lueck (1991, pp. 250, 251), in many (if not most) cases 'the contracting costs among landowners may eliminate the potential gains' from the private provision of wildlife habitat. Individual land holdings, meanwhile, tend to be 'small compared to the territories of most valued species.' Thus, private landowners suffer from a comparative disadvantage in wildlife regulation, which explains why wildlife are, for the most part, publicly owned and regulated. See also Lueck (1989) and Rasker, Martin and Johnson (1992). Some free market environmentalists, such as Nelson (1995), implicitly concede that scale economies sometimes favor public (state or federal) ownership of environmental goods, when they distinguish between public resources that should and should not be sold off to private owners.

Another criticism of free market environmentalists is that they tend to treat the market and private legal institutions, including the common law, far less critically than they treat public institutions, including politicians and bureaucrats. As Menell (1992, p. 505) puts it, their '[s]anguine view of markets and legal institutions contrasts sharply with their deeply cynical perception of public institutions.' They provide no reason to expect that common law courts should be immune from the public choice pressures that influence legislative decisions. See, e.g., Beerman (1991, 187–8) (noting the failure of Public Choice theorists to confront 'economic influences on judicial behavior'). Nor do they provide reason to believe that traditional common law remedies, such as nuisance and trespass, would efficiently internalize pollution costs. As Menell (1991), Brunet (1992), Thompson (1996) and many others have explained, common law remedies are highly imperfect and costly mechanisms for resolving most types of environmental disputes (especially those involving large numbers of parties).

The fundamental implication of all these criticisms is that the benefits of privatization and deregulation might not be worth the costs. This claim should, of course, be testable. But, despite their pronouncements about the relative benefits of privatization, free market environmentalists have provided no actual assessments of the costs. They do not deny that privatization would entail significant, perhaps even enormous, transaction costs. Anderson and Leal (1991, p. 167) concede that '[p]roperty rights are costly to define and enforce.' Anderson and Hill (1983, p. 438) even acknowledge that 'the definition and enforcement process may preclude whatever gains might have been realized by the establishment of [property] rights.' Compare Hanna, Folke, and Mäler (1996, p. 18) and Noll (1989). Nevertheless, one is hard pressed to locate in the free market environmentalist literature efforts to assess the potential transaction costs that privatization would entail. Libecap (1989) is exceptional in providing excellent empirical and historical studies that utilize transaction cost analyses to explain why some 'open access' resources have been subject to private ownership, while others have been subject either to public ownership or remain 'open access.'

In the absence of a detailed assessment of the costs and benefits of privatization, how could Anderson and Leal (1992, p. 165) possibly conclude, for example, that the privatization of roads together with strict liability rules for common law enforcement would *efficiently* resolve traffic congestion problems? In response to this policy prescription, Funk (1992, p. 512) has raised several pertinent questions: 'Who is going to sue for damages under this strict liability regime? The class of all persons in the greater metropolitan area? What damages are we talking about?. . . . And what about causation?' Ellickson (1993, p. 1385) notes that '[t]he laying out of a major road is a quintessential "large" event that private landowners and travelers cannot well coordinate on their own.'

Examples such as this may explain why some critics consider free market environmentalism to be an 'institutional fantasyland' (Menell, 1992). The danger is that fantasylands are designed to appear more attractive than the real world. As Schlager and Ostrom (1992, p. 260) have written, '[n]o real-world institution can win in a contest against idealized institutions.' Yet, the sheer lack of realism in much of the free market environmentalist literature may explain why their ideas, though widely disseminated in the academic and popular media, have not mined broader public, academic or political support.

13. Property-regime choice for environmental protection

The conclusion that private property rights are not always necessary or sufficient to conserve environmental goods over time does not mean that private property is never a useful or superior institution for that purpose. Even if other property regimes sometimes outperform private property for protecting environmental goods, they are just as fallible. As Ronald Coase (1964, p. 195) has written, in the real world all human institutions are 'more or less failures.' Coase was writing, in particular, about markets, firms, and governments, but he could as well have been writing about alternative property regimes for environmental governance. The goal in property-regime choice must be to maximize net social benefits, which can only be achieved through comprehensive *comparative institutional analyses* of alternative property regimes in the specific economic, technological, social, and ecological circumstances. Ostrom (1990) provides a fairly detailed set of conditions under which common-property regimes are likely to succeed (or fail). And Cole (2002) has provided a more general, but rudimentary, model of property-regime choice, based on relative costs of exclusion and coordination under alternative property arrangements. Importantly, these models are premised on understandings of property regimes that may not be wholly realistic. As noted in Section 3, the conventional typology of property systems entails many conceptual problems and confusions. Most importantly, property regimes, as they exist in the real world, may not conform to the conventional typology. For the most part, what we see are admixtures of property regimes that are shaped as much (or more) by historical forces as by the deliberate designs of policy makers. See Geisler (2000); Cole (2002, p. 13). In property regime choice, history, culture, and ideology all matter.

14. Conclusion

The great insight of Demsetz (1967) was that property rights regimes evolve over time, in response to social pressures and technological changes, to increase efficiency by minimizing the costs of coordinating human interactions (including those with nature). Contrary to the claims of free market environmentalists, however, this evolution does not run in only one direction toward more and more private ownership. As Horwitz (1977, p. 102) and Rose (1990) have shown in the context of water law, property rights sometimes evolve in the opposite direction – from more sharply-defined private rights to more ambiguous correlative rights. This reflects the fact that property rights themselves are costly (sometimes too costly) to impose and protect. See Coase (1960). In a given ecological and institutional context the question is whether and to what extent property rights – private, common or public – provide an efficient (or *more* efficient) means of accomplishing social goals.

This chapter has raised that question in the context of environmental policy: To what extent can property rights contribute to the efficient attainment of society's environmental protection goals? The first part of the entry focused on the evolution of property 'rights'-based approaches to environmental regulation, about which there is little controversy. The use of 'rights'-based regulatory mechanisms, such as pollution trading programs, can, in many circumstances, achieve environmental goals at far lower cost than traditional command-and-control regulations. Far more controversial is the contention that the complete privatization of environmental goods, assuming that were even possible, would in every ecological and institutional context obviate the need for state regulation beyond common law property rights protections. This claim brings to mind Solow's (1974) admonition that one ought to be equally suspicious of the uncritical centralization *and* the uncritical free-marketeering of environmental goods.

Bibliography

Ackerman, Bruce A. and Stewart, Richard B. (1985), 'Reforming Environmental Law,' *Stanford Law Review* **37**, 1333–65.

Anderson, Terry L. (1994), 'Enviro-Capitalism vs. Enviro-Socialism,' *Kansas Journal of Law and Public Policy* **4**, 35–40.

Anderson, Terry L. and Hill, P.J. (1975), 'The Evolution of Property Rights: A Study of the American West,' *Journal of Law and Economics* **12**, 163–79.

Anderson, Terry L. and Hill, Peter J. (1983), 'Privatizing the Commons: An Improvement?,' *Southern Economics Journal* **50**, 438–50.

Anderson, Terry L. and Hill, Peter J. (2002), 'Cowboys and Contracts,' *Journal of Legal Studies* **XXXI**, 489–514.

Anderson, Terry L. and Leal, Donald R. (1991), *Free Market Environmentalism*, Boulder, CO: Westview Press.

Anderson, Terry L. and Leal, Donald R. (1992), 'Free Market Versus Political Environmentalism,' *Harvard Journal of Law and Public Policy* **15**, 297–310.

Aristotle (1941), 'Politica,' Jowett, B. (trans.), in McKeon, Richard (ed.), *The Basic Works of Aristotle*, New York: Random House, 1113–1316.

Baden, John and Stroup, Richard (1990), 'Natural Resource Scarcity, Entrepreneurship, and the Political Economy of Hope,' in Block, Walter (ed.), *Economics and the Environment: A Reconciliation*, Vancouver, B.C.: The Fraser Institute, 117–36.

Bakken, Gordon Morris (2001), 'RECLAIM and Pollution Credit Trading: Aiming the Spotlight on the "Energy Crisis" Profiteers Who are Leaving the Public in the Dark,' *UWLA Law Review*, **33**, 175–90.

Barnes, David W. (1982–3), 'Enforcing Property Rights: Extending Property Rights Theory to Congestible and Environmental Goods,' *Environmental Affairs* **10**, 583–638.

Barzel, Yoram (1990), *Economic Analysis of Property Rights*, New York: Cambridge University Press.

Baumol, William J. and Oates, Wallace E. (1971), 'The Use of Standards and Prices for Protection of the Environment,' in Bohm, Peter and Kneese, Allen V. (eds.), *The Economics of Environment: Papers from Four Nations*, New York: St. Martin's, 53–65.

Baumol, William J. and Oates, Wallace E. (1988), *The Theory of Environmental Policy*, Cambridge: Cambridge University Press.

Beerman, Jack M. (1991), 'Interest Group Politics and Judicial Behavior: Macey's Public Choice,' *Notre Dame Law Review* **67**, 183–229.

Berkes, F., Feeny, D, McCay, B.J. and Acheson, J.M. (1989), 'The benefits of the commons,' *Nature* **340** (July 13), 91–3.

Block, Walter E. (1990), 'Environmental Problems, Private Property Rights Solutions,' in

Block, Walter E. (ed.), *Economics and the Environment: A Reconciliation*, Vancouver, B.C.: The Fraser Institute, 281–332.

Blumm, Michael C. (1992), 'The Fallacies of Free Market Environmentalism,' *Harvard Journal of Law & Public Policy* **15**, 371–89.

BNA Daily Environment Report, Aug. 12, 1996.

Borcherding, Thomas E. (1990), 'Natural Resources and Transgenerational Equity,' in Block, Walter E. (ed.), *Economics and the Environment: A Reconciliation*, Vancouver, B.C.: The Fraser Institute, 95–115.

Bromley, Daniel W. (1989), *Economic Interests & Institutions: The Conceptual Foundations of Public Policy*, Cambridge, Mass.: Basil Blackwell.

Bromley, Daniel W. (1991), *Environment and Economy: Property Rights and Public Policy*, Oxford: Blackwell.

Bromley, Daniel W. (ed.) (1992), *Making the Commons Work: Theory, Practice, and Policy*, San Francisco: Institute for Contemporary Studies.

Brunet, Edward (1992), 'Debunking Wholesale Private Enforcement of Environmental Rights,' *Harvard Journal of Law & Public Policy* **15**, 311–24.

Buchanan, James and Tullock, Gordon (1962), *The Calculus of Consent*, Ann Arbor: University of Michigan Press.

Burtraw, Dallas (1996), 'Cost Savings Sans Allowance Trades? Evaluating the SO_2 Emission Trading Program to Date,' Discussion Paper 95–30-REV, Washington, D.C.: Resources for the Future.

Burtraw, Dallas (2000), 'Innovation Under the Tradable Sulfur Dioxide Emissions Permits Program in the U.S. Electricity Sector,' Resources for the Future Discussion Paper 00–38.

Carl Bro International (1984), *An Evaluation of Livestock Management and Production with Special References to Communal Areas*, Glostrup, Denmark: Carl Bro International.

Carlson, Curtis, Burtraw, Dallas, Cropper, Maureen, and Palmer, Karen L. (2000), 'Sulfur Dioxide Control by Electric Utilities: What Are the Gains from Trade?,' *Journal of Political Economy*, **108**, 1292–1326.

Castle, Emery N. (1965), 'The Market Mechanism, Externalities, and Land Economics,' *Journal of Farm Economics* **47**, 542–56.

Chestnut, L.G. and Mills, D.M. (2005), 'A fresh look at the benefits and costs of the U.S. acid rain program,' *Journal of Environmental Management*, **77**, 252–6.

Ciriacy-Wantrup, S.V. and Bishop, Richard C. (1975), '"Common Property" as a Concept in Natural Resources Policy,' *Natural Resources Journal* **15**, 713–27.

Clark, Colin W. (1973a), 'Profit Maximization and the Extinction of Animal Species,' *Journal of Political Economy* **81**, 950–61.

Clark, Colin W. (1973b), 'The Economics of Overexploitation,' *Science* **181**, 630–34.

Clean Air Act, 42 U.S.C. §§ 7401 to 7671q (1996).

Coase, Ronald H. (1964), 'Discussion: The Regulated Industries,' *American Economic Review* **54**, 194–97.

Coase, Ronald H. (1960), 'The Problem of Social Cost,' *Journal of Law and Economics* **3**, 1–44.

Cole, Daniel H. (1999), 'Clearing the Air: Four Propositions About Property Rights and Environmental Protection,' *Duke Environmental Law & Policy Forum* **10**, 103–30.

Cole, Daniel H. (2002), *Pollution and Property: Comparing Ownership Institutions for Environmental Protection*, Cambridge: Cambridge University Press.

Cole, Daniel H. and Grossman, Peter Z. (1999), 'When is Command-and-Control Efficient? Institutions, Technology, and the Comparative Efficiency of Alternative Regulatory Regimes for Environmental Protection,' **1999** *Wisconsin Law Review*, 887–938.

Cole, Daniel H. and Grossman, Peter Z. (2002), 'Toward a Total-Cost Approach to Environmental Instrument Choice,' in Zerbe, R.O. and Swanson, T. (eds), *An Introduction to the Law and Economics of Environmental Policy: Issues in Policy Design, Research in Law and Economics*, **20**, 225–43.

Cox, Susan J.B. (1985), 'No Tragedy on the Commons,' *Environmental Ethics* **7**, 49–61.

Cropper, Maureen L., Evans, William N., Berard, Stephen J., Ducla-Soares, Maria M., and

Portney, Paul R. (1992), 'The Determinants of Pesticide Regulation: A Statistical Analysis of EPA Decision Making,' *Journal of Political Economy* **100**, 175–97.
Dahlman, Carl. J. (1979), 'The Problem of Externality,' *The Journal of Law and Economics* **22(1)**, 141–62.
Dales, J.H. (1968), *Pollution, Property and Prices: An Essay in Policy-Making and Economics*, Toronto: University of Toronto Press.
Dasgupta, Partha (1982), *The Control of Resources*, Cambridge, Mass.: Harvard University Press.
Davis, Otto A. and Kamien, Morton I. (1969), 'Externalities, Information, and Alternative Collective Action,' in Joint Economic Committee, United States Congress, *The Analysis and Evaluation of Public Expenditures: The PPB System, Vol. I*, Washington, D.C.: U.S. Government Printing Office, 67–86.
Demsetz, Harold (1964), 'The Exchange and Enforcement of Property Rights,' *Journal of Law and Economics* **7**, 11–26.
Demsetz, Harold (1967), 'Toward a Theory of Property Rights,' *American Economic Review* **57**, 347–59, reprinted in Demsetz, Harold (1988), *Ownership, Control and the Firm: The Organization of Economic Activity*, Vol. I, Cambridge: Basil Blackwell, 104–16.
Demsetz, Harold (1968), 'The Costs of Transacting,' *Quarterly Journal of Economics* **82**, 33–53.
Demsetz, Harold (1988), *Ownership, Control and the Firm, Volume I, The Organization of Economic Activity*, Oxford: Basil Blackwell.
Denman, D.R. (1978), *The Place of Property: A New Recognition of the Function and Form of Property Rights in Land*, The Keep, Berkhamsted, Herts., U.K.: Geographical Publications Ltd.
Dennis, Jeanne M. (1993), 'Smoke for Sale: Paradoxes and Problems of the Emissions Trading Program of the Clean Air Act Amendments of 1990,' *Ucla Law Review* **40**, 1101–44.
Downs, Anthony (1957), *An Economic Theory of Democracy*, New York: Harper.
Eggertsson, Thráinn (1990), *Economic Behavior and Institutions*, Cambridge: Cambridge University Press.
Eggertsson, Thráinn (1996), 'The Economics of Control and the Cost of Property Rights,' in Hanna, Susan S., Folke, Carl, and Mäler, Karl-Gören (eds.), *Rights to Nature: Ecological, Economic, Cultural, and Political Principles of Institutions for the Environment*, Washington, D.C.: Island Press, 157–75.
Ellickson, Robert (1991), *Order Without Law: How Neighbors Settle Disputes*. Cambridge, Mass.: Harvard University Press.
Ellickson, Robert C. (1993), 'Property in Land,' *The Yale Law Journal* **102**, 1315–1400.
Energy Information Administration (1997), *The Effects of Title IV of the Clean Air Act Amendments of 1990 on Electric Utilities: An Update*, Washington, D.C.: United States Department of Energy.
Environmental Protection Agency (1980), *Emissions Reduction Banking and Trading Update*, Washington, D.C.
Environmental Protection Agency (1986a), *Emissions Trading Policy Statement; General Principles for Creation, Banking, and Use of Emission Reduction Credits*, 51 Fed. Reg. 43,814.
Environmental Protection Agency (1986b), *Emissions Trading Technical Document*, 51 Fed. Reg. 43,837.
Environmental Protection Agency (1990), *Environmental Investments: The Cost of a Clean Environment*, Washington, D.C.
Environmental Protection Agency (1993), *Final Rule on the Acid Rain Program*, 58 Fed. Reg. 3,677–8.
Environmental Protection Agency (2006), *Acid Rain Program: 2005 Progress Report.*
Epstein, Richard (1995), *Simple Rules for a Complex World*, Cambridge, Mass.: Harvard University Press.
Epstein, Richard (1996), *Simple Rules for a Complex World*, Cambridge, Mass: Harvard University Press.

Ercmann, Sevine (1996), 'Enforcement of Environmental Law in United States and European Law: Realities and Expectations,' *Environmental Law* **26**, 1213–39.

Farber, Daniel A. and Frickey, Philip P. (1991), *Law and Public Choice: A Critical Introduction*, Chicago: University of Chicago Press.

Featherstone, Allen M. and Goodwin, Barry K. (1993), 'Factors influencing a farmer's decision to invest in long-term conservation improvements,' *Land Economics* **69**, 67–81.

Feeny, D., Berkes, F., McCay, B.J. and Acheson, J.M. (1990), 'The Tragedy of the Commons: Twenty-two years later,' *Human Ecology* **18**, 1–19.

Feeny, David, Hanna, Susan, and McEvoy, Arthur F. (1996), 'Questioning the assumptions of the "tragedy of the commons" model of fisheries,' *Land Economics* **72(2)**, 187–205.

Foster, Vivien and Hahn, Robert W. (1995), 'Designing More Efficient Markets: Lessons from Los Angeles Smog Control,' *Journal of Law and Economics* **38**, 19–48.

Funk, William (1992), 'Free Market Environmentalism: Wonder Drug or Snake Oil?,' *Harvard Journal of Law and Public Policy* **15**, 511–16.

Gaines, Sanford E. and Westin, Richard A. (1991), *Taxation for Environmental Protection: A Multinational Legal Study*, New York: Quorum Books.

Geisler, Charles (2000), 'Property Pluralism,' in Geisler, C. and Daneker, G. (eds), *Property and Values: Alternatives to Public and Private Ownership*, Washington, D.C.: Island Press.

Goetze, David (1987), 'Identifying Appropriate Institutions for Efficient Use of Common Pools,' *Natural Resources Journal* **27**, 187–99.

Gordon, H. Scott (1954), 'The Economic Theory of a Common Property Resource: The Fishery,' *Journal of Political Economy* **62(2)**, 122–42.

Gordon, Scott (1958), 'Economics and the Conservation Question,' *Journal of Law and Economics* **1**, 110–21.

Grapel, William (trans.) (1994 Reprint), *The Institutes of Justinian, with the Novel as to Successions*, Holmes Beach, Fla.: Wm. W. Gaunt & Sons, Inc.

Green, Donald P. and Shapiro, Ian (1994), *Pathologies of rational choice theory: a critique of applications in political science*, New Haven: Yale University Press.

Hahn, Robert W. and Hester, Gordon L. (1989a), 'Where Did All the Markets Go? An Analysis of EPA's Emissions Trading Program,' *Yale Journal on Regulation* **6**, 109–53.

Hahn, Robert W. and Hester, Gordon L. (1989b), 'Marketable Permits: Lessons for Theory and Practice,' *Ecology Law Quarterly* **16**, 361–406.

Hamilton, James T. (1995), 'Pollution as News: Media and Stock Market Reactions to the Toxics Release Inventory Data,' *Journal of Environmental Economics and Management* **28**, 98–113.

Hanna, Susan, Folke, Carl, and Mäler, Karl-Gören (1996), 'Property Rights and the Natural Environment,' in Hanna, Susan, Folke, Carl, and Mäler, Karl-Gören (eds.), *Rights to Nature: Ecological, Economic, Cultural, and Political Principles of Institutions for the Environment*, Washington, D.C.: Island Press, 1–10.

Hanna, Susan and Munasinghe, Mohan (eds.) (1995a), *Property Rights and the Environment: Social and Ecological Issues*, Washington, D.C.: The Beijer International Institute of Ecological Economics and The World Bank.

Hanna, Susan and Munasinghe, Mohan (1995b), 'An Introduction to Property Rights and the Environment,' in Hanna, Susan and Munasinghe, Mohan (eds.), *Property Rights and the Environment: Social and Ecological Issues*, Washington, D.C.: The Beijer International Institute of Ecological Economics and The World Bank, 3–11.

Hansen, Zeynep K. and Libecap, Gary D. (2004), 'Small Farms, Externalities, and the Dust Bowl of the 1930s,' *Journal of Political Economy*, **112**, 665–94.

Hardin, Garrett (1968), 'The Tragedy of the Commons,' *Science* **162**, 1243–8.

Hardin, Garrett (1978), 'Political requirements for preserving our common heritage,' in Brokaw, H.P. (ed.), *Wildlife and America*, Washington, D.C.: Council on Environmental Quality, 310–17.

Heinzerling, Lisa (1995), 'Selling Pollution, Forcing Democracy,' *Stanford Environmental Law Journal* **14**, 300–344.

Hines, N. William (1966), 'Nor Any Drop to Drink: Public Regulation of Water Quality,' *Iowa Law Review* **52**, 186–235.
Hohfeld, Wesley Newcomb (1913), 'Some Fundamental Legal Conceptions as Applied to Judicial Reasoning,' *Yale Law Journal* **23**, 16–59.
Hohfeld, Wesley Newcomb (1920), *Fundamental Legal Conceptions as Applied in Judicial Reasoning*, New Haven: Yale University Press.
Honoré, Toni (1961), 'Ownership,' in Guest, Anthony Gordon (ed.), *Oxford Essays in Jurisprudence*, London: Oxford University Press, 107–47.
Horwitz, Morton J. (1977), *The Transformation of American Law, 1780–1860: The Crisis of Legal Orthodoxy*, New York: Oxford University Press.
Hotelling, Harold (1931), 'The Economics of Exhaustible Resources,' *The Journal of Political Economy* **39**, 137–75.
Howe, Charles W. (1979), *Natural Resource Economics*, New York: John Wiley & Sons.
Huffman, James L. (1994), 'The Inevitability of Private Rights in Public Lands,' *University of Colorado Law Review* **65**, 241–77.
Hyde, William F. (1981), 'Compounding Clearcuts: The Social Failures of Public Timber Management in the Rockies,' in Baden, John and Stroup, Richard (eds.), *Bureaucracy Versus the Environment*, Ann Arbor: University of Michigan Press, 186–202.
Jung, Chulho, Krutilla, Kerry and Boyd, Roy (1996), 'Incentives for Advanced Pollution Abatement Technology at the Industry Level: An Evaluation of Policy Alternatives,' *Journal of Environmental Economics and Management* **30**, 95–111.
Kaplowitz, Michael D. (ed.) (2000), *Property Rights, Economics, and the Environment*, Stamford, Conn.: JAI Press.
Klyza, Christopher McGrory (1996), *Who Controls Public Lands?: Mining, Forestry, and Grazing Policies, 1870–1990*, Chapel Hill: University of North Carolina Press.
Komesar, Neil K. (1994), *Imperfect Alternatives: Choosing Institutions in Law, Economics, and Public Policy*, Chicago: University of Chicago Press.
Konar, Shameek and Cohen, Mark A. (1997), 'Information as Regulation: The Effect of Community Right to Know Laws on Toxic Emissions,' *Journal of Environmental Economics and Management* **32**, 109–24.
Krieger, Martin H. (1973), 'What's Wrong with Plastic Trees? Rationales for Preserving Rare Natural Environments Involve Economic, Societal, and Political Factors,' *Science* **179**, 446–55.
Larson, Bruce A. and Bromley, Daniel W. (1990), 'Property Rights, Externalities, and Resource Degradation: Locating the Tragedy,' *Journal of Development Economics* **33**, 235–62.
Latin, Howard (1985), 'Ideal Versus Real Regulatory Efficiency: Implementation of Uniform Standards and "Fine-Tuning" Regulatory Reforms,' *Stanford Law Review* **37**, 1267–332.
Leman, Christopher K. (1984), 'How the privatization revolution failed, and why public land management needs reform anyway,' in Francis, John G. and Ganzel, Richard (eds.), *Western Public Lands*, Totowa, N.J.: Rowman and Allanheld, 110–128.
Libecap, Gary D. (1981), *Locking Up the Range: Federal Land Controls and Grazing*, Cambridge, Mass.: Ballinger Publishing Co.
Libecap, Gary D. (1989), *Contracting for Property Rights*, New York: Cambridge University Press.
Liroff, Richard A. (1986), *Reforming Air Pollution Regulation: The Toil and Trouble of EPA's Bubble*, Washington, D.C.: The Conservation Foundation.
Lueck, Dean (1989), 'The Economic Nature of Wildlife Law,' *The Journal of Legal Studies* **18**, 291–324.
Lueck, Dean (1991), 'Ownership and the regulation of wildlife,' *Economic Inquiry* **29**, 249–60.
Maloney, Michael T. and McCormick, Robert E. (1982), 'A Positive Theory of Environmental Quality Regulation,' *Journal of Law and Economics* **25**, 99–121.
Mazurek, Henry E. (1994), 'The Future of Clean Air: The Application of Futures Markets

to Title IV of the 1990 Amendments to the Clean Air Act,' *Temple Environmental Law and Technology Journal* **13**, 1–33.

McCay, Bonnie J. (1997), 'Common and Private Concerns,' in Hanna, Susan, Folke, Carl, and Mäler, Karl-Gören (eds.), *Rights to Nature: Ecological, Economic, Cultural, and Political Principles of Institutions for the Environment*, Washington, D.C.: Island Press, 111–26.

McCay, Bonnie J. (2000), 'Property Rights, the Commons, and Natural Resource Management,' in Kaplowitz, Michael D. (ed.) (2000), *Property Rights, Economics, and the Environment*, Stamford, Conn.: JAI Press, 67–82.

McGee, Robert W. and Block, Walter E. (1994), 'Pollution Trading Permits as a Form of Market Socialism and the Search for a Real Market Solution to Environmental Pollution,' *Fordham Environmental Law Journal* **6**, 51–77.

McNeill, John R. (2002), 'Tragedies of Privatization: Land, Liberty, and Environmental Change in Spain and Italy, 1800–1910, in Richards, J.R. (ed.), *Land, Property, and the Environment*, Oakland: ICS Press, 222–34.

Menell, Peter S. (1991), 'The Limitations on Legal Institutions for Addressing Environmental Risks,' *Journal of Economic Perspectives* **5(3)**, 93–111.

Menell, Peter S. (1992), 'Institutional Fantasylands: From Scientific Management to Free Market Environmentalism,' *Harvard Journal of Law & Public Policy* **15**, 489–510.

Menell, Peter S. and Stewart, Richard B. (1994), *Environmental Law and Policy*, Boston: Little, Brown and Company.

Michaelman, Frank (1982), 'Ethics, Economics, and the Law of Property,' in Pennock, J.R. and Chapman, J.W. (eds), *Nomos 24: Ethics, Economics, and the Law*, New York: New York University Press, 3–40.

Miller, Kathleen A. (1996), 'Water Banking to Manage Supply Variability,' *Advances in Economics of Environmental Resources* **1**, 185–210.

Mostaghel, Deborah M. (1995), 'State Reactions to the Trading of Emissions Allowances Under Title IV of the Clean Air Act Amendments of 1990,' *Boston College Environmental Affairs Law Review* **22**, 201–24.

Nelson, Robert H. (1995), *Public Lands and Private Rights: The Failure of Scientific Management*, Lanham, Maryland: Rowman & Littlefield Publishers, Inc.

Niskanen, William A., Jr. (1971), *Bureaucracy and Representative Government*, Chicago: Aldine-Atherton.

Noll, Roger C. (1989), 'Economic Perspectives on the Politics of Regulation,' in Schmalensee, Richard and Willig, Robert D. (eds), *Handbook of Industrial Organization*, Amsterdam: North-Holland, 1253–87.

North, Douglass C. and Thomas, Robert C. (1973), *The Rise of the Western World: A New Economic History*, Cambridge: Cambridge University Press.

Olson, Mancur, Jr. (1965), *The Logic of Collective Action*, New York: Schocken Books.

Opschoor, J.B. and Vos, Hans B. (1989), *Economic Instruments for Environmental Protection*, Paris: Organization for Economic Co-operation and Development.

Ostrom, Elinor (1990), *Governing the Commons: The Evolution of Institutions for Collective Action*, Cambridge: Cambridge University Press.

Ostrom, Elinor (2007), 'A diagnostic approach for going beyond panaceas,' *Proceedings of the National Academies of Science*, **104**, 15181–7.

Orzechowski, William (1977), 'Economic Models of Bureaucracy: Survey, Extensions, and Evidence,' in Borcherding, T.E. (ed.), *Budgets and Bureaucrats: The Sources of Government Growth*, Durham, N.C.: Duke University Press, 199–259.

Ovid (1992), *Metamorphoses V–VIII*, Hill, D.E. (trans.), Warminster, Wiltshire, U.K.: Aris & Phillips Ltd.

Pashigian, B. Peter (1985), 'Environmental Regulation: Whose Self-Interests Are Being Protected?,' *Economic Inquiry* **23(4)**, 551–84.

Percival, Robert, Miller, Alan S., Schroeder, Christopher H., and Leape, James P. (1996), *Environmental Regulation: Law, Science, and Policy*, Boston: Little, Brown and Company.

Petersen, William F., Jr. (1994), 'The Limits of Market-Based Approaches to Environmental Protection,' *Environmental Law Reporter* **24**, 10173–6.

Polesetsky, Matthew (1995), 'Will a Market in Air Pollution Clean the Nation's Dirtiest Air? A Study of the South Coast Air Quality Management District's Regional Clean Air Incentives Market,' *Ecology Law Quarterly* **22**, 359–411.

Poole, Robert W., Jr. (1996), 'Privatization for Economic Development,' in Anderson, Terry L. and Hill, Peter J., *The Privatization Process: A Worldwide Perspective*, Lanham, MD.: Rowman & Littlefield Publishers, Inc., 1–18.

Portney, Paul R. (1990), 'Air Pollution Policy,' in Portney, Paul R. (ed.), *Public Policies for Environmental Protection*, Washington, D.C.: Resources for the Future, 27–96.

Posner, Richard A. (1992), *Economic Analysis of Law*, Boston: Little, Brown & Co.

Power, Thomas Michael (1996), *Lost Landscapes and Failed Economies: The Search for a Value of Place*, Washington, D.C.: Island Press.

Randall, Alan and Castle, Emery N. (1985), 'Land Resources and Land Markets,' in Kneese, A.V. and Sweeney, J.L. (eds), *Handbook of Natural Resource and Energy Economics, vol. II*, Amsterdam: Elsevier Science Publishers.

Rasker, Raymond (1994), 'A New Look at Old Vistas: The Economic Role of Environmental Quality in Western Public Lands,' *University of Colorado Law Review* **65**, 369–99.

Rasker, Raymond, Martin, Michael V., and Johnson, Rebecca L. (1992), 'Economics: Theory versus Practice in Wildlife Management,' *Conservation Biology* **6**, 338–49.

Revenue Procedure 92–91, October 29, 1992, 92 Fed. Reg. ¶ 46,595.

Revesz, Richard L. (1996), 'Federalism and Interstate Environmental Externalities,' *University of Pennsylvania Law Review* **144**, 2341–416.

Richards, John R. (2002), *Land, Property, and the Environment*, Oakland: ICS Press.

Rose, Carol M. (1990), 'Energy and Efficiency in the Realignment of Common-Law Water Rights,' *Journal of Legal Studies* **19**, 261–96.

Rose, Carol M. (1994), *Property and Persuasion: Essays on History, Theory and Rhetoric of Ownership*, Boulder, CO: Westview Press.

Rosenberg, Adam J. (1994), 'Emissions Credit Futures Contracts on the Chicago Board of Trade: Regional and Rational Challenges to the Right to Pollute,' *Virginia Environmental Law Journal* **13**, 501–36.

Royal Commission on Environmental Pollution (1971), *First Report*, London: Her Majesty's Stationery Office.

Samuelson, Paul A. (1980), *Economics*, 11th ed., New York: McGraw-Hill.

Sapp, William W. (1995), 'The Supply-Side and Demand-Side of Wetlands Mitigation Banking,' *Oregon Law Review* **74**, 951–93.

Schlager, Edella and Ostrom, Elinor (1992), 'Property-rights regimes and natural resources: a conceptual analysis,' *Land Economics* **68(3)**, 249–62.

Schroder, Robert L. and Johnson, S. Lee (1997), 'Using Market Forces to Reduce Pollution: Michigan's Emissions Reduction Credit and Emission Averaging Rules,' *Michigan Bar Journal* **76**, 70–73.

Scott, Anthony D. (1955), 'The Fishery: The Objectives of Sole Ownership,' *Journal of Political Economy* **63**, 203–15.

Seabright, Paul (1993), 'Managing Local Commons: Theoretical Issues in Incentive Design,' *Journal of Economic Perspectives* **7(4)**, 113–34.

Sohn, David and Cohen, Madeline (1996), 'From Smokestacks to Species: Extending the Tradeable Permit Approach from Air Pollution to Habitat Conservation,' *Stanford Environmental Law Journal* **15**, 405–451.

Solow, Robert M. (1974), 'Richard T. Ely Lecture: The Economics of Resources or the Resources of Economics,' *American Economic Association* **64(2)**, 1–14.

Squillace, Mark (1992), *3 Environmental Law: Air Pollution*, Cincinnati: Anderson Publishing Co.

State Utility Forecasting Group (1991), *Indiana Electricity Demand: The 1990 Forecast*. West Lafayette, Indiana: State Utility Forecasting Group.

Stavins, Robert N. and Whitehead, Bradley W. (1992), 'Dealing With Pollution: Market-Based Incentives for Environmental Protection,' *Environment* **34(7)**, 7–42.

Stewart, Richard B. and Krier, James E. (1978), *Environmental Law and Policy: Readings, Materials and Notes*, Indianapolis: The Bobbs-Merrill Company, Inc.

Stewart, Richard B. and Wiener, Jonathan B. (2003), Washington, D.C.: American Enterprise Institute.

Stroup, Richard L. and Baden, John A. (1973), 'Externality, Property Rights and the Management of Our National Forests, *Journal of Law and Economics* **16**, 303–12.

Stroup, Richard L. and Baden, John A. (1983), *Natural Resources: Bureaucratic Myths and Environmental Management*, San Francisco: Pacific Institute for Public Policy Research.

Stroup, Richard L. and Goodman, Sandra L. (1992), 'Property Rights, Environmental Resources, and the Future,' *Harvard Journal of Law and Public Policy* **15**, 427–41.

Swift, Byron (1997), 'The Acid Rain Test,' *Environmental Forum* **14(3)**, 17–25.

Taylor, Margaret, Rubin, Edward S., and Hounshell, David A. (2005), 'Regulation as the Mother of Invention: The Case of SO_2 Control,' *Law and Policy*, **27**, 348–78.

Terrebonne, R. Peter (1993), 'Privatizing the Commons: The Distribution of Total Product,' *Eastern Economic Journal* **19(2)**, 165–71.

Thompson, Andrew Mcfee (1996), 'Free Market Environmentalism and the Common Law: Confusion, Nostalgia, and Inconsistency,' *Emory Law Journal* **45**, 1329–72.

Thompson, Barton H. (1993), 'Institutional Perspectives on Water Policy and Markets,' *California Law Review* **81**, 673–764.

Thompson, Barton H. (1996), 'The Search for Regulatory Alternatives,' *Stanford Environmental Law Journal* **15**, 8–21.

Tietenberg, Thomas (1985), *Emissions Trading: An Exercise in Reforming Pollution Policy*, Washington, D.C.: Resources for the Future.

Tipton, Carrie A. (1995), 'Protecting Tomorrow's Harvest: Developing a National System of Individual Transferable Quotas to Conserve Ocean Resources,' *Virginia Environmental Law Journal* **14**, 381–421.

Toulmin, Stephen (2001), *Return to Reason*, Cambridge, Mass.: Harvard University Press.

Tripp, James T.B. and Dudek, Daniel J. (1989), 'Institutional Guidelines for Designing Successful Transferable Rights Programs,' *Yale Journal on Regulation* **6**, 369–91.

US General Accounting Office (1994), *Report to the Chairman, Environment, Energy, and Natural Resources Subcommittee, Committee on Government Operations, House of Representatives, Air Pollution: Allowance Trading Offers an Opportunity to Reduce Emissions at Less Cost*. Washington, D.C.

Utility Environment Report, March 14, 1997.

Warming, Jens (1911), 'Om "grundrente" af fiskegrunde,' *Nationalokonomisk Tidsskrift*, 495–506, translated in Andersen, P., 'On Rent of Fishing Grounds: A Translation of Jens Warming's 1911 Article, with an Introduction,' *History of Political Economy* **15(3)**, 391–6.

Wittman, Donald A. (1995), *The Myth of Democratic Failure: Why Political Institutions are Efficient*, Chicago: University of Chicago Press.

Yandle, Bruce (1992), 'Escaping Environmental Feudalism,' *Harvard Journal of Law and Public Policy* **15**, 517–39.

Cases

Fountainbleu Hotel Corp. v. Forty-five Twenty-five, Inc., 114 So.2d 357 (Fla.App. 1959).

Ormet Corporation v. Ohio Power Co., 98 F.3d 799 (4th Cir. 1996).

Prah v. Maretti, 321 N.W.2d 182 (Wis. 1982).

United States v. Causby, 328 US 256 (1946).

12 Security interests, creditors' priorities, and bankruptcy

James W. Bowers

A. The debt obligation

'Bankruptcy' and 'creditors' remedies' are the labels lawyers give to procedures the law uses to enforce debt obligations. Typically, a debt arises as a result of a civil obligation of the debtor to make a payment of money, most commonly because the debtor has promised payment, or less commonly, because the debtor has committed a tort or invaded some other civil entitlement of the creditor, for which the substantive law provides a payment obligation as a remedy. Failure to pay permits the creditor to initiate a process under which the state will seize an asset belonging to the debtor and sell it. The proceeds of the sale are turned over by the state's selling agent (typically in individual cases, a 'sheriff,' or in collective proceedings, a 'bankruptcy trustee') to the creditor, in payment of the debt obligation. Djankov, Hart, McLeish and Schleifer (2006) and Armstrong and Riddick (2003) study the economic consequences of differences in the details of collection law among jurisdictions.

1. Why debt contracts? The subordination of equity and the resulting perverse investment incentives

The fundamental postulate of financial economics holds that in a world with adequately functioning capital markets, capital structure is irrelevant. The way in which a project is financed does not affect the value of that project, or of the firm pursuing it (Modigliani and Miller, 1958). It is obvious, however, that many firms and individuals finance their activities by issuing debt. It follows from the postulate, then, that firms financed using debt must be motivated by some market failure or transaction costs: principally, asymmetric information, discussed in paragraph A.2. below.

The employment of debt creates some perverse investment incentives for debtor firms. Debt gives equity investors an incentive to invest in excessively risky projects, since if the project succeeds, all residual gains in excess of the principal amount of the loan plus earned interest accrue to the equityholders. On the other hand if the project fails, all of the loss is borne by the lender. This incentive to gamble with creditor's money is known as the Jensen and Meckling (1976) 'overinvestment' incentive. To mitigate the operation of this incentive, lenders typically require in their loan contracts that borrowers make a significant equity investment in the project which will be subordinated to the lender's claim if the project is liquidated, so that by selecting an excessively risky project, the equity investors will be risking a significant sum of their own funds as well.

The presence of debt with priority over equity also creates another perverse incentive, the so-called Myers (1977) debt-overhang, or 'underinvestment' risk, as well. As a firm nears insolvency, but encounters opportunities to invest in net positive value projects, the possibility exists that much of the gains from the project will eventually accrue to the higher priority creditors rather than the controlling equity investors who will, accordingly, forego those profitable investment opportunities. This perverse incentive is more difficult to deal with by contract since it will often be impossible for the parties to foresee and describe the relevant future investment opportunities in their loan contracts (Gertner and Scharfstein, 1991).

2. Debt enables the creation of credible commitments

Most debt is contracted for. Such debt obligates the debtor to make a payment to the creditor at a determinable time set forth in the contract. One might imagine circumstances in which the efficient obligation might be made contingent on any number of future eventualities, and that contracts which had such equity-like features would also be common. The typical impulse to create debt contracts, however, probably stems, instead, from information asymmetries between lenders and borrowers. In the commercial context, the borrower seeks capital needed to conduct some project about which the borrower is better informed than the lender. Although the borrower might assure the lender that the project will generate sufficient revenues to retire the debt, those assurances may not always be credible. If the debtor also promises that should the project fail and the project revenues do not retire the debt, the debtor will subordinate its interests in all of its assets to the creditor's debt, the debtor's statement of confidence in his or her project becomes more believable and the commitment to subordinate implicit in the debt contract works as a bonding device. Well-informed borrowers doubtful about the prospects of their future projects would be less inclined to promise to subordinate themselves. Similarly, the future contingencies in consumer debt contracts which might affect the probability of repayment tend to be within the control of the borrowing consumer, thus exposing the prospective lender to significant moral hazard. The consumer trying to assure that lender that the power to affect many of the future contingencies will not be exercised adversely to the creditor's interests will find his assurances more credible if accompanied by an agreement to subordinate should payment not be made as agreed. To the extent that these informational asymmetries give rise to transaction costs resulting from misalignment of the parties' incentives, then, the debt contract by enabling the making of credible commitments is an efficient way to realign them. Presumably we observe debt in cases where the parties believe gains from correct incentive alignment outweigh the risks from perverse investment incentives that debt creates.

B. Systems of debt enforcement and the four strands of the law and economics research agenda

Debt contracts are enforced using two differing systems of remedies existing concurrently: One, the nonbankruptcy system which, in the United States, is a creature of the law of each of the 50 sovereign states, provides legal proceedings in which individual creditors can pursue their claims against individual debtors. The other is the Federal Bankruptcy system which provides a number of collective proceedings which involve the debtor and all of the creditors together. The mission of Law and Economics scholarship is thus to explain the existence of and justify the architectures of each system. There is also the question of how to coordinate the two systems – the issue of which system should govern and in what circumstances. Existing law and economics analysis has tended to focus on four salient features of the nonbankruptcy system and how its outcomes tend to differ from the bankruptcy outcomes. The four strands of the literature can be described as follows:

1. Individual vs. collective proceedings?

First, the nonbankruptcy system can be fairly characterized as a system of remedies given to individuals. It focuses on a debtor and a creditor and on the procedures which affect *only* those two parties. Bankruptcy systems, in contrast, are inherently collective, involving all of the debtor's creditors in the same legal proceedings. Thus it is fundamental to explain how these two diametrically opposed approaches can both be justified and explained: are there identifiable environments in which one of these alternative systems is appropriate and others in which the converse is likely more efficient?

2. Asset or claimant-type based remedies?

Second, the nonbankruptcy creditors' remedy system focuses on discrete assets in the debtor's inventory. Creditors seize only specific assets, which are then auctioned off. Likewise, security interests convey fractionalized property rights only in identified assets which are the collateral for the secured loan or credit. The creation of collective remedies, on the other hand, opens the possibility that priority ranking could be determined by the characteristics of creditors and could be applied to all of the debtor's assets as a group analogously, for example, to the interests of common and preferred shareholders in a firm. The issue is then to explain when and how asset-based as against claimant-type based systems are appropriate.

3. Justifying priorities?

Third, the priority system is a mixed one. As among creditors using the ordinary legal process to enforce their debtor's obligations, the first to complete the process and seize an asset has a priority right to the proceeds of the auction of that asset over the second to seize. Holders of security interests can finish in the race system, on the other hand, not in the order in which they seek to enforce their rights, but rather in order roughly of the times at which they contracted for those rights. In a collective proceeding, on the other hand, it is administratively possible to conceive of other priority systems which, to note the common example, adopt ratable sharing distributions as opposed to lexicographic priorities. Explaining the contrasting systems, accordingly, requires the development of theories of priorities.

4. Reconfiguring contractual priorities ex post

Fourth, Chapter 11 of the US Bankruptcy Code, which is thought to be a model for collective collection law devices applicable to corporate debtors in the developed and developing world, features a system which alters contractually agreed priorities ex post. How can such a system be justified and explained? A complete economic analysis of creditors' remedies must explain each of these four features of the existing dual creditors' remedies system. It is fair to introduce the literature addressing these problems by observing that much explaining remains to be done. What we do know, so far, is discussed, issue by issue, in the rest of this chapter.

C. Should debt collection law provide individual remedies or should it provide collective proceedings?

1. The individualistic creation of debt obligations

Debtors usually incur the debt obligation on an individualized basis. They borrow from a single creditor at a single moment, they buy something from a single seller on credit at an identifiable moment in time or they breach some civil duty owed to a fellow citizen in a unique accidental or wrongful event. The circumstances differ for each debt, and efficiency probably requires that the obligations of the debtor or the remedies of the creditor vary with those circumstances. There are no general commercial norms which dictate that the terms granted to one creditor must match those granted to any other, and debt contracts, accordingly, tend to be heterogeneous. Indeed the ways in which heterogeneous contractual obligations are incurred strongly suggests that the pattern of debt obligations is driven by the economics of optimal assortive matching. In the case of debt contracts, debtors must select creditors who possess competitive advantages of supplying debt capital in the types of borrowing contexts they can offer, and such creditors must select the types of borrower to deal with for whom they believe they have a competitive advantage. Nevertheless, to date, the literature does not develop hypotheses about the ways debtors match up with creditors, and the kinds of competitive advantages that generate those matches. It is not difficult to infer, however, that lenders do invest in specializing in dealing with certain kinds of borrowers, or in extending credit to borrowers located in specific geographical areas or pledging certain kinds of collateral, for example. Small loan companies and retail credit sellers and credit card companies specialize in making loans to consumers. Commercial lending departments of banks and commercial finance companies specialize in business loans.

Even were we to better understand why borrower A chose to deal with lender B, however, an additional question would remain: Would the remedy the law offers to B in the event of default work at cross purposes with the parties' incentives to exploit their respective competitive advantages that motivated the loan transaction in the first place? To the extent that parties are enabled to custom design their own remedial schemes, the risk that the remedy might dilute the gains from optimal matching is likely minimal. Creditors' remedies, then, should probably only be default provisions. There is much in the literature that criticizes the mandatory one-size-fits-all character of bankruptcy legislation (Schwartz, 1994b, 1997b, 1998; Rasmussen, 1992). Since collective remedies, which we style bankruptcy, tend to be mandatory, and cannot easily be contracted away from, the burden on supporters of bankruptcy to show that the collective remedy is likely to be efficient for individually contracted-for debt ought to be substantial.

2. *Creation of collective debt*

Sometimes, debtors undertake collective obligations, issuing identical debt instruments (bonds) to numerous members of the general public in a public offering, or committing torts which injure a large number of people, as in failing to properly maintain an aircraft which crashes injuring a number of passengers. In these rarer cases, the obligations of the debtor to any creditor match those owed to any other creditor member of the collective. Debt will probably be collectively incurred whenever there are economies of scope and scale which create gains from aggregating the obligations of many participants, although the literature has yet to identify or theorize how those economies might operate.

Interestingly, one of the principle contexts in which debt has been collectively issued in markets over the last 30 years has been in connection with securitization transactions which specifically seek to avoid the inefficiencies of bankruptcy procedures (Kettering, 2008) Indeed the growth and importance of securitization furnishes some of the strongest empirical evidence against theories which claim that involuntary collective collection processes are likely efficient, even for collectively created debt obligations.

3. *Individual vs. collective legal remedies*

Bowers (1990) argues that it is likely to be excessively costly to involve creditors B, C. . .N in disputes between the debtor and creditor A. The default creditor's remedy provided under state law in the United States and as an individual remedy in most legal systems is, accordingly, to entertain a legal proceeding on behalf of an individual creditor against the individual debtor. The proceeding is designed to permit the court to take the individual circumstances giving rise to each debt into account in determining whether to grant a remedy, and, if so, what remedy to grant. In the case of bond issues or mass torts, typical civil procedure is grounded on the assumption that the special circumstances under which the debt obligation arose are identical as among all of the claiming creditors. When collective obligations are undertaken under contract, on the other hand, and the terms of the contracts do not vary as between the claimants, collective proceedings do not differ from individualistic ones, in theory. The circumstances underlying the collective obligation are identical as between the debtor and all the creditors so the collection process can take them fully into account.

4. *Collective proceedings for heterogeneous claims*

The creditors' remedies schemes of many developed nations, however, have created bankruptcy style procedures, collective creditors' remedy processes under which individually formed claims are processed in a collective proceeding. If the individual circumstances result in the denial of a remedy to creditor B, more assets may remain for distribution to creditor C. C thus has an interest in the outcome of the collection dispute between B and the debtor so that an efficient collection regime would offer C the opportunity to intervene in the proceedings whenever C felt the expense of participating was less than the value of the private gains his participation might create. Typical bankruptcy proceedings, however, *require* all creditors to participate, on pain of loss of all their collection rights.

It is intuitively plausible that an efficient law would provide a process involving only the debtor and the individual creditor to enforce individualized debt contracts. The mystery to be explained by law and economics of bankruptcy law is, then, to show how and when it is efficient for the law to provide a collective process involving the heterogeneous claims not only of creditor A, but also creditors B, C, D. . .N in enforcing A's claim against the debtor. A process which gives consideration to the singular features of each credit transaction imposes procedural costs on creditors who were not parties to the transaction. A collective procedure which ignores those individualized circumstances threatens to reduce the values created by the process of seeking optimal matches between borrowers and lenders. The mystery of bankruptcy law is that it creates but cannot solve this dilemma. To make an efficient cost saving choice ex post is to deter efficient ex ante transactional matching. Attending to the efficiency of each match, on the other hand, makes the process excessively costly for other creditors.

5. *What might justify collective bankruptcy processes?*

Kanda and Levmore (1994) reason that the collective process can be justified if economies of scale exist in the conduct of collection efforts so that creditors would agree to join and pay a share of the reduced costs. It is possible that there are a limited number of cases in which the efficient matching which occurs at the time the debt obligation is initially created establishes a relationship which, despite the individualistic motivations for creating it, possesses features which nevertheless create economies of scale from joining its enforcement with the enforcement of other claims against the same debtor. Unfortunately, however, the literature has yet to describe or theoretically derive the features of such a case. Bankruptcy law itself governs nearly all debt contracts, and does not appear to attempt either to define cases which possess the requisite scale economies or to limit its application to just such cases.

6. *The collective action problem model*

The most famous law and economics analyst of bankruptcy systems made his name by arguing that when a single debtor has multiple creditors, the creditors may have a collective action problem. The individual incentives of each are to act in ways contrary to the best interests of all (Jackson, 1982). He therefore proposed that the creation of a mandatory collective remedy, which reflected the terms of an idealized multiple-creditor contract to cooperate, could be justifiable as a means of overcoming the collective action problem. Bankruptcy law could be explained if it actually incorporated the terms of that idealized 'creditors' bargain.' The literature developed in three directions from Jackson's basic insight.

(a) Does the law correspond with the model? First, there is a question whether the quest for efficiency (for example providing a legal solution to the 'common pool' problem creditors face under his analysis) could plausibly be regarded as driving the substance of the actual, existing bankruptcy doctrine. This first line of inquiry was addressed by Jackson himself with his collaborator Douglas Baird. They first attempted to apply the creditors' bargain heuristic to predict the features that an efficient bankruptcy statute would contain. In a series of pathbreaking articles, however, they discovered that the manner in which American Bankruptcy Judges were applying the provisions of Federal Bankruptcy legislation differed from those predicted by their efficiency hypothesis (Jackson, 1984, 1985; Baird and Jackson, 1984, 1985). Jackson and Scott (1989) attempted to account for the previously observed inefficiencies as an insurance mechanism, but conceded that the mechanism was unlikely to prove workable.

(b) Is there really a serious collective action problem after all – is the model itself theoretically sound? Research in the second direction challenged the soundness of Jackson's initial analysis. The 'Creditors' Bargain' logic grew from the premise of an assumed 'common pool' problem in which, when the debtor neared insolvency, assets seized and sold by creditor A tended to directly harm creditor B because insufficient assets were left behind to satisfy all remaining claims. This premise is more than simply distributional. Jackson argued, for example, that creditor A would not take the costs to B, C, . . ., N into account in making his decision to collect. Thus A would not avoid taking actions which destroyed synergistic values to the assets in the debtor's portfolio. A creditor owed \$100 might take a valuable earring whose stone could be sold for \$100, even when it was a member of a matched pair worth \$300 when kept and sold together. Such losses were avoidable, under Jackson's analysis, by forcing all the creditors to act collectively. Thus, he argued, the nonbankruptcy system had created a system of perverse incentives which, on the occasion of insolvency, were cured by switching over to the bankruptcy model.

Influenced by empirical evidence that the adoption of bankruptcy law had resulted in zero payouts to the supposedly cooperating creditors, Bowers (1990) argued that Jackson's view was one-sided, because it looked only at the incentives facing the creditors and either ignored the existence of the debtors, or assumed implicitly that debtors were completely passive. Bowers argued that debtors had both the means at hand and the incentive to avoid the losses Jackson predicted would result from perverse creditor common pool incentives.

Among the means available to a debtor under the nonbankruptcy system was the power to optimally liquidate its assets and, indeed, subsequent empirical research on the behavior of financially distressed firms (LoPucki and Whitford, 1993b; Gilson, 1996) shows that they do, in fact, conduct substantial asset liquidations. Once the debtor's incentives are brought back into the picture, the hypothesized common pool problem fades, leaving us once again without a compelling economic justification for bankruptcy law.

(c) Are there other, better solutions to the collective action problem? The third line of argument spawned by the Jackson creditors' bargain thesis took the law and economics literature in a new direction. It argued that whatever ex post collective action problem the nonbankruptcy system might create can be avoided by the use ex ante of optimal credit contracts (Adler, 1993b). Picker (1992), for example, justified the invention of security devices such as mortgages by showing that the adroit use of security could eliminate common pool problems. Bowers (1991) argued that the default terms of the existing nonbankruptcy system of secured and unsecured credit *already* provided the terms of optimal credit contracts, which tended to induce efficient distributions of the distressed debtor's least critical assets first to its most vulnerable creditors, thus minimizing the size of aggregate distress losses.

Finally, a number of scholars began to argue that the common pool or other perverse incentive problems which might occur in the nonbankruptcy system could be handled by contract (Adler, 1994c). Since corporate debtors probably dominate the economic impact of the American bankruptcy system, corporate finance approaches to the problem of understanding bankruptcy law have argued that borrowing firms are capable of creating new kinds of securities with attendant options and covenants, which can obviate any common pool problem. Since this literature tends also to address the issue of alteration of contractual priorities ex post, it will be discussed below in connection with this last issue.

D. Remedies Based on Assets vs. Remedies based on creditor type (herein of the law and economics of security interests)

1. The legal justification for security

Simultaneously with the bankruptcy debate discussed above, the law and economics literature was also engaged in a vigorous debate about the justification for granting contracted-for priority rights to secured creditors. The legal view of the justification, as exemplified in Kripke (1985) and Carlson (1994) was that security, by reducing the credit risk borne by the secured lender, tended to make loans available that creditors would not make on any other basis and so security interests could be justified on the same grounds that justified the extension of credit itself. Recent empirical studies (Berger and Udell, 1995, Mann, 1997a), confirm that lenders seek security interests in order to control the levels of moral hazard they face in lending to debtors who have limited amounts of equity financing. In what is, perhaps, the most important article in the law and economics literature concerning priority and security issues, Jackson and Kronman (1979) first developed and used the creditors' bargain theory, so influential in the bankruptcy literature, to provide an economic explanation for the development and use of security devices. They argued that an aspect of the creditors' collective action problem was a perverse tendency for creditors to expend duplicate efforts thus over-monitoring the debtor. Security, they concluded, if issued to the least efficient monitors, relieved them of the impulse to monitor, curing the perverse incentive, reducing unnecessary monitoring costs because only the most efficient monitors would have any remaining incentive to do so.

2. The secured debt puzzle

In 1981, however, Alan Schwartz showed that given some typical theoretical economic assumptions (completely informed, risk neutral creditors, with homogeneous expectations of the probability of default), the grant of security to a secured creditor tended to do more than just reduce risk to that lender (thus reducing the incentive to conduct duplicative monitoring). In fact, the grant transferred risks onto unsecured creditors who, under these theoretical assumptions, would demand as much compensation for accepting the transfer as the secured party was likely to give as a discount on the interest premium for being granted the security. The corollary as applied to the Jackson and Kronman monitoring thesis was that to the extent secured creditors could safely reduce their monitoring efforts, the grant of security correlatively increased the need for unsecured creditors to monitor, so that the theory could not predict any savings in aggregate monitoring costs either. Following Scott (1977), Schwartz argued security was in theory simply a zero sum game. If the confection of security interests is costly, then, the mystery is, why would debtors ever grant them when they stand to gain nothing by it? This analysis, Schwartz pointed out, was simply an application of the famous Modigliani and Miller Theorem (1958) of the irrelevance of capital structure. The argument created what he named and what has since been known as 'The Puzzle of Secured Debt' (Schwartz, 1984). Just as firms obviously invest much energy in designing and adapting their capital structures, they also issue secured debt in the teeth of theories which predict they will not. Schwartz concluded, however, that none of the then-existing theoretical explanations for the employment of short-term security devices could be squared with the empirical evidence, the patterns of secured lending actually observed.

3. Possible efficient puzzle solutions

The Schwartz thesis, that granting security is costly to debtors and gains them nothing, is, of course, contradicted by the observation that much secured lending and borrowing actually occurs. Shupack (1989) has observed that the costliness question is relative – that is, the Schwartz argument loses some of its punch if it is more costly to contract for unsecured lending than to take a security interest. Nevertheless, any explanation for the grant of security must probably show that the issuing of security is likely to be efficient, so that some private gains to the borrower and secured lender must be hypothesized.

Theories which explain the private gain as coming from externalizing risks onto uncompensated unsecured creditors, of course, are normatively unattractive. Schwartz (1984) examined several more benign explanatory answers proposed to his original puzzle, including those of Levmore (1982) (proposing that secured parties receive priority in payment for the external benefits their monitoring of the debtor confers on other creditors) and White (1984) (arguing that creditors differ in their levels of risk aversion so that security is arguably an efficient means of reducing risk to the most risk averse). Schwartz dismissed such theories which, by explaining the existence of private gains to borrowers, however, generate predictions that all borrowing will be conducted on a secured basis, such that all of every borrower's available assets will be encumbered before any unsecured borrowing occurs. All such theories, Schwartz argued, will be embarrassed by the fact that much *unsecured* lending takes place to borrowers with unencumbered assets. It thus seems likely that an eventual persuasive theory will have to show that security is both costly and beneficial, or else that unsecured lending achieves previously unknown gains, in order for it to explain the observed mixture of types of borrowings. A number of such theories have been proposed, which argue that the institution of security is likely to be efficient, including Adler (1993a), Bowers (1991), Buckley (1986, 1992), Kanda and Levmore (1994), Picker (1992), Shupack (1989), Scott (1986), Stulz and Johnson (1985) and Triantis (1992, 1994, 2000). Without some strong empirical confirmation of any of the competing theories, however, none has yet commanded a general level of acceptance in the law and economics community. Indeed, the current majority view is probably that the debate over the puzzle of secured transactions has been inconclusive (Scott, 1997).

Nevertheless, work on solving the puzzle continues. Schwartz himself, the creator of the puzzle, has proposed that the grant of security interests in favor of early lenders can be explained as an efficient way of permitting debtors to bind themselves not to engage in future financing which might dilute the value of earlier loans, which benefits borrowers without injuring creditors (Schwartz, 1997a). A still more recent model generalizes Schwartz's logic, and entertains the assumption that later creditors must incur costs to discover rights granted to earlier lenders. It finds that in such a context several features of secured lending tend to be explainable as reducing the deadweight loss of those due diligence costs. Their model also expands to explain features of other inter-creditor relations found in the law of creditors' remedies such as the veil-piercing exception to corporate limited liability and the law of fraudulent conveyances (Ayotte and Bolton, 2007).

4. *Inefficient solutions to the puzzle*

The inconclusiveness of the search for 'benign' explanations for security devices, which explain the use of security as justified by the creation of efficient outcomes, has led to a recent spate of arguments that the institution of secured credit is not only unproven as an efficient practice, but, on the contrary, is positively exploitative and thus inefficient. Schwartz (1981) had initially considered that security devices were employed by lenders and borrowers as means of exploiting creditors, like tort claimants, or consumers who were unsophisticated about the impact that security might have on their claims and who would therefore not increase the risk premiums they charged for becoming unsecured creditors. The distributive thesis, Schwartz argued, could only be proven by showing that firms whose creditors were likely to be unsophisticated were more apt to grant security interests than were borrowers whose other creditors were less easy to exploit. Such behavior should even be evident and the fact that it is not led him to dismiss the exploitation hypothesis. Nevertheless, LoPucki (1994) and Bebchuck and Fried (1996, 1997) have proposed that the priority extended to secured lenders be partially or wholly abolished to prevent the externalization of risk onto unsophisticated unsecured lenders. Warren (1997) and Klee (1997) argue that even though some measure of priority might be due to secured lenders, the law of security interests should 'carve out' an arbitrary percentage of the value of the collateral to be distributed to unsecured creditors. Scott (1994) has also suggested that the incentive structures inherent in the private law-proposing organizations which produced the American uniform law on security devices may also create perverse legal doctrine. Adler (1994a) argues that the Scott hypothesis results from a one-sided analysis. Harris and Mooney (1994) and Carlson (1986) have urged that in view of the inconclusive nature of the economic debate, that the institution of secured credit can be justified by resort to the historical legal theories which have been accepted by courts and lawyers. None of the exploitative or political theories of secured lending have yet gained general acceptance among scholars as explanations for the institution of security. The puzzle, thus, still remains to be solved, or, to say the same thing in another way, none of the existing theories which attempt to explain the institution has yet been proven correct.

5. Asset-based security as an individual remedy

Schwartz (1989) attempted to change the focus of the argument he himself had created by arguing for the grant of first priority over *all* of the debtor's assets in favor of the borrowing firm's earliest-to-lend financier. Under his analysis, the grant of priority, which is the functional equivalent of the grant of security in *all* the borrower's assets, can be an efficient way for firms with good projects to signal that they differ from firms with poor prospects. Since the first-in-time priority scheme he proposed resembles the priorities created under the existing law of secured credit, his argument reduces to a plea that the priority system cut loose from the asset-based nature it carries under existing security device law and that a creditor-based priority scheme be substituted therefore. His argument for this change is based, in part, on his assessment that the process of tying public notice to particular assets in the current regime is unduly costly. Bowers (1995) discusses some theoretical reasons why filing systems might impose excessive costs. Kanda and Levmore (1994), on the other hand, argue that notice is especially important only in asset-based priority schemes and is thus not so important if priorities are based on creditor characteristics as Schwartz proposes. Schwartz does not address the inevitable aspect of his proposal, however, that it must necessarily trigger some sort of collective collection proceeding in almost every case of nonpayment. Any second-to-lend creditor whose contract entitles him to be first to collect (as for example when a short-term trade creditor is seeking to collect against a debtor who has financed himself with a relatively long-term loan from the first-to-lend financer) must involve the financier as well as the debtor in any claim that his debt ought to be satisfied out of any of the debtor's assets, in all of which, under Schwartz's proposal, the financier has a priority interest. Although Schwartz offered his proposal on a conceptual basis only and so cannot be faulted for not having worked through the multitude of legal details which its adoption would inevitably necessitate, it is difficult to imagine that the debtor could even voluntarily *pay* the second-to-lend creditor with assets in which the first-to-lend had a superior interest. This look into Schwartz's proposal, on the other hand, does generate an explanation for the character of current security device law which is asset-based and not creditor-based. In an asset-based system, in which all the debtor's assets are encumbered, every unsecured creditor must deal with the prior secured lender in order to realize payment of his claim out of any of the debtor's assets. In that kind of case, an asset-based priority system can be seen as requiring a collective determination of the relative rights of at least two creditors every time only one wishes to collect. Unlike a creditor-type based system, however, an asset-based system permits debtors to retain some unencumbered assets which creditors can resort to without having to trigger a collective proceeding. The choice of asset vs. claimant-based priority rules, then, can be seen as another aspect of the choice between adopting individualized vs. collective creditors' remedies. Particularly when priority rules are claimant- rather than asset-based and claimants exist in large classes (such as, for example, when there are many shareholders and many unsecured creditors who share strata of priority), for any individual member of any class to collect, a legal proceeding almost necessarily must involve all the members of the claimant's own class, as well as all the members of any competing class in the process.

E. The economic analysis of creditor priorities

1. Nonbankruptcy first-in-time priority

Under nonbankruptcy law, once a creditor completes the involuntary collection process by having one of the debtor's assets seized and sold, title to that asset passed to the buyer at the judicial sale, and the asset was no longer available to satisfy claims by other competing creditors. The asset was no longer part of the debtor's property. This property theory-based system resulted in a 'race' system of priorities. The first creditor to seize the asset obtained priority over later seizing creditors. The nonbankruptcy system of individual remedies is, principally, one of temporal priority. Early lending secured creditors and early seizing creditors prevail over later ones. There are, however, exceptions. One of the chief deviations is in favor of later lending secured parties whose loans financed the acquisition of the collateral. They are granted a 'purchase-money' priority over earlier lenders claiming security interests in such after-acquired collateral. Certain statutory lien claimants also prevail over earlier perfecting secured lenders. In admiralty, there are many later-in-time but first-in-priority claims to interests in vessels. Lawyers probably deem the first-in-time priority as the general rule and the last-in-time priority cases as exceptional. Probably for that reason, the law and economics analysis has begun by attempting to understand the general rule first. Very little progress has been made in explaining the last-in-time priority cases. Mann (1996) is one analysis. Before discussing what there is on that score in the literature, therefore, we will first address the temporal priority scheme in general.

(a) Capricious factors influencing racing outcomes The outcome of the race among unsecured creditors can be influenced by a variety of arbitrary factors. Among the most capricious is the variance among courts in time-lags for obtaining judicial relief. The race is normally won by successfully completing a lawsuit, after which a judgment can be entered. The right to seize and sell the debtor's assets is usually assertable only after judgment has been obtained. *Ceteris paribus*, then, creditors suing in jurisdictions which have a year or more delay between the time a suit is commenced and the time at which it will be called for trial, will be disadvantaged in the race as compared with competing creditors who are capable of maintaining their actions in venues with shorter trial calendars. Perhaps to eliminate the capricious effects of these arbitrary factors, the common law developed a set of devices under which a creditor can, at the time of commencing judicial proceedings, reserve an early place in the order of finish, conditional only on completing the judicial proceedings.

(b) Finishing-place reserving devices and investments in collection The race system's prejudgment finishing-place reserving devices such as writs of attachment or sequestration, or notices of *lis pendens*, if freely available, would make the race among unsecured creditors more closely resemble the order in which their causes of action arose and thus susceptible to more reliable planning at the time credit is initially extended. The creditor making the first loan to become due would be more likely to become the first-in-line. In the last 40 years, however, the use of prejudgment writs has been restricted in the United States on constitutional grounds in a series of important US Supreme Court cases: *Snaidach v. Family Finance Corp.* 395 US 337 (1967); *Fuentes v. Shevin* 407 US 67 (1972); *North Georgia Finishing, Inc. v. Di-Chem Inc.* 419 US 601 (1975). The court found the writs objectionable, however, only on grounds that they invaded constitutional interests of the debtor. Their impact on the priority as among creditors was not attacked and it is conceivable that constitutional, prejudgment priority-reserving devices could still be designed to meet that need. Indeed, however, the recording of public notice of a security interest under Article 9 of the Uniform Commercial Code is an equally effective way of reserving a priority position at the time credit is negotiated and thus may have rendered the prejudgment collection writs superfluous.

Much unsecured credit is extended on a demand basis, however, so that an initial lending unsecured creditor cannot easily assure itself a head-start in the race system if it lends for a fixed term. Later demand-basis lenders will always have a head-start. Typical loan agreements attempt to enhance the likelihood of a more nearly even starting time, however, by permitting lenders to accelerate the due date upon adverse information, for example the calling in of a demand loan by another creditor. Thus, while one might argue that the nonbankruptcy priority system has a tendency to favor the earliest to lend creditor, it is more likely that it favors the earliest to discover the circumstances putting the debtor in default. This tendency of the unsecured creditors' racing system to induce careful creditor monitoring of the debtor has been regarded in the literature as a mixed blessing. Monitoring tends to reduce debtor misbehavior, but the system also tends to induce creditors to monitor each other, a potentially wasteful expenditure in light of the possibilities that creditors could agree to cooperate rather than compete with each other in monitoring. Indeed, however, Picker (1992) has shown that the use of security devices tends to enable creditors to avoid some of the expenses of monitoring each other. Bowers (1991) on the other hand, has argued that those creditors who are most vulnerable to losses from debtor default will be apt to invest in contract terms which permit early starts in the race and will also make the greatest investment in racing and thus tend to obtain proportionately greater recoveries than will creditors who are less vulnerable. Thus, it is arguable that the tournament-like system of the race among unsecured creditors has a tendency to produce efficient outcomes. Those who invest in winning the race are presumably the more efficient creditors and will be rewarded by the existing nonbankruptcy system.

(c) Payments as priorities and the law of preferences Rather than planning on winning a race through the judicial process, a far more promising collection strategy for unsecured creditors is to create contract incentives in their loan contracts which will induce debtors to voluntarily repay their debts. Credit contracts can and do frequently contain provisions which are designed to induce a debtor to pay a particular debt instead of other ones. Discounts for prompt payments and penalty or late-fees are common such devices. Creditors with whom the debtor does repeat business are also in positions of leverage, capable of cutting off profitable future business if past debts remain too long unpaid. The utility companies, by threat to cut off power and water to their deadbeat customers, are only the most obvious examples of creditors who can effectively employ such strategies as substitutes for judicial collection. Nevertheless, even if the collection tournament includes such nonjudicial strategies, it is still arguable that those creditors most vulnerable to loss will invest the most in designing contractual inducements for voluntary preferential repayment, and will invest most in post-default collection activity and are thus likely to be preferred.

One typical structural feature of bankruptcy law, however, is a doctrine that sets aside preferences. In order to discourage premature dismemberment of potentially viable firms, Jackson (1986, p. 125) argues that measures need to be taken to discourage creditors from 'opting out' of the bankruptcy fixed priority scheme in advance of the bankruptcy proceedings. If the tournament-like results of debtor preferences are likely to produce efficient results (payments to the most vulnerable creditors first and in such a way as to maximize the value of the debtor's remaining portfolio left available to the remaining creditors), then the need for a collective regime, particularly one to be protected by preference law, is questionable. What is more, Adler (1995) has shown in addition that, for corporate borrowers, the existence of a collective action problem itself impedes the effectiveness of any rules which attempt to prohibit debtors from making preferential transfers to creditors and that preference prohibitions may in fact *diminish* the value of the debtor's estate available to satisfy the claims of its creditors.

2. *First-to-perfect priority among secured creditors*

The first-wins priority scheme for secured creditors is explainable on a more straightforward basis. In it, each creditor can fix his or her place in the race for the debtor's assets at the time credit is extended. Those making later loans will be on notice that they will come in second in the race and can thus adjust the amount they choose to lend and the terms of their credit contracts to account for that fact. A contrary priority in favor of the last to lend likely would impose high costs on early lenders. Since the facts about later loans cannot be learned at the time the early contracts are entered into those early contracts cannot easily include plans for adjusting to them. Thus, the basic secured creditor priority system can be explained as the one which permits the creditors to adjust to each other most cheaply. To the extent that this rationale is explanatory, however, it also makes the few instances in which last-to-lend creditors are given priority, even more mysterious.

3. *Nonbankruptcy later-in-time priorities*

The earliest attempt to provide an economic explanation for a later-in-time priority involved the so-called 'purchase-money priority' of lenders who take as collateral, the very assets purchased which their extensions of credit financed. In an asset-based lending system, this transaction might be viewed as a first-in-time transaction because the taking of security in the asset occurs at the very first instant at which the collateral became part of the debtor's estate. The American Uniform Commercial Code, however, contemplates that borrowers can grant security interests to earlier lenders in after-acquired assets. The priority of the purchase-money lender, consequently, simply means that the purchase-money financier prevails over the after-acquired property interest of the earlier lender. Thus, what looks like a last-in-time priority may also be seen as nothing more than a limitation on the powers of debtors to pledge and of lenders to take security in future assets. None of the investigations to date, however, has asked whether there are efficient limits to the pledge of after-acquired assets. Jackson and Kronman (1979) addressed purchase-money priority as if it were a preferred default clause in the credit contract which created the earlier security interest in after-acquired collateral. Unless it could grant purchase-money priority to future lenders, they argued, the debtor was effectively committed to obtain all future financing from the initial lender. Since few debtors would willingly grant situational monopolies to lenders without asking for significant other concessions, they hypothesized that the parties to the initial credit contract would choose a purchase-money escape hatch clause in their contract and were saved the expenses of doing so by the priority provisions of the Code. Schwartz (1989), in his proposal to permit first priority to the first significant financier in all of the debtor's assets, also argues that the parties might bargain for purchase-money priority exceptions for sufficiently insignificant after-acquired asset purchases.

An attempt to explain later-in-time wins priority provisions is Levmore and Kanda (1994). They begin by espousing the recent trend in the law and economics literature to assume that existing doctrine was intended to address the problems of corporate borrowers. They then argue that the basic first-in-time gets priority rule is justifiable as a means of protecting early lending creditors from the perverse incentives which attract the equity owners of corporate borrowers to overinvest in excessively risky projects. Not all investments by the firm necessarily respond to the overinvestment incentive, however and, Levmore and Kanda surmise, later lenders have an informational advantage over earlier lenders about new investments the firm is undertaking. When, then, the informational advantage is significant and the environment is such that overinvestment is not likely to be a serious risk, they argue, one might expect to see a later-in-time priority rule displace the basic scheme as a means of encouraging investment in the firm's latest prospects by its best-informed lenders. This approach to explaining the mystery of late-in-time priority rules seems promising. On the other hand, the argument that each existing later-lender-gets-priority rule can be explained as being confined to an environment in which overinvestment risk is minor, is empirically speculative. An analogous argument, that sometimes we might not be able to accurately estimate future contingencies, and therefore might wish to postpone making the priority decision until after all of the facts are in, is made in Bowers (2005), but in another contractual context. However, the need to postpone the decision does not necessarily indicate *which* decision is likely to be the most highly desired come the optimal decision-making time.

4. Liquidation bankruptcy priority

The shape of the asset-based, first-in-time nonbankruptcy priority system conforms to the underlying assumption that the collection of obligations should be regarded as an individual matter, strictly between the debtor and the creditor. They are free to write credit contracts which meet their individual needs and to pursue the remedies they have bargained for on the basis of their individual circumstances. Particularly, however, once the debtor nears insolvency, the actions taken by any individual creditor arguably create a risk of external impacts on the welfare of competing creditors. Nothing in the contracting system in which the extension of credit is bargained for requires any creditor to modify the terms of his contract in order to coordinate his contract rights, or his ultimate legal remedy, with others who may have an interest in the debtor's fortunes. American lawyers intuit that on the occasion of insolvency some sort of coordination among creditors is required, and on that basis have built their basic understanding of the justification for bankruptcy law.

The basic priority system in the collective regime is complicated by the fact that, in theory, bankruptcy is designed to partially enforce the rights creditors acquire in the nonbankruptcy system. Thus, for example, secured creditors are technically entitled to recover the value of the collateral securing their debt to the extent that it is less than or equal to the amount owed. The extent to which this entitlement is enforced in actual bankruptcy proceedings, however, depends on whether the particular bankruptcy is a reorganization or a liquidation case. Reorganizations are discussed in Section F below. Since the legal priority rules which nominally create the baselines for distributions in reorganizations are the priorities which prevail in liquidation cases, it is useful to discuss these rules first.

(a) Class-based distribution The archetypical bankruptcy proceeding is Chapter 7 of the US Bankruptcy Code. It can be initiated by either the debtor or a group of creditors and once the proceedings commence, all individual collection activity by all creditors is stopped by the issuance of an automatic injunction. Almost immediately the bankruptcy trustee, an agent to represent all the claimants, is appointed and given control over all of the debtor's assets. The trustee then liquidates the assets, either in the ordinary course of the debtor's business, or else by auction, converting all of them into cash. The proceeds from the sale of collateral are paid to secured creditors. The remaining cash is distributed to various creditors according to the Chapter 7 priority scheme, which first sets up a set of

several classes of creditors holding 'priority claims.' The claims of the first priority are paid in full and only in the event there is cash remaining are distributions made to the next class and so on until all claims are paid. Creditors in the last class for whom the assets are sufficient for a distribution, but not enough to satisfy all the claims in the class, receive partial payments of the sum left undistributed in the debtor's estate, but are paid among themselves in proportion to the size of their claims – the so-called 'pro-rata equality' formula.

The literature has not addressed the question whether the existing fixed priority scheme of liquidation bankruptcy regimes can be economically explained. The first priority class is for so-called 'administrative priority' claims. The preference shown to these claims can probably be understood best as answering the need that the costs of the collective proceeding must be paid if there is to be any proceeding, but in fact the bulk of all US bankruptcy cases are those of individual debtors whose assets have no remaining distributable value once they enter bankruptcy. Bowers (1990) argues that debtors attempting to maximize the value of their assets will self-liquidate before their creditors force them to do it involuntarily and that the result of such self-liquidations will be that only highly-specialized assets and those which have the highest transaction costs to liquidate will remain in the debtor's inventories as of the time they are surrendered to creditors. Schleifer and Vishny (1992) opine that if assets are specialized to an industry in distress, auctioning those of any bankrupt firm will likely yield only 'fire-sale' prices. The fact that the bankruptcy estates of individual debtors are basically empty can thus be explained. One study, Maksimovic and Phillips (1998), finds that manufacturers' assets auctioned by bankruptcies are efficiently redeployable in other industries.

(b) Sympathetic classes The remaining classes of priority claims are more difficult to justify on efficiency grounds. Unpaid employees, certain farmers and fishermen and some consumers having made deposits on undelivered merchandise are sympathetic creditors who might be expected to find favor in the legislative arena in which bankruptcy legislation has traditionally been crafted. Tax collectors get priority for similar easy-to-understand political reasons, even if they do not merit much sympathy. The existing list of priority creditors does not exhaust the list of possibly sympathetic claimants. The omissions inspire demands, for example, that tort-victims of the debtor be given priority, even over the claims of secured creditors (see LoPucki (1994); Warren (1997)).

(c) Behavior invariant loss sharing rules The principally important feature of the statutory priority system, however, including the catch-all

pro-rata formula for the bottom priority creditors, is that it is fixed in advance and, thus, will not vary with creditor behavior. In the nonbankruptcy race system, for example, a creditor stands to make gains from obtaining information earlier than competing creditors so as to get a head-start in the race for the debtor's assets. The payouts in the collective regime, however, are fixed in advance and will not vary much according to creditors' investments in monitoring or collection efforts. A creditor who carefully monitors the debtor thus must share with the other creditors the gains from early detection if a collective proceeding ensues. If over-monitoring is a potential problem (Jackson and Kronman, 1979), or if racing costs are viewed as potentially wasteful (Jackson, 1982), then the fixed priority system imposed by bankruptcy law might be justified as a cure for the adverse effects of those perverse incentives. On the other hand, it has been shown in other contexts that mandatory equal sharing rules can block co-owned assets from being moved to higher valued uses (Easterbrook and Fischel, 1991, p. 118; Harris and Raviv, 1988; Kahan, 1993). The sharing regime gives some creditors incentives to free ride on the efforts of other creditors to monitor and force an ultimate liquidation. In the face of empirical complaints that bankruptcy proceedings might thus not be initiated soon enough, there are proposals in the literature to pay a bounty to the creditor who triggers the collective proceeding (Jackson, 1986; LoPucki, 1982). Of course, bounties are difficult to design and may give rise to races for the bounty, over-monitoring so as to be able to win the race to the bounty, and so on. The perfectly designed, happy medium liquidation bankruptcy structure which avoids both sets of perverse incentives, however, has not yet been developed in the literature.

F. Corporate reorganization bankruptcies and ex post modification of contractual priorities

1. The problem of the corporate borrower

The most heavily studied aspect of the issues raised in this chapter, is the question of what should be done when *corporate* borrowers incur financial distress. Although the bankruptcy code applies to individuals and other kinds of entities which become borrowers, the law and economics literature on this question has typically attempted to explain bankruptcy solely as a means of solving the collective action problem which *corporate* investors will foreseeably face. Until recently, the literature has assumed that the archetypical corporate bankruptcy law was Chapter 11 of the US Bankruptcy Code. The collective action problem is seen as the result of the content of the borrower's ex ante credit contracts and the nonbankruptcy law of creditors' remedies which permits creditors to race for, seize and sell the firm's assets. Bankruptcy law could be justified and understood if it addresses the collective action problem by refusing to enforce the suboptimal prebankruptcy market credit contracts and altering their terms ex post so that the set of post-reorganization claims against any debtor firm will more closely approximate an optimal capital structure. Recently, however, the companion literature on comparative corporate governance has raised the interesting possibility that corporate reorganization might be just an American problem. Roe (1994, Ch. 11) has shown that German and Japanese firms, for example, are subject to a great deal of management control by their financing banks, who also wield influence with the firm's other suppliers and customers. The relational lending regimes which result have the potential to essentially privatize the process of reorganizing financially distressed firms. Roe points out that the relational techniques have been politically outlawed in the US which might explain the American preoccupation with corporate bankruptcy law.

2. The illusive problem of optimal capital structure design

Presumably since any given firm's optimal capital structure cannot be specified in advance, the law of corporate reorganization replaces the nonbankruptcy and liquidation bankruptcy result of predetermined priorities with a non-predetermined scheme. The priority rights in the reorganized firm are not spelled out in the statute. Rather, it provides an extensive set of procedures under which a 'plan of reorganization' is developed and adopted for each bankrupt firm. The actual priorities awarded the claimants holding prebankruptcy contracts, then, is specified only ex post in the plan. It is well understood that the procedures under which such plans are developed dilute the value of contracts which provide for the claimant to receive high priority and, correlatively, enhance the distributions to those whose contracts called for them to have the lowest priorities. Benjamin (2004) studies the ways bankruptcy procedures influence the bargaining over such plans. What is not so well understood, however, is how altering the prebankruptcy priority contracts contributes to the solution of any collective action problem (Adler, 1992). From a law and economics viewpoint, the efficacy of this legal strategy for avoiding the collective action problem depends on whether we have developed a comprehensive theory of optimal capital structure for any given type of firm in the first place. If a firm's optimal capital structure is determinable, on the other hand, the coherence of the bankruptcy scheme must rest on some unarticulated explanations for why the investors' contracts cannot be expected to have already provided for the optimal outcome such that the resulting contracted-for priorities should not be enforced in the bankruptcy reorganization. As the law and economics literature has refined its definition of the issues needed to understand bankruptcy's corporate reorganization provisions, it has become increasingly obvious that these questions have not yet been answered. The answers are likely to come from the subfield of corporate finance.

3. Nonbankruptcy organizational solutions to the structural problem
To begin with, firms need incur the prospect of collective action problems only by choice. Business projects can be organized in all-equity entities or those which are solely owned by a single investor and which pursue whatever projects that controlling investor deems most efficient (Baird, 1994). It is even probable, based on the beginnings of relational theory in the literature (Scott, 1986; Posner, 1996), to suppose that relational behavior can solve all the parties' collective action problems. Multiple investors who are also actively relationally involved with each other can join together in a business partnership venture and function as if they were a sole investor, so long as the necessary acts of relating reduce transaction costs sufficiently among them as to invoke the Coase Theorem (Coase, 1960). Since most corporate reorganizations in the United States are of small firms (Bufford, 1994) which are thus arguably unlikely to face significant collective action problems, it is probable that US Corporate Reorganization law cannot be justified and explained by the need to solve small firms' problems. A study by Morrison (2007) finds that small firm reorganization bankruptcies are concluded swiftly indicating their collective action problems are less severe than those of larger firms.

4. The contributions of well-functioning capital markets to the problem of capital structure design
The law and economics literature has focused almost entirely on the optimal capital structure problems of firms of significant size and thus has assumed that Corporate Bankruptcy Reorganization law must be intended to address the problems of such firms for whom serious collective action problems likely exist. The debate over the significance of these problems has been recounted earlier in Section D discussing the justifications for development of collective remedy systems. Nevertheless, early in the debate Douglas Baird (1986) argued that the existence of well-functioning markets largely mitigated the possibility of any serious collective action problems for large, listed firms. The debate over what purposes corporate reorganization bankruptcy might serve has been conducted ever since between groups who, on the one hand, believe that almost all market results are inferior to bureaucratic decision making (LoPucki, 1992; Warren, 1992a) and those, on the other hand, who are persuaded that the existing capital markets function fairly well (Bowers, 1993).

The latter scholars have concluded from the data that Chapter 11 of the Bankruptcy Code has been punishing to investors (Bradley and Rosenzweig, 1992), without obviously assisting other recognizable groups of claimants (Bowers, 1994b).

5. The valuation problem with bureaucratic solutions

The logic underlying the corporate reorganization provisions of the US Bankruptcy Code ('Chapter 11') has always been that firms, even those in financial distress, have so-called 'going concern' values which are lost if the firm is broken up by having its assets sold off piecemeal. The collective action problem is seen as the incentives of individual creditors to race to dismember the firm on the first suspicion that it is headed for insolvency thus possibly destroying that going concern value (Baird, 1987a; Eisenberg and Tagashira, 1994). The structure of Chapter 11 is consistent with this explanation. When a firm files for Chapter 11 relief, all individual creditor actions to seize any of the bankrupts' assets are automatically enjoined and the assets are never, in fact, liquidated. Instead, the firm is recapitalized, with its old creditors becoming its new shareholders. Stock in the reorganized firm is swapped for the original debt. This result cannot obtain in legal theory, however, unless the equities distributed to the former creditors exceed the estimated value the creditor would have obtained in a hypothetical liquidation bankruptcy. In other words, the expectation is that the claimants' new interests in the firm will exceed the liquidation value of their interest in the unreorganized firm, presumably by the amount of the saved going concern surplus (Balz, 2001). The theory behind the provisions, however, has failed the test of practical applicability. Since the going concern value is necessarily the present market value of the firm minus the amount the assets would have sold for if liquidated and the firm is never presently sold on the market nor are its assets ever liquidated, the going concern value for any firm in Chapter 11 is simply a hypothetical construct. Hypothetical liquidation values estimated for use in the proceedings, in particular, are quite problematical because they are apt to be extremely context contingent. If you ask me to estimate how much I can sell General Motors for, but specify that I must sell it in the next five minutes, its liquidation value is equivalent to my estimate of the maximum amount of cash in the heaviest purse of the 23 persons within hailing distance. Prebankruptcy holders of the lowest priority claims (usually common equity) have an incentive to overstate the hypothetical going concern value of the firm so as to buttress their claim to have part of the reorganized firm distributed to them. They likewise have a strong incentive to understate the liquidation value of the firm's assets because that minimizes the baseline distributional entitlements of the creditors in the reorganized firm. The costs of trying to value the firm, without conducting any actual market transactions, are thought to be extremely high (Altman, 1984; Bhagat, Brickley and Coles, 1994; Opler and Titman, 1994). Andrade and Kaplan (1998), however, find that the indirect costs of financial distress are mostly suffered prior to the bankruptcy and are not necessarily substantial. The actual values which the bankruptcy judge might determine the assets would have sold for and what the reorganized firm will be worth, are sufficiently uncertain that the multiple claimants are not inclined to want to litigate them. Since management representing the common shareholders remains in control of the firm while the renegotiation of its capital structure is ongoing, Chapter 11 confers on management and common equity something akin to a legal right to engage in holdout behavior. As a consequence, it is common knowledge that the interests in the reorganized firm are not distributed to the claimants in accordance with their prebankruptcy contract priority rights. Those empowered to hold out commonly improve their ex ante contractual priority at the expense of senior creditors (Eberhart, Moore and Roenfelt, 1990; LoPucki and Whitford, 1990; Warner, 1977; Weiss, 1990). Creditors, particularly those holding collateral as security have begun to respond to the resulting effect that bankruptcy reorganization redistributes wealth away from them, by developing strategies to use Chapter 11 only to ready the assets of the bankrupt firm for resale, or to gain control over the reorganization process themselves. Baird and Rasmussen (2002, 2003), argue that these unconventional uses of Chapter 11 are beginning to dominate, and that traditional recontracting and reorganizing of firms is becoming so infrequent that corporate reorganizations have virtually come to an end.

6. Proposals for curing the valuation problem

Much scholarly creativity has been thrown into the effort to develop a better way to avoid the collective action problem and at the same time cheaply and accurately value the firm, or avoid the incentives to engage in ex post rent-seeking built into the current Chapter 11. Roe (1983) proposed an initial public offering of a small portion of the securities intended to be distributed to claimants in the reorganization as a more accurate way of evaluating whether the securities being swapped for debt had incorporated any real going concern value. Bebchuck (1988) proposed instead that each claimant be granted an option to buy the rights of the next most superior priority level at their face value or else lose its interest. Thus, the lowest priority level not bought out would end up holding the residual claims to the firm. Merton (1990) offered a similar proposal. Aghion, Hart and Moore (1992, 1994) proposed still another refinement on the Bebchuck scheme. They suggested that the Chapter 11 court, once having identified the appropriate holders of the residual interest in the firm from the exercise of the Bebchuck-type options, hereafter permit them to vote on new capital structure proposals offered by competing management groups. Baird (1986) proposed that instead of elaborate and expensive recontracting, that the firm simply be auctioned off in Chapter 11, with the auction proceeds being distributed in accordance with priorities fixed in the claimants' pre-bankruptcy investment contracts. Whatever going concern values the firm had would presumably be saved by being included in the price the winning bidder was willing to pay, buying the firm as an intact unit. Since the auction proceeds could be distributed in accordance with all the claimants' prebankruptcy priority contracts, the auction argument also showed that the solution to the collective action problem did not necessitate ex post modification of those contracts. Auctions are, nevertheless, known to entail their own transaction costs and imperfections (Baird, 1993; Cramton and Schwartz, 1991; French and McCormick, 1984; Bhattacharyya and Singh, 1999).

Adler (1993b) and Bradley and Rosenzweig (1992) both proposed that firms might issue new types of securities which automatically erase the lowest priority claims upon a default of an obligation to the next higher priority class and simultaneously place that next-higher class in control of the firm. Adler's proposal also eliminated the individual collection rights of holders of any of the contingent securities, thus eliminating any right and therefore any incentive for individual creditors to take action to dismember the debtor, and powerfully eliminating any justification for Chapter 11 if it was designed to ameliorate the collective action problem which arises when creditors have rights to act individually. Adler and Ayres (2001) resorted to the mechanism design literature to develop a procedure which might induce the parties in a reorganization to forego strategic manipulation of uncertain asset valuation in a reorganization process.

All of these proposals to reform Chapter 11, on the other hand, seem implicitly to accept that permitting individual creditors to enforce their credit contracts under nonbankruptcy law creates such significant collective action problems that a mandatory collective type proceeding is required as a solution. Some proposals offer the possibility that hybrid collective/individual type processes might improve on Chapter 11. Baird and Picker (1991) proposed that a collective stay be imposed on smaller creditors while permitting a single major financing creditor to individually decide whether to liquidate or continue the firm. Perhaps the most comprehensive proposals were those of Rasmussen (1993) and Schwartz (1993) under which individual firms would be obliged to specify the details of the collective program claimants against them would be required to follow. All of these proposals share the strategic presupposition that firms themselves can, in the design of their credit contracts or securities, also include contract terms which will ameliorate the collective action problems which might arise thereafter, by specifying a collective procedure in which the claims would be processed (Adler, 1994b). The fact that firms never seem to have attempted to use these devices then gives rise to some interesting empirical inferences. Perhaps the theoretically alarming collective action problem is not, in practice, as dreadful as armchair theorists and congressmen have feared. Adler (1993a) argues that automatically recapitalizing securities, at least, may not have been adopted for a variety of unrelated tax, tort and corporate law reasons. Gilson (1996) showed the most astonishing difference between failing firms which recapitalized using Chapter 11 and those recontracting outside of a regulated bankruptcy proceeding was that the net-operating-loss carry forwards (NOLS) of the Chapter 11 firms were nearly five times larger than those which recapitalized privately. This suggests that Chapter 11 may provide a technique for obtaining favorable corporate income tax treatment, a justification far afield from those currently speculated about. It is not easy to see, however, why a distressed firm should be required to undergo the details of a Chapter 11 reorganization before being entitled to these particular tax benefits. Such an understanding would have to proceed first by elaborating on the desirability of the creation of NOLS in the first place.

7. Bankruptcy and investment incentives

As the previous discussion showed, the collective action problem faced by a firm's creditors can be addressed without altering the investors' prebankruptcy priority plans ex post (Schwartz, 1994b) and Rasmussen (1994b) proposed that refusing ex post to honor investors' prebankruptcy priority contracts might be explained by their affects on the firm's near-insolvency investment incentives. They both concluded that none of the proposed contractual means of addressing the potential collective action problems could be judged better on this a priori basis, however. The inconclusiveness of these affects they deemed as a strong argument for giving individual firms their own ability to choose among a 'menu' of different possibilities for the proposal which best suited the concerns of that particular firm. Even if a one-size-fits-all bankruptcy regime could be improved upon by allowing each firm to tailor-make its own procedure, however, in the absence of a comprehensive understanding of how to create an optimal capital structure it is not easy to know how investors could value the differing choices on the resulting menus. The theoretical difficulties of knowing why capital structures might even matter raised by the Miller/Modigliani irrelevance theorem (1958) have begun to be overcome, largely as an offshoot of the theory of agency costs (Jensen and Meckling, 1976). It is now understood that debt in a firm's capital structure contributes to the firm's value by imposing discipline on managers whose personal incentives do not coincide with the desires of their principals, the equity investors. Fixed obligations impose a measurable task on management either to operate the firm profitably enough to raise the cash needed to meet the fixed obligation, or else to subject themselves to the discipline of the financial market in order to obtain the funds they need to operate the business (Easterbrook, 1984; Grossman and Hart, 1982; Jensen, 1986; Triantis, 1994). Since only firms with debt can incur financial distress, the overall expected gains from reduction of management misbehavior must be greater than the prospective losses which the existence of debt may create.

(a) Entrenchment Aside from the ex post collective action problems supposedly met by Chapter 11, it is also known that the existence of debt in the firm's capital structure has some downsides. First, just as debt is thought to reduce agency costs by controlling management's powers over the firm's free cash flow, it is also recognized that the existence of debt gives rise to the positive probability of a financial default. Managers may fear that if the firm is to be liquidated upon default, they will lose their valuable positions, including some firm-specific investment in human capital. This reasoning gives rise to the perverse incentive known as management entrenchment. When the firm has issued debt, managers will tend to warp the firm's investment decisions in favor of those projects in which managers can make themselves indispensable, even though these projects are not necessarily those with the highest net present values to investors (Morck, Shleifer and Vishny, 1989; Bebchuck and Picker, 1993).

(b) Overinvestment Second, it is now well understood that especially as the firm nears insolvency, low priority claimants have a perverse incentive to gamble with the firm's assets, since they can pay off the higher priorities with the winnings and keep the profits for themselves, but all the losses will be imposed on the higher priority claimants. This set of perverse incentives is known as the Jensen and Meckling (1976) 'overinvestment' problem. The current bankruptcy regime is sometimes thought to ameliorate this incentive by refusing to enforce the investors' ex ante contracts which require that equity be totally subordinated to debt claimants. If, as is known to be the case, Chapter 11 distributions deviate from the absolute priority rule, then the managers and equity may be gambling with some of their own money when they undertake risky projects and will be less inclined to do so. Insofar as these risky investments were likely to be in negative net present value projects, then the deviation from absolute priority might even be applauded as a means of avoiding socially detrimental wasteful

investment decisions. On the other hand, it has also been shown that priority redistributions in bankruptcy create a classic case of moral hazard for *solvent* firms. By insuring management and equity against losses if insolvency eventuates, it is likely to aggravate the tendency of equity-holders and their managers to undertake undue risk during the periods when the firm is solvent (Adler, 1992; Bebchuk, 2002).

(c) Underinvestment The third perverse incentive known to haunt capital structures which contain debt is the so-called debt-overhang, or Myers's (1977) 'underinvestment' risk. If the firm is nearly insolvent and is presented with a promising investment opportunity, equity (and management, their agents) may decide to forgo investing in it because the payoffs are likely to be captured entirely by the higher priority creditors. In that way, the existence of debt may cause the firm to forgo the opportunity to invest in positive net present value projects. For firms with investible internal funds, then, eliminating the claims of the higher priority creditors ex post in order to make distributions to the lowest priority claimants (equity) is a way of permitting equity to share in the returns from those valuable projects (Rasmussen, 1994b). Once in bankruptcy proceedings, the bankruptcy judge may approve subordinating senior claims to those of new financiers in order to overcome this underinvestment incentive (Triantis, 1993a).

Nevertheless, Schwartz (1994b) has shown that if the firm must resort to the capital markets in order to obtain the financing for positive net present value projects, then the failure to enforce pre-bankruptcy priority contracts creates an underinvestment incentive even for *solvent* firms and exacerbates those incentives for nearly insolvent firms. Generally, he argues, outside financiers, aware that their nonbankruptcy priority will not be honored in a Chapter 11, will insist not only on market returns for their investments, but also will insist on extra returns for being forced to bear the costs of the bankruptcy redistribution. The extra returns they will insist upon will render otherwise positive net value projects not worthwhile to undertake at the margins. It is thus an empirical issue whether the extra underinvestment risks which bankruptcy reorganization imposes on solvent firms and on those who must resort to the capital markets to finance their projects and are near insolvency, are outweighed by the mitigation of those risks to nearly insolvent firms with internal investible capital.

In summary, the current American corporate reorganization scheme has not yet been satisfactorily explained. In the first place, the collective action problems it seems designed to address may not be so serious after all, and in the second place, even if they are serious, they are capable of being addressed more cheaply by altering the contractual terms of credit contracts and securities. Finally, corporate reorganization's failure to honor prebankruptcy contractual priorities does not seem to address management entrenchment, the first set of perverse incentives which inhere in corporate capital structures. The impact of denying enforcement to prebankruptcy contractual priority is, at best, ambiguous with respect to both the overinvestment and underinvestment perverse incentives.

8. Structures with preplanned liquidations

Adler (1997) has suggested that the failure of law and economics scholarship to develop a satisfactory explanation for corporate reorganization bankruptcy may to be due to a flawed initial premise generated by a faulty ex post point of view. He suggests that asking why and how investors would like to be able to salvage going concern values, as looked at from the point in time when the debt obligations of the firm go into default themselves, ignores a significant feature of any business's necessarily prior decision to select its capital structure. The ex ante point of view, from the time the structure is designed, he suggests might offer a more fruitful perspective. Investors at the time the firm is structured may purposely design it so that it experiences financial distress whenever it is also likely to become economically unviable. Bowers (1991) had, in a similar vein, proposed that firms might employ security interests in a manner which would build self-executing optimal liquidating plans into their capital structures. See also Cornelli and Felli (1997).

Firms whose projects have no economic value ought not to be reorganized. Instead their assets ought to be redeployed to higher and better uses. It is a commonplace that, ex post, managers (Rose-Ackerman, 1991) and lower priority claimants (Bebchuck and Chang, 1992) have an incentive to fuzz the distinctions between economic and financial viabilities simply to milk the higher priority creditors for the last available dime before the firm must cease business, and that they apparently succeed in doing so (White, 1994a, 1994b). Describing the optimal moment at which management's control over the assets should be eliminated is a formidable task (Buckley, 1992). Even if the initial capital structure design does not perfectly separate the economically from the merely financially unviable firms ex post, however, the gains from rehabilitating a few firms may not be worth the losses from attempting to save a multitude of unsalvageable ones. Chapter 11's record for rehabilitating firms is not a stellar one since many Chapter 11 firms must refile shortly after being recognised (Hotchkiss, 1995). Kahl (2002) argues, on the other hand, that serial refilings may simply be part of the process of finely sorting economically inviable firms from those who are merely financially distressed. The potential for an out-of-court workout also provides a failsafe mechanism if the capital structure turns out, ex post, to have been an especially bad predictor (Fitts, et al., 1991; Gilson, John and Lange, 1990; Haugen and Senbet, 1988).

9. Nonbankruptcy law's responses to perverse investment incentives

This insight might in fact explain the nonbankruptcy creditors' remedy system in which, if creditors are unpaid, they can trigger a liquidation which will send the firm's assets back into the market to be reallocated to better uses. The nonbankruptcy system also can address some of the perverse incentives built into typical capital structures having a debt component. The overinvestment incentive is addressed by permitting creditors to seize the assets of the firm. Once the assets are seized, equity and its management can no longer gamble them on risky ventures. Furthermore, even management entrenchment can be resisted under the nonbankruptcy system. Creditors who can effectively precommit to a version of the 'grim' strategy, to seize and sell whatever assets the managers invest in, can eliminate the incentives of managers to invest in them even if such investments owe a lot of their value to information which is private to the managers. It is only the prospect of a job in the reorganized project which permits the entrenchment incentive to operate. An absolute commitment to liquidate rather than reorganize thus makes entrenchment prospectively unprofitable. In that sense, then, one of the most serious of the perverse incentives is *created* by the law of bankruptcy reorganization.

The final perverse incentive that arises under capital structures which include debt, so-called underinvestment, may also not be of the sort which can easily be resolved by altering the terms of credit contracts. The potential positive net present value project which might not be exploited in the future is difficult for the initial investors to describe in their present contracts. The underinvestment incentive is not addressed by corporate reorganization bankruptcy doctrine either. The problem, thus, may be practically intractable.

In that case, the investors may conclude that if the firm suffers distress, its assets ought not to be deployed in any new projects in a firm still laden with the old capital structure. The best alternative may be to liquidate the old firm and to structure a new one in order to pursue the new investment opportunities. It seems unlikely that a satisfactory explanation and justification for any sort of corporate reorganization law will be possible until such time as a generally acceptable model of optimal initial organization is developed. While the shape of such a model might be inferable from the actual behaviors of investors and executives, the empirical literature to date has not succeeded in distinguishing the essentials from the noise. Nor has the theory of corporate financial structure yet advanced to the point of offering a satisfying understanding.

Bibliography

Adams, Michael (1980), *Ökonomische Analyse des Sicherungsrechte* (Economic Analysis of Security Law), Königstein/Ts, Athenäum, 322 p.

Adler, Barry E. (1992), 'Bankruptcy and Risk Allocation', 77 *Cornell Law Review*, 439–489.

Adler, Barry E. (1993a), 'An Equity Agency Solution to the Bankruptcy Priority Puzzle', **22** *Journal of Legal Studies*, 73–98.

Adler, Barry E. (1993b), 'Financial and Political Theories of American Corporate Bankruptcy', **45** *Stanford Law Review*, 311–346.

Adler, Barry E. (1994a), 'Limits on Politics in Competitive Credit Markets', **80** *Virginia Law Review*, 1879–1885.

Adler, Barry E. (1994b), 'A World Without Debt', **72** *Washington University Law Quarterly*, 811–827.

Adler, Barry E. (1994c), 'Finance's Theoretical Divide and the Proper Role of Insolvency Rules', **67** *Southern California Law Review*, 1107–1150.

Adler, Barry E. (1995), 'A Reexamination of Near-Bankruptcy Investment Incentives', **62** *University of Chicago Law Review*, 575–606.

Adler, Barry E. (1997), 'A Theory of Corporate Insolvency', **72** *New York University Law Review*, 343–382.

Adler, Barry E. and Ayres, Ian (2001) 'A Dilution Mechanism For Valuing Corporations in Bankruptcy', **111** *Yale Law Journal*, 83.

Adler, Barry, Polak, Ben and Schwartz, Alan (1999) 'Regulating Consumer Bankruptcy: A Theoretical Inquiry', **29** *Journal of Legal Studies*, 585–613.

Aghion, Philippe, Hart, Oliver D. and Moore, John (1992), 'The Economics of Bankruptcy Reform', **8** *Journal of Law, Economics and Organization*, 523–546.

Aghion, Philippe, Hart, Oliver D. and Moore, John (1994), 'Improving Bankruptcy Procedure', **72** *Washington University Law Quarterly*, 811–827.

Aivazian, Varouj A. and Callen, Jeffrey L. (1980), 'Corporate Leverage and Growth: The Game-Theoretic Issues', *Journal of Financial Economics*, 379–399.

Aivazian, Varouj A. and Callen, Jeffrey L. (1983), 'Reorganization in Bankruptcy and the Issue of Strategic Risk', **7** *Journal of Banking and Finance*, 119–133.

Albuquerque, Rui and Hopenhayn, Hugo A. (2004), 'Optimal Lending Contracts and Firm Dynamics', **71** *Review of Economic Studies*, 275–315.

Alderson, Michael J. and Betker, Brian L. (1995), 'Liquidation Costs and Capital Structure', **39** *Journal of Financial Economics*, 45–69.

Altman, Edward I. (1984), 'A Further Empirical Investigation of the Bankruptcy Cost Question', **39** *Journal of Finance*, 1067 ff.

Ancel, Steven H. and Markell, Bruce A. (1999), 'Hope in the Heartland: Chapter 11 Dispositions in Indiana and Southern Illinois', **50** *South Carolina Law Review*, 343–362.

Anderlini, Luca and Felli, Leonardo (2006), 'Transaction Costs and The Robustness of the Coase Theorem', **116** *Economic Journal*, 223–245.

Andrade, Gregor and Kaplan, Steven N. (1998), 'How Costly is Financial (not Economic) Distress? Evidence from Highly Leveraged Transactions that Became Distressed', **53** *Journal of Finance*, 1443–93.

Armstrong, Vaughn S. and Riddick, Leigh A. (2003) 'Bankruptcy Law Differences Across Countries, Managerial Incentives and Firm Value', Working Paper, Marriott School of Management, Brigham Young University and Kogod School of Business, American University.

Athanas, Jopsef S. (2000), 'Using Bankruptcy Law to Implement or Combat Hostile Takeovers of Targets in Chapter 11', **55** *Business Lawyer*, 593–623.

Ayotte, Kenneth and Bolton, Patrick (2007), 'Optimal Property Rights in Financial Contracting', NBER Working Paper No. 13316, Cambridge, MA.

Bainbridge, Stephen M. (1986), 'Comity and Sovereign Debt Litigation: A Bankruptcy Analogy', **10** *Maryland Journal of International Law and Trade.*

Baird, Douglas G. (1983), 'Notice Filing and the Problem of Ostensible Ownership', **12** *Journal of Legal Studies*, 53–67.

Baird, Douglas G. (1986), 'The Uneasy Case for Corporate Reorganization', **15** *Journal of Legal Studies*, 127–147.
Baird, Douglas G. (1987a), 'A World Without Bankruptcy', *Law and Contemporary Problems*, 173–193.
Baird, Douglas G. (1987b), 'Loss Distribution, Forum Shopping and Bankruptcy. A Reply to Warren', **54** *University of Chicago Law Review*, 815–834.
Baird, Douglas G. (1991), 'The Initiation Problem in Bankruptcy', **11** *International Review of Law and Economics*, 223–232.
Baird, Douglas G. (1993), 'Revisiting Auctions in Chapter 11', **36** *Journal of Law and Economics*, 633–653.
Baird, Douglas G. (1994), 'The Reorganization of Closely Held Firms and the "Opt-Out" Problem', **72** *Washington University Law Quarterly*, 913–930.
Baird, Douglas G. (1998), 'Bankruptcy's Uncontested Axioms', **108** *Yale Law Journal*, 573–599.
Baird, Douglas G. (2002), 'Four (or Five) Easy Lessons From Enron', **55** *Vanderbilt Law Review*, 1787–1812.
Baird, Douglas G. and Jackson, Thomas H. (1983), 'Possession and Ownership: An Examination of the Scope of Article 9', **35** *Stanford Law Review*, 175–212.
Baird, Douglas G, and Jackson, Thomas H. (1984), 'Corporate Reorganizations and the Treatment of Diverse Ownership Interests: A Comment on Adequate Protection of Secured Creditors in Bankruptcy', **51** *University of Chicago Law Review*, 97–130.
Baird, Douglas G. and Jackson, Thomas H. (1985), 'Fraudulant Conveyance Law and Its Proper Domain', **38** *Vanderbilt Law Review*, 829–855.
Baird, Douglas G. and Jackson, Thomas H. (1987), *Cases, Problems and Materials on Security Interests in Personal Property*, Mineola, NY, Foundation Press, 889 p.
Baird, Douglas G. and Picker, Ronald C. (1991), 'A Simple Noncooperative Bargaining Model of Corporate Reorganizations', **20** *Journal of Legal Studies*, 311–349.
Baird, Douglas G. and Morrison, Edward R. (2001) 'Bankruptcy Decisionmaking', **17** *Journal of Law, Economics and Organization*, 356–372.
Baird, Douglas G. and Rasmussen, Robert K. (2002), 'The End of Bankruptcy', **55** *Stanford Law Review*, 751–789.
Baird, Douglas G. and Rasmussen, Robert K. (2003), 'Chapter 11 at Twilight', **56** *Stanford Law Review*, 673.
Ball, Corrine (1998), 'Shifting Duties: The Impact of Insolvency on the Fiduciary Duties of Directors', Working Paper available at http://ssrn.com/abstract=81673.
Balz, Manfred (2001), 'Equity Auctions and a New Concept of Priority: Two Bankruptcy Reform Proposals', Working Paper available at http://ssrn.com/abstract=264511.
Barclay, Michael J. and Smith, Clifford W. (1995), 'The Priority Structure of Corporate Liabilities', **50** *Journal of Finance*, 899 ff.
Barondes, Royce de R. (1998), 'Fiduciary Duties of Officers and Directors of Distressed Corporations', **7** *George Mason Law Review*, 45–104.
Barondes, Royce de R. and Slawson, V. Carlos, Jr. (2005), 'Examining Compliance with Fiduciary Duties: A Study of Real Estate Brokers', **84** *Oregon Law Review*, 681–724.
Bebchuck, Lucian A. (1988), 'A New Approach to Corporate Reorganizations', **101** *Harvard Law Review*, 775–804.
Bebchuk, Lucian Arye (1994), 'Efficient and Inefficient Sales of Corporate Control', **109** *Quarterly Journal of Economics*, 957–993.
Bebchuk, Lucian Arye (1998), Essay, 'Chapter 11', **Vol. 1** *New Palgrave Dictionary of Law and Economics*, 551–554.
Bebchuk, Lucian Arye (2000), 'Using Options to Divide Value in Corporate Bankruptcy', **44** *European Economic Review*, 829–843.
Bebchuk, Lucian Arye (2002), 'Ex Ante Costs of Violating Absolute Priority in Bankruptcy', **57** *Journal of Finance*, 445–460.
Bebchuck, Lucian A. and Chang, Howard F. (1992), 'Bargaining and the Division of Value in Corporate Reorganization', **8** *Journal of Law, Economics and Organization*, 253–279.

Bebchuck, Lucian A. and Fried, Jesse M. (1996), 'The Uneasy Case for the Priority of Secured Claims in Bankruptcy', **105** *Yale Law Journal*, 857–934.

Bebchuk, Lucian Arye and Fried, Jesse M. (1997), 'The Uneasy Case for the Priority of Secured Claims in Bankruptcy: Further Thoughts and a Reply to Critics', **82** *Cornell Law Review*, 1279–1348.

Bebchuk, Lucian Arye and Fried, Jesse M. (2001), 'A New Approach for Valuing Secured Claims in Bankruptcy', **114** *Harvard Law Review*, 2386–2496.

Bebchuk, Lucian Arye and Guzman, Andrew T. (1999), 'An Economic Analysis of Transnational Bankruptcies', **49** *Journal of Law and Economics*, 775–808.

Bebchuck, Lucian A. and Picker, Randal C. (1993), 'Bankruptcy Rules, Entertainment and Human Capital', Working Paper.

Benjamin, David (2004), 'Fast Bargaining in Bankruptcy', 2004 Meeting Papers, Society for Economic Dynamics.

Berger, Allen N. and Udell, Gregory F. (1995), 'Relationship Lending and Lines of Credit in Small Firms', **68** *Journal of Business*, 351–381.

Berlin, Mitchell and Mester, Loretta J. (2001), 'Lender Liability and Large Investors', **10** *Journal of Financial Intermediation*, 108–137.

Bhagat, Sanjai, Brickley, James A. and Coles, Jeffery L. (1994), 'The Costs of Inefficient Bargaining and Financial Distress: Evidence from Corporate Lawsuits', **35** *Journal of Financial Economics*, 221–247.

Bhattacharyya, Sugato and Singh, Rajdeep (1999), 'The Resolution of Bankruptcy by Auction: Allocating the Residual Right of Design', **54** *Journal of Financial Economics*, 269–294.

Bigus, Jochen (2002), 'Bankruptcy Law, Asset Substitution Problem, and Creditor Conflicts', **22** *International Review of Law and Economics*, 109–132.

Bisdal, Joaquím (1986), *La Empresa en Crisis y el Derecho de Quiebras* (The Crisis of the Firm and Bankruptcy Law), Bolonia, Real Colegio de España, 383 p.

Bjerre, Carl S. (1999), 'Secured Transactions Inside Out: Negative Pledge Covenants, Property and Perfection', **84** *Cornell Law Review*, 305–393.

Block-Lieb, Susan (1997), 'Congress' Temptation to Defect: A Political and Economic Theory of Legislative Resolutions to Financial Common Pool Problems', **39** *Arizona Law Review*, 801–871.

Block-Lieb, Susan (1998), 'Permissive Bankruptcy Abstention', **76** *Washington University Law Quarterly*, 781–851.

Block-Lieb, Susan (2000), 'The Politics of Privatizing Business Bankruptcy Law', **74** *American Bankruptcy Law Journal*, 77–96.

Block-Lieb, Susan (2001), 'The Logic and Limits of Contract Bankruptcy', **2001** *University of Illinois Law Review*, 503–60.

Blum, Walter J. (1950), 'The Law and Language of Corporate Reorganizations', **17** *University of Chicago Law Review*, 565–603.

Bogart, Daniel (1998a), 'Finding the Still Small Voice: The Liability of Bankruptcy Trustees and The Work of the National Bankruptcy Review Commission', **102** *Dickenson Law Review*, 703–46.

Bogart, Daniel (1998b), 'Unexpected Gifts of Chapter 11: The Breach of a Director's Duty of Loyalty Following Plan Confirmation and the Postconfirmation Jurisdiction of Bankruptcy Courts', **72** *American Bankruptcy Law Journal*, 303–86.

Boone, Audra L. and Mulherin, J. Harold (2005) 'Valuing the Process of Corporate Restructuring', Working paper, University of Kansas School of Business Administration and University of Georgia Department of Banking and Finance.

Bowers, James W. (1990), 'Groping and Coping in the Shadow of Murphy's Law: Bankruptcy Theory and the Elementary Economics of Failure', **88** *Michigan Law Review*, 2097–2150.

Bowers, James W. (1991), 'Whither What Hits the Fan? Murphy's Law, Bankruptcy Theory and the Elementary Economics of Loss Distribution', **26** *Georgia Law Review*, 27–83.

Bowers, James W. (1993), 'The Fantastic Wisconsylvania Zero-Bureaucratic-Cost School of Bankruptcy Theory: A Comment', **91** *Michigan Law Review*, 1773–1792.

Bowers, James W. (1994a), 'Kissing Off Economics and Misunderstanding Murphy's Law: Carlson's On the Efficiency of Secured Lending', **80** *Virginia Law Review*, 2215–2231.
Bowers, James W. (1994b), 'Rehabilitation, Redistribution or Dissipation: The Evidence for Choosing Among Bankruptcy Hypotheses', **72** *Washington University Law Quarterly*, 955–977.
Bowers, James W. (1995), 'Of Bureaucrats' Brothers-in-Law and Bankruptcy Taxes: The Article 9 Filing System and the Market for Information', **79** *Minnesota Law Review*, 721–743.
Bowers, James W. (2005), 'Murphy's Law and the Elementary Theory of Contract Interpretation: A Response to Schwartz and Scott', **57** *Rutgers Law Review*, 587–629.
Bowers, James W. and Bigelow, John P. (1996), 'The Economics of Relationships and The Limits of the Law', Louisiana State University Law and Economics Working Group Discussion Paper, July 10, 1996.
Bradley, Michael (1997), 'A Re-Examination of the Effect of the 1978 Bankruptcy Reform Act on the Wealth of Corporate Stockholders', Working paper, George Mason University School of Law.
Bradley, Michael and Rosenzweig, Michael (1992), 'The Untenable Case for Chapter 11', **101** *Yale Law Journal*, 1043–1089.
Braham, Matthew and Steffen, Frank (2002), 'Voting Rules in Insolvency Law: A Simple Game Theoretic Approach', **22** *International Review of Law and Economics*, 421–442.
Bratton, Dale (1985), 'Note: The California Agricultural Producer's Lien, Processing Company Insolvencies and Federal Bankruptcy Law: An Evaluation and Alternative Methods of Protecting Farmers', **36** *Hastings Law Journal*, 609–644.
Bris, Arturo, Schwartz, Alan and Welch, Ivo (2005), 'Who Should Pay for Bankruptcy Costs?', **34** *Journal of Legal Studies*, 295–341.
Brown, David T. (1989), 'Claimholder Incentive Conflicts in Reorganization: The Role of Bankruptcy Law', **2** *Review of Financial Studies*, 109ff.
Brown, David T., James, Christopher M. and Mooradian, Robert M. (1993), 'The Information Content of Distressed Restructurings Involving Public and Private Debt Claims', **33** *Journal of Financial Economics*, 93–118.
Brubacher, Ralph (1999), 'One Hundred Years of Federal Bankruptcy Law and Still Clinging to an *in rem* Model of Bankruptcy Jurisdiction', **15** *Bankruptcy Developments Journal*, 261–284.
Brubacher, Ralph (2000), 'On the Nature of Federal Bankruptcy Jurisdiction: A General Statutory and Constitutional Theory', **41** *William and Mary Law Review*, 743–941.
Brunstad, G. Eric, Jr. (2000), 'Bankruptcy and the Problems of Economic Futility: A Theory on the Unique Role of Bankruptcy Law', **55** *The Business Lawyer*, 499–591.
Brunstad, G. Eric and Sigal, Mike (1999), 'Competitive Choice Theory and the Broader Implications of the Supreme Court's Analysis in *Bank of America vs. 203 North LaSalle Street Partnership*', **54** *The Business Lawyer*, 1475–1555.
Buckley, F.H. (1986), 'The Bankruptcy Priority Puzzle', **72** *Virginia Law Review*, 1393–1470.
Buckley, F.H. (1992), 'The Termination Decision', **61** *University of Missouri – Kansas City Law Review*, 243–289.
Buckley, F.H. (1995), 'The American Fresh Start', **4** *Southern California Interdisciplinary Law Journal*, 67–97.
Buckley, F.H. (1997), 'Free Contracting in Bankruptcy', in F.H. Buckley, ed., *The Rise and Fall of Contract*, Durham, NC: Duke University Press.
Bufford, Samuel L. (1994), 'What is Right About Bankruptcy Law and Wrong About its Critics', **72** *Washington University Law Quarterly*, 829–848.
Bufford, Samuel L. (2000), 'Introduction to the Articles Presented by Three Rising Stars in Bankruptcy Scholarship', **3** *Chapman Law Review*, 21–41.
Bulow, Jeremy and Shoven, John (1978), 'The Bankruptcy Decision', **9** *Bell Journal of Economics*, 437–456.
Bussel, Daniel J. (1996), 'Coalition-Building Through Bankruptcy Creditors' Committees', **43** *University of California at Los Angeles Law Review*, 1547–1633.

Bussel, Daniel J. (2004), 'Creditors' Committees as Estate Representatives in Bankruptcy Litigation', **10** *Stanford Journal of Business and Finance*, 29–37.
Cabrillo, Francisco (1987), *Análisis Económico del Derecho Concursal Español* (An Economic Analysis of Spanish Bankruptcy Law), Madrid, Fundación Juan March.
Cabrillo, Francisco (1989), *Quiebra y Liquidación de Empresas* (Bankruptcy and Closing Down of Firms), Madrid, Unión Editorial, 151 p.
Carlson, David G. (1986), 'Rationality, Accident and Priority Under Article 9 of the Uniform Commercial Code', **71** *Minnesota Law Review*, 207–268.
Carlson, David G. (1994), 'On the Efficiency of Secured Lending', **80** *Virginia Law Review*, 2179–2213.
Carruthers, Bruce and Halliday, Terence (1998), *Rescuing Business: The Making of Corporate Bankruptcy Law in England and the United States*, New York: Oxford University Press.
Cecil, Michelle Arnopol (2000), 'Reinvigorating Chapter 11: The Case for Reinstating The Stock-for-Debt Exception in Bankruptcy', **2000** *Wisconsin Law Review*, 1001–71.
Cecil, Michelle Arnopol (2004), 'Abandonments in Bankruptcy: Unifying Competing Tax and Bankruptcy Policies', **88** *Minnesota Law Review*, 723–82.
Chatterjee, Sris, Dhillon, Upinder S. and Rarirez, Gabriel G. (1995), 'Coercive Tender and Exchange Offers in Distressed High-Yield Debt Restructurings: An Empirical Analysis', **38** *Journal of Financial Economics*, 333–360.
Che, Yeon-Koo and Schwartz, Alan (1999), 'Section 365, Mandatory Bankruptcy Rules and Inefficient Continuence', **15** *Journal of Law, Economics and Organization*, 441–67.
Chen, Nan (2003), 'Chapter 11, Private Workouts and Corporate Debt Pricing Under Asymmetric Information', Working Paper, Division of Finance and Economics, Graduate School of Business, Columbia University, New York.
Claessens, Stijn, Djankov, Simeon and Klapper, Leora (2003), 'Resolution of Corporate Distress in East Asia', **10** *Journal of Empirical Finance*, 199–216.
Cornelli, Francesca and Felli, Leonardo (1997), 'Ex-Ante Efficiency of Bankruptcy Procedures', **41** *European Economic Review*, 475–85.
Cornelli, Francesca and Felli, Leonardo (1998), 'How to Sell a (Bankrupt) Company', Working Paper, The Wharton School, University of Pennsylvania and London School of Economics.
Cramton, Peter and Schwartz, Alan (1991), 'Using Auction Theory to Inform Takeover Regulation', **7** *Journal of Law, Economics and Organization*, 27–53.
Cuelenaere, L.M. and Leen, A.R. (1989), 'Een Rechtseconomisch Aspect van de Positie van de Crediteur in een Faillissement. Is Afschaffing van de Maximum Rente een Oplossing? (A Law and Economics Aspect of the Creditors Position in Bankruptcy. Abolishment of the Maximum Interest as a Solution?)', **38(10)** *Ars Aequi*, 834–836.
Dahiya, Sandeep, John, Kose, Puri, Manju and Ramirez, Gabriel (2003), 'The Dynamics of Debtor-in-Possession Financing and Bankruptcy Resolution: Empirical Evidence', **69** *Journal of Financial Economics*, 259–280.
Daigle, Katherine H. and Maloney, Michael T. (1994), 'Residual Claims in Bankruptcy: An Agency Theory Explanation', **37** *Journal of Law and Economics*, 157–192.
Dale-Johnson, David, Dietrich, J. Kimball and Langetieg, Terence G. (1987), 'A Legal and Economic Analysis of the Due-on-Sale Clause: A Retrospective Examination', **10** *Research in Law and Economics*, 105–127.
Dalhuisen, Jan Hendrik (1968), 'Compositions in Bankruptcy – A Comparative Study of the Laws of the E.E.C. Countries, England, and the U.S.A.', Leyden: A.W. Sijthoff.
Diamond, Douglas W. (1994), 'Corporate Capital Structure: The Control Roles of Bank and Public Debt with Taxes and Costly Bankruptcy', **80** *Federal Reserve Bank of Richmond Economic Quarterly*, 11 ff.
Dickerson, A. Mechele (1999), 'From Jeans to Genes: The Evolving Nature of Property of the Estate', **15** *Bankruptcy Developments Journal*, 285–319.
Dilger, Alexander (2006), 'The Market is Fairer than Bebchuk's Scheme', **21** *European Journal of Law and Economics*, 79–94.
Djankov, Simeon, Hart, Oliver R., McLeish, Caralee and Shleifer, Andrei (2006), 'Debt

Enforcement Around the World', Working Paper No. 12,897, National Bureau of Economic Research.
Domowitz, Ian and Sartain, Robert L. (1999), 'Incentives and Bankruptcy Chapter Choice: Evidence from the Reform Act of 1978', **28** *Journal of Legal Studies*, 61–87.
Drukarczyk, Jochen (1991), 'Secured Debt, Bankruptcy and the Creditors' Bargain Model', **11** *International Review of Law and Economics*, 203–221.
Duggan, A.J. (1994), 'Personal Property Security Interests and Third Party Disputes: Economic Considerations in Reforming the Law', in Gillooly, Michael (ed.), *Securities over Personality*, Sydney, The Federation Press, 234–290.
Easterbrook, Frank H. (1984), 'Two Agency-Cost Explanations of Dividends', **74** *American Economic Review*, 650–659.
Easterbrook, Frank H. (1990), 'Is Corporate Bankruptcy Efficient?', **27** *Journal of Financial Economics*, 411–417.
Easterbrook, Frank H. and Fischel, Daniel R. (1991), *The Economic Structure of Corporate Law*, Cambridge: Harvard University Press.
Eberhart, Allen C., Moore, William and Roenfelt, Rodney (1990), 'Securities Pricing and Deviations from the Absolute Priority Rule', **37** *Journal of Financial Economics*, 1457–1469.
Eckbo, B. Espen and Thorburn, Karin S. (2003), 'Control Benefits and CEO Discipline in Automatic Bankruptcy Auctions', **69** *Journal of Financial Economics*, 227–258.
Eckbo, B. Espen and Thorburn, Karin S. (2008), 'Automatic Bankruptcy Auctions', **89** *Journal of Financial Economics*, 404–422.
Eichengreen, Barry and Mody, Ashoka (2004), 'Would Collection Action Clauses Raise Borrowing Costs?', **114** *Economics Journal*, 247–264.
Eisenberg, Theodore and Tagashira, Shoichi (1994), 'Should we Abolish Chapter 11? The Evidence from Japan', **23** *Journal of Legal Studies*, 111–157.
Eskridge, William N., Jr (1984), 'One Hundred Years of Ineptitude: The Need for Mortgage Rules Consonant with the Economic and Psychological Dynamics of the Home Sale and Loan Transaction', **70** *Virginia Law Review*, 1083–1218.
Fan, Wei and White, Michell J. (2003), 'Personal Bankruptcy and the Level of Entrepreneurial Activity', **46** *Journal of Law and Economics*, 543–567.
Faure-Grimaud, Antoine (1999), 'Product Market Competition and Optimal Debt Contracts: The Limited Liability Effect Revisited', **44** *European Economic Review*, 1832–1840.
Fay, Scott, Hurst, Eric and White, Michelle J. (2002), 'The Household Bankruptcy Decision', **92** *American Economic Review*, 706–768.
Fisher, Timothy C.G. and Martel, Jocelyn (1995), 'The Creditors Financial Reorganization Decision: New Evidence from Canadian Data', **11** *Journal of Law, Economics and Organization*, 112 ff.
Fisher, Timothy and Martel, Jocelyn (2005), 'The Irrelevance of Direct Bankruptcy Costs to the Firm's Financial Reorganization Decision', **2** *Journal of Empirical Legal Studies*, 151–170.
Fitts, Peter, Luigs, Russell, Miller, Steve, Price, Michael, Rosen, Leonard, Ross, Wilbur, Schulte, David, Turner, David and Zell, Sam (1991), 'Bankruptcies, Workouts and Turnarounds: A Roundtable Discussion', **4** *Journal of Applied Corporate Finance*, 34–61.
Franks, Julian and Sussman, Oren (2003), 'Financial Distress and Bank Restructuring of Small to Medium Sized UK Companies', Working Paper, London: Centre for Economic Policy Research.
Franks, Julian and Torous, Walter (1989), 'An Empirical Investigation of US Firms in Reorganization', **44** *Journal of Finance*, 747–769.
Freirman, Michael and Viswanath, P.V. (1994), 'Agency Problems of Debt, Convertible Securities and Deviations from Absolute Priority in Bankruptcy', **37** *Journal of Law and Economics*, 455–476.
Fremault, Anne and Schary, Martha (1995), 'Default Risk in the Contingent Claims Model of Debt', in Lenos Trigeorgis, ed., *Real Options in Capital Investment: Models, Strategies, and Applications*, Westport, Conn.: Praeger.

French, Kenneth R. and McCormick, Robert E. (1984), 'Sealed Bids, Sunk Costs and the Process of Competition', **57** *Journal of Business*, 417–441.

Fried, Jesse M. (1996), 'Executory Contracts and Performance Decisions in Bankruptcy', **46** *Duke Law Journal*, 517–574.

Frierman, Michael (1994), 'Agency Problems of Debt, Convertible Securities and Deviations from Absolute Priority in Bankruptcy', **37** *Journal of Law and Economics*, 455–476.

Frost, Christopher W. (1997), 'Asset Securitization and Corporate Risk Allocation', **72** *Tulane Law Review*, 101–157.

Frost, Christopher W. (1998), 'The Theory, Reality, and Pragmatism of Corporate Governance in Bankruptcy Reorganizations', **72** *American Bankruptcy Law Journal*, 103–156.

Gangopadhyay, Shubhashis and Wihlborg, Clas (2001), 'The Impact of Bankruptcy Rules on Risky Project Choice and Skill Formation under Credit Rationing', Presented Paper, European Finance Association 2002 Berlin Meeting; CBS Department of Finance working paper no. 2001–5, available at http://ssrn.com/abstract=302594.

Gebbia-Pinetti, Karen M. (2000), 'Interpreting the Bankruptcy Code: An Empirical Study of the Supreme Court's Bankruptcy Decisions', **3** *Chapman Law Review*, 179–308.

Georgakopoulos, Nicholas L. (2002), 'Bankruptcy Law for Productivity', **37** *Wake Forest Law Review*, 51–96.

Gertner, Robert and Scharfstein, David (1991), 'A Theory of Workouts and the Effects of Reorganization Law', **46** *Journal of Finance*, 1189–1222.

Ghose, Aloke and Ruland, William (1997), 'Managerial Ownership, Method of Payment for Acquisitions and Executive Job Retention', **53** *Journal of Finance*, 785–798.

Gillette, Clayton (1998), 'Lock-In Effects in Law and Norms', **78** *Boston University Law Review*, 813–842.

Gilson, Ronald J. (1993), 'Regulating the Equity Component of Financial Structure: The SEC's Response to the One Share One Vote Controversy', in K. Lehn and R. Kamphuis, eds., *Modernizing United States Securities Regulation*, Burr Ridge, Ill: Irwin.

Gilson, Stuart C. (1993), 'Transaction Costs and Capital Structure Choice: Evidence from Financially Distressed Firms', **52** *Journal of Finance*, 161–196.

Gilson, Stuart C. and Warner, Jerold B. (2000), 'Private vs. Public Debt: Evidence from Firms that Replace Bank Loans with Junk Bonds', Working Paper, Harvard Business School and University of Rochester.

Gilson, Stuart C., Hotchkiss, Edith S. and Ruback, Richard S. (2000), 'Valuation of Bankrupt Firms', **13** *Review of Financial Studies*, 43–74.

Gilson, Stuart C., John, Kose and Lang, Larry (1990), 'Troubled Debt Restructurings: An Empirical Study of Private Reorganizations of Firms in Default', **27** *Journal of Financial Economics*, 315–353.

Goetz, Charles J. and Scott, Robert E. (1983), 'The Mitigation Principle: Toward a General Theory of Contractual Obligation', **69** *Virginia Law Review*, 967–1024.

Goldstein, Robert, Ju, Negliu and Leland, Hayne (2001), 'An EBIT Model of Dynamic Capital Structure', **74** *Journal of Business*, 483–512.

Grossman, Sanford J. and Hart, Oliver (1982), 'Corporate Financial Structure and Managerial Incentives', in John J. McCall (ed.), *The Economics of Information and Uncertainty*, Chicago: University of Chicago Press.

Hansen, Bradley (1998), 'Commercial Associations and the Creation of a National Economy: The Demand for Federal Bankruptcy Law', **72** *Business History Review*, 86–113.

Hansen, Bradley (2000), 'The People's Welfare and the Origins of Corporate Reorganization: The Wabash Receivership Reconsidered', **72** *Business History Review*, 377–405.

Hansmann, Henry B. and Kraakman, Reinier H. (1992), 'Hands-Tying Contracts; Book Publishing, Venture Capital Financing and Secured Debt', *Journal of Law, Economics and Organization*, 628–655.

Harris, Frederick H. (1987), 'Security and Penalty in Debt Contracts: Comment', **143** *Journal of Institutional and Theoretical Economics*, 168–174.

Harris, Milton and Raviv, Artur (1988), 'Corporate Control Contests and Capital Structure', **20** *Journal of Financial Economics*, 55–86.
Harris, Steven L. and Mooney, Charles W., Jr (1994), 'A Property-Based Theory of Security Interests: Taking Debtors' Choices Seriously', **80** *Virginia Law Review*, 2021–2072.
Harris, Steven L. and Mooney, Charles W., Jr. (2004), 'The Unfortunate Life and Merciful Death of the Avoidance Powers under Section 103 of the Durbin-Delahunt Bill: What were they Thinking?', **25** *Cardozo Law Review*, 1829–1893.
Hart, Oliver, LaPorta, Raphael, Lopez-de-Silanes, Florencio and Moore, John (1997), 'Bankruptcy Design in East and West: A New Bankruptcy Procedure that Uses Multiple Auctions', **41** *European Economic Review*, 461–473.
Harvey, Campbell R., Lins, Karl V. and Roper, Andrew H. (2004), 'The Effect of Capital Structure When Expected Agency Costs are Extreme', **74** *Journal of Financial Economics*, 3–30.
Haugen, Robert A. and Senbet, Lemma W. (1988), 'Bankruptcy and Agency Costs: Their Significance to the Theory of Optimal Capital Structure', **23** *Journal of Financial and Quantitative Analysis*, 27–38.
Heaton, J.B. (2000), 'Incomplete Financial Contracts and Non-Contractual Legal Rules: The Case of Debt Capacity and Fraudulent Conveyance Law', **9** *Journal of Financial Intermediation*, 169–183.
Hege, Ulrich and Mella-Barral, Pierre (2002), 'Reorganization Law and Dilution Threats in Different Financial Systems', in J.A. McCahery, P. Moreland, T. Raaijmakers, and L. Renneboog, eds., *Corporate Governance Regimes: Convergence and Diversity*, Oxford: Oxford University Press, pp.470–490.
Hess, James D. and Knoeber, Charles R. (1987), 'Security and Penalty in Debt Contracts', **143** *Journal of Institutional and Theoretical Economics*, 149–167.
Hill, Clair A. (1997), 'Why Financial Appearance Might Matter: An Explanation for "Dirty Pooling" and Other Financial Cosmetics', **22** *Delaware Journal of Corporation Law*, 141–196.
Hill, Clair A. (2002a), 'Is Secured Debt Efficient?', **80** *Texas Law Review*, 1117–1178.
Hill, Clair A. (2002b), 'The Future of Securitization: A Comment on Bell and Dawson', **12** *Duke Journal of Comparative & International Law*, 563–566.
Hill, Clair A. (2002c) 'Whole Business Securitization in Emerging Markets', **12** *Duke Journal of Comparative and International Law*, 521–531.
Hotchkiss, Edith Shwalb (1995), 'Postbankruptcy Performance and Management Turnover', **50** *Journal of Finance*, 3–22.
Hudson, John (1995), 'The Case against Secured Lending', **15** *International Review of Law and Economics*, 47–63.
Indro, Daniel C., Leach, Robert T. and Lee, Wayne Y. (1999), 'Sources of Gains to Shareholders from Bankruptcy Resolution', **23** *Journal of Banking and Finance*, 21–47.
Jackson, Thomas H. (1982), 'Bankruptcy, Non-Bankruptcy Entitlements and the Creditors' Bargain', **91** *Yale Law Journal*, 857–907.
Jackson, Thomas H. (1984), 'Avoiding Powers in Bankruptcy', **36** *Stanford Law Review*, 725–787.
Jackson, Thomas H. (1985), 'Translating Assets and Liabilities to the Bankruptcy Forum', **14** *Journal of Legal Studies*, 73–114.
Jackson, Thomas H. (1986), *The Logic and Limits of Bankruptcy Law*, Cambridge, MA, Harvard University Press, 287 p.
Jackson, Thomas H. and Kronman, Anthony T. (1979), 'Secured Financing and Priorities Among Creditors', **88** *Yale Law Journal*, 1143–1182.
Jackson, Thomas H. and Schwartz, Alan (1985), 'Vacuum of Fact or Vacuous Theory: A Reply to Professor Kripke', **133** *University of Pennsylvania Law Review*, 987–1001.
Jackson, Thomas H. and Scott, Robert E. (1989), 'On the Nature of Bankruptcy: An Essay on Bankruptcy Sharing and the Creditors' Bargain', **75** *Virginia Law Review*, 155–204.

Jaffe, Austin J. (1992), 'Kreditkontrakte, Zahlungsverweigerung und Zahlungsafschub (Contracting for Housing, Mortgage Default and Mortgage Foreclosure Moratoria)', Proceedings of Systeme der Wohnungs-Finanzierung Internationale Workshop.
Jaffe, Austin J. and Sharp, J. (1995), 'Contract Theory and Mortgage Foreclosure Moratoria', **10** *Journal of Real Estate Finance and Economics.*
Jensen, Michael C. (1986), 'Agency Costs and Free Cash Flow, Corporate Finance and Takeovers', **76** *American Economic Review. Papers and Proceedings*, 323–329.
Jensen, Michael C. (1993), 'Active Investors, LBOs and the Privatization of Bankruptcy', **2** *The Journal of Applied Corporate Finance*, 35–44.
Jensen, Michael C. and Meckling, William H. (1976), 'Theory of the Firm: Managerial Behavior, Agency Costs and Ownership Structure', **3** *Journal of Financial Economics*, 305–360.
Johnsen, D. Bruce (1995), 'The Quasi-Rent Structure of Corporate Enterprise: A Transaction Cost Theory', **44** *Emory Law Journal*, 1277–1356.
Jones, Edith H. and Zwicki, Todd J. (1999), 'It's Time for Means-Testing', **1999** *Brigham Young Law Review*, 177–250.
Kahan, Marcel (1993), 'Sales of Corporate Control', **9** *Journal of Law, Economics and Organization*, 368–379.
Kahan, Marcel (1995), 'The Qualified Case Against Mandatory Terms in Bonds', **89** *Northwestern University Law Review*, 565–622.
Kahan, Marcel, Lesham, Shemuel and Sundaram, Rangarajan (1999), 'An Economic Analysis of Rights of First Refusal', Working Paper, New York University Center for Law and Business.
Kahan, Marcel and Yermack, David (1998), 'Investment Opportunities and the Design of Debt Securities', **14** *Journal of Law, Economics and Organization*, 136–151.
Kahl, Matthias (2002), 'Economic Distress, Financial Distress, and Dynamic Liquidation', **57** *Journal of Finance*, 135–168.
Kahn, Charles and Huberman, Guy (1989), 'Default, Foreclosure and Strategic Renegotiation', **52(1)** *Law and Contemporary Problems*, 49–61.
Kanda, Hideki and Levmore, Saul (1994), 'Explaining Creditor Priorities', **80** *Virginia Law Review*, 2103–2154.
Keating, Daniel (1991), 'Pension Insurance, Bankruptcy and Moral Hazard', *Wisconsin Law Review*, 65–108.
Kettering, Kenneth C. (2008), 'Securitization and its Discontents: The Dynamics of Financial Product Development', **29** *Cardozo Law Review*, 1553–728.
Klee, Kenneth N. (1997), 'Barbarians at the Trough: Riposte in Defense of the Warren Carve-Out Proposal', **82** *Cornell Law Review*, 1466–1482.
Klee, Kenneth N. (2002), 'One Size Fits Some: Single Asset Real Estate Bankruptcy Cases', **87** *Cornell Law Review*, 1285–1332.
Klerman, Daniel (1991), 'Earth First? CERCLA Reimbursement Claims and Bankruptcy', **58** *University of Chicago Law Review*, 795–822.
Korobkin, Donald R. (1991), 'Rehabilitating Values: A Jurisprudence of Bankruptcy', **91** *Columbia Law Review*, 717–789.
Korobkin, Donald R. (1996a), 'Employee Interests in Bankruptcy', **4** *American Bankruptcy Institute Law Review*, 5–34.
Korobkin, Donald R. (1996b), 'The Role of Normative Theory in Bankruptcy Debates', **82** *Iowa Law Review*, 75–126.
Kripke, Homer (1985), 'Law and Economics: Measuring the Economic Efficiency of Commercial Law in a Vacuum of Fact', **133** *University of Pennsylvania Law Review*, 929–985. Reprinted in Corporate Practice Commentator, 1996, 28, 153–210.
Lacker, Jeffrey M. (2001), 'Collateralized Debt as the Optimal Contract', **4** *Review of Economic Dynamics*, 842–859.
Lawrence, William H. (1989), 'Lender Control Liability: An Analytical Model Illustrated with Applications to the Relational Theory of Secured Financing', **62** *Southern California Law Review*, 1387–1447.

Lennox, Clive (1997), 'Identifying Failing Companies: A Re-evaluation of the Logit, Probit and MDA Approaches', **51** *Journal of Economics and Business*, 347–364.
Levmore, Saul (1982), 'Monitors and Freeriders in Commercial and Corporate Settings', **92** *Yale Law Journal*, 49–83.
Levmore, Saul (1997), 'Efficiency and Conspiracy: Conflicts of Interest, Anti-Nepotism Rules, and Separation Strategies', **66** *Fordham Law Review*, 2099–2116.
Levmore, Saul and Kanda, Hideki (1994), 'Explaining Creditor Priorities', **80** *Virginia Law Review*, 2103.
Li, Kai (1999), 'Bayesian Analysis of Duration Models: An Application to Chapter 11 Bankruptcy', **63** *Economics Letters*, 305–312.
Longhofer, Stanley D. and Peters, Stephen R. (2004), 'Protection for Whom? Creditor Conflicts in Bankruptcy', **6** *American Economics Review*, 249–284.
LoPucki, Lynn M. (1982), 'A General Theory of the Dynamics of the State Remedies/Bankruptcy System', *Wisconsin Law Review*, 311–372.
LoPucki, Lynn M. (1992), 'Strange Visions in a Strange World: A Reply to Professors Bradley and Rosenzweig', **91** *Michigan Law Review*, 79–110.
LoPucki, Lynn M. (1994), 'The Unsecured Creditors Bargain', **80** *Virginia Law Review*, 1887–1965.
LoPucki, Lynn M. (1996), 'The Death of Liability? A Systems/Strategic Analysis', **106** *Yale Law Journal*, 1–92.
LoPucki, Lynn M. (1998), 'The Essential Structure of Judgement Proofing', 51 *Stanford Law Review*, 147–160.
LoPucki, Lynn M. (1999a), 'Contractual Bankruptcy: A Reply to Alan Schwartz', **109** *Yale Law Journal*, 317–342.
LoPucki, Lynn M. (1999b), 'Bankruptcy Contracting Revised: A Reply to Alan Schwartz's New Model', **109** *Yale Law Journal*, 1365–1379.
LoPucki, Lynn M. (1999c), 'Cooperation in International Bankruptcy: A Post-Universalist Approach', **84** *Cornell Law Review*, 696–762.
LoPucki, Lynn M. (1999d), 'The Irrefutable Logic of Judgment Proofing: A Reply to Professor Schwartz', **52** *Stanford Law Review*, 55–71.
LoPucki, Lynn M. (2002), 'Can the Market Evaluate Legal Regimes? A Response to Professors Rasmussen, Thomas, and Skeel', **54** *Vanderbilt Law Review*, 331–356.
LoPucki, Lynn M. and Doherty, Joseph W. (2002), 'Why are New York and Delaware Bankruptcy Reorganizations Failing?', **55** *Vanderbilt Law Review*, 1335–1385.
LoPucki, Lynn M. and Kallin, Sara D. (2001), 'The Failure of Public Company Bankruptcies in Delaware and New York: Empirical Evidence of a "Race to the Bottom"', **54** *Vanderbilt Law Review*, 231–282.
LoPucki, Lynn M. and Warren, Elizabeth (1996), 'Taking a New Look at Secured Transactions, Secured Credit: A Systems Approach', **96** *Columbia Law Review*, 759–787.
LoPucki, Lynn M. and Whitford, William C. (1990), 'Bargaining Over Equity's Share in the Bankruptcy Reorganization of Large Publicly-Held Companies', **139** *University of Pennsylvania Law Review*, 125–196.
LoPucki, Lynn M. and Whitford, William C. (1993a), 'Corporate Governance in the Bankruptcy Reorganizations of Large Publicly-held Companies', **141** *University of Pennsylvania Law Review*, 669–800.
LoPucki, Lynn M. and Whitford, William C. (1993b), 'Patterns in Bankruptcy Reorganization of Large, Publicly Held Companies', **78** *Cornell Law Review*, 597–618.
Maksimovic, Vojislav and Phillips, Gordon (1998), 'Asset Efficiency and Reallocation Decisions of Bankrupt Firms', **53** *Journal of Finance*, 1495–1532.
Mann, Ronald J. (1996), 'The First Shall be Last: A Contextual Argument for Abandoning Temporal Rules of Lien Priority', **75** *Texas Law Review*, 11–49.
Mann, Ronald J. (1997a), 'Explaining the Pattern of Secured Credit', **110** *Harvard Law Review*, 625–683.
Mann, Ronald J. (1997b), 'Searching For Negotiability in Payment and Credit Systems', **44** *University of California at Los Angeles Law Review*, 951–1007.

Mann, Ronald J. (1997c), 'Strategy and Force in the Liquidation of Secured Debt', **86** *Georgetown Law Journal*, 159–244.
Mann, Ronald J. (1997d), 'The Role of Secured Credit in Small Business Lending', **87** *Georgetown Law Journal*, 1–44.
Mann, Ronald J. (1999), 'Verification Institutions in Financing Transactions', **87** *Georgetown Law Journal*, 2225–2272.
Markell, Bruce A. (1998a), 'A New Perspective on Unfair Discrimination in Chapter 11', **72** *American Bankruptcy Law Journal*, 227–264.
Markell, Bruce A. (1998b), 'Changes in Attitudes, Changes in Platitudes: A Short Examination of Non-Uniform Approaches to Business Insolvency', **6** *American Bankruptcy Institute Law Review*, 35–43.
Markell, Bruce A. (1999), 'Introduction: Bankruptcy, Impeachment, and History', **15** *Bankruptcy Developments Journal*, 253–259.
McCoid, John C. II (1989), 'Setoff: Why Bankrupcty Priority', **75** *Virginia Law Review*, 15–43.
Meckling, William H. (1977), 'Financial Markets, Default and Bankruptcy: The Role of the State', **41(4)** *Law and Contemporary Problems*, 13–38.
Mehran, Hamid, Nogler, George E. and Schwartz, Kenneth B. (1998), 'CEO Incentive Plans and Corporate Liquidation Policy', **50** *Journal of Financial Economics*, 319–349.
Mendales, Richard E. (1996), "Looking Under the Rock: Disclosure of Bankruptcy Issues Under the Securities Laws', **57** *Ohio State Law Journal*, 731–807.
Merton, Robert C. (1990), 'The Financial System and Economic Performance', **4** *Journal of Financial Services Research*, 263 ff.
Milhaupt, Curtis J. (1996), 'A Relational Theory of Japanese Corporate Governance: Contract, Culture and The Rule of Law', **37** *Harvard International Law Journal*, 3–64.
Miller, Richard I. and Young, Michael R. (1997), 'Financial Reporting and Risk Management in the 21st Century', **65** *Fordham Law Review*, 1987–2064.
Miller, Walter W. and O'Rourke, Maureen A. (2001), 'Bankruptcy Law vs. Privacy Rights: Which Holds the Trump Card?', **38** *Houston Law Review*, 777–854.
Mooney, Charles W., Jr. (1990), 'Beyond Negotiability: A New Model For Transfer and Pledge of Interests in Securities Controlled by Intermediaries', **12** *Cardozo Law Review*, 305–427.
Mooney, Charles W., Jr. (2004a), 'A Normative Theory of Bankruptcy Law: Bankruptcy as (Is) Civil Procedure', **61** *Washington and Lee Law Review*, 931–1961.
Mooney, Charles W., Jr. (2004b), 'Insolvency Law as Credit Enhancement: Insolvency related Provisions of the Cape Town Convention and the Aircraft Equipment Protocol', **13** *International Insolvency Review*, 27–42.
Morellec, Erwan and Francois, Pascal (2004), 'Capital Structure and Asset Prices: Some Effects of Bankruptcy Procedures', **77** *Journal of Business*, 387–411.
Mooradian, Robert M. (1994), 'The Effect of Bankruptcy Protection on Investment: Chapter 11 as a Screening Device', **49** *Journal of Finance*, 1403 ff.
Mooradian, Robert M. and Hotchkiss, Edith S. (1998), 'Acquisitions as a means of Restructuring Firms in Chapter 11', **7** *Journal of Financial Intermediation*, 240–262.
Morck, Randall, Shleifer, Andrei and Vishny, Robert W. (1989), 'Alternative Mechanisms for Corporate Control', **79** *American Economic Review*, 842–852.
Morrison, Edward R. (2007), 'Bankruptcy Decision Making: An Empirical Study of Continuation Bias in Small Business Bankruptcies', **50** *Journal of Law and Economics*, 381–419.
Myers, Stuart C. (1977), 'Determinants of Corporate Borrowing', **5** *Journal of Financial Economics*, 147–175.
Nelson, Julianne (1991a), 'Legal and Economic Perspectives of Bankruptcy: A Comment', Working Paper #67 Columbia University School of Law.
Nelson, Julianne (1991b), 'The Limits of Liability to Input Suppliers and Bondholders:

Bankruptcy, Moral Hazard, and Production Choices', Working Paper #68, Columbia University School of Law.
Nickles, Steve H. and Epstein, David G. (2000), 'Another Way of Thinking About Section 105(a) and Other Sources of Supplemental Law Under the Bankruptcy Code', **3** *Chapman Law Review*, 7–20.
Opler, Tim C. and Titman, Sheridan (1994), 'Financial Distress and Corporate Performance', **49** *Journal of Finance*, 1015–1040.
Parlour, Christine A. and Rajan, Uday (1998), 'Competition in Loan Contracts', **91** *American Economic Review*, 1311–1328.
Picker, Randal C. (1992), 'Security Interests, Misbehavior and Common Pools', **59** *University of Chicago Law Review*, 645–679.
Picker, Randal C. (1997), 'Designing Verifiability: Implementing Mechanisms for Distributing Assets in Bankruptcy', Working Paper, University of Chicago Law School.
Plank, Thomas E. (1998a), 'The Outer Boundaries of the Bankruptcy Estate', **47** *Emory Law Journal*, 1193–1287.
Plank, Thomas E. (1998b), 'Why Bankruptcy Judges Need Not and Should Not Be Article III Judges', **72** *American Bankruptcy Law Journal*, 567–640.
Pomykala, Joe (2000), 'Bankruptcy's Origins in Debtor Perpetrated Crime', Working Paper, Department of Economics, Towson State University.
Poppo, Laura (1995), 'Strategic Coordination and Influence Activities: Two Distinctions of Internal and External Markets', **41** *Management Sciences*, 1845–1859.
Posner, Eric A. (1996), 'The Regulation of Groups: The Influence of Legal and Nonlegal Sanctions on Collective Actions', **63** *University of Chicago Law Review*, 33–197.
Posner, Eric A. (1997), 'The Political Economy of the Bankruptcy Reform Act of 1978', **96** *Michigan Law Review*, 47–126.
Posner, Eric A. and Kordana, Kevin A. (1999), 'A Positive Theory of Chapter 11', **74** *New York University Law Review*, 161–234.
Posner, Eric A., Hynes, Richard and Malani, Anup (2004), 'The Political Economy of Property Exemption Laws', **47** *Journal of Law and Economics*, 19–43.
Povel, Paul (1999), 'Optimal "Soft" or "Tough" Bankruptcy Procedures', **15** *Journal of Law, Economics and Organization*, 659–684.
Rapullo, Raphael and Suarez, Javier (1999), 'Entrepreneurial Moral Hazard and Bank Monitoring: A Model of the Credit Channel', **44** *European Economic Review*, 1931–1950.
Rasmussen, Robert K. (1991a), 'The Efficiency of Chapter 11', **8** *Bankruptcy Developments Journal*, 319–334.
Rasmussen, Robert K. (1991b), 'Bankruptcy and the Administrative State', **42** *Hastings Law Journal*, 1567–1610.
Rasmussen, Robert K. (1992), 'Debtor's Choice: A Menu Approach to Corporate Bankruptcy', **71** *Texas Law Review*, 51–121.
Rasmussen, Robert K. (1993), 'A Study of the Costs and Benefits of Textualism: The Supreme Court's Bankruptcy Cases'; **71** *Washington University Law Quarterly*, 535–598.
Rasmussen, Robert K. (1994a), 'An Essay on Optimal Bankruptcy Rules and Social Justice', **1994** *University of Illinois Law Review*, 1–43.
Rasmussen, Robert K. (1994b), 'The Ex Ante Effects of Bankruptcy Reform on Investment Incentives', **72** *Washington University Law Quarterly*, 1159–1211.
Rasmussen, Robert K. (1997), 'A New Approach to Transnational Insolvencies', **19** *Michigan Journal of International Law*, 1–36.
Rasmussen, Robert K. and Skeel, David A., Jr (1995), 'The Economic Analysis of Corporate Bankruptcy', **3** *American Bankruptcy Institute Law Review*, 85–115.
Rasmussen, Robert K. and Thomas, Randall S. (2001), 'Whither the Race? A Comment On The Effects of the Delawarization of Corporation Reorganizations', **54** *Vanderbilt Law Review*, 283–307.
Rea, Samuel A., Jr (1984), 'Arm-breaking, Consumer Credit and Personal Bankruptcy', *Economic Inquiry*, 188–208.

Rhodes-Kropf, Matthew (2005), 'Financing Auction Bids', **36** *Rand Journal of Economics*, 789–815.

Ribstein, Larry E. (1997), 'The Illogic and Limits of Partnership Liability in Bankruptcy', **32** *Wake Forest Law Review*, 31–77.

Robe, Michel A. (1998), 'Optimal versus Traditional Securities Under Moral Hazard', **34** *Journal of Finance and Quantitative Analysis*, 161–189.

Roe, Mark J. (1983), 'Bankruptcy and Debt: A New Model for Corporate Reorganization', **83** *Columbia Law Review*, 527–602.

Roe, Mark J. (1987), 'The Voting Prohibition in Bond Workouts', **97** *Yale Law Journal*, 232–279.

Roe, Mark J. (1989), 'Commentary on "On the Nature of Bankruptcy": Bankruptcy, Priority and Economies', **75** *Virginia Law Review*, 219–240.

Roe, Mark J. (1994), *Strong Managers, Weak Owners and the Political Roots of American Corporate Finance*, Princeton, NJ, Princeton University Press.

Roe, Mark J. (1996), 'Commentary: Chaos and Evolution in Law and Economics', **109** *Harvard Law Review*, 641–668.

Roe, Mark J. (1998a), 'Backlash', **98** *Columbia Law Review*, 217–241.

Roe, Mark J. (1998b), 'German Codetermination and German Securities Markets', **1998** *Columbia Business Law Review*, 167–183.

Rose-Ackerman, Susan (1991), 'Risk Taking and Ruin: Bankruptcy and Investment Choice', **20** *Journal of Legal Studies*, 277–310.

Rusch, Linda J. (1996), 'Bankruptcy as a Revolutionary Concept: Good Faith Filing and a Theory of Obligation', **57** *Montana Law Review*, 49–97.

Schleifer, Andrei (2003), 'Will the Sovereign Debt Market Survive?', May 2003 American Economic Review Papers and Proceedings.

Schleifer, Andrei and Vishny, Robert W. (1992), 'Liquidation Values and Debt Capacity: A Market Equilibrium Approach', **47** *Journal of Finance*, 1343–1366.

Schumann, Jochen (1987), 'Security and Penalty in Debt Contracts: Comment', **143** *Journal of Institutional and Theoretical Economics*, 175–179.

Schwarcz, Steven L. (1996), 'Rethinking a Corporation's Obligations to Creditors', **17** *Cardozo Law Review*, 647–690.

Schwarcz, Steven L. (1997a), 'Protecting Rights, Preventing Windfalls: A Model for Harmonizing State and Federal Laws on Floating Liens', **75** *North Carolina Law Review*, 403–470.

Schwarcz, Steven L. (1997b), 'The Easy Case for the Priority of Secured Claims in Bankruptcy: A Response to Professors Bebchuk and Fried', **47** *Duke Law Journal*, 425–489.

Schwarcz, Steven L. (1998), 'The Universal Language of Cross-Border Finance', **8** *Duke Journal of Comparative and International Law*, 235–254.

Schwarcz, Steven L. (1999a), 'The Inherent Irrationality of Judgment Proofing', **52** *Stanford Law Review*, 1–53.

Schwarcz, Steven L. (1999b), 'Judgment Proofing: A Rejoinder', **52** *Stanford Law Review*, 77–85.

Schwarcz, Steven L. (1999c), 'Rethinking Freedom of Contract: A Bankruptcy Paradigm', **77** *Texas Law Review*, 515–604.

Schwarcz, Steven L. (2005), 'Temporal Perspectives: Resolving the Conflict Between Current and Future Investors', **89** *Minnesota Law Review*, 1044–1091.

Schwartz, Alan (1981), 'Security Interests and Bankruptcy Priorities: A Review of Current Theories', **10** *Journal of Legal Studies*, 1–37.

Schwartz, Alan (1983), 'The Enforceability of Security Interests in Consumer Goods', **26** *Journal of Law and Economics*, 117–162.

Schwartz, Alan (1984), 'The Continuing Puzzle of Secured Debt', **37** *Vanderbilt Law Review*, 1051–1069. Reprinted in **27** *Corporate Practice Commentator*, 1985, 294–312.

Schwartz, Alan (1989), 'A Theory of Loan Priorities', **18** *Journal of Legal Studies*, 209–261.

Schwartz, Alan (1993), 'Bankruptcy Workouts and Debt Contracts', **36** *Journal of Law and Economics*, 595–632.
Schwartz, Alan (1994a), 'Taking the Analysis of Security Seriously', **80** *Virginia Law Review*, 2073–2087.
Schwartz, Alan (1994b), 'The Absolute Priority Rule and the Firms Investment Policy', **72** *Washington University Law Quarterly*, 1213–1229.
Schwartz, Alan (1997a), 'Priority Contracts and Priority In Bankruptcy', **82** *Cornell Law Review*, 1396–1419.
Schwartz, Alan (1997b), 'Contracting About Bankruptcy', **13** *Journal of Law, Economics and Organization*, 127–146.
Schwartz, Alan (1998), 'A Contract Theory Approach to Business Bankruptcy', **107** *Yale Law Journal*, 1807–1852.
Schwartz, Alan (1999), 'Bankruptcy Contracting Revisited', **109** *Yale Law Journal*, 343–364.
Schwartz, Alan (2005), 'A Normative Theory of Business Bankruptcy', **91** *Virginia Law Review*, 1199–1265.
Schwartz, Alan and Wilde, Louis L. (1983), 'Imperfect Information in Markets for Contract Terms: The Examples of Warranties and Security Interests', **69** *Virginia Law Review*, 1387–1485.
Scott, James H., Jr (1977), 'Bankruptcy, Secured Debt and Optimal Capital Structure', **32** *Journal of Finance*, 1–19.
Scott, James H., Jr (1979), 'Bankruptcy, Secured Debt and Optimal Capital Structure: Reply', **34** *Journal of Finance*, 253–260.
Scott, Robert E. (1986), 'A Relational Theory of Secured Financing', **86** *Columbia Law Review*, 901–977.
Scott, Robert E. (1994), 'The Politics of Article 9', **80** *Virginia Law Review*, 1783–1851.
Scott, Robert E. (1997), 'The Truth About Secured Financing', **83** *Cornell Law Review*, 1436–1465.
Sepinuck, Stephen L. (2000), 'Rethinking Unfair Discrimination in Chapter 13', **74** *American Bankruptcy Law Journal*, 341–398.
Shavell, Steven (2005), 'Minimum Asset Requirements and Compulsory Liability Insurance as Solutions to the Judgment Proof Problem', **36** *Rand Journal of Economics*, 63–77.
Shumway, Tyler (2001), 'Forecasting Bankruptcy More Accurately: A Simple Hazard Model', **2001** *Journal of Business*, 101–124.
Shupack, Paul M. (1989), 'Solving the Puzzle of Secured Transactions', **41** *Rutgers Law Review*, 1067–1129.
Skeel, David A. (1992), 'The Nature and Effect of Corporate Voting in Chapter 11 Reorganization Cases', **78** *Virginia Law Review*, 461–533.
Skeel, David A. (1993), 'Markets, Courts and the Brave New World of Bankruptcy Theory', **1993** *Wisconsin Law Review*, 465–521.
Skeel, David A., Jr. (1994), 'Rethinking the Line Between Corporate Law and Corporate Bankruptcy', **72** *Texas Law Review*, 471–557.
Skeel, David A., Jr. (1997), 'Public Choice and the Future of Public-Choice-Influenced Scholarship', **50** *Vanderbilt Law Review*, 647–676.
Skeel, David A., Jr. (1998a), 'Bankruptcy Judges and Bankruptcy Venue: Some Thoughts on Delaware', **1** *Delaware Law Review*, 1–45.
Skeel, David A., Jr. (1998b), 'The Law and Finance of Insurance Insolvency Regulation', **76** *Texas Law Review*, 723–780.
Skeel, David A., Jr. (1998c), 'An Evolutionary Theory of Corporate Law and Corporate Bankruptcy', **51** *Vanderbilt Law Review*, 1325–1398.
Skeel, David A., Jr. (1998d), 'Bankruptcy Lawyers and the Shape of American Bankruptcy Law', **67** *Fordham Law Review*, 497–522.
Skeel, David A., Jr. (1999a), 'The Genius of the 1898 Bankruptcy Act', **15** *Bankruptcy Developments Journal*, 321–341.
Skeel, David A., Jr. (1999b), 'The Market Revolution in Bank and Insurance Firm Governance: Its Logic and Limits', **77** *Washington University Law Quarterly*, 433–459.

Skeel, David A., Jr. (2000a), 'In Memoriam: Vern Countryman and the Path to Progressive (and Populist) Bankruptcy Scholarship', **113** *Harvard Law Review*, 1075–1129.
Skeel, David A., Jr. (2000b), 'Lockups and Delaware Venue in Corporate Law and Bankruptcy', **68** *University of Cincinnati Law Review*, 1243–1279.
Skeel, David A., Jr. (2001), 'What's so Bad about Delaware?', **54** *Vanderbilt Law Review*, 309–329.
Skeel, David A., Jr. (2004a), 'Bankruptcy's Home Economics', **12** *American Bankruptcy Institute Law Review*, 43–58.
Skeel, David A., Jr. (2004b), 'Inside the Black Box: How Should A Sovereign Bankruptcy Framework Be Structured?', **53** *Emory Law Journal*, 763–822.
Skeel, David A., Jr. (2004c), 'The Past, Present and Future of Debtor-in-Possession Financing', **25** *Cardozo Law Review*, 1905–1034.
Slain, John J. and Kripke, Homer (1973), 'The Interface between Securities Regulation and Bankruptcy: Allocating the Risk of Illegal Securities Issuance between Securityholders and the Issuer's Creditors', **48** *New York University Law Review*, 261–300.
Slovin, Myron B., Sushka, Marie E. and Waller, Edward (1994), 'Bankruptcy Resolution, Creditors Holding Private Debt and the Market for Corporate Control: Market-Based Evidence from Chapter 11 Filing Announcements', Discussion Paper, Law and Economics Working Group, Paul M. Hebert Law Center, Louisiana State University.
Smith, Clifford W., Jr and Warner, Jerold B. (1979), 'Bankruptcy, Secured Debt and Optimal Capital Structure: Comment', **34** *Journal of Finance*, 247–251.
Spier, Kathryn E. (2002), 'Settlement with Multiple Plaintiffs: The Role of Insolvency', **18** *Journal of Law, Economics and Organization*, 293–323.
Stulz, Rene M. and Johnson, Herb (1985), 'An Analysis of Secured Debt', **14** *Journal of Financial Economics*, 501–521.
Sward, Ellen E. (1987), 'Resolving Conflicts between Bankruptcy Law and the State Police Power', *Wisconsin Law Review*, 403–453.
Tabb, Charles Jordan (1999), 'A Century of Regress or Progress? A Political History of Bankruptcy Legislation in 1898 and 1998', **15** *Bankruptcy Developments Journal*, 343–381.
Thorburn, Karin S. (2000), 'Bankruptcy Auctions: Costs, Debt Recovery, and Firm Survival', **58** *Journal of Financial Economics*, 337–368.
Tracht, Marshall E. (1997), 'Contractual Bankruptcy Waivers: Reconciling Theory, Practice and the Law', **82** *Cornell Law Review*, 301–355.
Tracht, Marshall E. (2000), 'Insider Guarantees in Bankruptcy: A Framework for Analysis', **54** *University of Miami Law Review*, 497–562.
Triantis, Alexander J. and Triantis, George G. (1994), 'Conversion Rights and the Design of Financial Contracts', **72** *Washington University Law Quarterly*, 1231–1255.
Triantis, George G. (1992), 'Secured Debt under Conditions of Imperfect Information', **21** *Journal of Legal Studies*, 225–258.
Triantis, George G. (1993a), 'A Theory of the Regulation of Debtor-in-Possession Financing', **46** *Vanderbilt Law Review*, 901–935.
Triantis, George G. (1993b), 'The Effects of Insolvency and Bankruptcy on Contract Performance and Adjustment', **43** *University of Toronto Law Journal*, 679–710.
Triantis, George G. (1994), 'A Free-Cash-Flow Theory of Secured Debt and Creditor Priorities', **80** *Virginia Law Review*, 2155–2168.
Triantis, George G. (1995), 'Debt Financing, Corporate Decision Making and Security Design', **26** *Canadian Business Journal*, 93–105.
Triantis, George (2000), 'Financial Slack Policy and the Laws of Secured Transactions', **29** *Journal of Legal Studies*, 35–69.
Triantis, George G. and Daniels, Ronald J. (1995), 'The Role of Debt in Interactive Corporate Governance', **83** *California Law Review*, 1073–1113.
Trost, J. Ronald (1973), 'Corporate Bankruptcy Reorganization for the Benefit of Creditors or Stockholders?', **21** *UCLA Law Review*, 540–552.
Tung, Frederick (1999), 'Taking Future Claims Seriously: Future Claims and Successor Liability in Bankruptcy', **49** *Case Western Reserve Law Review*, 435–506.

Tung, Frederick (2000), 'The Future Claims Representative in Mass Tort Bankruptcy: A Preliminary Inquiry', **3** *Chapman Law Review*, 43–78.
Tung, Frederick (2001a), 'Fear of Commitment in International Bankruptcy', **33** *George Washington International Law Review*, 555–584.
Tung, Frederick (2001b), 'Skepticism About Universalism: International Bankruptcy and International Relations', Working Paper, University of San Francisco School of Law.
Vercammen, James (2000), 'Irreversible Investments Under Uncertainty and the Threat of Bankruptcy', **66** *Economics Letters*, 319–325.
Vilasuso, Jon and Minkler, Alanson (2000), 'Agency Costs, Asset Specificity, and the Capital Structure of the Firm', **44** *Journal of Economic Behavior and Organization*, 55–69.
Walsh, Cliff (1975), 'First-Party-Priority Revisited', **51** *Economic Record*, 275–277.
Warner, G. Ray (1996), 'American Bankruptcy Institute Report on the State of the American Bankruptcy System', Book, American Bankruptcy Institute, also available at http://www.abiworld.org/survey/reportfront.html.
Warner, Jerold (1977), 'Bankruptcy Costs: Some Evidence', **32** *Journal of Finance*, 337–347.
Warren, Elizabeth (1987), 'Bankruptcy Policy', **54** *University of Chicago Law Review*, 775–814. Reprinted in Bhandari (ed.) (1994), *Bankruptcy: Legal and Financial Papers*, Cambridge University Press. Reprinted in Wheeler, S. (ed.), *Company Law*, Dartmouth Publishing United Kingdom.
Warren, Elizabeth (1991), 'A Theory of Absolute Priority', *New York University Annual Survey of American Law*, 9–48.
Warren, Elizabeth (1992a), "The Untenable Case for Repeal of Chapter 11', **102** *Yale Law Journal*, 437–479.
Warren, Elizabeth (1992b), 'Why Have a Federal Bankruptcy System?', **77** *Cornell Law Review*, 1093–1098.
Warren, Elizabeth (1993), 'Bankruptcy Policymaking in an Imperfect World', **92** *Michigan Law Review*, 336–381.
Warren, Elizabeth (1997), 'Making Policy with Full Information: The Article 9 Full Priority Debates, **82** *Cornell Law Review*, 1373–1395.
Warren, Elizabeth and Westbrook, Jay (1994), 'Searching for Reorganization Realities', **72** *Washington University Law Quarterly*, 1257–1289.
Warren, Elizabeth and Westbrook, Jay Lawrence (1999), 'Financial Characteristics of Businesses in Bankruptcy', **73** *American Bankruptcy Law Journal*, 499–589.
Warren, Elizabeth, Sullivan, Teresa and Westbrook, Jay (1987), 'The Role of Empirical Data in Formulating a National Bankruptcy Policy', **50** *Law and Contemporary Problems*, 195–235.
Wassenaer Van Catwijck, A.J.O. Baron Van (1991), 'Op zeker spelen. Invloeden van zekerheden in het NBW op het financieringsbedrijf (Play it Safe. Influence of Dutch New Civil Code Security Articles on the Investment Firm)', in Coljee, P.D., Franken, H., Heertje, A. and Kanning, W. (eds), *Law and Welfare Economics*, Amsterdam, VU, 133–150.
Weiss, Lawrence (1990), 'Bankruptcy Resolution: Direct Costs and Violation of Priority Claims', **27** *Journal of Financial Economics*, 285–314.
Weiss, Lawrence A. and Wruck, Karen H. (1997), 'Information Problems, Conflicts of Interest and Asset Stripping: Chapter 11's Failure in the Case of Eastern Airlines', **48** *Journal of Financial Economics*, 55–97.
Welch, Ivo (1997), 'Why is Bank Debt Senior? A Theory of Priority Based on Influence Costs', **10** *Review of Financial Studies*, 1203–1236.
White, James J. (1984), 'Efficiency Justifications for Personal Property Security', **37** *Vanderbilt Law Review*, 473–508.
White, Michelle J. (1980), 'Public Policy toward Bankruptcy: Me-First and Other Priority Rules', **11** *Bell Journal of Economics*, 550–564.
White, Michelle J. (1989), 'The Corporate Bankruptcy Decision', **3** *Journal of Economic Perspectives*, 129–151.
White, Michelle J. (1994a), 'Corporate Bankruptcy as a Filtering Device: Chapter 11

Reorganizations and Out-of-Court Debt Restructurings', **10** *Journal of Law, Economics and Organization*, 268–295.
White, Michelle J. (1994b), 'Does Chapter 11 Save Economically Inefficient Firms?', **72** *Washington University Law Quarterly*, 1319–1340.
Woodward, William J. (1996), 'Empiricists and the Collapse of the Theory-Practice Dichotomy in the Large Classroom: A Review of LoPucki and Warren's Secured Credit: A Systems Approach', **74** *Washington University Law Quarterly*, 419–422.
Zywicki, Todd J. (2000), 'The Economics of Credit Cards', **3** *Chapman Law Review*, 79–172.

Other references

Coase, Ronald (1960), 'The Problem of Social Cost', **3** *Journal of Law and Economics*, 1–44.
Modigliani, Franco and Miller, Merton H. (1958), 'The Cost of Capital, Corporate Finance and The Theory of Investment', **48** *American Economic Review*, 261–297.
Nelson, Grant S. and Whitman, Dale A. (1985), *Real Estate Finance Law*, St. Paul, West Publishing Co.

Index